p 46 - A relic presentatio[n]
"Arial Unicode MS" ←
on Dell 8000, not on
    Dell 4000.
c:\windows\system\
    FM20.DLL
    on both

Unicode:™
A Primer

Unicode:™
A Primer

Tony Graham

M&T Books
An imprint of IDG Books Worldwide, Inc.

Foster City, CA ▪ Chicago, IL ▪ Indianapolis, IN ▪ New York, NY

Unicode: A Primer

Published by
M&T Books
An imprint of IDG Books Worldwide, Inc.
919 E. Hillsdale Blvd., Suite 400
Foster City, CA 94404
www.idgbooks.com (IDG Books Worldwide
Web site)

ISBN: 0-7645-4625-2

Printed in the United States of America

10 9 8 7 6 5 4 3 2 1

1O/SU/QT/QQ/FC

Distributed in the United States by IDG Books Worldwide, Inc.

Distributed by CDG Books Canada Inc. for Canada; by Transworld Publishers Limited in the United Kingdom; by IDG Norge Books for Norway; by IDG Sweden Books for Sweden; by IDG Books Australia Publishing Corporation Pty. Ltd. for Australia and New Zealand; by TransQuest Publishers Pte Ltd. for Singapore, Malaysia, Thailand, Indonesia, and Hong Kong; by Gotop Information Inc. for Taiwan; by ICG Muse, Inc. for Japan; by Intersoft for South Africa; by Eyrolles for France; by International Thomson Publishing for Germany, Austria and Switzerland; by Distribuidora Cuspide for Argentina; by LR International for Brazil; by Galileo Libros for Chile; by Ediciones ZETA S.C.R. Ltda. for Peru; by WS Computer Publishing Corporation, Inc., for the Philippines; by Contemporanea de Ediciones for Venezuela; by Express Computer Distributors for the Caribbean and West Indies; by Micronesia Media

Distributor, Inc. for Micronesia; by Chips Computadoras S.A. de C.V. for Mexico; by Editorial Norma de Panama S.A. for Panama; by American Bookshops for Finland.

For general information on IDG Books Worldwide's books in the U.S., please call our Consumer Customer Service department at 800-762-2974. For reseller information, including discounts and premium sales, please call our Reseller Customer Service department at 800-434-3422.

For information on where to purchase IDG Books Worldwide's books outside the U.S., please contact our International Sales department at 317-596-5530 or fax 317-596-5692.

For consumer information on foreign language translations, please contact our Customer Service department at 800-434-3422, fax 317-596-5692, or e-mail rights@idgbooks.com.

For information on licensing foreign or domestic rights, please phone +1-650-655-3109.

For sales inquiries and special prices for bulk quantities, please contact our Sales department at 650-655-3200 or write to the address above.

For information on using IDG Books Worldwide's books in the classroom or for ordering examination copies, please contact our Educational Sales department at 800-434-2086 or fax 317-596-5499.

For press review copies, author interviews, or other publicity information, please contact our Public Relations department at 650-655-3000 or fax 650-655-3299.

For authorization to photocopy items for corporate, personal, or educational use, please contact Copyright Clearance Center, 222 Rosewood Drive, Danvers, MA 01923, or fax 978-750-4470.

ABOUT IDG BOOKS WORLDWIDE

Welcome to the world of IDG Books Worldwide.

IDG Books Worldwide, Inc., is a subsidiary of International Data Group, the world's largest publisher of computer-related information and the leading global provider of information services on information technology. IDG was founded more than 30 years ago by Patrick J. McGovern and now employs more than 9,000 people worldwide. IDG publishes more than 290 computer publications in over 75 countries. More than 90 million people read one or more IDG publications each month.

Launched in 1990, IDG Books Worldwide is today the #1 publisher of best-selling computer books in the United States. We are proud to have received eight awards from the Computer Press Association in recognition of editorial excellence and three from Computer Currents' First Annual Readers' Choice Awards. Our best-selling ...For Dummies® series has more than 50 million copies in print with translations in 31 languages. IDG Books Worldwide, through a joint venture with IDG's Hi-Tech Beijing, became the first U.S. publisher to publish a computer book in the People's Republic of China. In record time, IDG Books Worldwide has become the first choice for millions of readers around the world who want to learn how to better manage their businesses.

Our mission is simple: Every one of our books is designed to bring extra value and skill-building instructions to the reader. Our books are written by experts who understand and care about our readers. The knowledge base of our editorial staff comes from years of experience in publishing, education, and journalism — experience we use to produce books to carry us into the new millennium. In short, we care about books, so we attract the best people. We devote special attention to details such as audience, interior design, use of icons, and illustrations. And because we use an efficient process of authoring, editing, and desktop publishing our books electronically, we can spend more time ensuring superior content and less time on the technicalities of making books.

You can count on our commitment to deliver high-quality books at competitive prices on topics you want to read about. At IDG Books Worldwide, we continue in the IDG tradition of delivering quality for more than 30 years. You'll find no better book on a subject than one from IDG Books Worldwide.

John Kilcullen
Chairman and CEO
IDG Books Worldwide, Inc.

Eighth Annual
Computer Press
Awards ≥1992

Ninth Annual
Computer Press
Awards ≥1993

Tenth Annual
Computer Press
Awards ≥1994

Eleventh Annual
Computer Press
Awards ≥1995

IDG is the world's leading IT media, research and exposition company. Founded in 1964, IDG had 1997 revenues of $2.05 billion and has more than 9,000 employees worldwide. IDG offers the widest range of media options that reach IT buyers in 75 countries representing 95% of worldwide IT spending. IDG's diverse product and services portfolio spans six key areas including print publishing, online publishing, expositions and conferences, market research, education and training, and global marketing services. More than 90 million people read one or more of IDG's 290 magazines and newspapers, including IDG's leading global brands — Computerworld, PC World, Network World, Macworld and the Channel World family of publications. IDG Books Worldwide is one of the fastest-growing computer book publishers in the world, with more than 700 titles in 36 languages. The "...For Dummies®" series alone has more than 50 million copies in print. IDG offers online users the largest network of technology-specific Web sites around the world through IDG.net (http://www.idg.net), which comprises more than 225 targeted Web sites in 55 countries worldwide. International Data Corporation (IDC) is the world's largest provider of information technology data, analysis and consulting, with research centers in over 41 countries and more than 400 research analysts worldwide. IDG World Expo is a leading producer of more than 168 globally branded conferences and expositions in 35 countries including E3 (Electronic Entertainment Expo), Macworld Expo, ComNet, Windows World Expo, ICE (Internet Commerce Expo), Agenda, DEMO, and Spotlight. IDG's training subsidiary, ExecuTrain, is the world's largest computer training company, with more than 230 locations worldwide and 785 training courses. IDG Marketing Services helps industry-leading IT companies build international brand recognition by developing global integrated marketing programs via IDG's print, online and exposition products worldwide. Further information about the company can be found at www.idg.com.   1/26/00

Credits

Acquisitions Editors
Judy Brief
Grace Buechlein
Ann Lush

Project Editor
Scott M. Fulton III
Terri Varveris

Technical Editors
Rick Jelliffe
Unicode Consortium Technical
Reviewers

Copy Editor
S.B. Kleinman

Project Coordinators
Linda Marousek
Joe Shines

Quality Control Specialist
Laura Taflinger

Graphics and Production Specialists
Robert Bihlmayer
Jude Levinson
Michael Lewis
Ramses Ramirez
Victor Perez-Varela
Dina F Quan

Book Designer
Kurt Krames

Illustrators
Mary Jo Richards
Clint Lahnen

Proofreading and Indexing
York Production Services

Cover Design
W. Lawrence Huck

About the Author

Tony Graham has been working with SGML for over seven years.
He has worked as an Editor and Document Analyst with Uniscope,
Inc., in Tokyo Japan for four years. He has also worked as an SGML
Consultant with ATLIS Consulting Group. He is currently a con-
sultant with Mulberry Technologies, Inc., a consultancy specializing
in SGML and XML training and design.

In loving memory of Grace Johnson,
an exemplary character standard.

Preface

Welcome to *Unicode: A Primer*! Many other books have included sections on Unicode, but usually as an adjunct to their main topic. In this book, the topic is Unicode.

Unicode is a character encoding standard that includes all of the major scripts of the world in a simple and consistent manner. It is an integral part of HTML 4.0 and XML, and the basis of the character model for the World Wide Web. In addition, Unicode support is being quietly added to the operating systems and programming languages that you use.

The Unicode Standard is the product of the Unicode Consortium, a non-profit organization that any company or individual can join. Major versions of the standard are published in book form, and intermediate versions are released as online updates. Version 3.0 is current at the time of this writing.

The Unicode Standard book is the definitive — and for many people, the only — source of information on Unicode. It is quite readable as standards go, but its scope, quite properly, is the definition of the standard. The Unicode Consortium also standardizes other aspects of handling Unicode without including them in the standard, which also means not including them in the Unicode Standard book. Furthermore, applications of the Unicode Standard — also quite properly — are outside the scope of the Unicode Standard book.

This book is a primer for Unicode and its uses. Whereas the coverage in the Unicode Standard is necessarily deep but narrow, the coverage in this book is broad. This book doesn't attempt to replicate the Unicode Standard. Instead, it does the following:

- Introduces the principles of Unicode.

- Describes both the Unicode Standard and the other material from the Unicode Consortium not included in the standard.

- Shows how the Unicode Standard is used on the Internet, in operating systems, and in programming languages.

Why I Wrote This Book

I have been interested in character sets and character set issues since I worked in Japan where I produced books and manuals in Simplified Chinese, Traditional Chinese, English, Japanese, and Korean. At the time, this required separate formatting programs and separate editors for each of these languages. Furthermore, even for Japanese, there were multiple encodings in common use, so that text files on different machines in the office were mutually unintelligible. In that environment, Unicode — a single, consistent encoding for all the major written scripts of the world — would have been a dream come true, but the tools weren't yet available.

Even after leaving Japan, I remained interested in Unicode, and I have written about Unicode and given presentations at conferences and user groups in the U.S. and Australia. This book, therefore, is an extension and expansion of that earlier work.

What You Need to Know

To begin reading this book, you don't need much more than familiarity with hexadecimal numbers and the ASCII character set. If that is your level, the Introduction will bring you up to speed, since it covers the basic concepts of character sets and encodings and provides a brief sketch of Unicode, its capabilities, and its software support.

A basic understanding of character set terminology is sufficient for the overview of the Unicode Standard and its design goals and principles covered in the first part of the book. This understanding is also needed for the close-up view of the Unicode Standard's details provided in the second part of this book.

Some knowledge of basic HTML will be useful in reading Chapter 9, "Unicode on the Internet," even though the HTML markup in the examples is very simple. Experience with one or more computer programming languages will help you appreciate Chapter 11, "Programming Language Support," which describes and demonstrates the Unicode support in nine languages. However, non-programmers will still benefit from the summaries of the languages' capabilities.

How this Book is Organized

This book begins with an introduction. It is divided into 3 parts that consist of 12 chapters. It also has 4 appendices, a bibliography, a glossary, and an index — all of which are described in this section.

Introduction

This is where to start if you're new to Unicode or to character sets. This portion introduces the basic concepts of characters, glyphs, and fonts, describes life before Unicode, and provides a distillation of the reasons for the Unicode Standard.

Part I: Unicode 101

This part is just two chapters that lay the groundwork for the rest of the book. Chapter 1 introduces the Unicode Standard and its near-twin, ISO/IEC 10646, and describes their common history. It also introduces the Unicode Consortium, the parent organization of the Unicode Standard. Chapter 2 describes the four design goals and ten design principles of the Unicode Standard.

Part II: Unicode CloseUp

This provides nitty gritty about the Unicode Standard, other material standardized by the Unicode Consortium but not included in the Unicode Standard, and ISO/IEC 10646. Chapter 3 provides three views of the structure of the character set: as character blocks, as characters with properties described in the Unicode Character Database, and as the character set defined by ISO/IEC 10646. Chapter 4 details the defined encodings for the characters of the Unicode Standard. Some of these are defined in the Unicode Standard itself, and others that are not part of the standard are defined in technical reports or IETF RFCs. Chapter 5 takes the opposite view and focuses on the details of handling specific characters. The next chapter, Chapter 6, changes the focus slightly and describes how to handle characters as runs of text. Chapter 7 goes beyond the general rules for handling characters and manipulating text and provides details about handling scripts such as the CJK ideographs and Korean Hangul. Finally, Chapter 8 describes the conformance requirements for the Unicode Standard and ISO/IEC 10646 and how to submit new characters and scripts to the two standards.

Part III: Use of Unicode

This part moves beyond describing Unicode to describing its use. Reliance on the Unicode Standard and ISO/IEC 10646 permeates the Internet, and Chapter 9 details some of the key IETF and W3C requirements for using Unicode on the Internet, including support in HTML 4.0 and XML, and the support implemented in current versions of the major Web browsers. Chapter 10 describes the level of Unicode support in different operating systems, including versions of Windows, Unix, and Mac OS. Chapter 11 describes the Unicode support in nine programming languages and, for most of the languages, provides sample code demonstrating how to manipulate Unicode text. Chapter 12 details how fonts relate to the Unicode character repertoire, lists some available Unicode fonts, and describes how some font suppliers are supporting the Unicode Standard.

Appendixes

Four appendixes round out the book:

- Appendix A describes each of the character blocks in the Unicode Standard, Version 3.0.

- Appendix B lists Unicode Consortium resources, including Unicode Technical Reports, versions of the Unicode Standard, and editions of the Unicode Standard book.

- Appendix C lists ISO/IEC 10646 resources, including where to buy the standard and lists of ISO/IEC 10646-1:1993 amendments and ISO/IEC 10646-1 block names.

- Appendix D lists URLs for web pages related to Unicode and its use.

The book ends with a bibliography that lists some of my information sources as well as a glossary and an index.

Conventions Used in This Book

Take a minute to skim this section and learn some of the terminology and typographic conventions used throughout this book.

Normative and Informative

When discussing a standard such as Unicode, "normative" and "informative" are two words of standard-speak that appear very frequently. "Normative" denotes a part of a standard that you must implement or support for your application to conform to the standard. "Informative" denotes a part of the standard that is provided *for your information*: you may act upon it or implement it, but whether or not you do will not affect your conformance to the standard. In this book, "normative" and "informative" are mostly used when describing: portions of the Unicode Standard and of ISO/IEC 10646, particularly the annexes (think *appendices*) of

ISO/IEC 10646; the technical reports published by the Unicode Consortium; and the character properties defined by the Unicode Standard.

Code Values and Character Names

The following conventions are used throughout for code values and character names:

- Unicode code values are shown as "U+" followed by the code value as four hexadecimal digits. For example, U+0030 is the code value for the space character.
- Unicode character names are shown in uppercase. For example, SPACE is the character name for U+0030.
- ISO/IEC 10646 code values follow the ISO/IEC 10646-1:1993 convention and are shown as four or eight hexadecimal digits. For example, 0030 and 0000 00030 are the two representations for the code value for the space character.
- ISO/IEC 10646 character names and Unicode character names are identical, so SPACE is also the ISO/IEC 10646 character name for the space character.
- Code values for other character sets are shown as "0x" followed by the code value in hexadecimal. For example, 0x30 is the ASCII code value for the space character.

Other Conventions

Monospaced text distinguishes URLs, e-mail addresses, and code excerpts. Blocks of code are shown in monospaced text set off from the surrounding paragraphs.

Italic text identifies terms used for the first time, plus it sometimes just adds emphasis to a word or phrase.

What the Icons Mean

Throughout the book, I've used *icons* in the left margin to call your attention to points that are particularly important.

Note

I use Note icons to tell you that something is important (e.g., a concept that may help you master the current topic or something fundamental for understanding subsequent material.)

Tip

I use the Tip icon to indicate a technique that is not so obvious.

Cross-Reference

I use the Cross-Reference icon to refer you to other chapters that have more to say on a subject or to the Unicode Standard itself.

Reach Out

My publisher and I both want your feedback. After you have had a chance to use this book, please take a moment to register this book on the http://my2cents.idgbooks.com Web site. (Details are listed on the my2cents page in the back of the book.) Please don't hesitate to let us know about any chapters that gave you trouble, or where you thought we could have made things more clear. Also let us know where we've done a particularly good job.

Despite my best efforts and the best efforts of my editors and technical reviewers, I do not expect that I have excised every error from this book. Errors are recorded on the Web site for this book at:

`http://www.mulberrytech.com/unicode/primer/`

If you find any errors or notice any omissions, please send me an e-mail at:

`tgraham@mulberrytech.com`

Acknowledgments

No man is an island, entire of himself; every man is a piece of the
continent.

John Donne

When writing this book, I was glad to be part of a large and capable
continent. Allow me to point out some of the landmarks. If I've
missed any, it's because of my poor eyesight, and not because they
are not noteworthy.

From IDG Books, thanks go to Ann Lush, my acquisitions editor, for seeing the need for a Unicode book and finding the germ of
a book in my conference paper. Debra Cauley Williams stepped in
as acquisitions editor while Ann was temporarily busy with a cre-
ative work of her own. Terri Varveris, my development editor, capa-
bly handled the minutiae and tried heroically to keep me on
schedule. Scott M. Fulton, III served as my second development
editor in the later stages of the book. S.B. Kleinman, my copy editor,
faithfully undangled my participles and kept me from using "references" as a verb. Shelley Lea handled my figures, and their wide
range of fonts, with aplomb.

I also thank my co-workers at Mulberry Technologies, Inc. for
their encouragement and support, particularly B. Tommie Usdin,
who reviewed some of the chapters.

Thanks also to Rick Jelliffe, who served as technical editor for
most of the chapters. Special thanks go to the technical reviewers
from the Unicode Consortium—principally Joe Becker, Mark
Davis, John Jenkins, Rick McGowan, Lisa Moore, and Ken
Whistler—for finding errors and suggesting examples. Any errors
that remain are my own.

To go back to the beginning, thanks go to Robin Masson of Uniscope, Inc. in Tokyo who got me started with this character set stuff.

Lastly and most importantly, I thank Mary for her love and support, and for putting up with poor company and interrupted sleep while I wrote this book.

Contents at a Glance

Preface ix
Acknowledgments xvii
Introduction xxvii

Part I: Unicode 101 1

Chapter 1: Introducing Unicode and ISO/IEC 10646 3
Chapter 2: Unicode Design Basis and Principles 19

Part II: Unicode CloseUp .29

Chapter 3: Structure of the Unicode Standard 31
Chapter 4: Encodings and Transcodings .79
Chapter 5: Characters and Character Properties 107
Chapter 6: Working With Text 139
Chapter 7: CJK Ideographs and Hangul .157
Chapter 8: Standard Issues 171

Part III: Use of Unicode 179

Chapter 9: Unicode on the Internet 181
Chapter 10: Operating System Support .229
Chapter 11: Programming Language Support 239
Chapter 12: Unicode and Fonts 311

Appendix A: Character Blocks 323
Appendix B: Unicode Consortium Resources 379
Appendix C: ISO/IEC 10646 Resources .395
Appendix D: Other Resources 411
Glossary 419
Bibliography 427
Index 431

Contents

Preface ix
Acknowledgments xvii
Introduction xxvii

Part I: Unicode 101 1

Chapter 1: Introducing Unicode and ISO/IEC 10646 3
The Unicode and ISO/IEC 10646 Timeline 3
The Unicode Standard 6
What is ISO/IEC 10646? 8
The Unicode Consortium 11
Unicode Membership 12
Speaking of Unicode 14
International Unicode Conferences 15
Unicode Technical Committee 16
The Unicode Consortium and Other Standards Bodies 16
Unicode Resources 17

Chapter 2: Unicode Design Basis and Principles 19
Design Basis 19
Unicode Design Principles 20
Sixteen-Bit Characters 21
Full Encoding 22
Characters, Not Glyphs 22
Semantics 23
Plain Text 23
Logical Order 24
Unification 25
Dynamic Composition 26
Equivalent Sequence 26
Convertibility 27

Part II: Unicode CloseUp 29

Chapter 3: Structure of the Unicode Standard 31
Major Allocation Areas 32

What are the Allocation Areas? 32
What's in the Pipeline? 47
The Unicode Character Database 51
UnicodeData.txt 53
SpecialCasing.txt 54
ArabicShaping.txt 55
Blocks.txt 56
LineBreaking.txt 57
EastAsianWidth.txt 57
CompositionExclusions.txt 59
PropList.txt 60
ISO/IEC 10646 Structure 61
Basic Multilingual Plane 62
Common Features of the Unicode Standard and
   ISO/IEC 10646 64
ISO/IEC 10646 Features Not in the Unicode Standard 69
ISO/IEC 10646–Unicode Terminology Translation 74
Features of Unicode Not In ISO/IEC 10646 76
Is Unicode a Universal Character Set? 76

Chapter 4: Encodings and Transcodings **79**
UCS-4 81
UCS-2 82
UTF-16 82
UTF-7 84
Base64 Encoding 86
Modified Base64 Encoding 88
UTF-8 90
UTF-EBCDIC 96
UTF-32 96
Endianness 97
SCSU 100
Transcoding 103
Using Unicode as "Pivot" 103
Transcoding Software 105

Chapter 5: Characters and Character Properties **107**
Unicode Scalar Value 108
Surrogates 109
Private Use Characters 110
Handling Unrecognized Characters 111
Character Properties 112

Alphabetical 117
Case 117
Case Mapping 118
Combining Class 121
Combining Jamo 122
Dashes 122
Decomposition 122
Directionality 124
East Asian Width 124
Ideographic 124
Jamo Short Name 125
Letter 125
Line Breaking 125
Mathematical 125
Mirrored 125
Numeric 126
Private Use 128
Space 129
Surrogate 129
Unicode 1.0 Name 129
Unicode Character Name 129
Additional Properties in PropList.txt 130
Special Characters 131
Byte Order Signature 132
Object Replacement Character 132
Interlinear Annotation Characters 133
Replacement Character 133
Control Characters 134
Normalization Forms 134
Chapter 6: Working With Text **139**
Language Identification 139
Language Tagging 140
Proper Inclusion of Language Identifiers 143
Bidirectional Text 145
Rendering 150
Regular Expressions 151
Sorting and Searching 152
Identifiers 154
Higher-Level Protocols 155

Chapter 7: CJK Ideographs and Hangul **157**

CJK Unified Ideographs 157

Sources for CJK Ideographs 159

CJK (Han) Unification 161

Ideograph Order 164

Unihan Database 165

Unihan Database Online 167

Ideograph Code Charts 168

Korean Hangul and Jamo 168

Chapter 8: Standard Issues **171**

Conformance 171

Unicode Transformation Formats 172

Invalid Code Values 173

Interpretation 174

Modification 174

ISO/IEC 10646 Conformance 175

Submitting New Scripts 175

Part III: Use of Unicode **179**

Chapter 9: Unicode on the Internet **181**

Character Model for the World Wide Web 181

The Changing Nature of the Web 182

The Push for Early Normalization 184

Where and How to Use Early Normalization 186

Implications of Early Normalization 188

HTML 189

HTML 4.0, HTML 4.01, and the Unicode Standard 189

Document Character Set 190

Numeric Character References 191

Specifying Character Encoding 191

UTF-16 and UTF-1 193

Language Indication 193

Directionality 194

Web Browsers 195

Internet Explorer 5 195

Netscape Communicator 4.7 199

XML 203

The Appeal of Extensible Markup 204

How XML Addresses the Issue of Characters 205

Supported Encodings 209
Referencing Characters Not in the Current Encoding 212
Language Identification 212
HTTP 215
SGML 220
The SGML Declaration 221
Numeric Character References 227

Chapter 10: Operating System Support 229
Windows 230
Windows 95/98 230
Windows NT 230
Windows 2000 230
Windows CE 231
Unix 231
Solaris 7 232
Linux 235
FreeBSD 236
Mac OS 236
Mac OS X Server 237

Chapter 11: Programming Language Support 239
Common Example 240
C/C++ 242
Class or Function Libraries 243
DSSSL 246
ECMAScript/JavaScript/JScript 250
What is ECMAScript Really? 251
ECMAScript's Handling of Unicode 252
Java 259
Standard Java 263
Microsoft Visual J++ 270
Perl 276
Python 286
Tcl 287
Visual Basic 292
VBScript 301

Chapter 12: Unicode and Fonts 311
Handling Typographic Conventions 312
Font Techniques 315
OpenType 315

Apple Advanced Typography 316
Solaris 316
Java AWT 317
Wide-Coverage Fonts 318
The Transition to Unicode 321

Appendix A: Character Blocks 323
Appendix B: Unicode Consortium Resources 379
Appendix C: ISO/IEC 10646 Resources 395
Appendix D: Other Resources 411
Glossary 419
Bibliography 427
Index 431

Introduction

If you are new to the concept of Unicode and why we need a Universal Character Set, or new to character sets and character handling in general, start here. This Introduction provides a distillation of the reasons the Unicode Standard was developed, plus a brief sketch of its current capabilities and software support. To prepare you for the material in the rest of the book, there's also a section on the basic concepts of characters, glyphs, and fonts, and a discussion of life in the character set world before the advent of Unicode.

What is Unicode?

The Unicode Standard is a character encoding specification published by, of all people, the Unicode Consortium. Unicode is designed to be a universal character set that includes all of the major scripts of the world in a simple and consistent manner. Version 3.0 of the Unicode Standard defines 49,194 characters from over 90 scripts. It covers alphabetic, syllabic, and ideographic scripts, including Latin scripts, Greek, Cyrillic, Thai; ideographs unified from the scripts of China, Japan, and Korea; and Hangul characters used for writing Korean. (It also assigns 8,515 other code values for private use, future expansion, and other purposes.) The Unicode Standard also defines properties of the characters and algorithms for use in implementations of the standard. Every major operating system, many programming languages, and applications such as HTML 4.0 and XML all support the Unicode Standard.

The Unicode Standard (and, as we will see, ISO/IEC 10646) departs from the practice of other character encoding standards by assigning character numbers using a uniform 16-bit (two-byte) character code. It does this without concern that either byte of a two-byte character code could be mistaken for ASCII. Even the existing multi-byte Chinese, Japanese, and Korean (CJK) encodings took care to maintain compatibility with ASCII, and thereby reduced the number of characters that they could address. With a uniform two-byte character code, the Unicode Standard can address over 65,000 characters, and with its extension mechanism, it can address over 1,000,000 characters.

The success of the Unicode Standard is self-evident. Not only are new applications of the standard appearing almost daily, the major desktop operating systems — including Windows in all its flavors, and Mac OS — are themselves becoming applications of the Unicode Standard. Even the World Wide Web is now an application of the Unicode Standard since HTML 4.0, and now XML, mandates support for the characters and encodings it has defined.

The following list is a sampling of current applications of the Unicode Standard from the list at `http://www.unicode.org/unicode/standard/UnicodeEnabledProducts.html`. Software that you write can also be an application of the Unicode Standard since many programming languages now support strings and files containing the characters in Unicode, and in languages such as Java and JavaScript *all* characters are Unicode characters. In addition, a number of toolkits and libraries are available for adding Unicode character handling to your programs. Even the word processor that I am using right now includes the ability to save files as "Unicode Text."

Ada 95
Apple MacOS 8.6, MacOS X
Server, MacOS X (forthcom-
ing), ATSUI
 Basis Rosette
 Bell Labs Plan 9
 BeOS
 Bitstream Cyberbit
 Chinese Star 3.0
 Citec DocZilla
 Compaq's Tru64 UNIX,
 OpenVMS
 Dynalab fonts
Ericsson A, R and T series
mobile phones
 FreeType
 GAWK 3.0.3
 IBM AIX, AS/400, OS/2
 IBM APL2
 IBM DB2 (UDB, AS/400)
 Java
 JavaScript (ECMAScript)
 Linux xterm (utf-8), qt,
 gscript
 Lotus Domino, Lotus Notes
Microsoft Internet Explorer,
Office 2000

Microsoft SQL Server
Microsoft VJ++, Visual
Studio 7.0 (forthcoming),
Visual Basic
Microsoft Windows CE,
Windows NT, Windows
2000
Monotype fonts
NCR Teradata
Netscape Navigator
Novell Distributed File
Services, NetWare Directory
Services, Storage Services
 Open Market Transact
 Oracle Oracle 8
 Palm OS
 Perl 5.005 (improved in 5.6)
 SCO UnixWare 7.1.0
 Sun Solaris
Sybase Adaptive Server
Anywhere, Adaptive Server
Enterprise
 Sybase PowerBuilder,
 Unicode Developer's Kit
TCL, TK

The Unicode effort was born out of frustration by software manufacturers with the fragmented, complicated, and contradictory character encodings in use around the world. The technical difficulties that
emerged from having to deal with different coded character sets meant
that software had to be extensively localized before it could be released
into different markets. This meant that the "other language" versions
of software had to be significantly changed internally because of the

different character handling requirements, which resulted in delays. Not surprisingly, the locale-specific character handling changes were regrafted onto each new version of the base software before it could be released into other markets.

Of course, character encoding is not the only characteristic of software to be changed during its localization, but it is an unavoidably large characteristic, and the one most likely to require a custom solution for each new language. As an example of these delays, Microsoft shipped the Japanese release of Windows 3.0 about 18 months after the US release, and only shortly before the US release of Windows 3.1. Once the English version of Windows 3.1 was announced, sales of the Japanese version of Windows 3.0 — not too surprisingly — plummeted, since it was all but obsolete. The difference that a comprehensive localization strategy and uniform character handling based on the Unicode Standard can make is shown when the English and Japanese versions of Windows 2000 use a single binary architecture. And, at the time of this writing, they are expected to ship almost simultaneously.

To help you understand why character handling and character encoding was and is such a problem, I'll talk about characters, glyphs, and fonts, and why the three are often conflated (to their and our detriment). I'll then provide more details about what character handling was like "pre-Unicode."

Characters, Glyphs, and Fonts

The following quote by Robert A. Heinlein characterizes what to expect when you deal with characters, glyphs, and fonts:

> Climate is what we expect; weather is what we get.

For much of the rest of the book, I'll be talking about characters and character sets, so it's good if you understand what precisely I mean by these terms. The problem isn't a lack of precise definitions for terms like "character," but rather an overabundance. Every existing text on the subject of character sets gives a slightly differing definition of "character" and those terms that follow from it. Since this is a book about Unicode, I will quote the definitions from the Unicode Standard, Version 2.0:

> *Character.* The smallest component of written language that has semantic value; refers to the abstract meaning and/or shape, rather than a specific shape (see also *glyph*), though in code tables some form of visual representation is essential for the reader's understanding.
>
> *Font.* A collection of glyphs used for the visual depiction of character data. A font is often associated with a set of parameters (for example, size, posture, weight, and serifness), which, when set to particular values, generates a collection of imagable glyphs.
>
> *Glyph.* (1) An abstract form that represents one or more glyph images. (2) A synonym for *glyph image*. In displaying Unicode character data, one or more glyphs may be selected to depict a particular character. These glyphs are selected by a rendering engine during composition and layout processing.

Characters are the fundamental building blocks — the "atoms" if you wish — of how we write. Some characters may be decomposed, but only into other characters. For example, Å may be disassembled into A and ° but no further. In the abstract, characters exist independently of their representation. The following figure shows many characters; they all look slightly or not so slightly different, but we recognize them all as representing the *a* character.

a a **a** ɑ a a a **a** a a a a ą **a** *a*
a ə a **a** a **a** *a* a a ʔ a a a ɑ **ɑɑ**a
a a *ɑ* a ɑ a **a** ᴀ a a ɑ **a** ɑ a ə

The various representations of the "a" character are its glyphs. There is, however, no fixed distinction between characters and glyphs, and one person's glyph might be another person's character. For example, in most applications and to most people, ℛ, ℜ, and ℝ are just different representations of the abstract "R" (LATIN CAPITAL LETTER R) character. In mathematical equations, however, the different representations mean different things, so in that context they are treated as three separate characters. In fact, for compatibility with their use in mathematics, three characters with these glyphs are included in the Unicode Standard in addition to LATIN CAPITAL LETTER R.

Abstract Character Repertoire

A *character repertoire* is a unordered set of characters that are used together. To begin these definitions at the beginning, as it were, the set of abstract characters defined by the Unicode Standard, therefore, is its *abstract character repertoire*. For example, the abstract *a* character is part of Unicode's abstract character repertoire.

Coded Character Set

At a slightly less abstract level, a *coded character set* (or *character encoding*) is an ordering and mapping of an abstract character repertoire onto a set of non-negative integers. The emphasis here is on "slightly less abstract:" we've gone from thinking about characters in the abstract to giving them a sequence and assigning them numbers, but the numbers don't have to be contiguous and are still several steps away from something that you can store in a computer or manipulate in a program.

The integer for a character is its *code point*, and, when it is so equipped, the character is an *encoded character*. The range of code points for the repertoire defines a *code space*.

In another retreat from abstraction, encoded characters are also frequently named. In fact, in the Unicode Standard and ISO/IEC 10646, every character has a unique name.

The *a* character, when encoded in the Unicode Standard, has the code value 0x61 and the name LATIN SMALL LETTER A. (The code value is written as U+0061 when using the Unicode convention.)

Character Encoding Form

A *character encoding form* (CEF) is a mapping from the integers used in the coded character set to sequences of regularly-size units of data (such as bytes) that you can represent on your computer. A *fixed width* encoding form uses data sequences of the same length for all encoded characters. A *variable width* encoding form uses different multiples of the basic data unit to represent different characters.

The two encoding forms associated with the Unicode Standard are UTF-8 and UTF-16. With UTF-8, which is a variable width encoding form using one to four bytes per character, the *a* character is represented as the 1-byte quantity 0x61. Using UTF-16, which is also a variable width encoding form, the *a* character is represented as 0x0061.

Glyphs

We've defined characters, character sets, and encoding forms, but what about glyphs? Many character encoding standards provide one or more sample glyphs for their characters. As we've seen, however, there can be a wide choice of glyphs for a single character, and the question of whether different glyphs represent the same or different characters isn't clear-cut. *Ligatures* — glyphs for a combination of multiple characters — blur this distinction yet again. For example, depending on the context and the sophistication of the software you choose to examine, the fi ligature (joined *f* and *i* drawn as a single character) is either a separate character or merely the visual representation of the *f* and *i* characters within the software's data. Since glyphs can represent one or more abstract characters, there can be one-to-many or many-to-one relationships between glyphs and characters.

A font is a collection of glyphs for representing characters. When working with metal type, a font is a set of characters at a particular size and weight, along with other characteristics. But for our purposes, a font is the visual representation of a character set. The glyphs in a font may or may not match a defined character set. Under MS-DOS, for example, the character set is, simply enough, the characters in a font. Under English Windows, the majority of fonts match Windows code page CP 1252, which is a superset of the ISO standard character set ISO 8859-1. Similarly, Mac OS Thai is a superset of the Thai Industrial Standard TIS 620-2529 character set, and I have worked with a Thai font that further extended Mac OS Thai with multiple variant glyphs for characters in TIS 620-2529.

We've seen that characters aren't always the same as glyphs, character sets aren't always the same as fonts, encodings aren't always the same as coded character sets, and character sets implemented by an operating system aren't always the same as the standard. Little wonder then that character handling before Unicode presented an array of problems.

Life Before Unicode

Character handling before the advent of Unicode — at least if you wanted to use characters from multiple scripts or use multiple hardware platforms — was never dull. Speaking bluntly, it was a morass of problems. The delights of pre-Unicode character encodings included:

- Multiple ways of representing the same characters
- Single code points representing different characters depending on the context
- Poor differentiation between abstract characters and their representations
- Multiple incompatible ways of handling combining characters

Note, however, that I expect "pre-Unicode" character encodings to be with us for as long as there's data or hardware that uses them, which could mean the next 50 years.

Pre-Unicode character encodings were a mixture of one-byte and two-byte encodings — Chinese, Japanese, and Korean (CJK) encodings need two bytes per character, and most other coded character sets use only one byte per character. Most coded character sets are more or less compatible with ASCII for the first 127 character numbers, but after 127, it's anybody's game. In those applications, changes between character encodings were signaled by escape sequences embedded in the text stream. Therefore, to determine a character's encoding, and in some cases, to determine how many bytes to read as a single character, the application had processed the entire text stream up to that point. The net result was that one transmission error or one misstep in applying encoding-translation software could garble an entire document.

When I was working in Japan, a co-worker had the following happen to him. When converting a number of files from the Shift-JIS encoding of Japanese with MS-DOS line endings to the EUC encoding with Unix-style line endings, he performed the conversion in the wrong sequence or applied the wrong conversion. As a result, he completely garbled his data. Since he deleted his Shift-JIS source before he discovered the error, one small mistake cost him a lot of unnecessary effort!

Character Encoding Standards

The first quote is from the Introduction to ISO (http://www.iso.ch/infoe/intro.htm), ISO. The second quote is from Ken Olsen (founder of Digital Equipment Corp., 1977).

> Standards are documented agreements containing technical specifications or other precise criteria to be used consistently as rules, guidelines, or definitions of characteristics, to ensure that materials, products, processes and services are fit for their purpose.

> The nicest thing about standards is that there are so many of them to choose from.

As we will see, there are a lot of pre-existing character sets — far too many to cover in a single book, let alone a single short chapter.

To make a sweeping generalization, character handling — and, therefore, character sets — started simple but increased in complexity. Successive generations of character sets typically increased their character count for either of two reasons:

1. A writing system may have used many new characters, and technology had to adapt in order to include them.

2. Some character sets — including Unicode — contain characters from multiple writing systems. Not surprisingly, these character sets are larger than any other character set that represents just one of the writing systems.

As an example, Japanese MS-DOS initially supported an 8-bit character set, which was room enough for JIS-Roman — the Japanese equivalent of ASCII — and half-width katakana characters (半角カタカナ).

You can write any Japanese word using katakana and you don't need a high-resolution display to render it, but katakana characters don't convey nearly as much information as do kanji. For example, katakana was used for the name and address on my electricity bills in Japan. I don't have a Japanese name, so the sound of my name, Tony Graham, was approximated in katakana as トニー　グラハム even when kanji was available. My old suburb, Kasugacho, is written in kanji as 春日町, which combines the characters for the spring season (春), the moon (日), and town (町). Kasugacho written in katakana is カスガチョ ウ, which tells you only the sound of the word but, thankfully, was enough for the postal service to be able to deliver my electricity bills.

The first standardized character set for Japanese that included kanji was JIS C 6226-1978. The current generation of that character set, JIS X 0208:1997, encodes 6,879 characters, including 6,355 kanji — not enough, however, to encompass all of written Japanese. A supplemental character set standard, JIS X 0212:1990, encodes a further 6,067 characters, including another 5,801 kanji. In addition, work is underway for a new, third character set standard, JIS X 0213, that may include approximately 5,000 kanji. That's not to say that all kanji will be encoded once JIS X 0213 is complete, but the gap is, at least, narrowing.

The case of the Japanese character serves as the most prominent example of how the complexity of character sets exceed the capabilities of the technology that renders them. Shift-JIS — one of the widely used encodings of Japanese characters and the one used on Japanese PCs, Macintoshes, and some Unix systems — has room for only JIS-Roman, half-width katakana, and the characters in JIS X 0208:1997.

Bytes versus Characters

This is not the place for a replete history of computing, but a measure of ancient history is in order here: Early computers used differing numbers of bits to represent a "word." When microprocessors arrived on the scene, the Intel 4004 — the first microprocessor, invented in 1971 — handled data in 4-bit chunks. The Intel 8008 used 8-bit words, as did later microprocessors from Intel, Motorola, Zilog, and others.

Computers that used other word lengths didn't suddenly wither and die; but an 8-bit word did become the common unit for representing information in a computer. The *Concise Oxford Dictionary*, Ninth Edition, defines "byte" as "a group of binary digits (usu. 8), operated on as a unit." The convention of working in 8-bit bytes has continued. This is although we now have 32-bit CPUs, are on the verge of having 64-bit CPUs, and have graphics subsystems that can operate on 128 or even 256 bits at a time.

The interesting feature of 8-bit bytes for this discussion is that they can represent 256 (2^8) different values. When working with characters, this means that a byte can represent any one of 256 different characters before you need to find a way to swap character encodings. For much of the history of computing, however, people made do with what the technology could support. Seven-bit encodings are still with us today because the Internet's e-mail protocols were standardized when seven bits per character was the norm, and the e-mail systems on the Internet cannot all be trusted to handle 8-bit characters.

The question when working with 16-bit characters in an 8-bit world is how to represent 16-bit values? Inevitably, computer architectures differ in the order in which they store their bytes and, consequently, the order in which these bytes are serialized for storage in a file or for passing between processes.

A 16-bit value — for example, 0xFEFF — is represented in an 8-bit world by two byte values: 0xFE and 0xFF. In this example, the byte 0xFE is termed the "most significant" byte because it represents the greatest value within the 16-bit quantity. The byte 0xFF is termed the "least significant" byte because it represents the least value.

The following figure shows how the two bytes representing a 16-bit value are stored and serialized in "big-endian" (BE) and "little-endian" (LE) systems. The big-endian system stores and serializes the most significant byte (in our example, 0xFE) before the least significant byte (0xFF). When the most significant byte is stored at location *n*, the least significant byte is stored at the following location, *n*+1. When the data is serialized — for instance, during a file transfer operation — the most-significant byte is followed by the least significant. Conversely, the little-endian system stores and serializes the least significant byte before the most significant byte: the byte order in memory and when serialized is the reverse of the big-endian byte order.

	Big-endian		Little-endian
	n+3 `01` 0x41 `0001`	n+3	`0000` 0x00 `0000`
In memory	n+2 `0000` 0x00 `0000`	n+2	`01` 0x41 `0001`
	n+1 `11` 0xFF `1111`	n+1	`11` 0xFE `101`
	n `11` 0xFE `101`	n	`11` 0xFF `111`

Serialized	...FEFF0041...	...FFFE4100...

ASCII

ASCII — American Standard Code for Information Interchange — is arguably the most widely implemented character encoding for representing the English language. There were coded character sets prior to ASCII, such as EBCDIC and the five-bit codes for Telex messages. (If you like, Morse Code can be considered an early character encoding.) However, ASCII now represents the departure point for many other coded character sets (some of which are described below) that modify or extend the common base.

ASCII is a seven-bit character encoding. Seven bits can represent the 128 values from 0 to 127. Actually, ASCII defines the 94 printable characters as shown below, and the non-printing control characters are defined in ISO 6429:1992, Information Technology – Control Functions for Coded Character Sets.

```
!"#$&'()*+,-./123456789:;<=>?
@ABCDEFGHIJKLMNOPQRSTUVWXYZ[\]^_
`abcdefghijklmnopqrstuvwxyz{|}~
```

ASCII includes the upper- and lower- case forms of the alphabet used to write the English language, but, obviously, other languages are written with the same characters. In deference to their origin, the alphabetic characters in ASCII are frequently referred to as Latin or Roman characters.

ISO 646

ISO 646 defines multiple seven-bit character sets. Each of these sets is essentially a variation of ASCII that is specific to a language or script. For example, RFC 1345, *Character Mnemonics & Character Sets*, lists 25 variants of ISO 646. The ISO standard allows variation of the characters encoded at the positions for ten ASCII characters (@, [, \,], ^, `, {, |, }, and ~) and a choice of two alternatives for each of the code points for the ASCII characters $ and #. The ASCII character set has been adopted as the International Reference Version (IRV) of ISO 646. Many other variants are identical to seven-bit character sets defined by other national standards bodies. Table I.1 shows the differences between ISO 646-IRV (ASCII), ISO 646-DK, which is equivalent to DS 2089 and used for Danish, and ISO 646-CN, which is equivalent to GB 1988 and used for Roman characters in Chinese text.

Table I.1 *Differences between ISO 646-IRV, ISO 646-DK, and ISO 646-CN*

Code point (Hex)	ISO 646-IRV (ASCII)	ISO 646-DK (DS 2089)	ISO 646-CN (GB 1988)
5B	[	Æ	[
5C	\	Ø	\
5D	]	Å	]
7B	{	æ	{
7C	|	ø	|
7D	}	å	~

ISO/IEC 8859

ISO 646-IRV is also the basis for a series of eight-bit coded character sets defined in the multi-part standard ISO/IEC 8859, *Information processing — 8-bit single-byte coded graphic character sets*. Each part defines a different set of characters for code points 0x80 to 0xFF. Table I.2 lists the parts of ISO/IEC 8859, their names, and

the languages that they cover as identified in an informative document (i.e., provided for information) entitled Annex A of ISO/IEC
8859-15:1999. Note that some of these eight-bit character sets were
initially standardized by ECMA, and then parts 1–8 were published
between 1987 and 1988 as ISO standards. At the time of this writing, only ISO 8859-7:1987 had not yet been republished as an
ISO/IEC standard. (Incidentally, 8859-11 — currently a committee
draft — will cover Thai.)

Table I.2 *ISO/IEC 8859 parts*

Part	Year	Name	Languages
1	1998	Latin alphabet No. 1	Albanian, Basque, Breton, Catalan, Cornish, Danish, Dutch, English, Faroese, Frisian, Galician, German, Greenlandic, Icelandic, Irish Gaelic (new orthography), Italian, Latin, Luxemburgish, Norwegian, Portuguese, Rhaeto-Romanic, Scottish Gaelic, Spanish, and Swedish
2	1999	Latin alphabet No. 2	Albanian, Croatian, Czech, English, German, Hungarian, Latin, Polish, Slovak, Slovenian, and Sorbian
3	1999	Latin alphabet No. 3	English, Esperanto, German, Italian, Latin, Maltese, and Portuguese
4	1998	Latin alphabet No. 4	Danish, English, Estonian, Finnish, German, Greenlandic, Latin, Latvian, Lithuanian, Norwegian, Sámi, Slovenian, and Swedish
5	1999	Latin/Cyrillic alphabet	Bulgarian, Byelorussian, (Slavic) Macedonian, Russian, Serbian, and Ukrainian
6	1999	Latin/Arabic alphabet	Arabic
7	1987	Latin/Greek alphabet	Greek
8	1999	Latin/Hebrew alphabet	Hebrew
9	1999	Latin alphabet No. 5	Albanian, Basque, Breton, Catalan, Cornish, Danish, Dutch, English, Frisian, Galician, German, Greenlandic, Irish Gaelic (new orthography), Italian, Latin, Luxemburgish, Norwegian, Portuguese, Rhaeto-Romanic, Scottish Gaelic, Spanish, Swedish, and Turkish

Continued

Table I.2 *Continued*

Part	Year	Name	Languages
10	1998	Latin alphabet No. 6	Danish, English, Estonian, Faroese, Finnish, German, Greenlandic, Icelandic, Irish Gaelic (new orthography), Latin, Lithuanian, Norwegian, Sámi, Slovenian, and Swedish
13	1998	Latin alphabet No. 7 (Baltic Rim)	English, Estonian, Finnish, Latin, Latvian, Lithuanian, and Norwegian
14	1998	Latin alphabet No. 8 (Celtic)	Albanian, Basque, Breton, Catalan, Cornish, Danish, English, Galician, German, Greenlandic, Irish Gaelic (new orthography), Irish Gaelic (old orthography), Italian, Latin, Luxemburgish, Manx Gaelic, Norwegian, Portuguese, Rhaeto-Romanic, Scottish Gaelic, Spanish, Swedish, and Welsh
15	1999	Latin alphabet No. 9	Albanian, Basque, Breton, Catalan, Danish, Dutch, English, Estonian, Faroese, Finnish, French, Frisian, Galician, German, Greenlandic, Icelandic, Irish Gaelic (new orthography), Italian, Latin, Luxemburgish, Norwegian, Portuguese, Rhaeto-Romanic, Scottish Gaelic, Spanish, and Swedish

Not surprisingly, using one of the Latin alphabet parts of ISO 8859 makes it is easier to mix characters from multiple scripts than does mixing multiple ISO 646 encodings. Neither standard, however, is sufficient for every script. There is, however, an ISO standard for switching among character sets: ISO/IEC 2022:1994.

ISO/IEC 2022:1994

ISO/IEC 2022:1994, *Information technology — Character code structure and extension techniques*, defines a structure for switching among multiple seven-bit or eight-bit coded character sets. This standard is designed for use when exchanging data between an originating device and a receiving device. The standard relies upon escape sequences, called "designating sequences," to identify the character sets, and upon special characters or sequences of special characters to permanently or temporarily switch between the multiple coded character sets.

When working with seven-bit character sets, as in the following figure shows, ISO/IEC 2022 allows definition of one or two sets of control (non-visible) characters and up to four sets of graphic (printing) characters. The base set of control characters, using the range 0x00–0x1F, is designated C0, and the alternate, which may be selected with escape sequences, is designated C1. The base graphic character set, using the range 0x20–0x7F, is designated G0, and the alternates are designated G1, G2, and G3. Most G0–G3 character sets, however, use the range 0x21–0x7E, with 0x20 reserved for SPACE and 0x7F reserved for DELETE.

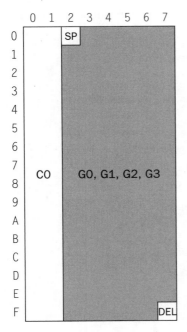

SP: SPACE   DEL: DELETE

You can use either a "locking shift" or a "single shift" when switching among graphic character sets. A locking shift changes to the G1, G2, or G3 character set until another shift sequence selects a different graphic character set, and a single shift selects a different character set for only the single character following the single shift sequence.

As the following figure shows, when working with eight-bit character sets, the C0 control characters use the range 0x00–0x1F, the G1 character set uses 0x20–0x7F (or 0x21–0x7E), the C1 control characters use 0x80–0x9F, and the G1, G2, and G3 character sets use 0xA0–0xFF (or 0xA1–0xFE). For reasons that become obvious when you look at the figure, the code points in the range 0x00–0x7F are sometimes referred to as the "left half" or "left half-plane," and the range 0x80–0xFF, the "right half" or "right half-plane." Similarly, the graphic characters in the range 0x20–0x7F are sometimes referred to as "Graphic Left" (GL), and those in the range 0x80–0xFF, as "Graphic Right" (GR).

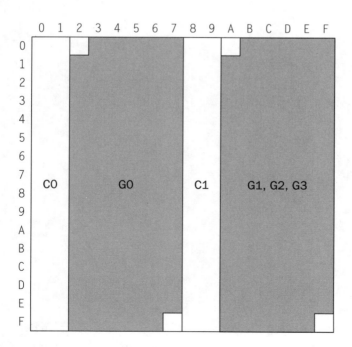

Since many control and graphic character sets have their own unique designating sequences registered with the ISO International Registry (see http://www.itscj.ipsj.or.jp) it is possible, with some terminal software, to mix arbitrary character sets using the techniques of ISO 2022. You begin by typing the escape sequence that indicates the character set (C0, C1, G0–G3) to which you are shifting. The final character of the escape sequence is the byte value that indicates which coded character set you are going to use. Just using the correct escape sequence with the proper final character, you can also mix in many multi-byte character sets, or even the encodings associated with ISO/IEC 10646 (some of which could apply to Unicode). An example of ISO/IEC 2022 in action is the multilingual extensions to the Emacs text editor that are included with Emacs 20.3 and subsequent versions.

In practice, several applications of ISO/IEC 2022 choose simplicity (and more reliable software) over flexibility and hard-wired the character sets they support. RFC 1557, for example, defines a Korean character encoding, referred to as "ISO-2022-KR," for use in e-mail (and now on the Web). In ISO-2022-KR, the G0 character set is always ASCII, the G1 character set is always the Korean standard KSC 5601, and the G2 and G3 character sets are not used. The RFC provides the designating sequence for specifying KSC 5601 as the G1 character set plus the standard characters for shifting between the G0 and G1 character sets, and no others. Similarly, other RFCs define ISO-2022-CN and ISO-2022-CN-EXT for Chinese and ISO-2022-JP, ISO-2022-JP-1, and ISO-2022-JP-2 for Japanese.

ISO/IEC 2022 is very powerful, but it is also very complex. It can also be fragile, since a missed bit or a garbled byte can change an escape sequence, which could completely change the interpretation of a long sequence of characters. The standard was designed principally for exchanging data between an originating device and a receiving device. So it does sterling work as the transmitted representation of Chinese, Japanese, Korean, and other texts, but it is not well suited for use as a storage representation. Random access into an ISO/IEC 2022 string — in other words, reading a string of characters starting at any random point, perhaps in the middle — is problematic. For a program to be able to interpret a character at any point in the middle of a string, it must read first from the beginning of the string and continue to read up until the desired character. This is because the program must determine, first, what character sets are being encoded, secondly, what character set is active for that desired character, and, thirdly, how many bytes it should interpret as representing a single character.

Vendor Character Sets

Character sets created by a single vendor instead of by a standards organization or industry group — including the character sets used on Windows — are also frequently referred to as "code pages."

Vendor implementations frequently differ, to varying degrees, from the national or international standard for a coded character set. For example, the following figure shows the Windows CP 1252 code page, which is a superset of ISO 8859-1. The characters in CP 1252 that are not in ISO 8859-1 are shown in bold text against a gray background.

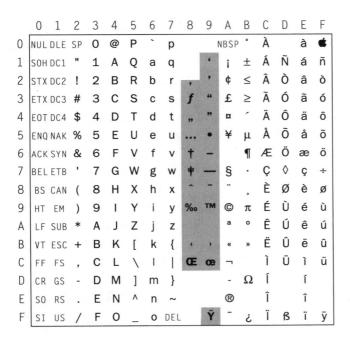

The World Wide Web

The World Wide Web, in a sense, really began its existence as the "Western European Web" since early versions of HTML either explicitly or implicitly limited the character set to ISO 8859-1. The HTML 2.0 RFC (`ftp://ftp.isi.edu/in-notes/rfc1866.txt`) from November 1995 specifies only that conforming HTML documents include ISO 8859-1 in their character set. A note in the RFC, however, does mention encoding documents in ISO 2022-JP (which doesn't include all the characters in ISO 8859-1) and numeric character references to ISO 10646 characters, but a strict interpretation of the SGML Declaration provided in the RFC would disallow both possibilities. The earlier HTML+ discussion document and the later HTML 3.2 Recommendation (`http://www.w3.org/TR/REC-html32.html`) both only mention the ISO 8859-1 character set. HTML 4.0 made HTML officially internationalized when it specified ISO/IEC 10646 as its document character set but also allowed you to use any encoding to represent the characters.

Of course, the Web was being used with other scripts and other character sets than ISO 8859-1 long before HTML 4.0 was published in 1998. Without the underpinning of a universal character set such as ISO/IEC 10646, however, Web browsers were much the same as any other pieces of software. As the following two figures show, a Web browser could handle the script or scripts for which it had been built, but viewing a Web page in an encoding that it did not understand resulted in gibberish. The first figure below shows some Japanese text (which translates as "This is Japanese") viewed from Internet Explorer with the correct encoding selected, and the second figure shows the same text viewed as ISO 8859-1 encoded text.

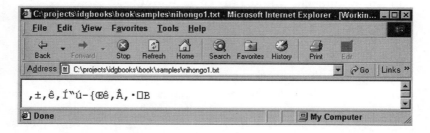

Later versions of browsers have add-on language kits that give the ability to view Web pages in a select range of other scripts, but the support is by no means universal. This leads to work-arounds like that mentioned in a *MultiLingual Computing & Technology* article on Tibetan, where the author suggests using the font tag to select a Tibetan font when the browser does not support a Tibetan encoding.

Personal History

Let me tell you a bit of personal history that pertains to my work prior to the advent of Unicode. In 1994, when I was working in Japan, we produced printed documents from SGML in English, Japanese, Korean, Simplified Chinese, and Traditional Chinese. To do this, we used the TEX formatter in Japanese, Korean, and two flavors of Chinese, plus a separate formatter for English and European language documents, plus the Japanese version of the Emacs editor, plus a Korean version of the vi editor, and finally, specialized Chinese editors. This also required separate Japanese, Korean, and two styles of Chinese fonts for both on-screen display and the printer. We ran the Japanese version of SunOS 4.1.3 on Sun workstations, an English-language version of Unix on a 386 PC, and the Japanese version of Mac OS on an Apple Macintosh.

The various problems of writing Chinese and Korean on Japanese versions of SunOS and Mac OS notwithstanding, both operating systems used the same Japanese characters, although their Japanese text files were mutually unintelligible because they used different encodings to represent those characters. Of course even the Japanese text was unintelligible on the 386 unless you used kterm, the Japanese terminal program, or nemacs (Nihongo Emacs), the Japanese version of Emacs. Even then, you had to use files in the EUC (Extended Unix Code) encoding (which SunOS used), not Shift-JIS (which MacOS used).

Having Unicode supported by the formatters, the operating system, and the editors wouldn't have solved all our problems, but it would have made life a lot easier. Using Unicode all around would have obviated problems with different character encodings on the different machines, and we may have been able to use a single editor no matter what language a document was being written in.

Unicode reduces your character handling problems, but it's not a panacea or a substitute for proper localization or internationalization of your software. If we had a single editor, we would still have needed different input methods for the different scripts. While we may have been able to get away with a single Unicode font for working with the documents on-screen, we would still have needed different fonts when formatting each of the scripts. We would have also needed a formatter (or formatters) that implemented the proper line-breaking rules for each language.

Unconventional mixing of characters also caused problems when we developed a mailing list database for a Tokyo importer of Danish furniture. The database included addresses from not just Japan, but also Denmark, Sweden, Norway, Germany, and other parts of Europe. Pre-Unicode, most software that handled Japanese couldn't also handle the non-ASCII characters used in writing European languages. The operating system and Japanese version of the database that we used were no exception. They worked quite well when we mixed Japanese and English, but neither natively supported the æ, ø, and å characters that are used in Danish but not English, or the other characters such as ä and ö, needed for Swedish names and addresses, or ß, needed for German. All of those are included in the ISO 8859-1, or Latin-1, encoding, but we couldn't input the Latin-1 characters. Even if we could, a properly encoded Latin-1 character would, on our Japanese system, have been interpreted as one of the two bytes for a kanji character. There are ways to mix encodings, using ISO/IEC 2022, but our software was localized, not internationalized, and it didn't support anything other than ASCII (actually, JIS-Roman) and EUC-JP.

Our eventual — and quite proprietary — solution was to replace the half-width katakana font on that machine with one that included the required Latin-1 characters necessary to replace some of the katakana, and to assign function keys for inserting those characters. When creating our font, we had to be careful to avoid writing those characters that the Japanese input method would alter if we were to insert two or more of them in sequence. We also needed to filter the printer output to replace the special characters with the following, in order of their appearance:

- The escape sequence to switch to the Latin-1 encoding.
- The correct character number for the character.
- The escape sequence to switch back to the Japanese encoding.

If our operating system and our database had both supported Unicode, we could have used the correct code values for the Latin-1 characters instead of abusing the role of the half-width katakana characters. Of course, we would have needed a different input method for Danish and the other Western European languages from the one we used for Japanese. However, once the data was in the computer, it would have displayed, sorted and printed without a problem, and without clumsy kludges.

Part I

Unicode 101

Chapter

| 1 | Introducing Unicode and ISO/IEC 10646 |
| 2 | Unicode Design Basis and Principles |

1

Chapter 1

Introducing Unicode and ISO/IEC 10646

Although this is a book about the Unicode Standard, the past, present, and future of the Unicode Standard is inextricably intertwined with that of ISO/IEC 10646. As we will see, the two standards merged their character repertoires in 1991, and today new characters and scripts are added to both standards concurrently. This chapter introduces the two standards and provides a little of their separate origins and common history. The chapter concludes with a summary of the activities of the Unicode Consortium, the parent of the Unicode Standard and the other major influence on the development of the standard.

The Unicode and ISO/IEC 10646 Timeline

A Universal Character Set is an idea whose time has come, or, to borrow a line that Robert Heinlein attributed to Charles Fort:

> You railroad only when it comes time to railroad.

The ISO effort and the Unicode effort started at about the same time, with very similar goals. This is an indication that a truly comprehensive, even universal, character set is an idea whose time has come. It is to their credit and our advantage that the two groups recognized the futility of *two* universal, but incompatible, character sets and so, in 1991, reconciled the differences between their character sets. Table 1-1 shows the timeline of the development of the Unicode Standard and ISO/IEC 10646.

Table 1-1 *Unicode Standard and ISO/IEC 10646 timeline*

Year	Occurrence
1984	ISO/IEC working group formed.
1989	DP 10646 distributed independently of Unicode. "Unicode Han character set" proposed for ISO 10646 by "Unicode Working Group."
1990	Unicode 1.0 published.
1990	DIS-1 10646 balloted.
1991	Unicode and ISO/IEC 10646 agree to merge. Unicode, Inc. formed.
1992	Unicode Standard modified for merger. Unicode 1.0.1 published.
1992	ISO 10646 merged with Unicode. DIS-2 10646 balloted.
1993	Merged standard, ISO 10646-1:1993, balloted.
1993	Unicode 1.1 revised to match ISO 10646-1:1993.
1995	ISO 10646 amended.
1996	Unicode 2.0 published.
1998	Unicode 2.1 published, incorporating euro and correcting errors.
1999	Unicode 3.0 published.
2000	ISO/IEC 10646-1:2000 balloted. ISO/IEC 10646-2:2000 expected.

Note

Table 1.1 refers to ISO/IEC 10646-1:2000 since, at the time of this writing (early 2000), publication of the next revision of ISO/IEC 10646 was expected in 2000.

Ever since the merger in 1991, the Unicode Technical Committee (UTC) and WG2 (the ISO/IEC working group responsible for ISO/IEC 10646) have worked side by side in developing and expanding the character repertoire. The UTC ratifies decisions made by WG2 for inclusion in the Unicode Standard, and the UTC has a C-liaison with WG2, so it is involved with the WG2 decision-making, and can present submissions to WG2.

To the common observer, an international standard like ISO/IEC 10646 presents a different image from an industry standard like Unicode. ISO standards are highly respected for their stability and their independence from vendor influences, but the ISO standards process is frequently thought of as slow-moving (although it often isn't slow). Industry consortiums and industry standards, on the other hand, are often seen as more rapid and responsive, but the industry standards process is sometimes thought of as influenced by the big players in an industry (although it often isn't influenced).

ISO/IEC 10646 and the Unicode Standard largely escape the negative perceptions for their type of standard and benefit from the positive perceptions. As an example of the responsiveness of WG2, adding the 11,172 Hangul script characters took less than six months from submission to approval.

Both the Unicode Standard and ISO/IEC 10646 have benefited from WG2 and the UTC working in tandem. Adoption of the Universal Character Set has benefited from the combination of the two groups because other ISO and IEC standards can reference ISO/IEC 10646 where it is against their rules to reference an industry standard. Similarly, many major projects — particularly government projects — prefer to reference international standards in their contract requirements. The existence of an international standard paralleling the Unicode Standard has helped the adoption of the Unicode character repertoire. Alternately, you could just as easily say that the existence of the Unicode Standard has helped the adoption of the ISO/IEC 10646 character repertoire. Furthermore, some standards, such as the XML Recommendation, normatively reference both the Unicode Standard and ISO/IEC 10646.

The Unicode Standard

The Unicode Standard defines a fixed-width, 16-bit uniform encoding scheme for written characters and text. The standard defines 49,194 distinctly coded characters, including characters for the major scripts of the world, as well as technical symbols in common use. Figure 1-1 shows the major allocations of the Unicode Standard, which are discussed in more detail in Chapter 3.

Work on Unicode began in the late 1980s as a response by multilingual software developers at Xerox and Apple to early drafts of ISO 10646. The term *Unicode* was first used in December 1987. As part of their contribution to ISO 10646, Xerox and Apple joined efforts to create a Han character cross-reference database. In September 1989, the Unicode Working Group (as it was then known) proposed the merged information, entitled the Unicode Han character set, for inclusion in ISO 10646. The formation of the Unicode Consortium was announced in December 1990, at the same time as the second draft of the Unicode Han character repertoire was released for review, and the Consortium was incorporated as Unicode, Inc. in 1991.

 Note

Although the "Unicode" as we know it now was first used in 1987, Nelson Beebe's Unicode bibliography at http:www. math.utah.edu/pub/tex/bin/unicode.html notes eight other uses of the term, including "'Unicode': the universal telegraphic phrase-book," first published in London in 1889.

The Unicode Standard, Version 1.0, was published in 1990. In 1993, Version 1.1 was published, incorporating the changes resulting from the merger with the ISO/IEC 10646 character repertoire. While incremental revisions of the Unicode Standard were available from the Unicode Consortium's Web site, the next printed version of the standard — Version 2.0 — would not be released until 1996. Version 2.0 was code-for-code identical to ISO/IEC 10646-1:1993 (plus amendments).

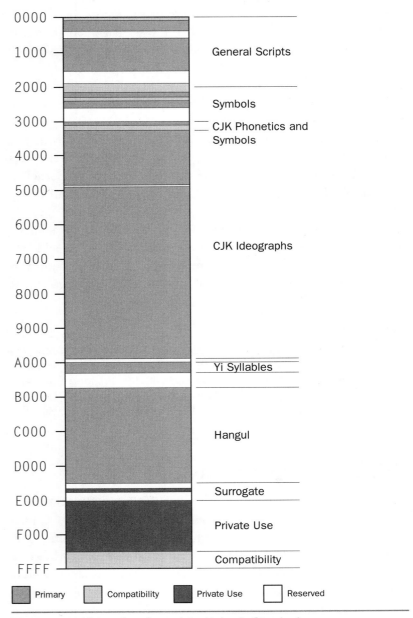

Figure 1-1 *Major allocations of the Unicode Standard*

At the time of this writing, the current version of the Unicode Standard is 3.0, published in 2000. It is a 1040-page book that lists every character with a definition and an example glyph. Version 3.0 defines 49,194 characters, 10,309 more than version 2.0. Unicode 3.0 is identical with the forthcoming ISO/IEC 10646-1:2000. Maintaining compatibility between the Unicode Standard and ISO/IEC 10646 is very important to everyone involved.

The printed Unicode Standard 3.0 book, combined with any online updates (see Appendix B), is its ultimate reference. It covers the definition and handling of the defined character properties in more detail than I can in a primer (for example, it lists all of the characters with the "mirror" property, whereas, in Chapter 5, I only explain it). However, the book cannot completely include as much information on ISO/IEC 10646 or on different programs' and languages' support for the Unicode Standard as I can include in this primer. After you've read this book, the next step is to go to the source and read the published Unicode Standard.

Note

The Unicode Standard is open-ended, and new characters are likely to be added with each new release. For example, the euro   character was added with the Unicode Standard, version 2.1. Appendix B lists the versions of the Unicode Standard to date, and the Web site for this book will track future changes.

What is ISO/IEC 10646?

The full name for this standard is "ISO/IEC 10646-1:1993, Information Technology — Universal Multiple-Octet Coded Character Set (UCS) — Part 1: Architecture and Basic Multilingual Plane." ISO/IEC 10646-1:2000 is expected to be approved in Spring 2000, and ISO/IEC 10646-2, which will define characters outside the Basic Multilingual Plane (BMP), should be approved shortly after that. The Unicode Technical Committee has a liaison membership with the ISO/IEC Working Group responsible for computer character sets. Unicode version 3.0 is code-for-code identical to ISO/IEC 10646-1:2000, although it does define more semantics for characters than ISO/IEC 10646 does.

Figure 1-2 illustrates the multiple portions of the identifiers for ISO and joint ISO/IEC standards. As the figure shows, each portion serves a purpose, and, reading from left to right, each identifies the standard in ever-increasing detail. In many situations when referring to the ISO standard, it is sufficient to omit the part number and year; but to be specific, the full "ISO/IEC 10646-1:2000" identifier should be used.

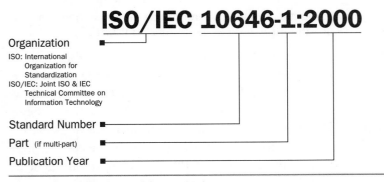

Figure 1-2 *Identifying ISO standards*

ISO/IEC 10646 is the work of ISO/IEC JTC1/SC2/WG2, or Working Group 2 of Subcommittee 2 of the Joint Technical Committee 1 (covering Information Technology) of the International Organization for Standardization (ISO) and the International Electrotechnical Commission. Now you know why people prefer to call it WG2!

WG2 was chartered in 1984 with the goal of developing an international character set standard as an alternative to the multitude of national or regional standards that existed at that time. Interest among nations in the work of WG2 has grown over the years, from seven nations participating in its initial development work, to a reported 19 national bodies and several liaison organizations represented at a 1999 meeting.

The ISO/IEC 10646 standard defines a four-octet (32-bit) coded character set (UCS-4) and a two-octet (16-bit) coded character set (UCS-2) — more on these in Chapter 3. The standard also defines the UTF-8 and UTF-16 formats, thereby establishing how they are commonly used with respect to the Unicode Standard; these encodings are discussed in Chapter 4.

Note

ISO standards refer to *octets* as the eight-bit units commonly called "bytes." Since I have seen newsgroups become paralyzed by raging discussions over whether a byte is or is not an octet, and which term to use in normal conversation, I'll use the ISO terms while discussing ISO/IEC 10646.

The focus of ISO/IEC 10646, far more so than the Unicode Standard, is on the transmission and interchange of the coded characters. Whenever I read ISO/IEC 10646-1:1993, I am always struck by the emphasis on "coded-character-data-elements" being interchanged between an originating device and a receiving device. I am also struck by the use of designating sequences (escape sequences) to indicate the form of the data being exchanged. By contrast, the Unicode Standard focuses on encoding characters and their semantics while, for the most part, not codifying which subsets an application can support. It helps, therefore, to remember that ISO/IEC 10646 is interoperable with ISO/IEC 2022 and other encoding standards. Chinese, Japanese, and Korean encodings of ISO/IEC 2022, for example, are widely used as the information interchange codes for e-mail. ISO/IEC 10646 is, in effect, the next step in the ISO work on encodings for information interchange.

Perhaps another facet of the differences between the standards is that ISO/IEC 10646 defines only the name and character number for each character, along with a short list of properties and the characters with those properties. The standard does provide a graphic symbol for each character but, as you by now expect, it describes these as typical representations, and it does not attempt to prescribe the exact shape of each character. By contrast, the Unicode Standard specifies additional semantics for characters (still without specifying the exact shape of each character) as well as rules for collation — i.e., sorting rules, bidirectional text, etc. — that apply to the character set as a whole.

The essential feature of ISO/IEC 10646 is that characters are uniquely specified by their names; for example, SPACE, LATIN CAPITAL LETTER A, CYRILLIC CAPITAL LETTER ZHE, and CJK UNIFIED IDEOGRAPH 5E73. The name of a character does one of the following:

- Gives the character's meaning
- Describes the character's glyph
- Identifies it as a Hangul glyph or CJK unified ideograph (whose name includes its character number)

Unique names allow unambiguous translation of characters, or *transcoding*, between ISO/IEC 10646 and another coded representation of these characters. To this end, ISO/IEC 10646 uses the same guidelines for composing character names as the ISO/IEC 646, ISO/IEC 6937, ISO 8859, and ISO/IEC 10367 character set standards. Where any of these standards define the same character, they will all use the same character name. Note also that the character names used in the Unicode Standard are the same as those in the English-language version of ISO/IEC 10646.

You've just seen how ISO/IEC 10646 relates to the Unicode Standard. The other major influence on the standard, of course, is its parent organization, the Unicode Consortium. The next section introduces the Consortium and describes its activities.

The Unicode Consortium

The Unicode Consortium is incorporated as by the legal entity "Unicode, Inc.," a California non-profit corporation. (See Appendix

B for how to contact the Consortium.) The Consortium's income from membership fees and sales of the Unicode Standard books covers the administrative and support costs of the Consortium. Development and enhancement of the Unicode Standard continues, however, because of the time, energy, and expertise volunteered by member companies and by individual experts from around the world. By one unofficial estimate, the assessed annual value of the work effort put in by UTC members, member companies, and support staff is two or three times the annual budget of the Unicode Consortium. The time donated by individuals and by member-company employees working on their off hours is incalculable.

Unicode Membership

The Unicode Consortium is made up of companies, organizations, and individuals interested in the promotion and advancement of Unicode. Anyone, including you or your company, can join the Unicode Consortium. There are four levels of membership: Full, Associate, Specialist, and Individual. Only corporations and organizations may be Full or Associate members; individuals may be either Specialist or Individual members. You can join at any time, and membership is renewable yearly. The membership rates, not surprisingly, vary with your membership type.

Several other organizations, including the World Wide Web Consortium, maintain liaison membership with the Unicode Consortium. The composition of the membership list may surprise you. However, it represents a cross-section of the companies (from Apple to Xerox), organizations (such as the Internet Mail Consortium and the Research Libraries Group), and people (such as myself) with an interest in the major scripts of the world. The membership list changes over time. Versions of the Unicode Standard book each list the members current at the time; the up-to-date list is available online at http://www.unicode.org/unicode/consortium/memblist.html. For your reference, the Full, Associate, and Liaison members as of January 2000 are listed in Appendix B.

Membership benefits at the time of this writing include:

- Full members name a Primary and two Alternates to represent them to the Unicode Consortium and at Unicode Technical Committee (UTC) meetings. Only Full members may attend the Annual Meeting of the Consortium, elect the Board of Directors, or take office in the Consortium. Full members are also the only ones to vote on motions and proposals of the Unicode Technical Committee (UTC). Full members have a link from the Consortium's members' page to their site, have company-wide access to the members-only "Unicore" e-mail list and members-only portions of the Web and FTP sites.

- Associate members also name a Primary and two Alternate representatives to the Consortium and the UTC. The members also have a link from the Consortium's members' page to their Web site, but their access to members-only material is restricted to the Primary and Alternate representatives.

- Specialist members — such as I — are their own representatives to the Consortium and the UTC. They are listed on the members' page (without a link to their site), and have access to members-only material.

- Individual members are not listed by name on the Web site, do not have access to members-only material, and may only participate at UTC meetings as space permits.

- All members receive a number of free copies of the Unicode Standard according to their membership category, as well as discounts at the semiannual International Unicode Conferences (IUC).

Note

The Unicode Consortium operates multiple mailing lists. One such list, unicode@unicode.org, is available to members and non-members alike. See Appendix B for details on subscribing to unicode@unicode.org.

Speaking of Unicode

The name "Unicode" and the Unicode logo are trademarks of the Unicode Consortium, and there are restrictions on where and how you may use them.

You may only use the Unicode logo with the written consent of the Unicode Consortium. Non-commercial use of the logo is free, and there is a nominal application fee, but no royalties, for the commercial license to use the logo. You should, however, apply to the Unicode Consortium and receive permission before you use the logo for any purpose, even if it is non-commercial.

An example of non-commercial use of the logo would be if it were to accompany a description of the Unicode Standard or the Unicode Consortium in an article or news report. On the other hand, since commercial products must license their use of the Unicode logo, you cannot use the logo in product reviews or descriptions without a license.

You can license use of the logo for a specific product or product revision for a two-year period to designate that you, the manufacturer, certify that the product supports the Unicode Standard. Once you have licensed it, you may use the logo in marketing materials, product announcements, product reviews or descriptions, and advertisements. The Unicode Consortium may revoke your license at any time if the logo is not used in accordance with its terms and conditions.

You should also use the word "Unicode" correctly. Since it is a trademark, use "Unicode™" when referring to the Unicode Standard, and "Unicode®" when referring to the Unicode Consortium and the Unicode logo. You should also attribute the ownership of the trademarks as follows:

Unicode™	Unicode is a trademark of Unicode, Inc.
Unicode®	Unicode is a registered trademark of Unicode, Inc.
The Unicode logo	Unicode and the Unicode logo are trademarks of Unicode, Inc.

The "Unicode™" attribution for the trademark appears on the cover. In the eyes of the law, that and the legal notice at the beginning of the book are sufficient to cover all occurrences of "Unicode" in this book. Table 1-2 shows additional requirements for correct use of "Unicode."

Table 1-2 *Additional requirements for correct use of "Unicode"*

Rule	Correct	Incorrect
Never use in product or service name		Tony's Unicode Editor tkg/unicode
Use as proper adjective	Unicode™ Standard Unicode® Consortium	
Do not combine with improper generic names	Application of the Unicode™ Standard	Unicode™ application
Do not use in possessive form	Characters in Unicode™	Unicode's™ characters
Do not use in plural form	Read the next two characters	Read the next two Unicodes

International Unicode Conferences

The Unicode Consortium hosts semiannual International Unicode Conferences in San Jose, California, each September and at another location each March. In recent years, the March conference has been held in Mainz, Germany; in Tokyo, Japan; in Boston, Massachusetts; and in Amsterdam, Netherlands. Global Meeting Services, Inc., organizes these conferences; however, you can find information on both recent and future conferences on the Unicode Consortium's Web site at http://www.unicode.org/unicode/ conference/about-conf.html.

Recent conferences have featured two days of tutorials plus two days of presentations. When not in plenary, the presentations have been three simultaneous tracks. Looking at the proceedings from the Ninth to the Fifteenth International Unicode Conferences, both the tutorials and presentations have had extremely high quality content. Unfortunately the Unicode Consortium recently changed its practice, and you can no longer buy copies of past conferences' proceedings from the Consortium.

Unicode Technical Committee

This is the engine that powers the Unicode machine. The UTC produces the Unicode Standard as well as Unicode Technical Reports (UTR). A UTR may be make normative changes to the Unicode Standard: for example, UTR #8 — The Unicode Standard, Version 2.1 — details the changes and additions that were made between the Unicode Standard, Version 2.0, and the Unicode Standard, Version 2.1. A UTR may instead simply provide information for implementers of the Unicode Standard. Some UTRs have been superseded by later versions of the Unicode Standard; a complete list is provided in Appendix B of this book, and the content of current UTRs is covered in later chapters.

Although the quarterly UTC meetings are held in the United States, the committee is made up of experts and member representatives from around the globe. Like most collaborative efforts these days, much of the UTC's work takes the form of e-mail discussions. Files for many discussion items are posted on the members-only Web and FTP sites long before the completed works are publicly available.

The Unicode Consortium and Other Standards Bodies

As noted previously, several standards bodies have liaison membership with the Unicode Consortium, and the Unicode Technical Committee has C-liaison status with the ISO/IEC JTC1/SC2/WG2, the ISO/IEC working group responsible for ISO/IEC 10646.

Note also that many of the Unicode Consortium's members are also members of consortia and industry groups such as the W3C and the Internet Society (http://www.isoc.org/) that have liaisons with some of these standards organizations. Furthermore, there is some overlap between the membership of the UTC and the membership of some of the ISO/IEC and other committees, including, for example, the internationalization working group of the World Wide Web Consortium (w3c-i18n-wg). This doesn't lead to a conspiracy theory, but rather to the realization that many people and many organizations are committed to and working together toward achieving interoperable standards.

Unicode Resources

The Unicode Consortium makes public on its Web and FTP sites many files related to the Unicode Standard. Chief among these is the Unicode Character Database. This is a set of text files containing information on all of the characters in the Unicode Standard plus their defined semantics. Most files detail one character per line so they are easily grepped (if you like using Unix tools). The Unicode Character Database is covered in detail in Part 2. A comprehensive list of available resources appears in Appendix B.

Before you read up on the technical details, however, I suggest you read the next chapter. It covers the design basis and principles of the Unicode Standard, so you can understand the "why" as well as the "how."

Chapter 2

Unicode Design Basis and Principles

The design basis for the Unicode Standard gave it a solid foundation that established it as universal, efficient, uniform, and unambiguous. These qualities were largely missing from prior character encoding standards. Building on this design basis, the Unicode Standard defines ten design principles that have guided its development throughout its history.

This chapter introduces the basis and principles of the Unicode Standard's design. With this chapter under your belt, you will be better able to appreciate the following chapters on the structure of the standard and the technical details of its implementation.

Design Basis

The design basis of the Unicode Standard reflects a desire to avoid many of the pitfalls of prior standards. As you may recall from the Introduction, early character sets used seven bits or fewer per character. Later character sets used eight bits. Eventually, multi-byte character sets for large character repertoires such as Chinese, Japanese, and Korean were developed. There was, and still is, a multitude of character sets — such as the ISO 646 variants or the different parts of ISO/IEC 8859 — that use the same code point ranges as each other, yet represent different characters. There are also techniques, such as the one described by ISO/IEC 2022, for mixing character sets within a single stream of bytes. ISO/IEC 2022 — when you consider it along with all of the character sets that came before it — is well on its way toward being able to handle nearly every major written script in the world. ISO/IEC 2022 is, however, a complex and comparatively fragile mechanism best suited for the transmission of character data rather than for its storage.

Against this background, the Unicode Consortium developed a four-part basis for the design of the Unicode Standard. The Unicode Standard should be:

- *Universal.* The repertoire has to be large enough to encompass all characters likely to be used in general text interchange.

- *Efficient.* Plain text, composed of a sequence of fixed width characters, is simple to parse, and software does not need to maintain state, look for special escape sequences, or search forward or backward through text to identify characters.

- *Uniform.* A fixed-length character code allows efficient sorting, searching, display, and editing of text.

- *Unambiguous.* Any given 16-bit value always represents the same character.

Unicode Design Principles

Building on this design basis, the architecture of the Unicode Standard presently reflects ten particular design principles, which will be introduced in this section. Note, however, that during the development of the Unicode Standard, these design principles had yet to be followed, and some had yet to be discovered. In some areas, compromises were reached — such as including presentation forms of characters for compatibility with existing standards — that reflect the proper application of one design principle ahead of others that competed with it. In general, whatever principle that would enable easier adoption of the Unicode Standard took precedence.

Sixteen-Bit Characters

Unicode character codes are a uniform 16 bits in length. For compatibility with existing computer systems that can't handle 16-bit characters, the Unicode Standard defines the UTF-8 format for lossless transformation between Unicode characters and 8-bit character sequences

Cross-Reference

See Chapter 4 for more information on lossless transformation between Unicode characters and 8-bit character sequences

In practice, creating a Universal Character Set requires more characters than you can represent using 16-bit character numbers. Accordingly, the Unicode Standard has adopted the UTF-16 encoding, which can represent over 1,000,000 additional characters. When characters outside the ordinary 16-bit range U+0000 to U+FFFF are eventually defined, they will be encoded in UTF-16 as a sequence of two 16-bit values. This will add a level of complexity to character handling, but it remains simpler than some other encoding schemes. This is because there is no ambiguity between the 16-bit code values for characters and those for representing code values beyond U+FFFF.

Cross-Reference

UTF-16 and the "surrogates" extension mechanism are described in Chapters 4 and 5, respectively.

UTF-32, a 32-bit fixed-width encoding defined in UTR #19 (in draft at the time of this writing), to some extent breaks from all four key design principles — universality, efficiency, uniformity, non-ambiguity.

Cross-Reference

The reasons why the UTF-32 breaks from all four design principles are explored in Chapter 4.

Other standards, such as XML and HTML, combine the Unicode Standard's character repertoire with any formally recognized character encoding. In XML and HTML, characters that cannot be represented in the current encoding are coded as numeric character references to the Unicode code value.

Full Encoding

The original design principle that led to using 16-bit values to represent characters was that it enabled 65,536 code positions to be assigned to characters. The expectation is that this would far exceed the expected requirements for all modern and most archaic languages.

As of Unicode 2.1, there were still over 18,000 unassigned code positions, and Unicode 3.0 has nearly 8,000 unassigned 16-bit code values, but it is already recognized that this is not enough. Later versions of the Unicode Standard and of ISO/IEC 10646 will assign code values in the range U-0001000 to U-000FFFFF. Reasons for the expansion beyond 64,000 characters include:

- The practice of assigning characters in blocks, with the result that many blocks contain unassigned code values that will never be assigned

- The large number of characters included for one-to-one mapping between the Unicode Standard and existing character sets, even though many of them could be composed from a smaller number of base and combining characters

- The large number of CJK ideographs

- The large number of written scripts that potentially could be included

Characters, Not Glyphs

Unicode is generally concerned with characters, not glyphs. The distinction between characters and glyphs was made in the Introduction. Encoding characters rather than glyphs made developing the

Unicode Standard into a merely gigantic effort, rather than an infinite one. This also made the previous design principle realistic, at least for a time.

The Introduction contained a figure that showed a wide variety of glyphs for the "a" (LATIN SMALL LETTER A, to give it its Unicode name) character. If I can find that many glyphs just for "a" with little effort, imagine how many possible glyphs there are for all the characters in the written scripts of the world. Cataloging the characters is a Herculean task, but cataloging the glyphs would be a never-ending one.

Semantics

The Unicode Standard provides well-defined semantics for each character, including numeric, spacing, combination, and directionality properties. Several new property types were added to the Unicode Standard, Version 3.0; in addition, many property assignments were made. Full lists of characters with each property are included in the book of the Unicode Standard, Version 3.0. The property information is also included in the Unicode Character Database, available from the Unicode Consortium's FTP site and detailed in Chapter 3.

 Cross-Reference

Property types are detailed in Chapter 5

The specification of these semantics is not currently included in ISO/IEC 10646, and the writers of the Unicode Standard see this as a major feature of Unicode over ISO/IEC 10646.

Plain Text

Plain Unicode text is a sequence of character codes. The Unicode Standard does not currently define any codes for specifying font, etc., although there are character codes that provide hints about directionality of the text and the language.

The recent Unicode Technical Report #7, while not part of Unicode 3.0, defines the use of characters from Plane 14 for use in tagging the language of the text. Since the markup for the language tags cannot be confused for textual content, in theory parsing for them is easier, than, say, using SGML or XML, and they are seen as a lighter-weight mechanism for specifying language.

Cross-Reference

The Unicode Technical Report #7 is detailed in Chapter 6.

In Unicode terms, HTML, XML, and other such Internet "markup languages," are "fancy texts" or "higher-level protocols" since their markup codes represent additional data structures interspersed in the stream of plain Unicode characters. However, both HTML and XML define standardized mechanisms for specifying the origin of their file's contained written language (see Chapter 9); enormous amounts of textual data around the world are currently represented as HTML and, increasingly, as XML. When HTML and XML are used, it is *strongly* advised to not use the Plane 14 language tags because mixing the two forms of markup complicates parsing of the data.

Logical Order

Characters are stored in their logical order: in the sequence in which they are read, which is not always the sequence in which they are displayed. For example, Arabic and Hebrew are read right to left. Since the logical start of the right-to-left text is the character closest to the right margin, as Figure 2-1 shows, that character is the first character in the Unicode character stream.

Display order

Example of "tfel ot thgir" text

Logical order

Example of "right to left" text

Figure 2-1 *Display versus logical order for right-to-left text*

The characters' directionality properties, and use of character codes specifying changes in direction when mixing characters of different dominant direction, provide sufficient information for correct rendering of the text.

The Unicode Standard also specifies that each combining mark (see "Dynamic Composition" later in this chapter) always follows its base character. In contrast, existing encodings are not standardized, and some require the combining characters before the base character and some after.

Unification

Unicode unifies characters within scripts across languages so that characters with equivalent form are given a single code. For example, common letters, punctuation marks, symbols, and diacritics were each given one code. In addition, over 130,000 ideographs used in Chinese, Japanese, and Korean were unified to 27,786 Han character codes.

To give specific examples:

- The German umlaut dots, diaeresis, and the mathematical double derivative sign are unified as U+0308, COMBINING DIAERESIS.

- The prime symbol ('), the symbol for seconds, and the symbol for feet are unified as U+2032, PRIME.

Not all characters that look alike are unified. For example, the Greek capital omega and the ohm symbol remain as two separate characters. Such exceptions are "compatibility characters" that could have been unified but instead remained at separate code positions, often in support of round-trip mapping between Unicode and an existing code set. As explained in Chapter 7, additional rules were applied when unifying Chinese, Japanese, and Korean characters.

The downside of the unification process is that a "Unicode" font would use the same glyph for the same character number, no matter what glyph variations existed for the "un-unified" forms of the character. At best, this leads to homogenized fonts that use generic representations of the characters and please no one; at worst, this leads to the occasional "wrong" appearance when the font uses the wrong glyph variant for a user's locale.

Extra information can be added to the document, using the Unicode language tags or, preferably, a higher-level protocol such as XML markup and the `xml:lang` attribute, to specify the correct language and/or locale for the text. This practice can be used to key the selection of fonts for representing the characters, but this also leads to more complex software and detracts from the "Characters, not Glyphs" design principle.

Dynamic Composition

Instead of allowing just well-known accented characters such as Ö, the Unicode Standard allows dynamic composition of accented forms where any base character plus any combining character (or sequence of combining characters) can make an accented form. Figure 2-2 shows four examples of dynamic composition. The first is the "O" and "¨" example that I've been using, and the other three are legal but rather more unusual examples just to show what is possible.

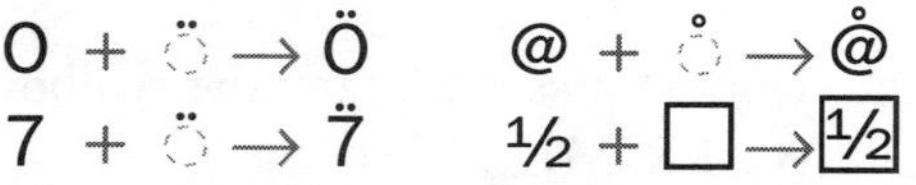

$$\text{O} + \ddot{\circlearrowright} \rightarrow \ddot{\text{O}} \qquad @ + \overset{\circ}{\circlearrowright} \rightarrow @\overset{\circ}{}$$

$$7 + \ddot{\circlearrowright} \rightarrow \ddot{7} \qquad \tfrac{1}{2} + \square \rightarrow \boxed{\tfrac{1}{2}}$$

Figure 2-2 *Dynamic composition examples*

Equivalent Sequence

Since some characters may be represented in precomposed or dynamically composed forms, the Unicode Standard defines equivalent sequences for each precomposed form. The Unicode Standard, Version 3.0, also includes character decomposition mappings that can be recursively followed to reach the maximal decomposition of a character. Figure 2-3 shows some examples of character sequences and their decomposed equivalents. Note how the combining character follows the base character in both examples.

ãu → a + ̃ + u

aü → a + u + ̈

Figure 2-3 *Equivalent sequence examples*

Since sequences of combining characters can follow a base character, the Standard also defines a canonical ordering for combining characters.

Cross-Reference

Character decomposition and canonical ordering of characters is discussed more in Chapter 5.

Note that the Unicode Standard does not prescribe one particular internal representation of composed characters or one particular sequence of combining characters. Systems may choose to normalize Unicode text to one particular representation, and the W3C character model for the World Wide Web standardizes the normalization form for the entire Web, but in the Unicode Standard, all sequences of characters are permitted.

Convertibility

Round-trip conversion between Unicode and many pre-existing standards is possible since each character has a unique correspondence with a sequence of one or more Unicode characters. When a base standard includes multiple variant forms of a single character, the variants are not unified to ensure that there will always be a mapping between Unicode and the base standard.

While accurate convertibility is guaranteed, many conversions require a mapping table. This is since the corresponding Unicode characters may not be in the same sequence as in the base standard or a base standard character may map to a sequence of Unicode characters.

Guaranteeing convertibility has required compromises such as the inclusion of many compatibility characters. This does mean that the Unicode Standard can become a replacement or alternative for these pre-existing standards. It also means that an application can read or write using a pre-existing coded character set and also be "Unicode inside." In the chapters that follow, you'll see in more detail what it means to be "Unicode inside." The next chapter describes the encodings associated with the Unicode Standard, and later chapters show you how to work with characters and text.

Part II

Unicode CloseUp

Chapter

3	Structure of the Unicode Standard
4	Encodings and Transcodings
5	Characters and Character Properties
6	Working With Text
7	CJK Ideographs and Hangul
8	Standard Issues

Chapter 3

Structure of the Unicode Standard

Now that you know something of the history of the Unicode Consortium and of the principles governing the design, I can go into some detail about the structure of the Unicode Standard and its character repertoire.

Since the purpose of the Unicode standard is to encode the major written scripts of the world, it is not surprising that its character repertoire is divided into blocks of characters associated with specific scripts. The following section identifies the major allocation areas within the repertoire, and the second section introduces each of the blocks in the Unicode Standard. To keep this chapter a reasonable length, I've only provided bare details about the blocks here.

Cross-Reference

More detailed descriptions about blocks appear in Appendix A.

The real source for information about characters and blocks, of course, is the Unicode Standard itself, and, in particular, the text files making up the Unicode Character Database. This chapter's third section describes `UnicodeData.txt` and associated files and how to use them.

`Unihan.txt`, one of the Unicode Character Database files, specifies the mappings between the unified Han characters in the

Unicode Standard and the corresponding characters in each of the source standards. It is described in the section on Han unification in Chapter 7.

It bears repeating that the Unicode Standard is character for character identical with ISO/IEC 10646. The two standards have other things in common, but there are also significant differences in terminology and even conceptual differences about the purpose and use of this universal character set. This chapter includes a discussion of the ISO/IEC view of the character set's structure and use.

Finally, the chapter concludes with a discussion of whether the Unicode Standard and ISO/IEC 10646 really are universal.

Major Allocation Areas

The Unicode Standard divides its character repertoire into allocation areas that group related blocks together. Successive versions of the Standard, however, have reduced the emphasis on organization by allocation area. The Unicode Standard, Version 2.0, organized its block descriptions by allocation area, but the Version 3.0 book only names the areas, and does not organize its entire document around them.

What are the Allocation Areas?

Table 3-1 provides descriptions of the major allocation areas of the Unicode 3.0 character repertoire. Compared to the Unicode 2.0 areas, the Unicode Standard, Version 3.0, changed some allocation area boundaries and added the Yi Syllables allocation area.

Table 3-1 *Major Allocation Areas*

Name	Start	End	Description
General Scripts	0000	1FFF	Latin and other non-ideographic scripts: for example, Greek, Hebrew, Thai, Bengali, Tibetan, and Lao. These each have comparatively small character sets.

Name	Start	End	Description
Symbols	2000	2DFF	Symbolic characters and dingbats for punctuation, mathematics, chemistry, etc. This also includes, for example, OCR characters and characters for representing control codes.
CJK Phonetics and Symbols	2E00	33FF	Phonetic characters, punctuation marks, and symbols used in Chinese, Japanese, and Korean.
CJK Ideographs	3400	9FFF	Ideographic Han characters unified from Chinese, Japanese, and Korean sources.
Yi Syllables	A000	A4CF	Yi syllables and Yi radicals.
Hangul Syllables	AC00	D743	Precomposed Korean Hangul syllables.
Surrogates	D800	DFFF	Low- and high-surrogate code points used in the UTF-16 encoding (see Chapter 4) to address characters in the next 16 planes (where the code points addressed by a 16-bit code value represent a plane, and the currently defined characters are all in plane 00).
Private Use	E000	F8FF	Reserved for user-defined characters.
Compatibility and Specials	F900	FFFD	Alternate representations of characters from existing standards. These duplicates of characters defined elsewhere in the Unicode Standard are included for compatibility and round-trip mapping. This are also includes several special-use characters.

Tables 3-2 to 3-10 and Figures 3-1 to 3-9 show the layout of the blocks within each of the major allocation areas of the Unicode Standard's character repertoire. They also show the code value range and the name of each of those blocks. Although minimal information is given here, each of the blocks is discussed in more detail in Appendix A. If you need further information on the scripts mentioned, some additional sources are listed in the Bibliography.

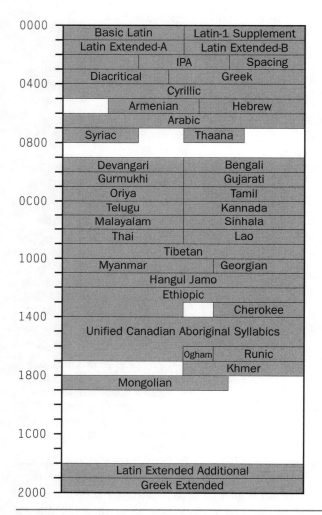

Figure 3-1 *General Scripts area*

Table 3-2 *General Scripts Area Character Block*

Start	End	Character Block Name
0000	007F	Basic Latin. This is the same as ASCII (ISO 646-IRV).
0080	00FF	Latin-1 Supplement. This is the same as the corresponding character numbers in ISO 8859-1.
0100	017F	Latin Extended-A. Additional letters that extend the Basic Latin and Latin-1 Supplement blocks to support additional languages such as Afrikaans, Polish, and Welsh.
0180	024F	Latin Extended-B. Additional letters required for supporting additional languages such as Azerbaijani, Ewe, Fulani, Hausa, Zhuang, and Zulu, etc.
0250	02AF	IPA Extensions. Symbols of the International Phonetic Alphabet (IPA) that are not encoded elsewhere.
02B0	02FF	Spacing Modifier Letters. Signs indicating modification of a preceding letter.
0300	036F	Combining Diacritical Marks. Diacritical marks for use with any script. Remember that in the Unicode Standard, combining characters can be used with any base character.
0370	03FF	Greek. Modern Greek, archaic Greek, and Coptic letters.
0400	04FF	Cyrillic. Letters for Russian and other languages, including some historic Cyrillic letters rarely used in modern forms.
0530	058F	Armenian. Used primarily for writing the Armenian language.
0590	05FF	Hebrew. Used for Hebrew, Yiddish, Judezmo, and other languages.

Continued

Table 3-2 *Continued*

Start	End	Character Block Name
0600	06FF	Arabic.
		Used for Arabic, and also for other languages such as Persian and Urdu.
0700	074F	Syriac.
		Script for the Syriac language that grew out of Aramaic and is now mainly used as the liturgical language for certain Christian churches.
0780	07BF	Thaana.
		Script for the Dhivehi language used in the Maldives.
0900	097F	Devanagari.
		Used for Hindi and classical Sanskrit.
0980	09FF	Bengali.
		A North Indian script derived from Sanskrit and used for Bengali plus other languages such as Assamese.
0A00	0A7F	Gurmukhi.
		Used to write the Punjabi language.
0A80	0AFF	Gujarati.
		Used to write Gujarati and Kacchi.
0B00	0B7F	Oriya.
		Another North Indian script related to Devangari that is used for the Oriya language and also for Khondi and Santali.
0B80	0BFF	Tamil.
		Used for the Tamil language, which is used in southern India, Sri Lanka, Singapore, and parts of Malaysia.
0C00	0C7F	Telugu.
		Used for the Telugu language of Andhra Pradesh state in India and also for minority languages such as Gondi and Lambadi.
0C80	0CFF	Kannada.
		Used for the Kannada language of Karnataka state in India and also for minority languages such as Tulu.

Start	End	Character Block Name
0D00	0D7F	Malayalam.
		Used for the Malayalam language of Kerala state in India.
0D80	0DFF	Sinhala.
		Used for Sinhalese, the official language of Sri Lanka.
0E00	0E7F	Thai.
		Used for the Thai language and other languages such as Kuy, Lavna, and Pali.
0E80	0EFF	Lao.
		Used for Lao, the official language of Laos.
0F00	0FFF	Tibetan.
		Used for Tibetan and other languages such as Ladakhi and Lahuli.
1000	109F	Myanmar.
		Used for Burmese and other languages spoken in Myanmar such as Mon, Karen, and Shan.
10A0	10FF	Georgian.
		Used for the language of Georgia on the southeastern corner of the Black Sea.
1100	11FF	Hangul Jamo.
		Alphabetic components that are combined, or conjoined, to form the syllables of the Hangul script for the Korean language.
1200	137F	Ethiopic.
		Used for Amharic and other languages of East Africa.
13A0	13FF	Cherokee.
		Syllabary of the Cherokee language.
1400	167F	Unified Canadian Aboriginal Syllabics.
		Syllabic characters for languages such as Cree, Ojibwe, Athabaskan, and Inuit.
1680	169F	Ogham.
		Archaic Irish script.
16A0	16FF	Runic.
		Archaic Norse script.

Continued

Table 3-2 *Continued*

Start	End	Character Block Name
1780	17FF	Khmer.
		Script for the national language of Cambodia.
1800	18AF	Mongolian.
		Traditional script for the Mongolian language.
1E00	1EFF	Latin Extended Additional.
		Precomposed combinations of Latin letters included in the Unicode Standard for compatibility with the developing ISO 10646 standard.
1F00	1FFF	Greek Extended.
		Precomposed combinations of Greek letters included in the Unicode Standard for compatibility with the developing ISO 10646 standard.

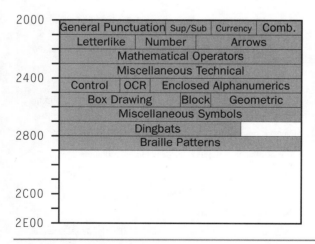

Figure 3-2 *Symbols area*

Table 3-3 *Symbols Area Character Blocks*

Start	End	Character Block Name
2000	206F	General Punctuation.
		Punctuation characters, some of which are used by many different scripts.
2070	209F	Superscripts and Subscripts.
		Superscript and subscript characters included for compatibility with existing character sets.
20A0	20CF	Currency Symbols.
		Currency symbols not encoded in other blocks.
20D0	20FF	Combining Marks for Symbols.
		Diacritical marks that are generally applied to mathematical or technical symbols.
2100	214F	Letterlike Symbols.
		Symbols derived from letters of alphabetic scripts.
2150	218F	Number Forms.
		Number forms, e.g., Roman numerals, included for compatibility with existing character sets.
2190	21FF	Arrows.
2200	22FF	Mathematical Operators.
2300	23FF	Miscellaneous Technical.
2400	243F	Control Pictures.
		Representations of the names of the C0 control characters, and the space, delete, and new-line characters.
2440	245F	Optical Character Recognition.
		OCR-A characters that are not otherwise encoded and MICR symbols used in check processing.
2460	24FF	Enclosed Alphanumerics.
		Enclosed numbers and letters included for compatibility with existing standards.

Continued

Table 3-3 *Continued*

Start	End	Character Block Name
2500	257F	Box Drawing.
		Box drawing characters included for compatibility with existing standards.
2580	259F	Block Elements.
		Graphic characters representing various filled or stated blocks included for compatibility with existing standards.
25A0	25FF	Geometric Shapes.
		Graphic characters representing various geometric shapes.
2600	26FF	Miscellaneous Symbols.
2700	27BF	Dingbats.
		Characters from the well-known ITC Zapf Dingbats font that are not otherwise encoded.
2800	28FF	Braille Patterns.
		Braille pattern symbols.

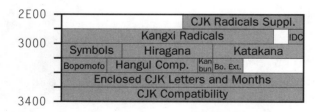

Figure 3-3 *CJK Phonetics and Symbols area*

Table 3-4 *CJK Phonetics and Symbols Area Character Blocks*

Start	End	Character Block Name
2E80	2EFF	CJK Radicals Supplement. Additional radicals not included in the 214 Kangxi radicals.
2F00	2FDF	Kangxi Radicals. 214 characters for the traditional indexing of Han ideographs.
2FF0	2FFF	Ideographic Description Characters. Characters used for describing the layout of an ideographic character.
3000	303F	CJK Symbols and Punctuation Punctuation marks and symbols used in China, Japan, and Korea.
3040	309F	Hiragana. Syllabary used in writing Japanese.
30A0	30FF	Katakana. Syllabary used in writing Japanese.
3100	312F	Bopomofo. Phonetic characters used for Chinese, principally the Mandarin language.
3130	318F	Hangul Compatibility Jamo. Additional Jamo included for compatibility with KSC 5601.
3190	319F	Kanbun. Literally "Chinese writing by/for Japanese," these are marks used in Japanese text to indicate the Japanese reading order of classical Chinese text.
31A0	31BF	Bopomofo Extended. Additional Bopomofo characters.
3200	32FF	Enclosed CJK Letters and Months
3300	33FF	CJK Compatibility

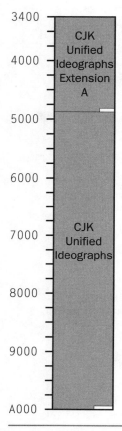

Figure 3-4 *CJK Ideographs area*

Table 3-5 *CJK Ideographs Area Character Blocks*

Start	End	Character Block Name
3400	4DB5	CJK Unified Ideographs Extension A.
		Additional ideographs added with Version 3.0.
4E00	9FFF	CJK Unified Ideographs.
		Han ideographs unified from Chinese, Japanese, and Korean sources.

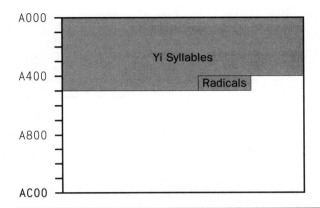

Figure 3-5 *Yi Syllables area*

Table 3-6 *Yi Syllables Area Character Blocks*

Start	End	Character Block Name
A000	A48F	Yi Syllables.
		Yi, also known as Lolo, is a script resembling Chinese in overall shape that is used in the Yunnan province of China.
A490	A4CF	Yi Radicals.
		Basic units of the Yi syllables.

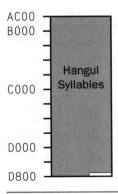

Figure 3-6 *Hangul Syllables area*

Table 3-7 *Hangul Syllables Area Character Blocks*

Start	End	Character Block Name
AC00	D7A3	Hangul Syllables. Composed syllables for the Korean writing system.

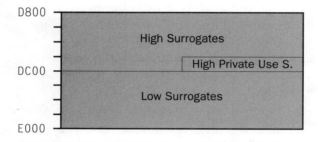

Figure 3-7 *Surrogates area structure*

Table 3-8 *Surrogates Area Structure Character Blocks*

Start	End	Character Block Name
D800	DB7F	High Surrogates. The first code value in a surrogate pair. See Chapter 5.
DB80	DBFF	High Private Use Surrogates. The first code value in a surrogate pair that addresses the private use areas that are accessible with UTF-16. See Chapter 5 and the section in this chapter on ISO/IEC 10646 structure.
DC00	DFFF	Low Surrogates. The second code value in a surrogate pair. See Chapter 5.

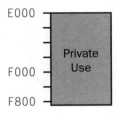

Figure 3-8 *Private Use area*

Table 3-9 *Private Use Area Character Blocks*

Start	End	Character Block Name
E000	F8FF	Private Use.
		Reserved for characters defined by private agreement between users.

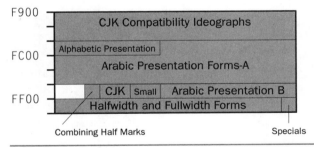

Figure 3-9 *Compatibility and Specials area*

Table 3-10 *Compatibility and Specials Area Character Blocks*

Start	End	Character Block Name
F900	FAFF	CJK Compatibility Ideographs.
		Ideographs included for compatibility with existing standards.
FB00	FB4F	Alphabetic Presentation Forms.
		Presentation forms of Armenian, Hebrew, and Latin characters.

Continued

Table 3-10 *Continued*

Start	End	Character Block Name
FB50	FDFF	Arabic Presentation Forms-A.
		Presentation forms – for example, contextual variants, ligatures, and ornate forms – of Arabic characters included for compatibility with existing standards.
FE20	FE2F	Combining Half Marks.
		Pairs of characters that are each the presentation form of one half of a combining mark that applies to multiple base characters.
FE30	FE4F	CJK Compatibility Forms.
		Presentation forms of symbols that are already encoded by the standard.
FE50	FE6F	Small Form Variants.
		Small variants of ASCII punctuation characters included for compatibility with CNS 11643.
FE70	FEFE	Arabic Presentation Forms-B.
		Arabic presentation forms included for compatibility with existing standards.
FEFF	FEFF	Specials.
		The Byte Order Mark (BOM) character, which also has significance as an encoding form signature. See Chapter 5.
FF00	FFEF	Halfwidth and Fullwidth Forms.
		Presentation forms included for round-trip mapping with existing CJK character sets.
FFF0	FFFD	Specials.
		Characters with special significance for Unicode processing.

Within most blocks, there are unassigned code values that are reserved for future standardization. Gaps between blocks are likewise reserved.

Notice also there is not a one-to-one correspondence between blocks and scripts covered by the Standard. For example:

- Characters from the Basic Latin block can be used to write English and many African languages, plus most of the characters are used in other scripts.

- Characters from the Latin-1 Supplement can be used for multiple European orthographies plus, for example, Hawaiian, Indonesian, and Swahili.

- The International Phonetic Alphabet (IPA) is written with characters from the IPA Extensions block plus many symbols found outside the block, since the IPA characters were unified as much as possible with other characters. In addition, some IPA characters are incorporated into writing systems for many written languages.

Note that U+FFFE and U+FFFF are regarded as non-characters and will not be encoded by either the Unicode Standard or ISO/IEC 10646. U+FFFE has significance as the byte-swapped form of U+FEFF, Byte-Order Mark, and it is used as an indicator of the encoding. U+FFFF is available to applications for use as an error code or a non-character value.

Cross-Reference

See the ISO/IEC 10646 section and the discussion of "endianness" in Chapter 4 for details.

What's in the Pipeline?

Table 3-11 lists the scripts proposed for inclusion in the Unicode Standard at the time of this writing. Some of these have been provisionally approved by the Unicode Technical Committee (UTC) or by both the UTC and, for inclusion in ISO/IEC 10646, WG2. The Consortium also accepts proposals for new characters.

Cross-Reference

For information on the submission process, see Chapter 8.

Note

This table shows the range of scripts proposed for inclusion at the time of this writing. The chance of a script being included by the time you read this ranges from nearly certain to nearly zero. See `http://www.egt.ie/standards/iso10646/ucs-roadmap.html` for information on the status of current proposals.

Table 3-11 *Scripts Proposed for Inclusion in the Unicode Standard*

Name	Description
Avestan	An ancient Iranian language that was the sacred language of the Zoroastrians.
Basic Egyptian Hieroglyphics	Used by scholars to write Ancient Egyptian.
Blissymbolics	A symbol system developed by Charles Bliss as a visual supplement to speech.
Brahmi	Script used in ancient India.
Buginese	Language spoken on the island of Celebes in Indonesia.
Byzantine Musical Symbols	An ancient musical notation dating back to ancient Greece and used since the 7th Century C.E. for religious choral music hand-scribed in the literature of the Byzantine and Benedictine (Orthodox) churches.
Cham	One of the minor languages spoken in Vietnam.
Cirth	Script invented by J. R. R. Tolkien and used in *Lord of the Rings* and *The Silmarillion*.
CJK Unified Ideographs, Extension B	Approximately 41,000 rare ideographs unified from currently unencoded ideographs present in a variety of sources.
Coptic	Liturgical language of the Coptic Church.
Cypriot Syllabary	Syllabary for the Cypriot dialect of Greek that was used from about 800 B.C.E. to 200 B.C.E.

Name	Description
Deseret Alphabet	Phonetic alphabet for English used by The Church of Jesus Christ of Latter-day Saints. Created in the 19th century, it has never been widely used.
Etruscan	Script for the Etruscan and Oscan languages. The script was used from the 7th century B.C.E. to the first century C.E..
Glagolitic	Alphabet ascribed to St. Cyril used for the Old Church Slavonic language.
Gothic	Phonetic alphabet used by the Germanic tribe of the Goths, invented in the 4th century C.E. by the Gothic bishop, Wulfila.
Javanese	Language spoken in central and eastern Java. (No connection with the computer language.)
Linear B	Oldest known Greek syllabic system that was used on Crete until at least 1375 B.C.E.
Meroitic	Script used by the ancient Meroites in what is now Sudan.
Old Hungarian Runic	The writing system of the Pálos religious order and Székely culture of early Hungary, prior to the end of the Turkish Wars in 1526.
Old Permic	A language from northeastern Russia.
Old Persian Cuneiform	Used by the scholarly community to write Old Persian.
Phillipine Scripts	Scripts for writing Tagalog, Hanunóo, Buhid, and Tagbanwa.
Phoenician	Script of ancient Phoenicia.
Pollard	Script invented by Samuel Pollard and used for about a dozen languages in Southeast Asia.
Rong	Script based on Tibetan writing that was devised in 1720.
Shavian	Phonetic alphabet designed by Kingsley Read that won a competition for a new alphabet established under the terms of George Bernard Shaw's will. Also known as "Shaw's alphabet" and the "Proposed British Alphabet."
Sinaitic	An ancient Semitic script

Continued

Table 3-11 *Continued*

Name	Description
South Arabian	Ancient script from southern Arabia.
Soyombo	A script invented in 1686 by Zanabazar, a Mongolian monk, and immortalized by a symbol on the present Mongolian flag.
Tai (Dai) scripts	A family of languages from Southeast Asia. Thai and Lao are both offshoots of Tai.
Tengwar	Script invented by J. R. R. Tolkien and used in *Lord of the Rings* and *The Silmarillion*.
Tifinagh (Berber)	Writing system consisting only of consonants used by the Tuareg tribesmen.
tlhingan Hol	Klingon script, invented by Marc Okrand for use in the *Star Trek* television series and movies.
Ugaritic Cuneiform	Used by the scholarly community to write Ugaritic.
Western Musical Symbols	Symbols from the Western musical tradition.

You should check the current versions of the Unicode Standard and ISO/IEC 10646 to see whether any or all of these proposed scripts have been approved since the time of this publication. You can also check for new proposals on the Unicode Consortium's Web site at http://www.unicode.org/pending/pending.html.

It has already been decided that, if approved, several of these scripts will be encoded in Plane 1. This is to say that their characters will be accessed using surrogate pairs (see Chapter 5) rather than with single 16-bit code values. Neither the Unicode Standard, Version 3.0, nor ISO/IEC 10646-1 includes characters from Plane 1. Later versions of the Unicode Standard and ISO/IEC 10646-2, however, will.

Note that scripts are not included in the Unicode Standard until they are approved by both the UTC and WG2. Note also that the industry-based UTC is frequently able to approve scripts faster than WG2, which must issue an amendment to an international standard to add scripts to ISO/IEC 10646.

Neither the Unicode Consortium nor WG2 guarantees that all proposed scripts will be approved for inclusion in the standards, and scripts have been rejected before. Even when the UTC publishes a proposed allocation for a script, the script can still be rejected or have its allocation changed.

The Unicode Character Database

Another way to approach the structure of the Unicode Standard is to say that the standard is defined by the text files making up the Unicode Character Database. These files—which are available from the Consortium's FTP site—contain the number, name, canonical mappings, and assigned properties for every character in the Unicode Standard. About the only thing missing is a sample glyph for each character.

While some files define characters or character properties and others, for example, define the character blocks, the file formats are the same. Each line of a file contains information about a single character (or block, etc.). The lines of a file all contain the same number of semicolon-delimited fields containing data about the character (or block). The fields are numbered starting from 0, although ending numbers may vary. In some files, there are additional space characters around the semicolons, and these can be ignored when parsing the data. Comments—which begin with a "#" character and continue to the end of the current line—can be ignored, as can blank lines.

A separate version of the Unicode Character Database is produced for each revision of the Unicode Standard. Table 3-12 shows the general names and the descriptions of the Unicode Character Database files for Version 3.0. This includes several files that are new with this version of the standard. Note that the real filenames also include their version number, but the numbers have been omitted from the table to avoid tying the descriptions to a single version of the Unicode Character Database. The numeric portion of the filenames is usually the version of the Unicode Standard to which the file applies — for example, the UnicodeData.txt file for Version 3.0 is named UnicodeData-3.0.0.txt. For some files that do not change very often, the numeric portion of the filename just indicates the revision number for the file.

Table 3-12 *Unicode Character Database files*

File	Description
UnicodeData.txt	The main file in the Unicode Character Database.
SpecialCasing.txt	Additional case mappings that cannot be expressed in the fields of UnicodeData.txt.
ArabicShaping.txt	Shaping information for right-joining and dual-joining Arabic characters.
Blocks.txt	Start and end code values and name for each of the blocks of the Unicode Standard. The blocks are listed in the previous section.
Jamo.txt	Code value, short name, and Unicode character name for each of the combining Jamo. Just as the Jamo are combined to form a Hangul syllable, the short names are combined to generate the Unicode character name for the resulting syllable. See Chapter 7.
Unihan.txt	Information about the unified Han ideographs and their sources. See Chapter 7.
LineBreak.txt	Line breaking properties for use with the rules in Unicode Technical Report #14.
EastAsianWidth.txt	Character width properties for use with the rules in Unicode Technical Report #11.
CompositionExclusions.txt	Code values of characters excluded from composition under the normalization forms defined in Unicode Technical Report #15 and the Unicode Standard, Version 3.0.
PropList.txt	Lists of code values with specific properties; for example, all the space characters or all the unassigned code values.

The files and their formats are explained further in the following sections.

UnicodeData.txt

Each line in UnicodeData.txt contains the following information for a character in the Unicode Standard, in the order presented here:

0. Code value

1. Unicode character name

2. General category

3. Canonical combining class

4. Bidirectional category

5. Character decomposition mapping

6. Decimal digit value

7. Digit value

8. Numeric value

9. Mirrored

10. Unicode 1.0 name

11. 10646 comment field

12. Uppercase mapping

13. Lowercase mapping

14. Titlecase mapping

All fields are normative — which means that applications purporting to support the Unicode Standard must use the information — except fields 10–14 and some of the values of field 2, General Category, which are informative.

Cross-Reference

The character properties specified in these fields are explained in Chapter 5.

Five sample lines of UnicodeData.txt are shown below:

```
04D4;CYRILLIC CAPITAL LIGATURE A IE;Lu;0;L;;;;;N;;;;04D5;

04D5;CYRILLIC SMALL LIGATURE A IE;Ll;0;L;;;;;N;;;04D4;;04D4

04D6;CYRILLIC CAPITAL LETTER IE WITH BREVE;Lu;0;L;0415 0306;;;;N;;;;04D7;
```

```
04D7;CYRILLIC SMALL LETTER IE WITH BREVE;Ll;0;L;0435 0306;;;;N;;;04D6;;04D6
04D8;CYRILLIC CAPITAL LETTER SCHWA;Lu;0;L;;;;;N;;;;04D9;
```

For example, U+04D6, CYRILLIC CAPITAL LETTER IE WITH BREVE, is categorized as an uppercase letter (Lu) and a member of the spacing (0) combining class. Its bidirectional category is Left-to-Right (L). It can be decomposed into U+0415, CYRILLIC CAPITAL LETTER IE, followed by U+0306, COMBINING BREVE. It is not mirrored (N) in a right-to-left context. Its lowercase equivalent is U+04D7, CYRILLIC SMALL LETTER IE WITH BREVE. The fields with no value between the semicolons indicate properties that are inapplicable in the context of their respective character. For example, a character may have no digit or numeric properties. Also, it may either not have been included in Unicode 1.0 or did not have its name changed as part of the merger with ISO 10646 or it may map to itself for uppercase or titlecase.

SpecialCasing.txt

This file provides additional information for only those characters with case mappings that cannot be adequately documented using the one-to-one uppercase mapping, lowercase mapping, and titlecase (first letter capitalized) mapping fields of `UnicodeData.txt`. Each line in `SpecialCasing.txt` contains the following information for a character in the Unicode Standard, in the order presented here:

0. Source character code value

1. Code value or values for the lowercase mapping of the source character

2. Code value or values for the titlecase mapping of the source character

3. Code value or values for the uppercase mapping of the source character

4. If present, additional locale and context information indicating when the mapping should be applied

Five sample lines of `SpecialCasing.txt` are shown below:

```
00DF; 00DF; 0053 0073; 0053 0053; # LATIN SMALL LETTER SHARP S

# Ligatures

FB00; FB00; 0046 0066; 0046 0046; # LATIN SMALL LIGATURE FF

# Turkish

0049; 0131; 0049; 0049; TR; # LATIN CAPITAL LETTER I
```

The first example is the well-known case of the ß character, which maps to two characters when converted to uppercase (or titlecase). The titlecase mapping of U+00DF, LATIN SMALL LETTER SHARP S, is U+0053, LATIN CAPITAL LETTER S, followed by U+0073, LATIN SMALL LETTER S. More succinctly, ß → Ss, and for the uppercase mapping, ß → SS.

The third example shows the special I → ı (U+0131, LATIN SMALL LETTER DOTLESS I) mapping that should apply only in the Turkish (TR) locale.

ArabicShaping.txt

Arabic characters are drawn joined to their neighbors, and characters have different appearances depending on their adjacent characters. The file `ArabicShaping.txt` contains joining information for each of the characters in the Arabic and Syriac blocks that are either right-joining or dual-joining. When used according to the shaping rules detailed in the Unicode Standard, the information guides selection of the correct glyph for an Arabic character in each context.

Each line in `ArabicShaping.txt` contains information for a separate character. The fields are, in order of their appearance:

0. Unicode code value

1. Abbreviated form of the character name, used in textual descriptions of the Arabic ligatures

2. Arabic joining class, abbreviated to "R" and "D" for right-joining and dual-joining, respectively

3. Name of a group of characters with similar shaping behavior. When there is no shaping behavior, the value is "<no shaping>"

The first five lines of `ArabicShaping.txt` are shown below:

```
# Unicode; Schematic Name; Link; Link  Group
0622; MADDA ON ALEF; R; ALEF
0623; HAMZA ON ALEF; R; ALEF
0624; HAMZA ON WAW; R; WAW
0625; HAMZA UNDER ALEF; R; ALEF
```

For example, the second line specifies that U+0622, ARABIC LETTER ALEF WITH MADDA ABOVE, is abbreviated as MADDA ON ALEF, is right-joining, and has the shaping behavior of characters in the ALEF group.

Blocks.txt

This file lists every block in the Unicode Standard, Version 3.0, and its start and end code values. Each line in `Blocks.txt` contains the following information for a character block, in the order of their appearance:

0. First code value in block

1. Last code value in block

2. Block name

The first five lines of `Blocks.txt` are shown below:

```
# Start Code; End Code; Block Name
0000; 007F; Basic Latin
0080; 00FF; Latin-1 Supplement
0100; 017F; Latin Extended-A
0180; 024F; Latin Extended-B
0250; 02AF; IPA Extensions
```

For example, the Basic Latin block starts at U+0000 and ends at U+007F, and the Latin-1 Supplement block starts at U+0080 and ends at U+00FF.

LineBreaking.txt

This file contains data used by the line-breaking algorithm described in Unicode Technical Report #14 and the Unicode Standard, Version 3.0. Each line in `LineBreaking.txt` contains the following information for a character in the Unicode Standard, in the order of their appearance:

0. Code value

1. Line breaking property identifier

2. Unicode character name

Five sample lines of `LineBreaking.txt` are shown below:

```
001F;CM;<control>
0020;SP;SPACE
0021;EX;EXCLAMATION MARK
0022;QU;QUOTATION MARK
0023;AL;NUMBER SIGN
```

For example, U+0020, SPACE, has the Space (SP) line-breaking property, and U+0021, EXCLAMATION MARK, has the Exclamation/Interrogation (EX) property. Characters with the SP property present an opportunity to insert a line break when formatting text, whereas characters with the EX property must be kept with the preceding character.

EastAsianWidth.txt

East Asian ideographic and other characters are traditionally written to each fit within a square cell. By contrast, Roman alphabet characters are typically taller than they are wide, and approximately half the width of ideographic characters of the same height. In a fixed-pitch font, characters that fill the square cell are termed *full-width* (*zenkaku* in Japanese), and other characters that take up half the space are termed *half-width* (*hankaku* in Japanese). The distinction between full-width and half-width characters isn't necessarily related to the character's origin. Some existing East Asian character sets include full-width versions of the Roman alphabet, and others include halfwidth versions of, for example, the Katakana syllabary.

In general, the Unicode Standard encodes characters, not glyphs, but to support round-trip mapping between existing character sets and the Unicode Standard, the standard includes explicit half-width and full-width forms of some characters. The file `EastAsian Width.txt` contains the East Asian Width property value for each Unicode character. This property is used when mapping between the Unicode Standard and existing East Asian character sets and when formatting mixtures of Western and East Asian characters.

Each line in `EastAsianWidth.txt` contains the following information for a character in the Unicode Standard, in the order of their appearance:

0. Code value

1. East Asian Width property identifier

2. Unicode character name

Five non-contiguous lines from `EastAsianWidth.txt` are shown below:

```
0041;Na;LATIN CAPITAL LETTER A
30AB;W;KATAKANA LETTER KA
30AD;W;KATAKANA LETTER KI
FF76;H;HALFWIDTH KATAKANA LETTER KA
FF77;H;HALFWIDTH KATAKANA LETTER KI
```

In this example, "A" (U+0041) has the East Asian Narrow (Na) property because it has a full-width equivalent. "カ" (U+30AB) and "キ" (U+30AD) have the East Asian Wide (W) property, and their half-width equivalents "ｶ" (U+FF76) and "ｷ" (U+FF77) have the East Asian Half-width (H) property.

CompositionExclusions.txt

Normalization forms C and KC, defined in Unicode Technical Report # 15, include both decomposition and composition steps. The composition process either replaces, where possible, sequences of base plus combining characters with composed characters, or replaces one character with the character to which it is a compatibility decomposition. However, blindly applying all possible compositions rarely, if ever, yields the best result. Some possible compositions will yield precomposed characters that are not the generally preferred form for particular scripts, whereas others will just replace one precomposed character with another.

 Cross-Reference

See "Dynamic Composition" in Chapter 2 and "Normalization Forms" in Chapter 5. for more information on normalization forms and composition.

The file `CompositionExclusions.txt` lists the code values of precomposed characters that should not be produced when applying the normalization forms defined in UTR #15. That is to say, these code values should be excluded from composition.

Each line in `CompositionExclusions.txt` contains a single field:

0. Unicode code value

Each code value is followed by the # comment delimiter and the character's Unicode character name.

Characters whose exclusion from composition can be determined based on data in other files in the Unicode Character Database are listed in `CompositionExclusions.txt`, but they are commented out. If your application cannot compute those code values, you can uncomment the lines in the file.

Five non-contiguous sample lines of `CompositionExclusions.txt` are shown below:

```
0958 # DEVANAGARI LETTER QA
0959 # DEVANAGARI LETTER KHHA
FB1F # HEBREW LIGATURE YIDDISH YOD YOD PATAH
# 0340 COMBINING GRAVE TONE MARK
# 0341 COMBINING ACUTE TONE MARK
```

The first three lines contain code values of precomposed characters that are not preferred forms. Whether a character is a preferred form cannot be determined from the Unicode Character Database, so these lines are not commented out.

The last two lines are commented out, since the characters with these code values have compatibility decompositions to other single characters. These "singleton decompositions" are excluded from composition. The characters are included in the `Composition Exclusions.txt`, but since singleton decompositions can be determined from the character decomposition mapping field in `UnicodeData.txt`, their lines are commented out.

PropList.txt

This file contains a list of properties of characters, along with the code values of characters that have each property. `PropList-3.0.0.txt` — which is the version current at the time of this writing — lists 56 properties. Each property is identified by a number followed by a name in parentheses; for example, `0x10000001` (`Zero-width`). The meaning of the numbers, the choice of properties, and the algorithms for assigning characters to properties is not, to my knowledge, publicly documented. Some properties, such as `Zero-width` and `Paragraph Separator`, are derived from property values or combinations of property values in `UnicodeData.txt` and, possibly, other Unicode Character Database files. Others, such as `Unassigned Code Value`, are derived from the absence of information in the Unicode Character Database files.

The first property dump in `PropList.txt` is shown below:

```
Property dump for: 0x10000001 (Zero-width)

070F
180B..180E   (4 chars)
200B..200F   (5 chars)
202A..202E   (5 chars)
206A..206F   (6 chars)
FEFF
FFF9..FFFB   (3 chars)
```

Isolated characters with the property are listed one per line. Ranges of characters with the property are listed on a single line, which shows the start, end, and length of the range.

In this example, all the characters that have a `Cf` value in the General Category field in `UnicodeData.txt` are listed. One addition, U+200B, has a set of property values that is unique within `UnicodeData.txt`.

ISO/IEC 10646 Structure

ISO/IEC 10646-1:1993, Information Technology – Universal Multiple-Octet Coded Character Set (UCS) – Part 1: Architecture and Basic Multilingual Plane, defines a 4-octet (32-bit) coded character set. It also defines a 2-octet form of the UCS that is identical to the Unicode Standard's coded character set.

Note

ISO standards define the eight-bit units commonly called bytes, as octets. As before, I'll use the ISO terms when discussing ISO/IEC 10646.

The canonical 4-octet UCS (UCS-4) is a coded character set with space for 2,147,483,648 characters. UCS-4 does not use the most significant bit — bit 8 of the most significant octet — so the available space for encoding characters is $128 \times 256 \times 256 \times 256 =$

2,147,483,648. The UCS standard will never come close to defining that many characters, but that number is certainly impressive when you first come across it.

As Figure 3-10 shows, the UCS is conceptually 128 three-dimensional groups. Each group contains 256 planes, and each plane contains 256 rows, each of which contains 256 cells. Plane 00 of Group 00 is called the Basic Multilingual Plane (BMP). As you may realize, the BMP comprises the characters in UCS-2, and it corresponds to the characters that can be addressed with 16-bit Unicode code values. The next 16 planes—Planes 01 to 10_{16} of Group 00—contain the characters that can be represented with UTF-16 (and represented using surrogates).

Cross-Reference

See Chapters 4 and 5 for more information on UTF-16 and surrogates, respectively.

The four octets of a UCS-4 character's number represent its group, plane, row, and cell, respectively. Figure 3-11 shows both the order of the octets and their full and abbreviated names. When you refer to characters within a plane, the digits for the group and plane may be omitted. Characters referred to by only the four hexadecimal digits of their Row and Cell octets are termed RC-elements. Characters in the BMP are frequently referred to by only the R- and C-octets, and are only referred to by those octets when being encoded as UCS-2. Strictly speaking, UCS-2 is the "two-octet BMP form of the UCS."

Basic Multilingual Plane

It should be obvious by now that the characters in the BMP of ISO/IEC 10646 are the same as the characters defined by the Unicode Standard, Version 3.0. Of course, when the Unicode Standard defines characters that are represented with surrogate pairs, ISO/IEC 10646 will also define characters outside the BMP. The two standards will remain in step with one another even after they break the 16-bit/2-octet barrier.

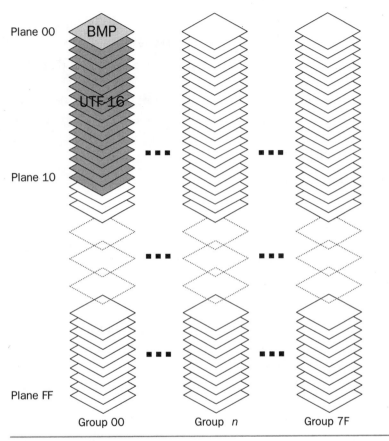

Plane 00

Plane 10

Plane FF

Group 00   Group *n*   Group 7F

Figure 3-10 *UCS structure*

m.s.   l.s.

Group-octet	Plane-octet	Row-octet	Cell-octet
G-octet	P-octet	R-octet	C-octet
G	P	R	C

Note:
m.s. = most significant bit
l.s. = least significant bit

Figure 3-11 *Octet order in a UCS-4 character number*

Common Features of the Unicode Standard and ISO/IEC 10646

Unicode defines more semantics for the same characters than does ISO/IEC 10646, even though their characters reside at the same code points within the same blocks. However, ISO/IEC 10646 does share some character semantics with the Unicode Standard. The common features of the Unicode Standard and ISO/IEC 10646 include the following:

- Character names
- Character code points
- Representative glyphs
- Semantics of formatting characters such as ZERO WIDTH SPACE and LEFT-TO-RIGHT MARK
- Identification of characters with mirror properties
- Identification of combining characters
- Identification of the source for CJK unified ideographs
- Optional use of FEFF as a signature to indicate encoding
- UTF-16 (if surrogates are used)
- UTF-8
- UCS-2 (if surrogates are not used)
- Private Use areas
- Division of the repertoire into blocks, although the blocks are not always identical

Character names and numbers

Character names in the Unicode Standard are identical to character names in the English version of ISO/IEC 10646. Character numbers for UCS-2 and the Unicode Standard are also identical.

Representative glyphs

Both standards provide a representative glyph for each of the characters that they define.

Character properties and semantics

The characters in the Unicode Standard and ISO/IEC 10646 are defined to have properties, such as directionality or whether a character can combine with other characters. The Unicode Standard defines more properties for characters than does ISO/IEC 10646.

Cross-Reference

The properties and their meanings are explained in Chapter 5.

Encodings

ISO/IEC 10646 and the Unicode Standard share the same 16-bit representation of the characters in UCS-2. In ISO/IEC 10646, this encoding is also called UCS-2; and in the Unicode Standard, it is rarely, if ever, named.

The two standards also share the 8-bit safe UTF-8 encoding format and the 16-bit format, UTF-16, for representing characters in planes 00 to 10. In ISO/IEC 10646, UTF stands for "UCS Transformation Format"; in the Unicode Standard, it stands for "Unicode Transformation Format."

Cross-Reference

These formats are explained in detail in Chapter 4.

Private use areas

Both ISO/IEC and the Unicode Standard reserve blocks of code values for characters defined by private agreement between interested parties. Figure 3-12 shows the areas of the UCS reserved for private use:

- Code positions E000 to F8FF of the BMP (same as the Unicode Standard)
- Planes 0F and 10 of Group 00 (which can be represented with UTF-16)
- Planes E0 to FF of Group 00
- Groups 60 to 7F

ISO/IEC 10646 defines private use areas that are outside the range of characters covered by the Unicode Standard. Use of the planes that cannot be represented with UTF-16 is strongly discouraged by the Unicode Standard since characters in those character positions are not interchangeable with implementations of the Unicode Standard.

Signatures

Annex F of ISO/IEC 10646-1:1993 describes a convention for using a ZERO WIDTH NO-BREAK SPACE character as the first character in a stream of coded characters. As Table 3-13 shows, an application can then determine the character stream's encoding based on the "signature" of octets used to encode the ZERO WIDTH NO-BREAK SPACE character: FF FE.

Table 3-13 *ZERO WIDTH NO-BREAK SPACE Signatures*

Signature	Encoding
00 00 FE FF	UCS-4, big-endian
FF FE 00 00	UCS-4, little-endian
EF BB BF	UTF-8
FE FF	UCS-2 or UTF-16, big-endian (UTF-16BE)
FF FE	UCS-2 or UTF-16, little-endian (UTF-16LE)

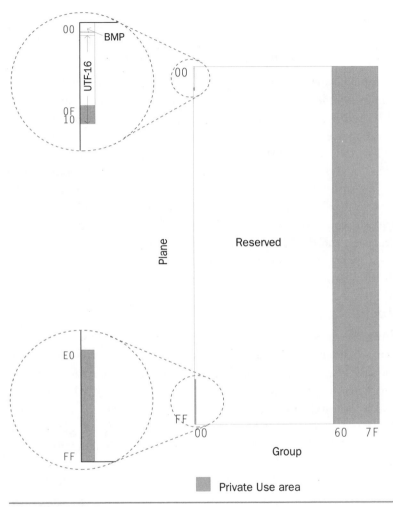

Figure 3-12 *Private Use areas*

The octets in reverse order are FF FE, which is not a valid character in any plane in ISO/IEC 10646 (or in the Unicode Standard). Receiving FF FE in the first two (or four) octets in a character sequence is a strong hint that the octets are in the reverse order from what you expect.

Cross-Reference

For more information on receiving octets in a character sequence, see the section on "Endianness" in Chapter 4.

Applications that use the Byte Order Mark to indicate the file format include Microsoft text files encoded in UTF-16 and XML. XML relies on the presence of the BOM to distinguish between documents encoded with UTF-16 and documents encoded with UTF-8 (since all XML processors must support both encodings). The Unicode FAQ (http://www.unicode.org/unicode/faq/) offers useful advice on when to use the BOM and when not to. In essence, if you know the encoding and whether it is big-endian or little-endian, you don't need to use the BOM. In applications like databases, the BOM just takes up space, and the BOM may interfere with sorting and equality matching of strings if one string has the BOM and the other string doesn't.

Blocks

Much like the Unicode Standard, ISO/IEC 10646 divides the character repertoire into blocks of related characters, typically characters in a single script. However, there is not always a one-to-one correspondence between the ISO/IEC 10646 blocks and the Unicode blocks. For example, the three ISO/IEC 10646-1:1993 blocks, HEBREW EXTENDED-A, BASIC HEBREW, and HEBREW EXTENDED-B, encompass the same range of characters as the Hebrew block in the Unicode Standard.

Compared to ISO/IEC 10646-1:1993, the block labels defined in ISO/IEC 10646-1:2000 more closely match the block names used in the Unicode Standard. Appendix C includes a table of the ISO/IEC 10646-1:1993 and ISO/IEC 10646-1:2000 blocks and their corresponding Unicode 3.0 blocks.

ISO/IEC 10646 Features Not in the Unicode Standard

Features of ISO/IEC 10646 that are not supported by the Unicode Standard include:

- UCS-4, although the forthcoming UTF-32 format is a compatible subset
- Characters outside the BMP and the planes represented with UTF-16
- Subsets
- Implementation levels
- Identification of features
- Reserved planes
- BMP Zones

The following sections explain some of the ISO/IEC 10646 features.

Subsets

ISO/IEC 10646 allows a transmitting or receiving device to specify the subset or subsets of the full repertoire that it supports. Subsets may be any of the following:

- A *limited subset*, where the supported characters are listed by name or character position
- A *selected subset*, being one or more of the collections listed in Annex A of each part of ISO/IEC 10646
- A combination of the two

ISO/IEC 10646-2 will also have an Annex A that lists its defined subsets.

All selected subsets, by definition, automatically include the characters of the BASIC LATIN collection — code positions 0020–007E of the BMP.

The collections defined in ISO/IEC 10646-1:1993 and ISO/IEC 10646-1:2000 are listed in Appendix C. The majority of the collections each correspond to a single block. The exceptions are: merged blocks; subdivisions of other blocks, such as FORMAT SEPARATORS; and other collections, such as COMBINING CHARACTERS.

Although the collections define ranges of character positions, most ranges include some positions that have not been assigned characters and are still reserved for future use. ISO/IEC 10646 does not include instructions for handing the reserved characters within a collection. An originating or receiving device, I believe, should handle all of the character positions within the range for a collection that it supports, whether or not the character position is reserved, and regardless of whether that position has been assigned a character.

Note that there are gaps in the numbered sequence of the collections to accommodate numbers for blocks of code added with ISO/IEC 10646-1:2000. The collections to be defined in Annex A of ISO/IEC 10646-2 will start at 1001, and will not conflict with the collections enumerated in ISO/IEC 10646-1.

Implementation levels

ISO/IEC 10646 defines three levels of combining character support to which applications may conform:

1. No combining characters or Hangul Jamo. This restriction includes characters in the three combining character subsets of ISO/IEC 10646 plus additional combining characters listed in clause B.1 of the standard.

2. Restricted use of combining characters and no Hangul Jamo. This restriction includes characters in the combining character subsets plus a shorter list of additional characters listed in clause B.2 of the standard.

3. No restrictions. Data may include any character defined by the standard, including combining characters and Hangul Jamo.

Note that the Unicode Standard conforms to Implementation Level 3 since it does not specify subsets, and conforming applications of the Unicode Standard are required to accept and retransmit even those characters that they cannot understand.

Identification of features

In keeping with its focus on data being sent between an originating and a receiving device, ISO/IEC 10646 defines ISO/IEC 2022-compatible escape sequences, or *designation sequences*, for indicating the features supported by a device. These include sequences for indicating the encoding and the implementation level, the subsets used, and the control functions used. The standard also defines an escape sequence for a return from a character sequence conforming to ISO/IEC 10646 to a character sequence conforming to ISO/IEC 2022.

In all cases, the escape sequences are defined as single octets padded with 00 octets to make them match the character size specified by the current encoding. For example, the ESCAPE character, written "ESC" in these designation sequences, is 1B as a single octet. When part of a UCS-2 character stream, it is represented by 00 1B, and when part of a UCS-4 character stream, it is represented by 00 00 00 1B.

Reserved planes

Planes 11 to DF in Group 00 and planes 00 to FF in Groups 01 to 5F — all the planes except for the BMP, the planes accessible with UTF-16, and the Private Use areas — are reserved "for future standardization" and may not be used.

BMP zones

ISO/IEC 10646-1:1993 divides the Basic Multilingual Plane into the five "zones," which are different from the Unicode Standard's division of the character repertoire into multiple "areas." Figure 3-13 shows the five zones overlaid on the Unicode Standard's areas, and Table 3-14 details the extent and content of the zones.

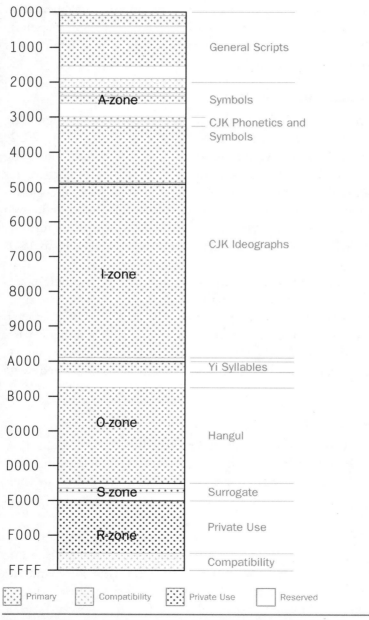

Figure 3-13 The ISO/IEC 10646-1:1993 BMP is divided into five zones

Table 3-14 *ISO/IEC 10646-1:1993 BMP Zones*

Name	Start	End	Character Positions	Description
A-zone	0000 0000	0000 4DFF	19,903	Alphabets, symbols, miscellaneous CJK, Hangul, ideographs. This zone appears shortchanged with only 19,903 character positions instead of 19,968, but the characters in the C0 and C1 control character regions and character number 0000 007F are reserved and do not count towards the total for the A-zone.
I-zone	0000 4E00	0000 9FFF	20,992	Unified Chinese, Japanese, and Korean ideographs.
O-zone	0000 A000	0000 D7FF	14,336	Hangul
S-zone	0000 D800	0000 DFFF	2,048	Reserved for use with UTF-16.
R-zone	0000 E000	0000 FFFD	8,190	"Restricted use" zone containing private use characters, presentation forms of other characters in the repertoire, and compatibility characters. 0000 FFFE and 0000 FFFF are not included since code positions FFFE and FFFF on any plane are not used. FFFE is reserved for use as an encoding signature, and FFFF is guaranteed to not be a character. FFFF, therefore, is available to programs to represent the end of text strings, etc.

Although Table 3-14 shows the number of assignable character positions in each zone, as you know, not all character positions in the BMP have been assigned characters.

Note

Note that the character position ranges are inclusive so that, for example, 0000 4E00 to 0000 9FFF is 20,9992 character positions even though in hexadecimal arithmetic 9FFF (4E00 is 51FF, or 20,991 decimal.

As Figure 3-14 shows, ISO/IEC 10646-1:2000 has almost completely dropped the concept of zones. That standard refers only to the "S-zone," comprising the Surrogate code values, and the "private use zone."

ISO/IEC 10646–Unicode Terminology Translation

The following table shows the equivalent Unicode terminology for several terms specific to ISO/IEC 10646. Note that some ISO/IEC 10646 terms do not have Unicode equivalents, and that some are only used in ISO/IEC 10646-1:1993.

ISO/IEC 10646	Unicode
A-zone (10646-1:1993)	General Scripts area + Symbols area + CJK Phonetics and Symbols area
Block	Character block
CC-data-element	–
Code position	Code point
Collection	–
High-half zone	High surrogate
Implementation level	–
I-zone (10646-1:1993)	CJK Ideographs area
Low-half zone	Low surrogate
O-zone (10646-1:1993)	Hangul Syllables area (+ reserved code points)
RC-element	Surrogate code point
R-zone (10646-1:1993)	Private Use area + Compatibility and Specials area
Subset	–
S-zone	Surrogates area
Zone	–

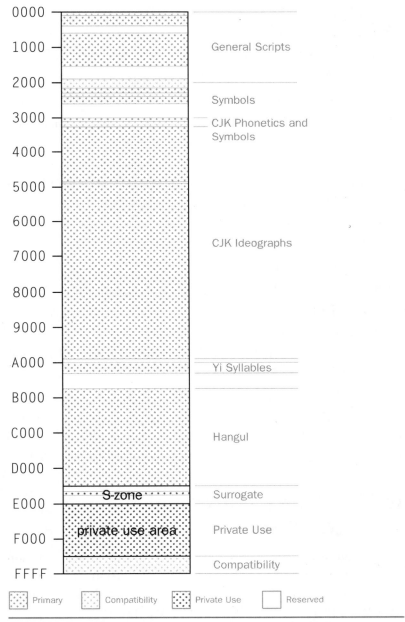

Figure 3-14 *The ISO/IEC 10646-1:200 BMP identifies only two zones*

Features of Unicode Not in ISO/IEC 10646

Features of the Unicode Standard and other work by the UTC that are not supported by ISO/IEC 10646 include:

- Implementation guidelines
- Additional character properties, such the mathematical property
- Canonical and compatibility decompositions
- Explicit mappings between the Unicode Standard and existing character encoding standards
- Aliases for character names
- Case mappings
- Cross-references to related characters
- Informative notes as part of character definitions
- Standard compression scheme
- Language indication
- Radical/stroke index for CJK unified Unified Ideographs (See Chapter 7)

Now you've been formally introduced to ISO/IEC 10646. I can now talk in the next section about how well or badly the character repertoire shared by the Unicode Standard and ISO/IEC 10646 represent their common goal of being a universal character set.

Is Unicode a Universal Character Set?

Not yet, but it's getting closer. I had a different response for Version 2.0, but the additions to the standard for Version 3.0, plus the scripts in the pipeline for inclusion, bring the Unicode Standard and ISO/IEC 10646 closer to their stated design goals.

There are still scripts that are not covered by the repertoire, but in some cases the languages for those scripts can be written in scripts that are included in the repertoire.

You may also think that including many of the lesser-known scripts in the pipeline — for example, Shavian or Ugaritic — is unnecessary. It may seem self-indulgent for languages of scholarly interest to be included when there are living languages that are not included. However, there are people who work with these languages daily and who want to input, sort, search, and display these languages on their computers. I have a colleague who got his start in computers in 1979 trying to establish a formal encoding for biblical Hebrew syntax. People that use these languages have the same hurdles trying to get computers to handle their languages, as do users of living but minority languages. Would Unicode be a universal character set if we all used Unicode and the scholars used a different system, or different systems for each specialty, for their work?

Will it ever be a universal character set? No, since it's impossible to catalog all the characters that are used or ever will be used. For example, new ideographs are being invented in Taiwan each year, plus there's the open-ended question of whether any two glyphs are the same character or different characters that should have separate code values. Furthermore, new scripts are still being invented, some as practical alternatives to English and other scripts, and some, such as tlhingan Hol, as truly artificial languages.

Despite it being impossible to create a universal character set, the Unicode Standard and ISO/IEC 10646 represent a very practical approach to encoding all of the major scripts of the world. This, after all, is the pragmatic goal of the Unicode Consortium. Accordingly, the next part of the book focuses on the practical side of using the Unicode Standard.

Chapter 4

Encodings and Transcodings

While the Unicode Standard is, at its core, a collection of characters, it is an ordered collection, and part of a character's definition is its character number. As was mentioned in the Introduction, a character encoding form is a mapping of a coded character set — such as Unicode's collection of characters — onto a set of regularly sized units of data. The default encoding form used by the Unicode Standard maps each character to a specific 16-bit unit, defined by its character number. Version 2.0 of the standard referred to this mapping as "Unicode text" or "Unicode-encoded text."

The Unicode Standard was initially designed with only 16-bit character codes and an upper limit of 2^{16} (i.e. 65,536) characters. ISO/IEC 10646, on the other hand, was designed for 32-bit (four-octet) characters with an upper limit of 2^{31} characters (since the most significant bit is always 0). The four-octet UCS-4 form is the default form for ISO/IEC 10646, but that standard also defines the two-octet UCS-2, which is compatible with "Unicode-encoded text." In addition, ISO/IEC 10646 was the first of the two standards to standardize a format for addressing characters in Planes 1 to 16 (the Basic Multilingual Plane (BMP) is Plane 0) using multiple 16-bit data units. This happened when the definition of UTF-16 was added in its first amendment. The Unicode Standard, Version 2.0, supported the same mechanism for addressing characters outside the BMP, but it referred to the mechanism as "Surrogates" (see "UTF-16" in this chapter and "Surrogates" in Chapter 5). The standard only used "UTF-16" when discussing the relationship between the Unicode Standard and ISO/IEC 10646.

As the Unicode Standard moves closer to defining characters outside of the Basic Multilingual Plane, it has stopped making artificial distinctions between UTF-16 and the use of Surrogates. The Unicode Standard, Version 3.0, now refers to Unicode text being encoded in UTF-16. Also, the Unicode Technical Committee has released a technical report (in draft at the time of this writing) detailing the UTF-32, 32-bit form for representing Unicode characters. UTF-32 is effectively a subset of UCS-4 that limits itself to the character codes in the BMP and the next 16 planes — the same planes that are covered by UTF-16.

The computing world does not uniformly support 16-bit character encodings, let alone 32-bit encodings. Organizations that needed to use Unicode characters in seven-bit and eight-bit systems have, therefore, developed the UTF-7 and UTF-8 encodings, respectively, that were subsequently adopted by the Unicode Standard and/or ISO/IEC 10646.

UTF-8 works well in most 8-bit systems because its first 128 characters are the same as ASCII (actually, the same as the graphic characters defined by ASCII plus the control codes defined by ISO 6429). Not all computer systems are ASCII-based, however, so a user at IBM developed the UTF-EBCDIC encoding for use in IBM mainframes and other EBCDIC-based systems. UTF-EBCDIC is the subject of UTR #16.

Lastly, the Unicode Technical Committee has designed the Standard Compression Scheme for Unicode (SCSU). This is not intended as an interchange format, but it is another, rather more dynamic encoding of sequences of characters from the Unicode Standard.

UCS-4

UCS-4 is the four-octet (32-bit) form of the Universal Character Set (UCS). ISO/IEC 10646 and the makeup of the UCS were introduced in Chapter 3.

UCS-4 is also referred to as the canonical form of the UCS since it is the only encoding capable of representing all of the possible characters in the coded character set. It is not expected that anything close to the maximum number of characters will ever be assigned to any character set, but if they were, UCS-4 would represent them.

The UCS defined by ISO/IEC 10646 is a 31-bit coded character set, so, when written to a file, the most significant bit in UCS-4 character numbers is always 0. This also leaves the most significant bit of a 32-bit in-memory representation of a UCS-4 character available for a program's own processing purposes.

Conceptually, the UCS is divided into 128 three-dimensional groups. Each group contains 256 planes comprising 256 rows of 256 cells. The four octets of a UCS-4 code point, therefore, represent its group, plane, row, and cell, respectively. The ISO/IEC 10646 term for the most significant octet of a UCS-4 code point is "Group-octet," but it is often abbreviated as "G-octet" or sometimes just "G." The names and abbreviations of the other octets are constructed similarly.

The characters currently defined by the Unicode Standard and ISO/IEC 10646 are all in the Basic Multilingual Plane, which is Plane 00 of Group 00. This means that the values of the G-octet and P-octet for all currently defined characters are both 0x00. For example, the UCS-4 representation of HEBREW LETTER BET is 0000 05D1.

Code values in the range 0000 D800 to 0000 DFFF, which are used for representing Surrogate Pairs in UTF-16, are not valid UCS-4 code values. UTF-16 requires two Surrogate code values to address the characters in Planes 1 to 16. Surrogate Pairs are unnecessary in UTF-4 since it represents the characters in Planes 1 to 16 using a single code value.

UCS-2

As was mentioned in Chapter 3, UCS-2 is the two-octet (16-bit) BMP form of the UCS. All of the characters defined in the Unicode Standard, Version 3.0, are in the BMP, so you can represent them all with UCS-2. This will not always be true, and future versions of the Unicode Standard and ISO/IEC 10646 will require that you use UTF-16 or some other encoding to represent all the defined characters.

In ISO/IEC 10646 terms, UCS-2 characters comprise a Row-octet (R-octet) and a Cell-octet (C-octet). These correspond to the most significant eight bits and least significant eight-bits of a 16-bit Unicode code value, respectively. For example, the Unicode code value and the UCS-2 representation for HEBREW LETTER BET is 0x05D1. Its R-octet value is 0x05, and its C-octet is 0xD1.

A distinction is often made between UCS-2 — which addresses only the BMP — and UTF-16. Although UTF-16 also contains 16-bit values, it can address not only the BMP but also the next 16 planes. There is no difference between the UCS-2 value and the UTF-16 value for any character in the BMP, although a conforming UCS-2 application will not use code values in the Surrogates area. The difference is that, in UTF-16, pairs of 16-bit values in the Surrogates area ("S-zone," in ISO/IEC 10646 terms) are interpreted as representing code points outside the BMP. The magic, therefore, isn't in the numbers, but in what those numbers represent.

UTF-16

UTF-16 stands for "UCS Transformation Format for Planes of Group 00." As noted above, pairs of code points from the Surrogates area (S-zone) are used to represent characters encoded in planes 1 to 16, which are the next 16 planes "after" the Basic Multilingual Plane (Plane 0).

UTF-16 is defined in Annex Q of ISO/IEC 10646-1:1993, which was published in 1996 as the first amendment to that standard. The encoding is also referred to by the Unicode Standard, Version 2.0, although for the most part it refers to the encoding of the characters in planes 1 to 16 as "the Unicode Standard with the use of surrogates." The Unicode FAQ and the Unicode Standard, Version 3.0, are more forthright about Unicode characters being encoded as UTF-16. Of course, the Unicode Consortium is now closer to defining characters in Plane 01 than it was when the Unicode Standard, Version 2.0, was published.

The Surrogates area — a.k.a., the S-zone — covers the range 0xD800 to 0xDFFF. It is divided into the High Surrogates and High Private Use Surrogates blocks (or "high-half zone") ranging from 0xD800 to 0xDBFF, and the Low Surrogates block ("low-half zone"), from 0xDC00 to 0xDFFF. The sequence of a code value from the High (or High Private Use) surrogates followed by a code value from the Low surrogates identifies a character in Planes 1 to 16. An unpaired surrogate code value or a Low surrogate followed by a High surrogate has no meaning, and thus no specified error handling or error recovery.

For the Surrogate Pair (H, L), the calculation of the code value being referenced (N) is:

```
N = (H - 0xD800) * 0x400 + (L - 0xDC00) + 0x10000
```

The code value N is also referred to as the Unicode Scalar Value of the Surrogate Pair. The code value of a non-surrogate character is its Unicode Scalar Value. Putting together the values that represent themselves and the values represented by surrogates, Unicode Scalar Values cover the ranges 0x00–0xD7FF and 0xE000–0x10FFFF.

Cross-Reference

The Unicode Scalar Value of the Surrogate Pair is covered in Chapter 5.

There are 1,024 (2^{10}) High Surrogate code values and 1,024 (2^{10}) Low Surrogate code values. Surrogate Pairs, therefore, can represent 1,048,576 (2^{20}) characters. Since a plane has 256 (2^8) rows containing 256 (2^8) cells, there are $2^8 \times 2^8 = 2^{16}$ code points in a plane. With 2^{20} possible characters to represent and 2^{16} code points in a plane, UTF-16 has room to handle 16 planes, since $2^{20} \div 2^{16} = 2^4 = 16$. Effectively, the eight least-significant bits in the Low Surrogate value determine the C-octet. The next two bits of the Low Surrogate value and the six least-significant bits of the High Surrogate value determine the R-octet. The next four bits of the High surrogate value determine the P-octet. The value 0x10000 is added to offset the P-octet value, so that the Surrogate Pairs address code values in planes 1 to 16 instead of planes 0 to 15.

Planes 15 and 16 are defined as Private Use areas (see Chapter 5). Code values from the High Private Use Surrogates block (128 code values in the range U+DB80–U+DBFF) combined with any Low Surrogate value can address into the Private Use planes.

ISO/IEC 10646 states that code values FFEF and FFFF on any plane are not used for representing characters (and are, therefore, available for use by your application for its own purposes, such as marking the end of strings). Accordingly, those code values in the 16 planes addressed by UTF-16 will not be assigned characters, and the Surrogate Pairs for those code points should also not be used.

UTF-7

The UTF-7 encoding uses a variable number of bytes per character and, unlike with other UTF encodings, the same character is not always encoded the same way every time. This runs counter to the current emphasis from the Unicode Consortium that UTF encodings always represent the same character the same way, and may partly explain why UTF-7 is quietly being dropped.

"Unicode Transformation Format, 7-bit form," "UCS Transformation Format, 7-bit form," and "Mail-Safe Transformation

Format for Unicode" are all valid long-form names for the encoding more conveniently entitled UTF-7. This encoding is defined in RFC 2152, and was mentioned in the Unicode Standard, Version 2.0. It is not given, however, any prominence in the Unicode Standard, Version 3.0, or in ISO/IEC 10646-1.

To understand why UTF-7 exists, you have to be acquainted with some ugly facts about the history of data interchange. The Internet's electronic mail protocols were developed when 7-bit character sets such as ASCII were the norm. As a result, much of the early e-mail software (like much other software of the time and, sadly, some of today's) was not "8-bit clean" and did not distinguish between two characters that differed only in their eighth bit. Many experts would advise you to forget about UTF-7 and use UTF-8 instead, arguing that e-mail systems are now 8-bit clean. Such advice reflects a great deal of blind faith in the integrity of e-mail systems, which may be justified for those systems limited to North America. When the topic of 8-bit cleanliness came up on the Unicode mailing list, one respondent recounted still using a VAX with 7-bit mail software at his facility in Iran.

UTF-7 is safe for use in message bodies (provided line length and line break restrictions are observed) and as the Q (quoted-printable) encoding for headers. Its MIME character set identifier is the somewhat anachronistic UNICODE-1-1-UTF-7.

The design of UTF-7 heeds well the warnings in the guidelines for sending e-mail data in Appendix B of RFC 1521, Mechanisms for Specifying and Describing the Format of Internet Message Bodies. Minimal UTF-7 uses only the US-ASCII characters known to work with all mail agents. Actually, UTF-7 does not use "=", even though RFC 1521 lists it as a safe character, mainly because of the character's use in quoting characters in headers.

UTF-7 directly encodes some Unicode characters as their "safe" US-ASCII equivalents, and optionally some with not-so-safe US-ASCII equivalents, and it encodes any other Unicode characters with a modified Base64 encoding. A "+" indicates a shift into a modified Base64 sequence, and the sequence ends at the next non-Base64 character. The non-Base64 "-" character is a special case. It is absorbed when it ends a Base64-encoded sequence. For example, "+" is encoded as "+-" but ends up being read as simply "+" because of the vanishing "-" character. Carriage returns and line feeds are not Base64 characters, so Base64-encoded sequences also end at the end of a line.

UTF-7 encoding follows three simple rules:

1. **Direct encoding.** The following characters are directly encoded as their US-ASCII equivalents:

   ```
   ABCDEFGHIJKLMNOPQRSTUVWXYZabcdefghijklmnopqrstuvwxyz
   0123456789'(),-./:?
   ```

   By comparison, the following characters may optionally be encoded as their US-ASCII equivalents, even though they may be mangled by some e-mail software and may be illegal within header fields:

   ```
   !"#$%&*;<=>@[]^_`{|}
   ```

2. **Modified Unicode encoding.** Any Unicode character (including those that can be directly encoded) can be encoded in a sequence of Modified Base64 characters.

3. **Control code encoding.** The SPACE, TAB, LINE FEED, and CARRIAGE RETURN characters are directly encoded by their ASCII equivalents.

Characters encoded according to Rules 1 and 3 are encoded with one byte per character, and characters encoded according to Rule 2 average 2 2/3 bytes per character (plus one byte to switch into Base64 encoding and, optionally, one byte to signal the end of the sequence).

Base64 Encoding

Base64 encoding—defined in RFC 1521—uses a 65-character subset of the US-ASCII characters to safely encode binary data before consigning it to the tender mercies of software that only handles text. Specifically, the characters used are:

- Safe for use in mail systems
- Included in all ISO 646 variants, so there is no ambiguity about the character being encoded
- Represented identically in all versions of EBCDIC, so there are no problems when transferring Base64-encoded data between ASCII-based and EBCDIC-based systems

The Base64 method divides the binary data into 24-bit groups then encodes each 24-bit input group into four 6-bit characters, which are selected from the Base64 "alphabet" shown in the following table. Since 2^6 = 64, 64 characters in the alphabet represent the 6-bit values.

Value	Encoding	Value	Encoding	Value	Encoding	Value	Encoding
0	A	17	R	34	I	51	z
1	B	18	S	35	j	52	0
2	C	19	T	36	k	53	1
3	D	20	U	37	l	54	2
4	E	21	V	38	m	55	3
5	F	22	W	39	n	56	4
6	G	23	X	40	o	57	5
7	H	24	Y	41	p	58	6
8	I	25	Z	42	q	59	7
9	J	26	a	43	r	60	8
10	K	27	b	44	s	61	9
11	L	28	c	45	t	62	+
12	M	29	d	46	u	63	/
13	N	30	e	47	v		
14	O	31	f	48	w	(pad)	=
15	P	32	g	49	x		
16	Q	33	h	50	y		

Strings of Base64 characters, as defined in RFC 1521, are always a multiple of four characters. This works well since each three bytes (24 bits) of input data is encoded as four Base64 characters. When the last input group is not 24 bits, it is padded with zero bits to form an integral number of 6-bit groups (6, 12, 18, or 24 bits). This last input group is then converted to between one and four Base64 characters — as few as necessary to adequately encode the group. But if this group ends up being fewer than four characters, it is padded with "=" characters so the total number of characters in the group is always four.

The maximum length of a line of Base64-encoded data is 76 characters. Any CARRIAGE RETURN or LINE FEED characters within the input data are encoded just like any other character. So a line break appearing in a Base64-encoded file is merely for the benefit of e-mail systems that cannot parse long lines. Accordingly, any CARRIAGE RETURN, LINE BREAK or other non-Base64 characters appearing in the encoded file are ignored by Base64 decoding software.

Lines of Base64-encoded data in UTF-7 can be any length, and the size of the Base64 data file does not have to be a multiple of four. In fact, UTF-7 does not use the "=" pad character since "=" has a different meaning from an escape character in the Q content transfer encoding of mail headers.

Modified Base64 Encoding

Figure 4-1 shows two Unicode characters, THAI DIGIT NINE and HEBREW LETTER BET, and their equivalent Modified Base64 encoding as DlmF0Q. Notice how enough zero bits were added to the right of the binary stream to make its bit count an exact multiple of six. In RFC 1521 Base64 encoding — though not in UTF-7's modified Base64 encoding — the encoded character file would be padded with enough "=" characters to make its length a multiple of four.

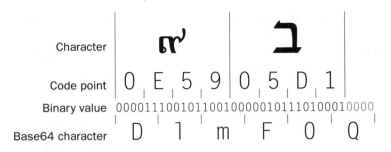

Character	אי	ב
Code point	0 E 5 9	0 5 D 1
Binary value	00001110010110010000010111010001 0000	
Base64 character	D l m	F 0 Q

Figure 4-1 *Modified Base64 encoding of THAI DIGIT NINE and HEBREW LETTER BET*

If we had been encoding a longer sequence of Unicode characters, the first four bits of the next character would have been used to
determine the sixth letter of the encoded sequence. So the sixth letter of the encoded sequence would not have been Q unless the first
four bits of the third UTF-16 encoded character were 0000.

Figure 4-2 shows a sequence of UTF-16 encoded characters
re-encoded as UTF-7 — i.e., as a sequence of ASCII characters.
The UTF-16 sequence begins with ZERO WIDTH NO-BREAK
SPACE (represented here by "ZWN BSP") acting as a *byte order
mark* (BOM) to indicate the order of the bytes in the 16-bit characters that follow it (see the section on UTF-16). When the BOM is
the first code value in a string, it does not count as a character, so it
is not included in the re-encoded UTF-7 sequence. The next two
UTF-16 characters, LATIN CAPITAL A and LATIN SMALL
LETTER B, are re-encoded into their ASCII equivalents according
to UTF-7 Rule 1. The SPACE character ("SP") is also encoded as
its ASCII equivalent according to UTF-7 Rule 3. Next, the UTF-7
re-encoding adds a "+" to indicate the start of a modified Base64
sequence. The next six characters in the UTF-7 should be familiar
to you from Figure 4.1: DlmFOQ, which stands for the two UTF-16
characters THAI DIGIT NINE and HEBREW LETTER BET.
Next, the UTF-7 re-encoding attaches a "-" — a minus sign (ASCII
0x2D), not a non-breaking hyphen (0x1E), not an en-dash (0x96),
and not an em-dash (0x97) — to indicate the end of the modified

Base64 sequence. When converting the UTF-7 sequence to another encoding (for example, back to UTF-16), neither the "+" nor the "-" will be included in the result. This is because they were only included in the UTF-7 as signals for the start and end of the Base64 sequence.

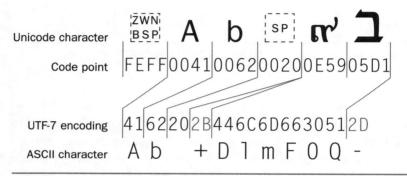

Figure 4-2 *Sample conversion from UTF-16 to UTF-7*

UTF-8

The term "UTF-8" stands for either "UCS Transformation Format, 8-bit form" or "Unicode Transformation Format, 8-bit form." The definition of UTF-8 in Appendix A of the Unicode Standard, Version 2.0 used "UCS," but the glossary in the same edition defined it as "Unicode (or UCS) Transformation Format, 8-bit form." In ISO/IEC 10646, it is known only as "UCS Transformation Format, 8-bit form." UTF-8 was developed by the X/Open consortium as File System Safe UTF (FSS-UTF). It was later known as UTF-2, but has since been renamed UTF-8. It is an integral part of ISO/IEC 10646, and has been included in the Unicode Standard since version 2.0. It is the preferred UCS encoding of many Unix variants and of programming languages such as Perl.

Unlike UTF-7, UTF-8 encodes each Unicode character as a sequence whose length is a precise multiple of eight bits, and totals between one and four bytes (between one and six bytes for UCS-4 characters). Table 4-1 demonstrates how the bits of any Unicode character's code point are translated into one or more UTF-8 encoded bytes. Here, certain bits from the Unicode character's pattern are represented in the "Bit pattern" column by placeholders x, y, z, u, and w. The new location of these bits in the UTF-8 encoding are represented by the same placeholders within the corresponding bytes.

The last rows of Table 4-1 are a bit complex, because UTF-8 is capable of encoding the Unicode Scalar Value represented by a Surrogate Pair. Unicode's High Surrogate and Low Surrogate bit patterns both come into play. Note that the value of $wwww$ from the High Surrogate bit pattern is incremented to make the $uuuuu$ bit pattern in the scalar value so that Surrogate Pair don't address the BMP. If you did not add 1 to the value of the four $wwww$ bits, the Surrogate Pair would address code values in Planes 0 to 15. However, Plane 0 is the BMP, and you can already address the BMP characters with a single 16-bit code value. Adding 1 to the $wwww$ values shifts the range of code values that you can address using Surrogate Pair "up" one plane, so the Surrogate Pair address characters in Planes 1 to 16. There are four $wwww$ bits and five $uuuuu$ bits since, when the $wwww$ bits are 1111_2 (0xF), adding one gives you 10000_2 (0x10).

Figure 4-3 shows the code value ranges that are encoded in UTF-8 as one, two, three, or four bytes. The ranges are superimposed on the ranges for the allocation areas.

Table 4-1 *Relationship Between Unicode Code Value and UTF-8 Bytes*

Unicode			UTF-8			
From	To	Bit pattern	Byte 1	Byte 2	Byte 3	Byte 4
0000	007F	00000000xxxxxxx	0xxxxxxx			
0080	07FF	00000yyyyyxxxxxx	110yyyyy	10xxxxxx		
0800	FFFF	zzzzyyyyyyxxxxxx	1110zzzz	10yyyyyy	10xxxxxx	
High Surrogate						
D800	DBFF	110110wwwwzzzzyy	11110uuu	10uuzzzz	10yyyyyy	10xxxxxx
Low Surrogate						
DC00	DFFF	110111yyyyxxxxxx				
Unicode Scalar Value						
100000	10FFFF	000uuuuuzzzzyyyyyyxxxxxx where uuuuu = wwww + 1				

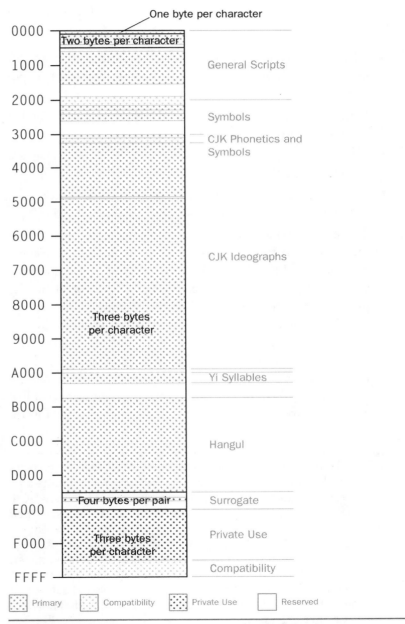

Figure 4.3 *Numbers of bytes required to encode UTF-8 characters*

The following facts may be ascertained from both Figure 4-3 and Table 4-1:

- The Latin characters corresponding to the ASCII character set, and only those characters, are encoded using one byte per character.

- Some of the blocks in the General Scripts area are encoded using two bytes per character.

- The remaining blocks, except for the Surrogate area, are encoded using three bytes per character.

- Surrogate Pairs are encoded using four bytes per pair — i.e., four bytes for every two Unicode code values.

These facts make UTF-8 very efficient for text containing many Latin characters. It also means that ASCII has become a subset of UTF-8. So if, like much of the English-speaking world, you only use ASCII text, that text is acceptable to any program that accepts UTF-8 input. If you use more than the ASCII characters — as much of the rest of the world does — then your mileage will vary. If you use only characters with Unicode code values less than 0x07FF, then UTF-8 will be at least as efficient as UTF-16. If you use any other characters, including any Han or Hangul characters, then using UTF-8 will require more bytes per character than will using UTF-16.

Tip

UTF-8 is one of the two encodings that all XML processors must support, and many XML processors will output text as UTF-8 by default. If your XML files are not encoded in ASCII, UTF-8, or UTF-16, make sure that you do indicate their encoding in the XML Declaration since other encodings – even ISO 8859-1 – are not compatible with UTF-8. Also, make sure that you know the encoding of the data produced by your XML application. This is because your ISO 8859-1 input may be output as UTF-8, and the only indication you may have of that fact will be that your accented characters will have changed.

Using UTF-8 makes your Unicode text safer in systems that handle data in 8-bit chunks but can't reliably handle characters as 16-bit chunks. In principle, any system that can handle 8-bit data can handle 16-bit data as two 8-bit chunks, but handling 16-bit data as two 8-bit pieces of text isn't nearly so reliable. Moreover, software that isn't designed to handle 16-bit characters could insert, for example, a line feed between the two bytes of a 16-bit character. This would potentially garble the rest of the 16-bit character sequence. UTF-8 doesn't magically solve all problems of 8-bit software handling multi-byte characters, but it does limit the damage that can be wrought by unequipped software to single characters.

The first byte of a UTF-8 encoded character indicates its own size in bytes: A 1-byte character has "0" in the most-significant bit, and 2-, 3-, and 4-byte characters have different bit patterns in the highest-order positions. A single error — such as a line feed inserted in the middle of a multiple-byte character — will affect only that character. Correct conversion from UTF-8 into Unicode characters can resume at the next byte that does not have "10" in the two highest order bit positions. This also makes random access into a sequence of UTF-8 characters comparatively simple, since you need only need to scan backward four bytes at most to find an initial byte.

In addition, UTF-8 uses the bit combinations for the C0 control characters (described in Chapter 3) and the ASCII characters only for the Unicode equivalents of those characters. This avoids a lot of grief in 8-bit systems compared to using UTF-16. For example, the UTF-16 code value for SYRIAC QUSHSHAYA is 0x0741. Interpreted as two ASCII (and ISO 6429) characters, this value is the equivalent of the Bell character — which could ring the terminal's bell or cause the screen to flash — followed by "A." Using the UTF-8 encoding in 8-bit systems safely avoids this sort of confusion.

Note

When you evaluate a product for Unicode conformance, you should check whether it is handling data as Unicode characters or fudging UTF-8 as sequences of single bytes. Soon after XML was developed, some SGML software vendors announced that they supported XML *provided it was encoded with UTF-8.* This was because XML's delimiter characters are encoded as their ASCII equivalents in UTF-8 and the bytes for the encoded non-Basic Latin characters can be handled as single bytes by 8-bit software.

UTF-EBCDIC

UTF-EBCDIC stands for EBCDIC-friendly Unicode (or UCS) Transformation Format. It is for use on or between computer systems using IBM's Extended Binary Coded Decimal Interchange Code (EBCDIC). It is not, however, intended as an open interchange format for use between disparate systems. UTF-EBCDIC is specified in UTR #15.

UTF-32

The encoding called "UTF-32" doesn't have a defined expansion. It is defined in UTR #19, which is in draft at the time of this writing, and therefore is not part of the Unicode Standard, Version 3.0, or of ISO/IEC 10646. The title of UTR #19 is "Interoperable 32-bit serialization," and the UTR does go so far as to note: "Notationally, the term 'UTF-32' is parallel to 'UTF-16' and 'UTF-8.'"

UTF-32 is a 32-bit form for representing Unicode characters. UTF-32 characters are indistinguishable from UCS-4 characters over the range of code values covered by UTF-32. Since they're identical, why bother mentioning UTF-32? Because UTF-32 has several constraints and some freedoms that the UCS-4 encoding does not have:

- UTF-32 code values are restricted to the range 0x0000000–0x0010FFFF, which is the range addressable with UTF-16. By contrast, although no characters will be assigned outside this range, ISO/IEC 10646 applications may use UCS-4 to access the Private Use planes and groups outside the UTF-16 range.

- UTF-32 characters are subject to the additional semantics defined by the Unicode Standard over those defined by ISO/IEC 10646. Specifying the encoding as UTF-32 makes it explicit that Unicode characters are being used.

- UTF-32 has named UTF-32, UTF-32BE, and UTF-32LE variants because different computers natively handle data with different "endianness" (defined shortly).

- UTF-32 can encode invalid Unicode Scalar Values — such as 0xFFFE, 0xFFFF, and unpaired Surrogates — that UCS-4, by definition, cannot. Use of these scalar values is not correct, but if they appear in the data, they must be able to be transformed into UTF-32 and transformed back into another encoding without loss of information.

Endianness

UCS-4, UCS-2, UTF-16, and UTF-32 all use 16 or 32 bits to represent a character. As noted in the Introduction, different computer architectures store the two bytes of a 16-bit quantity in a different order. "Big-endian" computers, such as those with Motorola or PowerPC processors, store and handle 16-bit quantities as the most-significant byte followed by the least significant. "Little-endian" computers, such as those with Intel processors, store and handle 16-bit quantities as the least-significant byte followed by the most significant. These computer types are frequently abbreviated as BE and LE, respectively.

Adhering to the theory that it is most efficient for a computer to process data stored in the computer's native form, the Unicode Standard and ISO/IEC 10646 do not specify the order of the bytes within a 16-bit quantity. Instead they support both. To avoid confusion when, for example, data is transferred from a big-endian computer to a little-endian, both standards also support the use of an "encoding signature" that indicates the endianness of the data.

When it is the first code value of a Unicode data stream, the Unicode Scalar Value 0xFEFF is treated as the Byte Order Mark (BOM), not as the ZERO WIDTH NO-BREAK SPACE character. It may, in fact, be dropped from any consideration of the data as characters. 0xFEFF is stored on big-endian computers as FE followed by FF, and on little-endian computers as FF followed by FE.

When the endianness of the data being read is the same type expected by the processor, the BOM is read as FE FF. When the data has the opposite endianness, the BOM is read as FF FE, which is not a Unicode or ISO/IEC 10646 character. Reading the BOM as FF FE indicates that the bytes within 16-bit quantities in the data need to be reversed before your program attempts to interpret the data as characters.

ZERO WIDTH NO-BREAK SPACE may also be the first character in a UTF-8 encoded sequence, where it is encoded as EF BB BF. ISO/IEC 10646, but not the Unicode Standard, documents using this three-byte sequence as a signature to identify the encoding rather than just the endianness of the byte stream.

 Tip

With XML files encoded with UTF-16, you should always include ZERO WIDTH NO-BREAK SPACE as the first character since XML processors rely on the presence of the BOM both to determine the endianness and to distinguish UTF-16 from UTF-8.

The Unicode Standard, Version 3.0, defines explicit big-endian, little-endian, and what I'll call "uncommitted" variants of UTF-16 and UTF-32. Table 4-2 shows examples of each of these. UTF-16BE and UTF-32BE are big-endian formats. Similarly, UTF-16LE and UTF-32LE are little-endian formats. The UTF-16 and UTF-32 formats, however, may be either big-endian or little-endian with the BOM or big-endian without the BOM. The BOM, however, is not required to signal the encoding of a format with explicit endianness. If ZERO WIDTH NO-BREAK SPACE occurs as the first character in one of the encodings with explicit endianness— UTF-16BE, UTF-16LE, UCS-32BE, or UCS-32LE—it is preserved as that character, not dropped like the BOM.

Table 4-2 *Example Encodings of HEBREW LETTER BET (0x05D1)*

Encoding	Byte Sequence	Interpreted as
UTF-16	05 D1	ב
UTF-16	FE FF 05 D1	ב
UTF-16	FF FE D1 05	ב
UTF-16BE	05 D1	ב
UTF-16BE	FE FF 05 D1	⟨ZWNBSP⟩ ב
UTF-16LE	D1 05	ב
UTF-16LE	FF FE D1 05	⟨ZWNBSP⟩ ב
UTF-32	00 00 05 D1	ב
UTF-32	00 00 FE FF 00 00 05 D1	ב
UTF-32	FF FE 00 00 D1 05 00 00	ב
UTF-32BE	00 00 05 D1	ב
UTF-32BE	00 00 FE FF 00 00 05 D1	⟨ZWNBSP⟩ ב
UTF-32LE	D1 05 00 00	ב
UTF-32LE	FF FE 00 00 D1 05 00 00	⟨ZWNBSP⟩ ב

In short, if you know the "endianness" of your data, you can specify it as part of the encoding and you don't need the BOM. If you don't, you can either discover it from the BOM or assume that it is big-endian.

SCSU

SCSU stands for "Standard Compression Scheme for Unicode," and it is defined in UTR #6. One of SCSU's goals is to compress Unicode strings to approximately the storage size of traditional character sets. When you consider that many of the pre-Unicode character sets used eight bits per character, and that Unicode is conceptually a 16-bit character set, you can see that Unicode looks bad when the file size counts. (And although in this chapter we've seen a variety of other fixed- and variable-length encodings of Unicode, 16 bits per character is the minimum you would use when presenting all of Unicode's characters using any of the previous encodings.)

SCSU's compression scheme makes two presumptions. The first presumption is that it is compressing a single document mostly using the same alphabet or script. The second presumption is that characters in an alphabet or script are mostly encoded in contiguous blocks in the Unicode coded character set.

The UTR defines sixteen 128-byte "windows" within the coded character set: eight fixed and eight dynamically movable. When the data includes many characters from the same script, you can set a dynamic window so it spans the code values for that script. For a sequence of data characters within a single window's range, re-encoding the data as SCSU requires only a single byte to select the window and one byte for each character, whereas encoding the same characters as UTF-16 requires 16 bits per character.

A compression program is expected to analyze its own input data and position its dynamic windows to achieve the best compression. For example, when the data contains many characters from the Armenian block and none from the Thaana block, it makes sense to position a dynamic window so it spans the Armenian block. It doesn't make sense to position one on the Thaana block.

The predefined static windows span ranges of characters that are likely to be used frequently but that tend to be used in isolation. You can only select characters from a static window one character at a time. However, specifying a static window and the character within the static window in combination takes fewer bytes than does moving a dynamic window, selecting a single character within the window, and moving the window again.

When there are characters within the data that don't fit within the current window, a compression program should do one of the following:

- Shift into (i.e., "select") another static or dynamic window for a single character.

- Shift permanently (i.e., make a "locking shift") into another dynamic window (permanently, that is, until you select another window)

- Define a new dynamic window and shift into it

- Quote a single two-byte Unicode character so it is represented as itself

- Make a locking shift into Unicode mode, where every character is represented by two bytes

- Define a window in the extended range 0x100000 to 0x10FFFF (from Planes 1 to 16) and shift into it.

The 128 characters in a window are encoded with the byte values 0x80 to 0xFF. Byte values 0x20 to 0x7F (as well as TAB, CR, and LF) always correspond to Basic Latin (or control) characters. The remaining byte values in the range 0x00 to 0x1F are used as tag bytes that select or define other windows or signal a shift into Unicode mode.

The dynamic windows' positions are not arbitrary. Instead of using two bytes to encode a window's starting offset, SCSU predefines the possible window positions and uses a single byte to select the offset. Table 4-3 shows the predefined window offsets.

Table 4-3 *Predefined SCSU Window Offsets*

Byte *x*	Offset	Comment
00	Reserved	Reserved for internal use
01–67	*x* (0x80	Half-blocks from U+0080 to U+3380
68–A7	*x* (0x80 + 0xAC00	Half-blocks from U+E000 to U+FF80
A8–F8	Reserved	Reserved for future use
F9	0x00C0	Latin-1 letters and half of Extended-A
FA	0x0250	IPA Extensions
FB	0x0370	Greek
FC	0x0530	Armenian
FD	0x3040	Hiragana
FE	0x30A0	Katakana
FF	0xFF60	Halfwidth Katakana

Table 4-4 shows the predefined static windows' offsets. Static windows 1–7 can only be used with non-locking shifts. As you can see, the windows cover ranges of commonly used characters that are more likely to be interspersed among other characters than part of a run of, say, general punctuation characters. When there is such a run, however, you can always position a dynamic window to any of the following starting offsets.

A 128-character window is effective for most alphabetic scripts but is ineffective for the large number of Han ideographs and Hangul characters. Consequently, neither the dynamic nor the static windows' positions cover the Han or Hangul blocks. Note, however, that static window 7 covers the CJK Symbols & Punctuation block, and that, for optimal compression of Japanese, the dynamic windows can span the Hiragana, Katakana, and Halfwidth Katakana blocks.

Table 4-4 *Predefined SCSU Static Windows*

Window	Starting Offset	Major Area Covered
0	0000	C0 control characters (Used for quoting of tags used in single-byte mode)
1	0080	Latin-1 Supplement
2	0100	Latin Extended-A
3	0300	Combining Diacritical Marks
4	2000	General Punctuation
5	2080	Currency Symbols
6	2100	Letterlike Symbols and Number Forms
7	3000	CJK Symbols & Punctuation

Unlike the other encodings (except for UTF-7), SCSU does not fit the recent emphasis that a UTF (Unicode Transformation Format) should always encode the same character the same way.

Transcoding

"Transcoding" refers to changing from one encoding to another. In this context, it involves changing from a Unicode encoding into another character set's encoding. It is fairly obvious that the Universal Character Set defined by the Unicode Standard and ISO/IEC 10646 is larger than that of any other existing character encoding standard. Therefore, at best, you can convert some portion of the repertoire of the Unicode Standard into any other single encoding.

Using Unicode as "Pivot"

You can use the Unicode Standard's character repertoire as a "pivot" when converting between two other encodings by converting from the source encoding into Unicode, and then converting from Unicode into the target encoding. The payoff for using the Unicode

Standard as a pivot comes when you need to convert between multiple encodings. For direct conversion between n different encodings, converting from one encoding to all other encodings requires $n + 1$ converters (one converter for every encoding except the current one). Converting between all possible source/target pairs requires $n + 1$ converters for each of n encodings, or $n^2 - n$ converters. Using Unicode as a pivot for n encodings requires a converter from each encoding to Unicode and a converter from Unicode to each encoding — $2n$ converters total. That makes using Unicode as a pivot more efficient when you're dealing with four or more encodings.

As you know from Chapter 2, the Unicode Standard encodes characters, not glyphs; that it has defined semantics for characters; and that it includes many characters only for the sake of convertibility between the Unicode Standard and existing standards. The net result is that transcoding from an existing standard to the Unicode Standard is usually straightforward, but transcoding from Unicode text to an existing standard may require choices. For example, should the uncomposed sequence o¨ be transcoded to ISO 8859-1 as o¨ or as ö? The ISO 8859-1 character ö is usually transcoded into the Unicode compatibility character ö, but what about the other way? The UTC publishes tables of mappings from many existing standards to Unicode, and they can be used for mapping in reverse. But it's really up to the conversion program to decide when to transcode an uncomposed sequence into either a composed character or another uncomposed sequence which might not mean exactly the same thing in the target encoding.

Note

UTR #22, which is a proposed draft at the time of this writing, defines an XML format for mapping tables. Using this format, you can specify alternative mappings within the same file for handling special cases such as context-sensitive mapping between \ and ¥ or \ when converting to JIS-Roman.

Even when a mapping table exists, the specified translation may not be the optimal translation, and there also may be inconsistencies between vendors' mapping tables. For example, the ISO 8859-1 mapping table maps the ISO 8859-1 apostrophe ', to 0x0027, APOSTROPHE. However, the apostrophe has mixed usage, as the Unicode Standard notes. Depending on the context, the ISO 8859-1 apostrophe may be better mapped to MODIFIER LETTER PRIME, MODIFIER LETTER APOSTROPHE, MODIFIER LETTER VERTICAL LINE, COMBINING ACUTE MARK, LEFT SINGLE QUOTATION MARK, RIGHT SINGLE QUOTATION MARK, or PRIME.

As you also know, the Unicode Standard unifies many characters and, for example, groups many similar characters into the General Punctuation block, Currency Symbols block, etc., as well as placing many compatibility characters in the Compatibility area. Because of this, it is generally better to use a mapping table rather than an algorithmic solution when transcoding between the Unicode Standard and another standard. The Unicode Standard provides advice about structuring mapping tables, including flat tables and two-stage tables. Transcoding techniques are also a frequent topic of discussion at Unicode conferences.

Transcoding Software

You don't have to do it all yourself. Your application or programming language may have built-in support for reading and writing multiple non-Unicode encodings, and Appendix D lists several transcoding software libraries and stand-alone products.

Java programs, for example, can use the `FileReader` class to read files as characters in the default encoding for the default locale, or they can use an `InputStreamReader` and specify the encoding in use. XML processors typically support multiple encodings and, based upon the encoding specified in the XML Declaration, will transparently convert non-Unicode input into a Unicode representation internally. While a transcoding program may drop characters that are not available in an output encoding, you need not lose any data when using XML, since you can make numeric character references to any Unicode character.

Cross-Reference

See Chapter 5 for more information on numeric character references.

Encodings, transcodings, and compression schemes all treat characters as numbers to be tweaked, torn apart, or squeezed to produce another way of looking at the same thing. There is, however, more to the Unicode Standard than inventing new ways to represent code values. The following chapters provide details about characters, their properties, and how they are handled as individual characters and as sequences of text.

Chapter 5

Characters and Character Properties

The previous chapter discussed the encodings that you can use to represent the characters of the Unicode Standard. By contrast, this chapter focuses on the specific details of handling characters. This chapter is concerned only with properties of single characters.

Cross-Reference

Chapter 6 addresses handling sequences of characters as runs of text.

Aspects of single characters include:

- Unicode Scalar Value
- Undefined characters
- Private Use characters
- Character properties
- Special characters, such as the Byte Order Mark
- Controls and control sequences
- Combining characters

Unicode Scalar Value

Every character has a Unicode Scalar Value, which is a single numeric value that identifies it. For characters within the Basic Multilingual Plane, this is the character's code value. The exceptions, of course, are code values within the Surrogates block, where a High Surrogate and a Low Surrogate combine to address a character in the next 16 planes.

The Unicode Scalar Value of a Surrogate Pair is the code value of the character addressed by the pair. Strictly speaking, it is the abstract character that has the Unicode Scalar Value, not the Surrogate Pair, since a character has the same Unicode Scalar Value whether it is encoded with UTF-16, UTF-32, or UCS-4 (oops, I'm back to talking about encodings again). The Unicode Standard has limited its scope to the BMP and the next 16 planes, but the code value of a UCS-4 character could also be treated as its (non-Unicode) Scalar Value.

The calculation for the Unicode Scalar Value (N) of a Surrogate Pair (H, L) is therefore the same as the calculation of the code point of the referenced character that was introduced in Chapter 4:

```
N = (H - 0xD800) * 0x400 + (L - 0xDC00) + 0x10000
```

And for code points outside the Surrogates block:

```
N = U
```

where U is the code value of the character.

As was also noted in Chapter 4, the ranges of Unicode Scalar Values are 0x00–0xD7FF and 0xE000–0x10FFFF. What wasn't noted in Chapter 4 is why the Unicode Scalar Value is a useful concept.

Unicode Scalar Values are useful in systems like SGML, HTML, and XML, that can make numeric references to characters. Whether an HTML 4.0 or XML document is encoded as UTF-8, UTF-16, UTF-32, Shift-JIS, or ISO 8859-8, the character sequence 一 refers to the Unicode character U+4E00.

Cross-Reference

The mechanics of SGML character references are covered in Chapter 9.

Note

In XML, a numeric character reference to a code value in the Surrogate block will be treated as an error. For example, 0x10000 – which is the first character outside the BMP – is represented in UTF-16 by the Surrogate Pair U+D800 and U+DC00. In XML, `&#x10000;` is a reference to 0x10000, but `&#D800;&#DC00;` is simply two illegal character references in a row.

Surrogates

Single code values from the Surrogate area do not represent characters. However, in the UTF-16 encoding, a High Surrogate (including a High Private Use Surrogate) followed by a Low Surrogate together represent a character.

Although no characters have been assigned outside the BMP, other than planes 0x0F and 0x10 being assigned as Private Use areas, there will eventually be characters assigned in planes other than the BMP. Once that happens, applications will become categorized by three levels of Surrogate support:

- *None* — Doesn't recognize Surrogate Pairs as characters, and integrity of pairs is not maintained.

- *Weak* — Recognizes at least some Surrogate Pairs as characters, but integrity of pairs is not guaranteed.

- *Strong* — Recognizes at least some Surrogate Pairs as characters, and integrity of pairs is guaranteed.

Undefined Characters

Just so you know, any code value for which a character is not defined is reserved for future expansion. It is not safe, or even well mannered, to assign your own meaning just because it hasn't been assigned one by the Unicode Consortium. Use the code values in the Private Use areas if you need to assign your own characters.

An application recognizing the two code values for a Surrogate Pair as a character means the difference between displaying one glyph or two. An application may or may not have the correct font for a Surrogate Pair character, but a strong implementation should use a single glyph for any pair. This is so even if it's just the fallback glyph for the "unknown character" (veterans of Microsoft Word will recall the square box that it shows you when it can't display a character). A weak implementation, on the other hand, is expected to use the correct glyph for the Surrogate Pair characters that it does support but may default to displaying two "unknown character" glyphs for other Surrogate Pairs.

Integrity of pairs refers to an application's ability to keep Surrogate Pairs together and not, for example, allow another code value to be inserted between the two code values of the Surrogate Pair when the text is being edited. Strong support for Surrogates includes maintaining this integrity, which is not expected of implementations with weak or no support for Surrogate Pair characters.

Private Use Characters

Private Use code values will not be assigned characters by the Unicode Consortium and are available for user-defined assignments. The Private Use block within the BMP covers the range U+E000 to U+F8FF. Additionally, planes 0F and 10, which comprise more than 128,000 code values, are reserved for private use.

"Private Use" effectively means "by private agreement" since you can share the details of your use of Private Use code values with the people with which you interchange data. Just think how confusing it would be if you used a Private Use code value and didn't tell your recipient what it meant!

There's no limit on how many people can be privy to this "private" agreement. For example, the W3C MathML Recommendation (http://www.w3.org/TR/REC-MathML/chapter6.html) has made interim assignments in the Private Use area to represent many mathematical symbols that have not yet been standardized by the Unicode Consortium. This "private use" is publicly posted on one of the busiest sites on the Web, and the character assignments are in daily use by an increasing number of people. Actually, since the assignments are expected to be temporary, the MathML Recommendation makes clever use of XML's text entities to avoid hard-coding code values or character references in MathML files.

By convention, the Private Use area is divided into a "Corporate Use Subarea," which extends downwards from U+F8FF, and an "End User Subarea," which extends upwards from U+E000. The expectation expressed by the authors of the Unicode Standard is that software vendors will use the corporate area and make some portion of the End User Subarea available for user applications. The extent to which this is true, and the proportions of the subarea allocations, will vary from platform to platform and vendor to vendor. No one — least of all the Unicode Consortium — guarantees that there won't be collisions between the two subareas.

Handling Unrecognized Characters

Sometimes an application receives code values that it does not recognize, such as:

- Unassigned code values
- Private Use area code values
- Code values that are simply unsupported by the application

The rule in this case is, "First, do no harm." The application should not transform the unrecognized code value into something else. When it writes out the data, it should go ahead and write the unrecognized code values along with the rest of the data. When displaying the data, the application should make its best effort to display something to represent the code values, possibly a black or white box, or a distinctive glyph indicating either that the code value is unassigned or the block that contains the code value. Similarly, applications may be able to make an effort to sort the unrecognized code values correctly.

Character Properties

In the Unicode Standard, *semantics* are expressed as properties of its characters. These properties are defined in the Unicode Standard and in Unicode Technical Reports, and the property values for each character are contained in the text files comprising the Unicode Character Database.

Cross-Reference

The Unicode Character Database – introduced in Chapter 3 – in a sense defines the structure of the Unicode Standard. Note that the Unicode Character Database defines the blocks comprising the repertoire as well as the properties of its characters.

Properties are normative or informative. Normative properties must be handled correctly by all implementations. Informative properties are not as critical. They are provided, in essence, "for your information," and an application may use or not use (or support or not support) any informative property without jeopardizing the application's conformance to the Standard.

Usually all values of a property apply normatively or all apply informatively, but the General category field in UnicodeData.txt has some possible values that are normative and some that are merely informative. This is confusing at first, but some character properties are mutually exclusive — for example, if a character is an uppercase letter, it is not also a punctuation character. Many of the mutually exclusive properties are grouped into the General category field — for example, two of its possible values are "Lu" (indicating "uppercase letter") and "Po" (indicating "other punctuation"). Some of these mutually exclusive properties are normative. In other words, if the character has the property, an application must "Do the Right Thing" or it won't be conformant. Some are informative. In other words, if the application doesn't support it, that doesn't affect whether the application is considered conformant. The "General category" field is described in Section 4.5 of the Unicode Standard, Version 3.0.

Table 5-1 lists each property; the section of the Unicode Standard, Version 3.0, in which it is defined; whether it is normative or informative, and the Unicode Character Database file that records its property value assignments. The properties are further explained in the following sections.

Table 5-1 *Properties and Their Sources*

Property	Unicode 3.0 Section	Normative	Unicode Character Database File	Unicode Character Database Field
Alphabetic	4.10	No	PropList.txt	–
Case	4.1	Yes	UnicodeData.txt	General category
Case mapping	4.1, 5.18	No	UnicodeData.txt	Uppercase mapping, Lowercase mapping, Titlecase mapping
			SpecialCasing.txt	–
Combining class	3.10, 4.2	Yes	UnicodeData.txt	Canonical combining class
Conjoining Jamo	3.11	Yes	Jamo.txt	–
Dashes	6.1	No	UnicodeData.txt	General category

Continued

Table 5-1 *Continued*

Property	Unicode 3.0 Section	Normative	Unicode Character Database File	Unicode Character Database Field
Decomposition	3.6	Yes	UnicodeData.txt	Character decomposition mapping
Directionality	3.12	Yes	UnicodeData.txt	Bidirectional mapping
East Asian width	10.3	No	EastAsianWidth.txt	
Ideographic	4.10	No	PropList.txt	–
Jamo short name	3.11, 4.4			
Letter	4.10	No	UnicodeData.txt	General category
Line breaking	13.1, 13.2	Yes/No	LineBreak.txt	–
Mathematical	4.9	No	PropList.txt	–
Mirrored	3.4, 4.7	Yes	UnicodeData.txt	Mirrored
Numeric	4.6	Yes	UnicodeData.txt	General category
Private use	3.4, 13.5	Yes	UnicodeData.txt	General category
Space	6.1	No	UnicodeData.txt	General category
Surrogate	3.7, 13.4	No	UnicodeData.txt	General category
Unicode 1.0 name	4.8	No	UnicodeData.txt	Unicode 1.0 name
Unicode character name	14.1	Yes	UnicodeData.txt	Character name

As noted above, the "General" category in `UnicodeData.txt` is a special case because some of its possible values apply normatively, and some informatively. Beyond that, some values indicate that the character has a certain property. As Table 5-2 shows, in some cases, multiple "General" category values can indicate the presence of a property, and some values can indicate the presence of multiple properties. Here, properties are listed only for the category values to which they apply. Where a property is not listed for a category value, then a character with that category value does not have that property.

Table 5-2 *UnicodeData.txt "General" category values*

Abbreviation	Description	Normative	Case	Dashes	Letter	Numeric	Private Use	Space	Surrogate
Cc	Other, Control	✔							
Cf	Other, Format	✔							
Cn	Other, Not Assigned	✔							
Co	Other, Private Use	✔					✔		
Cs	Other, Surrogate	✔							✔
Ll	Letter, Lowercase	✔	✔		✔				
Lm	Letter, Modifier	✔			✔				
Lo	Letter, Other	✔			✔				
Lt	Letter, Titlecase	✔	✔		✔				
Lu	Letter, Uppercase	✔	✔		✔				
Mc	Mark, Spacing Combining	✔							
Me	Mark, Enclosing	✔							
Mn	Mark, Non-Spacing	✔							
Nd	Number, Decimal Digit	✔				✔			
Nl	Number, Letter	✔				✔			

Continued

Table 5-2 *Continued*

Abbreviation	Description	Normative	Case	Dashes	Letter	Numeric	Private Use	Space	Surrogate
No	Number, Other	✓				✓			
Pc	Punctuation, Connector								
Pd	Punctuation, Dash			✓					
Pe	Punctuation, Close								
Pf	Punctuation, Final quote								
Pi	Punctuation, Initial quote								
Po	Punctuation, Other								
Ps	Punctuation, Open								
Sc	Symbol, Currency								
Sk	Symbol, Modifier								
Sm	Symbol, Math								
So	Symbol, Other								
Zl	Separator, Line	✓							
Zp	Separator, Paragraph	✓							
Zs	Separator, Space	✓						✓	

Note

No characters are currently assigned the "Co" value in their "General" category field.

Alphabetical

This informative property of letters in alphabetic scripts is defined in Section 4.10 of the Unicode Standard, Version 3.0, and characters with this property are listed in PropList.txt.

Case

This is a normative property of alphabetic characters (and not just Basic Latin characters) that have different case forms. The property is defined to be normative since an alphabetic character's case is a fixed, inherent feature of the character — for example, an *a* is always lowercase, and an *A* is always uppercase.

Characters with Lu, Ll, or Lt values in the "General" category field of UnicodeData.txt have the case property. Characters with other values do not. The Case property is defined in Section 4.1 of the Unicode Standard, Version 3.0, and the characters with each the three values are listed in PropList.txt.

"Lu" specifies an uppercase character. These generally are larger than their lowercase equivalents. The Unicode names for most of these characters contain "CAPITAL," but there are also many characters without this property whose names contain "CAPITAL," and a couple of uppercase characters (e.g., OHM SIGN, whose names don't contain the magic string "CAPITAL").

"Ll" specifies a lowercase character. These generally are smaller than their uppercase equivalents, though exceptions are conceivable. Most but not all of the characters with this property contain "SMALL" in their names, but there are also many characters whose names contain "SMALL" that are not lowercase letters.

"Lt" specifies a titlecase character. "Titlecase" refers to capitalizing only the first letter of a word. For example, "UNICODE", "unicode", and "Unicode" are the uppercase, lowercase, and titlecase forms of the word "Unicode." For compatibility with existing standards, the Unicode Standard includes several composite characters — such as the Croatian digraph U+01C9, LATIN SMALL LETTER LJ — that are effectively two characters that are always written together. When a word beginning with one of these composite characters is initialized (first letter capitalized), however, only the first of these two composite characters becomes capitalized. The Unicode Standard supports the titlecase value of the case property to correctly handle mapping between the lowercase or uppercase form of the composite characters and this initialized form.

Case Mapping

This is a multipart informative property. One-to-one uppercase, lowercase, and titlecase mappings, if they exist, are specified by the "Uppercase mapping," "Lowercase mapping," and "Titlecase mapping" fields of UnicodeData.txt, respectively. Additional case mappings are provided in SpecialCasing.txt. That file contains data for characters that have a case mapping from one character to two or even three characters, such as LATIN SMALL LETTER SHARP S that has titlecase and uppercase mappings to "Ss" and "SS", respectively. It also includes data for locale-specific mappings, such as mapping LATIN CAPITAL LETTER I to LATIN SMALL LETTER DOTLESS I in the TR (Turkish) locale.

Case mapping is an informative property (unlike the case property) because, as the examples above show, case mappings are neither invariant nor inherent in a character. The mapping can change based on the locale or the context of the character.

Implementation guidelines for case conversion, case detection, and caseless matching are described in UTR #21.

Canonical Ordering

We're getting into a sticky area in our discussion of character properties, so before we go on, it's important that we stop and examine the concept of canonical ordering in some depth. A *combining character* is what your eyes would consider to be a *part* of a printed character – like an accent, an umlaut, or a cedilla – that actually has a code point reserved for it in the Unicode sequence. A combining character always *follows* a base character, and multiple combining characters can follow a base character in any sequence. There is, however, a *canonical ordering* (the Unicode Standard's way of stating "pecking order"), governing the relative positions of a base character and its combining marks. Canonical ordering becomes relevant when comparing two sequences of a base character plus combining characters where the sequences differ only in the order of the combining characters' appearance. The sequences can only be recognized as identical once you put the combining characters in the same order in both sequences.

The way an application should interpret combining character sequences, particularly for rendering, follows several simple rules:

- Combining characters follow their base character; they never precede it

- Enclosing non-spacing marks – such as U+20DD, COMBINING ENCLOSING CIRCLE – surround all previous characters up to and including their base character

- Double diacritics – such as U+0360, COMBINING DOUBLE TILDE – are lower in the pecking order than almost all other non-spacing marks and are usually rendered above other diacritics

- Combining marks with the same combining class generally stack outwards in sequence from their base character, unless their Combining Class property is such that it specifically overrides the ordinary stacking behavior

Continued

- When combining characters have different classes, the order in which they occur after the base character isn't important for the presentation or meaning of the compound character (i.e., base + combining characters)

As noted later in the "Properties" section, characters have a normative Combining Class property that determines their interaction. Base characters, enclosing characters, and spacing combining characters have a Combining Class property value of zero, indicating that they don't combine with the other characters. Related non-spacing combining characters have the same numeric combining class property values. U+0345, COMBINING GREEK YPOGE-GRAMMENI, then the double diacritics – noted above as among the lowest in the pecking order – currently have the two highest Combining Class property values. This is so that they are last in any character ordering based on combining class.

The figure below shows some example canonical reorganizations of combined characters. As the figure demonstrates, the canonical ordering algorithm consistently produces the same arrangement of uncomposed characters, given any arrangement of precomposed or combining characters including the same elements. The order of the uncomposed characters will always be sorted by their combining class property values. In the figure, the combining class value is shown beneath each character. Notice how the precomposed å character is decomposed to a and the non-spacing ° prior to the canonical ordering algorithm ever seeing them. Notice also how characters with the same combining class – such as ¨ and ° – do not have any predefined sequence.

Original	Decomposition	Canonical order
å + ◌̦	→ a + ◌̊ + ◌̦	→ a + ◌̦ + ◌̊
0 202	0 230 202	0 202 230
a + ◌̦ + ◌̊ →		→ a + ◌̦ + ◌̊
0 202 230		0 202 230
ä + ◌̈	→ a + ◌̊ + ◌̈	→ a + ◌̊ + ◌̈
0 230	0 230 230	0 230 230
a + ◌̈ + ◌̊ →		→ a + ◌̈ + ◌̊
0 230 230		0 230 230
a + ◌̊ + ◌̈ →		→ a + ◌̊ + ◌̈
0 230 230		0 230 230

Example canonical ordering of composed and precomposed character sequences

Combining Class

This normative property is specified in the "Canonical combining class" field of `UnicodeData.txt`. Its value is an integer specifying the character's combining class for the purposes of the canonical ordering algorithm (see the sidebar on Canonical Ordering). The integers do not have any intrinsic meaning; only their relative magnitudes are important, since the canonical ordering algorithm sorts sequences of combining characters by their combining class.

Cross-Reference

A list of combining characters and their classes is provided in Chapter 4 of the Unicode Standard and in the HTML file accompanying the Unicode Character Database files.

Combining Jamo

This is a normative property of the characters in the Hangul Jamo block. All of the Jamo characters have this property, and no non-Jamo have it. The property assignment is stated in the Unicode Standard, Version 3.0. It is not indicated in the Unicode Character Database, unless you consider it sufficient indication that only combining Jamo are referenced in Jamo.txt.

Cross-Reference

For more information on the Hangul Jamo characters, see Chapter 7.

Dashes

This informative property is specified by a "Pd" value in the "General category" field of UnicodeData.txt. Characters with this property are listed in PropList.txt, as are characters with the undocumented "Hyphen" property. Descriptions of the dash and hyphen characters are provided in Section 6.1 of the Unicode Standard, Version 3.0.

Decomposition

This normative property is described in Section 3.6 of the Unicode Standard, Version 3.0. A character's value for this property is specified in the "Character decomposition mapping" field of UnicodeData.txt. If present, it specifies either a canonical mapping or a compatibility mapping.

A *compatibility mapping* maps the character to one or more other characters that you could use as a replacement for the first character. This is provided you don't mind losing something in the process and don't mind that the process isn't necessarily reversible. Compatibility mappings are indicated by including a "tag," such as <font> or <compat> in the field's value. For example, the character decomposition property for U+02DA, RING ABOVE, is <compat> 0020 030A, indicating a compatibility mapping to the two-character sequence U+0020, SPACE, and U+030A, COMBINING RING ABOVE.

A *canonical mapping* maps the character to its canonical equivalent character or characters (see sidebar for example). A canonical mapping is reversible without losing any information. For instance, the character decomposition mapping property for U+212B, ANGSTROM SIGN is 00C5, indicating a canonical mapping to the single character U+00C5, LATIN CAPITAL LETTER A WITH RING ABOVE. The canonical decomposition mapping for U+00C5 is 0041 030A, indicating a canonical mapping to the two-character sequence U+0041, LATIN CAPITAL LETTER A, and U+030A, COMBINING RING ABOVE.

Think of the process of canonical decomposition as being comprised of several individual levels of mapping. With each level, compound characters are stripped to their baser elements, and the order in which those baser elements are arranged is determined by the reordering algorithm. Each character decomposition mapping provides a single level of mapping. If you recursively apply canonical mappings for a character until the resulting character or characters can only be re-mapped to themselves, and then rearrange the order of those characters according to the canonical reordering algorithm, you eventually are left with that original character's canonical decomposition. Similarly, if you recursively apply both canonical and compatibility mappings to that same character, then apply the canonical reordering algorithm, you have that character's compatibility decomposition. See UTR #15, Unicode Normalization Forms, and the Normalization Forms section in this chapter.

Directionality

This is a normative multivalue property specified in the "Bidirectional mapping" field of UnicodeData.txt. This property is used by implementations of the Bidirectional Behavior algorithm specified in Section 3.12 of the Unicode Standard, Version 3.0, and in UTR #9 to determine the displayed order of characters when there is a mixture of left-to-right and right-to-left text. The characters with each value of the bidirectional mapping property are listed in PropList.txt.

Cross-Reference

The descriptions of the bidirectional categories are provided in Section 3.12 of the Unicode Standard, in UTR #9, in the HTML file accompanying the Unicode Character Database files, and in Chapter 6 of this book.

East Asian Width

This informative property is specified in EastAsianWidth.txt. The meaning of the property values is provided in UTR #11, East Asian Width Property.

Ideographic

This is an informative property of the Unified Ideographs as well as Compatibility Han characters, IDEOGRAPHIC NUMBER ZERO, IDEOGRAPHIC CLOSING MARK, and the Hangzhou-style numerals (used in China for keeping of accounts, etc.). The assignments are recorded in Section 4.10 of the Unicode Standard, Version 3.0, and the characters with this property are listed in PropList.txt.

Jamo Short Name

This normative property of the characters in the Hangul Jamo block is specified in `Jamo.txt`. This information, along with sample glyphs, is also provided in Section 4.4 of the Unicode Standard, Version 3.0.

Letter

This informative property of characters with an Ll, Lm, Lo, Lt, or Lu value in the "General category" field of `UnicodeData.txt` is defined in Section 4.10 of the Unicode Standard, Version 3.0.

Line Breaking

This sometimes normative, sometimes informative property is specified in `LineBreak.txt`. The meaning of the property values and the breakdown of the values into normative and informative is provided in UTR #14, Line Breaking Properties.

Mathematical

This informative property of characters used as operators in mathematical formulas. It is defined in Section 4.9 of the Unicode Standard, Version 3.0, and characters with this property are listed both there and in `PropList.txt`.

Mirrored

This normative property is specified in the "Mirrored" field of `UnicodeData.txt`. Paired characters—such as LEFT SQUARE BRACKET and RIGHT SQUARE BRACKET—that require different glyphs in a right-to-left context than in a left-to-right context, have this property. In a left-to-right context, LEFT SQUARE BRACKET—which usually opens a bracketed sequence of characters—appears as "[". In a right-to-left context, where characters are displayed in the reverse order, this "opening" square bracket appears as "]".

Numeric

This is a normative property of characters representing numbers. It is specified by an "Nd," "Nl," or "No" value in the "General category" field in UnicodeData.txt. The property is defined in Section 4.6 of the Unicode Standard, Version 3.0.

"Nd" specifies a decimal digit—i.e., one that can form a base-10 number. The digits 0–9 (DIGIT ZERO to DIGIT NINE), sometimes called "European digits," have this property as do other groups of digits. Fractions, superscript and subscript digits, and Roman numerals do not have this property. Table 5-3 shows the sets of decimal digits in the Unicode Standard, Version 3. The group names are unofficial designations derived from the characters' Unicode character names. Note that some of these groups of digits, such as the Fullwidth digits, are used with multiple scripts.

Table 5-3 *Groups of Decimal Digits*

Start	End	Group
0030	0039	European digits
0660	0669	Arabic-Indic digits
06F0	06F9	Eastern Arabic-Indic digits
0966	096F	Indic (Devanagari) digits
09E6	09EF	Bengali digits
0A66	0A6F	Gurmukhi digits
0AE6	0AEF	Gujarati digits
0B66	0B6F	Oriya digits
0BE7	0BEF	Tamil digits (Use DIGIT ZERO for zero)

Continued

Start	End	Group
0C66	0C6F	Telugu digits
0CE6	0CEF	Kannada digits
0D66	0D6F	Malayalam digits
0E50	0E59	Thai digits
0ED0	0ED9	Lao digits
0F20	0F29	Tibetan digits
1040	1049	Myanmar digits
1369	1371	Ethiopic digits (No zero)
17E0	17E9	Khmer digits
1810	1819	Mongolian digits
FF10	FF19	Fullwidth digits

"Nl" specifies numbers written with letters. For example, the characters for Roman numerals, ideographic zero, and the Hangzhou-style numerals have this property.

"No" specifies other forms of numerals. For example, characters for superscript and subscript digits, fractions, and circled and parenthesized numbers have this property. Some script-specific characters, such as special characters for ten or one hundred, etc., Tibetan half digits, and Bengali currency numerators, also have this property.

Characters with the Numeric property have values in zero or more of the "Decimal digit value," "Digit value," and "Numeric value" fields in `UnicodeData.txt`. Some characters have no values defined but most have a numeric value. Some characters representing numbers in the range 0–9 have both a digit value and a numeric value, and a smaller number have a decimal digit value, a digit value, and a numeric value. No other combinations exist.

The relationship between the numeric properties and the Digit value and Numeric value fields reflects the separate development of different scripts and, to my mind, defies any formula. Table 5-4 shows some of the combinations, including "No" characters without any assigned value and "No" characters with decimal digit, digit, and numeric values.

Table 5-4 *Sample combinations of decimal and numeric values*

Code value	Character name	General category	Decimal digit value	Digit value	Numeric value
0031	DIGIT ONE	Nd	1	1	1
00B9	SUPERSCRIPT ONE	No	1	1	1
00BC	VULGAR FRACTION ONE QUARTER	No	–	–	1/4
0F21	TIBETAN DIGIT ONE	Nd	1	1	1
0F2A	TIBETAN DIGIT HALF ONE	No	–	–	–
137C	ETHIOPIC NUMBER TEN THOUSAND	No	–	–	10000
2160	ROMAN NUMERAL ONE	Nl	–	–	1
2460	CIRCLED DIGIT ONE	No	–	1	1
2469	CIRCLED DIGIT TEN	No	–	–	10
3220	PARENTHESIZED IDEOGRAPH ONE	No	–	–	–
3280	CIRCLED IDEOGRAPH ONE	No	–	–	1

Private Use

For characters in the Basic Multilingual Plane, this normative property is specified by a "Co" value in the "General category" field of UnicodeData.txt. Only the characters in the Private Use Area — which are represented in UnicodeData.txt by their first and last code values — are listed as having this property.

The code values for characters in planes 0F and 10, which are reserved for Private Use, would also have this property, except they are not listed in UnicodeData.txt.

Space

This informative property is specified by a "Zs" value in the "General category" field of UnicodeData.txt. Characters with this property are listed in PropList.txt.

Surrogate

This normative property is specified by a "Cs" value in the "General category" field of UnicodeData.txt. Not surprisingly, only the characters in the High Surrogates, High Private Use Surrogates, and Low Surrogates blocks are listed as having this property, although only the first and last character of each block is listed in the file. "Low Surrogate," "High Surrogate," and "High Private Use Surrogate" are listed as separate properties in PropList.txt and, not surprisingly, the character ranges for their respective blocks are listed for each of the properties.

Unicode 1.0 Name

This informative property is specified in the "Unicode 1.0 name" field of UnicodeData.txt. As explained in Section 4.8 of the Unicode Standard, Version 3.0, many Unicode 1.0 character names were changed when the Unicode Standard merged with ISO/IEC 10646. The Unicode 1.0 name, however, is only provided when it is significantly different from the Unicode 3.0 name.

Unicode Character Name

This normative property is specified in the "Character name" field of UnicodeData.txt. Character names serve as unique identifiers, and they should not be seen as favoring one culture over another. The Unicode character name matches the character's name in the English language version of ISO/IEC 10646, and ISO/IEC 10646 follows the same guidelines for composing character names as ISO/IEC 646, ISO/IEC 6937, ISO 8859, and ISO/IEC 10367.

By convention, names contain only Latin capital letters A to Z, space, and hyphen characters. The following exceptions are character names containing digits:

- CJK Unified Ideographs, which include the character number as part of the character name

- Braille Patterns, which include the digits indicating the character's dots as part of the name

- Characters, such as U+201A, SINGLE LOW-9 QUOTATION MARK, where the digit indicates the shape of the character

Names of Hangul syllables are generated algorithmically, but the generated names do not contain digits. Surrogate and Private Use code values have no names.

Cross-Reference

See Chapter 7 for more detail on the algorithm for generating the names of Hangul syllables.

C0 and C1 control characters are all named <control> because their uses are not standardized across all platforms and all applications. However, the character tables in the Unicode Standard, Version 3.0, do include their ISO 6429 meanings as alternative names.

Additional Properties in PropList.txt

The file PropList.txt lists, for each of 56 properties, the ranges of characters with that property.

Cross-Reference

Some sample properties are listed in the description of PropList.txt in Chapter 3.

Most of the properties defined in Chapter 4 of the Unicode Standard are listed in PropList.txt; however, the "Letter" property, for example, is not. In some cases, each of the possible values of a field in UnicodeData.txt appears as a separate property. For example, each of the values of the "Bidirectional mapping" field appear separately. Furthermore, some properties in `PropList.txt`, such as "Hex Digit," are not defined in the text of the Unicode Standard or do not directly correspond to a defined property. For example, `PropList.txt` lists a "Left of Pair" property while not listing the "Mirrored" property.

Special Characters

Section 3.9 and, for some characters, Chapter 13 of the Unicode Standard, Version 3.0, identify characters with special properties that are not part of a single script or that have special consequences when processing Unicode characters. The special character categories are shown below:

- Line boundary control
- Hyphenation control
- Fraction formatting
- Special behavior with non-spacing marks
- Double non-spacing marks
- Joining
- Bidirectional ordering
- Alternate formatting
- Syriac abbreviation
- Indic dead-character formation
- Mongolian variant selectors
- Ideographic variant indication
- Ideographic description
- Interlinear annotation
- Object replacement
- Code conversion fallback
- Byte order signature

Because of space constraints, the characters in each of these listed categories are not shown here. However, they are listed in the Unicode Standard, Version 3.0. Some of the categories are further explained in the following sections or in other applicable parts of this book.

Byte Order Signature

The use of U+FEFF, ZERO WIDTH NO-BREAK SPACE, as the Byte Order Mark (BOM) indicates the "endianness" of 16-bit and 32-bit encodings of Unicode characters.

Cross-Reference

This above-described use of U+FEFF, ZERO WIDTH NO-BREAK SPACE, is discussed in Chapter 4.

Object Replacement Character

U+FFFC, OBJECT REPLACEMENT CHARACTER, is intended as a placeholder for an external object — for instance, an image — referenced from within a stream of text. No information about the object is maintained in the text stream. It is expected that software will track the offsets of any object replacement characters and associate the correct filename, display size, and other formatting information with each character. An example use (which I don't recommend implementing) is to replace the HTML tag `<img src="picture.gif" width="100" height="50" alt="Company logo">` with a U+FFFC character and store the source, width, height, and alternate text information outside the stream of text. Of course, the software would also have to maintain the correspondence between the U+FFFC character and its related data *without* adding anything else to the steam of text.

Caution

U+FFFE and U+FFFF are not characters. For information on U+FFFE, see the section on "endianness" in Chapter 4. U+FFFF is not, and never will be, a character, as guaranteed by ISO/IEC 10646. It is, therefore, available to programs for internal use as a string delimiter, etc.

Interlinear Annotation Characters

Code values U+FFF9 to U+FFFB are intended for use in an application's internal representation of Japanese Ruby (small characters that appear above text) and similar annotations. (For information on Ruby, see *CJKV Information Processing* by Ken Lunde.) As with the object replacement character, the formatting information for the annotation characters is expected to be maintained elsewhere by the application program. However, the interlinear annotation characters do not convey enough information to be usable in plain text, nor do they convey as much information as the Ruby markup proposed by the W3C in `http://www.w3.org/TR/WD-ruby`.

Caution

Use of the alternate formatting characters, U+206A to U+206F, is strongly discouraged in the Unicode Standard, Version 3.0, so they will not be covered here.

Replacement Character

When transcoding into the Unicode Standard's character repertoire, U+FFFD, REPLACEMENT CHARACTER, is used as a catchall replacement for characters in the original encoding that do not have equivalents in the Unicode Standard. Information conveyed by the original characters is lost, but there remains an indication that a character, albeit unknown, was present at that point in the text stream. This is better than just dropping unknown characters.

If you know what your "unknown" characters are, you can instead transcode them to code values in the Private Use area. This does, of course, require more work on your part to ensure that you use the Private Use code values consistently. It may also require specialized transcoding software, but it can be a good alternative to throwing away information.

Control Characters

Historically, the meaning or use of the ASCII control characters has varied from application to application. Accordingly, the control characters in the Unicode Standard — U+0000 to U+001F and U+007F to U+009F — do not have any particular meaning. Also, it is up to users and applications to generate or interpret them according to their own requirements.

Some control characters — U+0009 to U+000D and U+001C to U+001F — do, however, have significant bidirectional mappings. U+0009, U+000A, U+000C, and U+000D — which are generally used as the tab, line feed, form feed, and carriage return control characters, respectively — also have significant line breaking roles.

There are no shortcuts when encoding control characters. They are represented using the same encoding as the rest of the characters in a sequence of Unicode characters. That means that the LINE FEED character, 0x0A in ASCII/ISO 6429, is encoded as the 8-bit value 0x0A in UTF-8, the 16-bit value 0x000A in UTF-16, and the 32-bit value 0x0000000A in UTF-32.

Normalization Forms

UTR #15, Unicode Normalization Forms, defines four forms of normalized text. As Table 5-5 shows, the D, C, KD, and KC normalization forms differ both in whether they are the result of an initial canonical or compatibility decomposition, and in whether the decomposed text is recomposed with canonical composed characters wherever possible.

Table 5-5 *Decomposition and Canonical Composition Steps for Normalization Forms*

	If NOT followed by Canonical Composition	If followed by Canonical Composition
Canonical Decomposition	D	C
Compatibility Decomposition	KD	KC

Canonical and compatibility decompositions were covered in the earlier Decomposition section. Canonical decomposition recursively applies canonical mappings to the text and then reorders the characters using the canonical ordering algorithm to sort combining characters into a sequence based on each character's combining class. Compatibility decomposition recursively applies both canonical and compatibility mappings (decomposition mappings containing a "tag" such as <font>) before reordering.

Canonical composition (as opposed to canonical decomposition) replaces, where possible, sequences of a base plus combining characters with precomposed characters. For example, the two-character sequence U+0041, LATIN CAPITAL LETTER A, and U+030A, COMBINING RING ABOVE has a canonical composition to U+00C5, LATIN CAPITAL LETTER A WITH RING ABOVE. Note, however, that the two-character sequence is also the canonical decomposition of U+212B, ANGSTROM SIGN. U+212B has a *singleton* (single-character to single-character) decomposition mapping to U+00C5, which has the decomposition mapping to U+0041 and U+030A. Canonical compositions are the reverse of decompositions, but they never reverse singleton decompositions since characters with singleton decompositions are only included in the Unicode Standard for round-trip compatibility with pre-existing standards.

Singletons are one of four classes of characters that are excluded from compositions:

- Script-specific precomposed characters that are generally not the preferred form for their script
- Precomposed characters added to the Unicode Standard after the composition version is fixed (see below)
- Characters with singleton decompositions
- Precomposed characters whose decompositions begin with a non-starter character, e.g., with a combining mark

The characters in each of these four classes are listed in `CompositionExclusions.txt` in the Unicode Character Database (see Chapter 3). However, since the singleton decompositions and the non-starter decompositions are computed from the Unicode Character Database, the characters in those classes are listed in the file but are also commented out. If your application can compute the character classes directly from the Unicode Character Database, it should; otherwise you can uncomment and use the lists in `CompositionExclusions.txt`.

Precomposed characters added to the Unicode Standard after the composition version is fixed are included within a class in `CompositionExclusions.txt` to avoid different, incompatible normalization forms being produced from different versions of the Unicode Character Database. The composition version is defined as version 3.0.0 of the Unicode Character Database, and, not too surprisingly, there are currently no characters in this class since the version 3.0.0 is the current version of the database. Any precomposed characters added in future versions of the Unicode Standard, however, will be added to this character class.

If the Unicode Standard, Version 4.0, adds another precomposed character, that character will have a decomposition mapping. Canonical compositions based on the version 4.0.0 decomposition mappings, therefore, could be different from those based on the version 3.0.0 decomposition mappings. However, since the new precomposed character will be added to `CompositionExclusions.txt`, the version 4.0 software will not use the new mapping and will continue to return the same normalized text as current version 3.0 software. Since text normalization will be built into a huge amount of software in the future, it is a very good thing that future versions of the Unicode Standard will not automatically break existing normalization software.

Cross-Reference

For more on text normalization, see the discussion of the character model for the World Wide Web in Chapter 9.

Normalization will break, however, if an existing character's decomposition mapping changes. Because of this, the Unicode Technical Committee has publicly committed to a policy of careful review of proposals to change decompositions, and will only make changes where the benefits outweigh the drawbacks.

Figure 5-1 shows each of the normalization forms of *affairé* (French adjective for "busy" or "involved") when using U+FB00, LATIN SMALL LIGATURE FF, in place of two U+0066, LATIN SMALL LETTER F, characters. Note that the compatibility decomposition of U+FB00 is U+0066 + U+0066, and that the canonical decomposition of U+00E9, LATIN SMALL LETTER E WITH ACUTE, is the two-character sequence U+0065, LATIN SMALL LETTER E, and U+0301, COMBINING ACUTE ACCENT.

Form	Normalization
D	a + ff + a + i + r + e + ´⟡
C	a + ff + a + i + r + é
KD	a + f + f + a + i + r + e + ´⟡
KC	a + f + f + a + i + r + é

Figure 5-1 *Normalization forms of affairé*

In normalization form D, U+00E9 is decomposed since it has a canonical decomposition, but U+FB00 is not decomposed because it has a compatibility decomposition. In normalization form C, the decomposed canonical sequence of U+0065 and U+0301 is composed back into U+00E9. An example with multiple combining marks that are subject to canonical ordering would perhaps have been more impressive, but real-life examples are a bit hard to come by.

In normalization form KD, both the compatibility and canonical decompositions are made, so U+FB00 is decomposed to U+0066 and U+0066. In normalization form KC, the same decompositions are made, but only canonical compositions are made, so U+0065 and U+0301 are composed back into U+00E9 but U+0066 and U+0066 are not composed into U+FB00.

An understanding of character properties, decompositions, and normalization forms is essential for an understanding of how to work with the characters of the Unicode Standard. Handling individual characters, however, isn't everything you need to know, so the next chapter describes how to work with characters as runs of text.

Chapter 6

Working With Text

This chapter addresses the topic of working with sequences of characters as runs of text. You have already seen that individual characters have defined properties. In this chapter, you will see some examples of the following:

- Text can have properties imposed upon it, such as identified language or directionality
- Text can be sorted and searched
- Text can be interpreted as identifiers or as matching a regular expression
- Text can mean something in a higher-level protocol

Language Identification

Language identification has an obvious, though often overstated, role in the process of selecting glyphs to represent unified characters, and the CJK Unified Ideographs serve as the most obvious example of this. There are, however, other important uses for language identification, such as selecting the right spelling dictionary, hyphenation dictionary or grammar checker. It is also useful when searching multilingual text. Section 5.11 of the Unicode Standard, Version 3.0, discusses requirements for language tagging and working with language tags.

Language Tagging

Despite its utility, a mechanism for identifying the principal language in which a body of text is written, has was only recently been proposed by the Unicode Technical Committee. Up to and including Version 2.0, the Unicode Standard maintained that language identification was the function of a higher-level protocol, such as SGML, since the Unicode Standard encodes scripts, not languages. Many higher-level protocols and markup schemes, including HTML, XML, and many SGML applications, do support language identification—for example, XML has a standardized xml:lang attribute—but there were still calls for a lower-level scheme applicable to all applications of the Unicode Standard.

In response to this, Unicode Technical Report #7, Plane 14 Characters for Language Tags (http://www.unicode.org/unicode/reports/tr7/), defines a simple protocol for specifying language using characters from Plane 14. The Technical Report is not part of the Unicode Standard, Version 3.0, nor is it part of ISO/IEC 10646-1:2000. (However, at the time of this writing, it is being balloted as part of ISO/IEC 10646-2.)

You should, however, still use the higher-level mechanisms such as xml:lang wherever possible. The Plane 14 language tags are *only* intended as for use in string-oriented protocols, such as LDAP, that cannot support language identification in a higher-level protocol.

Language tagging is actually one application of an extensible scheme for using Plane 14 characters for embedding information about Unicode-encoded text within the text itself. No further uses have been proposed at the time of this writing. The general scheme defines a series of "tag" characters. One class of tag character—"Identification characters"—identifies a scheme, although only LANGUAGE TAG is currently defined, and 95 Plane 14 clones of the ASCII characters make up the tags within a scheme. Tags within a scheme do not nest, but multiple schemes (once more are defined) can concurrently mark up the same text since the tags for the schemes will not interact.

Table 6-1 shows the code values and names of several of the tag characters, where ellipses imply the presence of code values in between. You can see that the ASCII clone characters have a strict correspondence with the ASCII characters defined in the Basic Latin block: The clone characters are in the same order (displaced by 0xE0000) and the character names are identical except for the "TAG " prefix. The code values in the table have a direct correspondence in the UTF-32 encoding, but the tags can be expressed equally well in the UTF-16 and UTF-8 encodings.

Table 6-1 *Plane 14-tag characters*

Code Value (Hexadecimal)	Character Name
E0000	<reserved>
E0001	LANGUAGE TAG
E0002	<reserved>
...	...
E001F	<reserved>
E0020	TAG SPACE
E0021	TAG EXCLAMATION MARK
...	...
E002D	TAG HYPHEN-MINUS
...	...
E0041	TAG LATIN CAPITAL LETTER A
...	...
E0061	TAG LATIN SMALL LETTER A
...	...
E007A	TAG LATIN SMALL LETTER Z
...	...
E007E	TAG TILDE
E007F	CANCEL TAG

Plane 14 characters were chosen for the tagging scheme since they cannot be mistaken for "normal" text. Only 128 code values— 0xE0000 to 0xE007F—are reserved for the tagging scheme, so detecting the tag characters requires just a range check. This is simple for UTF-32 data, and, as the C code examples in UTR #7 show, is straightforward for UTF-16 and for UTF-8, even though UTF-8 is a variable-length encoding. Tags comprise an identification character followed by ASCII clone characters spelling out the language (or, eventually, a tag name in a different scheme).

Tags terminate at the first non-clone character; i.e., either a "normal" Unicode value or another identification character. The exception is the CANCEL TAG character. When following an identification character, CANCEL TAG cancels the current tag for that scheme (and doesn't affect any other scheme); when used alone, the CANCEL TAG character cancels *all* tags for *all* schemes. Its intended use is at the end of strings to reset one or all schemes. This avoids unexpected results when, for example, two strings are concatenated. Without canceling, the initial characters of the second string will be identified as being in whatever language was current at the end of the first string. This could, for example, identify Italian text as French, English as German, or, with more obvious formatting consequences, Japanese as Korean. There is, of course, nothing stopping you from identifying Japanese text as Korean when you create the text, but using CANCEL TAG can save you from making additional errors when you work with the text.

Tags in the language identification scheme are language identifiers as specified in RFC 1766. Both registered identifiers and user-defined identifiers, which start with x-, may be used. Registered identifiers are either an ISO 639 language ID, such as en, or a language ID followed by an ISO 3166 country ID, such as en-us or en-au. Since RFC 1766 language identifiers are not case-sensitive, UTR #7 recommends using only lowercase language identifier tags. For example, the UTF-32 code values for the complete language tag, including identifier, for English (en) is:

```
0x000E0001 0x000E0065 0x000E006E
```

and the `en-au` language tag for Australian English is:

```
0x000E0001 0x000E0065 0x000E006E 0x000E002D 0x000E0061
0x000E0075
```

With software that uses the language identifier to select spelling dictionaries, I could use the `en-au` language tag so that, for example, when I use "colour" instead of "color," I do not have my usual disagreement with the spell-check software.

Language identifier tags mark the text following them until any of the following occurs:

- The next language identifier tag establishes a new language
- The tag is canceled by a CANCEL TAG character
- The text goes out of scope; e.g., in a line-oriented protocol, the end of line is reached

As noted above, tags do not nest, so when a language identifier is canceled or goes out of scope, no language identification is in effect.

Proper Inclusion of Language Identifiers

Figure 6-1 shows a simple example of rendering two ideographs both with and without language identifiers. Without the language identifiers, there is not enough information for an editor application to do anything but render the two characters identically. With the language identifiers, however, an application that supports the identifiers can display a Japanese-style glyph when the language tag is `jp`, and display a Korean-style glyph when the language tag is `kr`. Language identifiers normally are not displayed, but some applications may choose to display the text of the tag when the user is editing or debugging the text.

UTR #7 recommends using ASCII character glyphs for the tag text, preferably glyphs that are visually different from "normal" ASCII character glyphs. Unless an application is designed to support the language identifiers, however, the characters in an identifier are likely to be treated like any other non-BMP characters that the application does not recognize. In that case, many applications will display each of the tag characters with a default "unknown character" glyph, or, in the case of UTF-16 text and an application that does not support surrogates, two glyphs. One alternative would be an application that recognizes the language identifiers, and doesn't do anything with them but also doesn't display "unknown character" glyphs for the tags.

No language identifier		
Character	平 平	
UTF-32	0000 0000 5E73 5E73	
Rendering	平平	

Language identifier		
Character	⌐LANG⌐ ⌐TAG⌐ ⌐TAG⌐ 平 ⌐LANG⌐ ⌐TAG⌐ ⌐TAG⌐ 平 ⌐TAG⌐ ⌐ j ⌐ ⌐ p ⌐ ⌐TAG⌐ ⌐ k ⌐ ⌐ o ⌐	
UTF-32	000E 000E 000E 0000 000E 000E 000E 0000 0001 006A 0070 5E73 0001 006B 006F 5E73	
Supported	平平	
Editor view	j p 平 k o 平	
Non-supported	■■■平■■■平	
Aware	平平	

Figure 6-1 *Rendering characters with and without language identifiers*

The use of the Plane 14 characters to identify language was designed to be a low-level alternative to higher-level protocols or markup mechanisms such as XML or HTML. If you are using XML or HTML, however, it makes sense for you to only use the xml:lang or html:lang attribute, as appropriate. Using one mechanism to indicate the structure of your text and a different one to indicate the language just creates more overhead, both for you when you create the text and for any software that has to parse and process your text. Plane 14 language indication tags are also less likely to be noticed by an XML or HTML search engine than are the standardized language attributes.

Also, how software is supposed to behave when a substring extracted from a longer string begins or ends inside a language tag is not something that is defined by UTR #7. Nor are any requirements expressed for replicating or maintaining the language information of a substring extracted from a longer string. I don't know what it means, for example, to extract one of the ideographs from the second example in Figure 6-1. An application might choose to carry the "ko" language tag with the substring, or it might not.

Bidirectional Text

The Unicode Standard includes several scripts whose characters are normally written right-to-left, as opposed to English and other languages whose scripts are written left-to-right. Arabic and Hebrew are probably the most widely used right-to-left scripts, but the Syriac and Thaana scripts are also written right-to-left, as well as some ligatures used only in Yiddish.

The Unicode Standard also specifies that applications store and transmit characters in their *logical* order. For left-to-right text, this means storing the leftmost character first, and for right-to-left text, this means storing the rightmost character first. This is straightforward when the text is all left-to-right or all right-to-left, but life becomes more interesting when the two forms are mixed. To ensure that applications of the Unicode Standard correctly and consistently handle mixing of text with different directionality, the Unicode Standard specifies the *bidirectional algorithm* (i.e., handling text in two directions) in Section 3.12 of the Unicode Standard, Version 3.0, and in UTR #9, Unicode 3.0 Bidirectional Algorithm. The Unicode Standard, Version 3.0, requires merely that applications display text as if the bidirectional algorithm had been applied, in the absence of higher level protocols. This means that you can use a different algorithm provided the results are the same. It also means that you can, for example, override the effects of the bidirectional algorithm by using XML markup that indicates text direction.

Handling bidirectional text isn't as simple as saying that all Arabic or Hebrew or Syriac or Thaana text, and only that text, runs right-to-left, or that changes in text direction are only one level deep. Your text, for example, may be based in Hebrew but may contain an English quotation containing an Arabic word (or English containing an Arabic phrase containing an English word, etc.). You may also want to break or override the rules and, for example, make an English word (e.g., a product name) display as right-to-left text within a run of Hebrew text. Also, some characters, such as some numbers and punctuation characters, do not have the same strong directionality as, for example, English and Arabic letters, so their directionality depends upon that of the characters in their vicinity.

Correctly handling direction levels, explicit overrides, and characters with weak or neutral directionality makes for a bidirectional algorithm too complex to cover here. If you are interested in implementing the algorithm, the details are available in the Unicode Standard, Version 3.0, and online at http://www.unicode.org/unicode/reports/tr9/.

Note

The Unicode Consortium has published the source code for Java and C++ reference implementations of the bidirectional algorithm. The programs are known to produce identical results, and you use them check the conformance of your own implementation. The code is included on the CD-ROM accompanying the Unicode Standard, Version 3.0, book, and is also available online as part of UTR #9.

The bidirectional algorithm relies upon each character's Bidirectional category defined in `UnicodeData.txt` and, for explicit setting of directionality, upon a handful of zero-width characters from the General Punctuation block. For your reference, Table 6-2 shows the characters with explicit effect on the directionality of displayed text, and Table 6-3 shows the Bidirectional category values ranked into strong, weak, and neutral directionality groups.

Table 6-2 *Characters Affecting Directionality*

Code value (Hex)	Character name	Abbr.	Role
200E	LEFT-TO-RIGHT MARK	LRM	Behaves like a printing left-to-right character for the purposes of the bidirectional algorithm
200F	RIGHT-TO-LEFT MARK	RLM	Behaves like a printing right-to-left character for the purposes of the bidirectional algorithm
202A	LEFT-TO-RIGHT EMBEDDING	LRE	Treats the following text up to the next PDF as left-to-right text embedded within right-to-left text
202B	RIGHT-TO-LEFT EMBEDDING	RLE	Treats the following text up to the next PDF as right-to-left text embedded within left-to-right text
202C	POP DIRECTIONAL FORMATTING	PDF	Removes the bidirectional state imposed by the previous LRE, RLE, LRO, or RLO
202D	LEFT-TO-RIGHT OVERRIDE	LRO	Forces the following text as strongly left-to-right
202E	RIGHT-TO-LEFT OVERRIDE	RLO	Forces the following text as strongly right-to-left

Table 6-3 *Bidirectional Category Values Ranked by Strength*

Category	Type	Description	Scope
Strong	L	Left-to-Right	LRM and most other characters and unassigned code values not otherwise mentioned in this table. Does not include European or Arabic digits or unassigned code values among the ranges for the right-to-left scripts and their presentation forms
	LRE	Left-to-Right Embedding	LRE
	LRO	Left-to-Right Override	LRO
	R	Right-to-Left	RLM, the Hebrew alphabet, most Hebrew-specific punctuation, and all unassigned code values in the Hebrew block and among the Hebrew presentation forms in the range FB1D–FB4F
	AL	Right-to-Left Arabic	Arabic, Thaana, and Syriac alphabets and their script-specific punctuation, plus all unassigned code values in the Arabic, Syriac, Thaana, Arabic Presentation Form-A, and Arabic Presentation Form-B blocks
	RLE	Right-to-Left Embedding	RLE
	RLO	Right-to-Left Override	RLO
Weak	PDF	Pop Directional Format	PDF
	EN	European Numberand	European digits, Eastern Arabic-Indic digits, full-width, circled, superscript, subscript, etc. forms of the European digits
	ES	European Number Separator	SOLIDUS ("/") and FULLWIDTH SOLIDUS
	ET	European Number Terminator	Plus and minus signs and their presentation forms, currency symbols, and some other punctuation and other symbols

Continued

Category	Type	Description	Scope
Weak (continued)	AN	Arabic Number	Arabic-Indic digits, and the Arabic decimal and thousands separators
	CS	Common Number Separator	Colon, comma, and fullstop characters and their presentation forms, plus NO-BREAK SPACE
	NSM	Non-Spacing Mark	Characters with "Mn" or "Me" values in their "General category" field in UnicodeData.txt
	BN	Boundary Neutral	All other formatting and control characters
Neutral	B	Paragraph Separator	PARAGRAPH SEPARATOR plus control characters that conventionally indicate ends of paragraphs
	S	Segment Separator	Tab
	WS	Whitespace	Space characters
	ON	Other Neutrals	All other characters, including OBJECT REPLACEMENT CHARACTER

The specification of the bidirectional algorithm notes how a higher-level protocol can supplement or override the behavior specified by the algorithm. Some protocols, such as HTML 4.0, also document how their directionality controls interact with the bidirectional algorithm. When you use both a higher-level protocol and the Unicode Standard's bidirectional algorithm, however, there is enormous opportunity for error. Mixing the embedded controls — LRE, RLE, LRO, RLO, and PDF — with a higher-level protocol is especially problematic. As the HTML 4.0 Specification dryly notes:

> If both methods are used, great care should be exercised to insure proper nesting of markup and directional embedding or override, otherwise, rendering results are undefined.

Using a protocol — such as HTML or XML — that can separate a document's content from its formatting frequently requires a stylesheet for correct presentation of your text. Specifying directionality properties in the stylesheet adds welcome or unwelcome interaction with the behavior of the bidirectional algorithm. You should be especially careful with specifying directionality properties in the stylesheet, since stylesheets are typically used with entire classes of documents. The more frequently a stylesheet is associated with a document, the greater the chance for a bad interaction with the bidirectional algorithm.

Note also that some protocols, such as XML, reference the character repertoire of the Unicode Standard without requiring that applications fully conform to the Unicode Standard. An application supporting such a protocol may, in fact, support the bidirectional behavior specified by that protocol and not support the bidirectional behavior implicit in the Bidirectional category properties of the text.

Rendering

If you are going to implement a rendering engine for Unicode characters, and particularly if you are going to implement an editor, then you need more information than I can provide here. Some of the necessary information is provided in Chapter 5 of the Unicode Standard, Version 3.0, but many additional, script-specific details have to be gleaned from the character block descriptions in Chapters 6 to 13 of the standard. Fortunately, newer operating system versions, particularly for Windows and MacOS, are improving their built-in support for rendering the characters in the Unicode Standard.

 Cross-Reference

Overviews of operating systems' current levels of support are provided in Chapter 10 of this book.

Reasons why rendering characters is so tough include the following:

- There is obviously a large number of characters in the Unicode Standard.

- Operating systems must pay attention to the need to handle both composed and precomposed characters.

- In some scripts, characters have different glyphs depending on their position in a word, along with other factors.

- Combining marks can be used in *any* sequence with *any* base character.

- A full-featured operating system is expected to include an API that recognizes word and line boundaries.

- When multiple languages are involved, there's the possibility of intermingling left-to-right and right-to-left text.

Reasons why implementing an editor is particularly tough include:

- The definition of character and word boundaries differs between scripts

- A truly compliant editor should handle input of combining marks

- Precomposed characters (for example, Å) may need to be edited as if they were composed from sequences of characters, (A ˚).

Regular Expressions

UTR #18, which is a draft report at the time of this writing, describes guidelines for regular expressions. Several aspects of the Unicode Standard make life interesting for someone implementing regular expression support. These include:

- The character repertoire is *large*.

- Many characters have a decomposition mapping into an equivalent sequence of base plus combining character or characters.

- The Unicode Standard covers many scripts with very different characteristics from each other.

- The characters within a script are not necessarily located within a contiguous block of code values in the Unicode Standard. In one case where this might occur, the punctuation characters may be in the General Punctuation block even though the alphabetic characters are together.

- The Unicode Standard is an open standard that changes from version to version as new characters are added and, to a lesser extent, properties of existing characters are redefined.

- Properties of some characters, or even the collation order of the characters, vary from language to language and locale to locale.

The draft UTR defines three implementation levels for regular expression engines:

- *Basic Unicode Support* Minimal, locale-independent support for characters as 16-bit (or 32-bit) units.

- *Extended Unicode Support.* Still locale-independent, but supports canonical equivalents and surrogates.

- *Locale-Sensitive Support.* Additionally provides locale-sensitive treatment of characters.

I won't go into details about the regular expression guidelines, not only because they are complex but also because they may have changed by the time you read this. The latest version of the guidelines is available at `http://www.unicode.org/unicode/reports/tr18/`.

Sorting and Searching

Sorting and searching are grouped under Section 5.17 of the Unicode Standard, Version 3.0. The reason is because the job of locating a passage of text in a larger body and the job of sorting several textual strings, are similar in that they share one important process: They both involve pattern matching.

Note

ISO/IEC 10651 (under development at the time of this writing) specifies the default string ordering of ISO/IEC 10646 data.

Sorting Unicode text as opposed to sorting 8-bit character strings is a complex job but not an insurmountable one, especially since UTR #10 defines the Unicode Collation Algorithm and the Unicode Consortium provides the Default Unicode Collation Element Table for use with the algorithm. (The table is, however, limited to the Unicode 2.1.9 repertoire at the time of this writing.) Some of the complexity of the task stems from the quirks that different scripts have developed (or accreted) during their development. Aspects of culturally expected sorting include:

- Single characters treated as multiple — in English, *æ* may sort as *ae*

- Multiple characters treated as single — in traditional Spanish, *ch* is treated as a single letter

- French accents — when sorting French, accents later in a string are more important than accents earlier in the string

- Characters not in logical order — in Thai and Lao, some vowels are coded *before* the character that they logically follow

- Uppercase and lowercase forms — in many languages, uppercase and lowercase forms of characters are treated equally. So although *A* may have an earlier code value than *a*, a book title starting with lowercase *a* would be sorted along with those with uppercase *A* rather than following uppercase *Z*.

Ordinary binary sorts by initial code values may not necessarily result in sets of strings that are arranged in their culturally expected order. To address this problem, the Unicode Standard recommends, and the Unicode Collation Algorithm specifies, a multilevel comparison using several categories of sort keys. For the Latin script, the sort keys (in order of decreasing importance) are alphabetic ordering, diacritic ordering, and case ordering.

The two-part Default Unicode Collation Element Table provides, as the name says, a default set of sort keys. However, you can modify the table; for example, you can use French sorting of accented characters.

Identifiers

Programming languages such as C, Perl, etc., have rules about what characters can and cannot be used in identifiers such as variable and function names. Similarly, markup schemes such as SGML have rules about what characters may be used as tag names, etc. In the not-too-distant past, when most programming languages supported ASCII and not much else, the rules for identifiers were simple. Typically only A–Z, a–z, maybe 0–9, and maybe a handful of punctuation characters were allowed in identifiers. However, the rules vary from programming language to programming language, particularly the rules involving punctuation characters and the choice of characters that may start an identifier.

Even with the ASCII character set, programming language designers have made many different choices regarding what constitutes an identifier. Those choices may be multiplied by 500 when it comes time for you to decide which characters from the Unicode Standard to allow or disallow in identifiers. Language designers can make informed choices about which characters from their own script to allow in identifiers, but few, if any, language designers will be able to make similarly informed choices when considering the entire repertoire of the Unicode Standard.

To make life simpler, and possibly even consistent, Section 5.16 of the Unicode Standard provides guidelines for which characters should and should not be used in identifiers. Features of these guidelines—which I won't duplicate here—include proper handling of combining marks, and the option to ignore layout and format control characters when parsing identifiers.

Note

The guidelines in the Unicode Standard, Version 3.0, are considerably simpler than the guidelines specified in the Unicode Standard, Version 2.0.

The identifier guidelines break up identifiers into a set of allowable start characters and a larger set of characters that may follow the initial character, as do many languages, including XML.

Note

The XML 1.0 character classes are based, in part, upon the identifier guidelines from the Unicode Standard, Version 2.0.

Characters are considered identifiers, whether initial or subsequent, based upon their properties. "Identifier start" characters are those with a Lu, Ll, Lt, Lm, Lo, or Nl value in the General category field of UnicodeData.txt. "Identifier extend" characters are those with a Mn, Mc, Nd, Pc, or Cf value in the General category field of UnicodeData.txt. Only "identifier start" characters may start an identifier, but subsequent characters may be either "identifier start" or "identifier extend" characters.

A protocol or application can extend or otherwise modify these assignments. For example, adapting these guidelines for use with XML would require, at a minimum, allowing the colon and underscore characters as "identifier start" characters.

Higher-Level Protocols

The Unicode Standard is primarily concerned with plain text — i.e., sequences of its own characters. As far as the Unicode Standard is concerned, higher-level protocols such as XML or HTML, which attach additional meaning to some characters, are "fancy text" and are outside its scope.

The characters used for the higher-level markup for your text, however, should use the same encoding as the content of your text.

It would not be feasible for you to encode the text of your HTML document in UTF-16 (because it contains ideographs) and then use single-byte ASCII characters for the HTML tags surrounding the text (because the tags only use Latin characters). At the lowest level, your text is a sequence of Unicode characters. Only when the bits and bytes of your encoded text make sense as encoded characters will your software be able to parse the text for the higher-level markup.

A common fallacy along those lines is the belief that the XML Declaration at the start of an XML file has to be in ASCII, and that the Declaration indicates the encoding of the text that follows it. An XML processor doesn't do any magic switching of encodings; the whole file, including the XML Declaration, should be in the same encoding. An XML processor typically contains code for recognizing the byte sequence for the characters in an XML Declaration in each of its supported encodings. It first applies heuristics until it can properly parse the Declaration. Upon locating a proper Declaration, it then picks up the encoding psuedo-attribute and switches to the encoding listed there.

Here's a real-life example of parsing text as characters before the advent of parsing for higher-level markup: I once had a sizable XML file containing a single non-ASCII character about halfway down the file. When I parsed the file, my XML processor assumed the text was encoded as UTF-8 (as it should have), and complained that there was an invalid character in the file (as it should have). However, the parser error message stated that the error was on line 1 — rather than halfway down the file — which was an indication that the XML processor was parsing the characters at an even lower level than it was breaking up text into lines.

Cross-Reference

The other half of the picture – the dependencies of XML and HTML upon the Unicode Standard – is covered in Chapter 9.

Chapter 7

CJK Ideographs
and Hangul

This chapter describes the principles guiding the encoding of the CJK ideograph and Hangul characters in the Unicode Standard. Here, the rules governing the inclusion and sequence of the CJK ideographs — the unification of characters from Chinese, Japanese, Korean, and Vietnamese sources — are explained in detail.

By design, the sequence of the Hangul characters in the Unicode Standard reflects a formulaic relationship between the composed syllables in the Hangul Syllables block and their component Jamo in the Hangul Jamo block. This chapter describes the history of Hangul characters and the relationship between Jamo and composed Hangul syllables.

Cross-Reference

This chapter thoroughly describes only the CJK Unified Ideograph blocks and the Hangul blocks. Appendix A mentions every block in the Unicode Standard, Version 3.0.

CJK Unified Ideographs

The characters in the CJK Unified Ideographs block were unified from multiple Chinese, Japanese, and Korean sources. In all, over 130,000 ideographs were unified into 27,786 character codes in the

Unicode Standard, Version 3.0. Additional unified ideographs are in the pipeline for inclusion in Plane 2 in a future version of the Unicode Standard.

The characters are often called *Han ideographs*, which is a reference to the Chinese origin of the ideographic system. They are also called CJKV ideographs in other contexts since similar ideographs were are used (and, to a lesser extent, still are used) in Vietnam. The characters are called *hanzi* in Chinese, *kanji* in Japanese, *hanja* in Korean, and *chu Han* in Vietnamese. Ideographs are frequently identified, sorted, and indexed by their *radicals*—small, primitive units comprising all or part of the ideograph—or by their *stroke count*—the number of lines comprising the character.

The principle of unification was introduced in Chapter 2. The CJK ideographs are prime candidates for unification because multiple standards have encoded many similar, if not identical, characters with common roots. Most ideographs originated in China and were adopted by the inhabitants of Japan, Korea, and Vietnam when the countries adopted, adapted, or borrowed the Chinese writing system. This sometimes occurred gradually over a period of centuries. For example, the Japanese borrowing of the Chinese writing system occurred during three waves of Chinese influence, each spanning centuries, all between 222 C.E. and 1279 C.E. There are, however, some ideographs invented in Japan and Korea, as well as some transfer in the opposite direction. Ken Lunde in *CJKV Information Processing* notes one kanji that was created in Japan and subsequently borrowed by China. Furthermore, new ideographs are still being created.

Note

The history of the development and spread of the ideographic writing systems and the similarities and differences between Chinese, Japanese, and Korean writing systems is very interesting, but beyond the scope of this book. If you are interested, see *CJKV Information Processing* by Ken Lunde or *The World's Writing Systems*, edited by Peter T. Daniels and William Bright.

Sources for CJK Ideographs

The ideographic repertoire was developed by the CJK Joint Research Group (CJK-JRG) ad hoc committee of ISO/IEC JTC1/SC2/WG2, later made a formal subgroup and renamed Ideographic Rapporteur Group. See Appendix A of the Unicode Standard, Version 3.0, for a detailed history of Han unification.

The ideographs primarily came from a number of existing Chinese, Taiwanese, Japanese, Korean, and Vietnamese character set standards. These standards were grouped by country of origin, and a standard contributed a source character only if the character hadn't been included in a previously evaluated standard from the same group. Several other secondary source standards were included without the application of the source separation rule (see below). Table 7-1 shows the sources for the CJK Unified Ideographs included in the Unicode Standard, Version 3.0. Sources are generally identified by the country submitting the standard to the IRG. G sources are submissions to the IRG from mainland China, the Hong Kong SAR, and Singapore. T, J, K, and V sources are submissions from Taiwan, Japan, Korea. and Vietnam, respectively. U sources, which don't have two-character designations, are additional standards used by the Unicode Consortium that were not submitted to the IRG by a member body.

Table 7-1 *Source Standards for CJK Unified Ideographs*

Name	Source
G0	GB2312-80 – Code of Chinese graphic character set for information interchange, primary set
G1	GB12345-90 – Code of Chinese ideogram set for information interchange, supplementary set – with 58 Hong Kong and 92 Korean "Idu" characters
G3	GB7589-87 – Code of Chinese ideograms set for information interchange, second supplementary set – unsimplified forms
G5	GB7590-87 – Code of Chinese ideograms set for information interchange, fourth supplementary set – unsimplified forms

Continued

Table 7-1 *Source Standards for CJK Unified Ideographs (continued)*

Name	Source
G7	General Purpose Hanzi List for Modern Chinese Language, and General List of Simplified Hanzi
GS	Singapore characters
G8	GB8565-88 – Coded character sets for text communication
GE	GB16500-95
J0	JIS X 0208-1990 – Code of the Japanese character set for information interchange
J1	JIS X 0212-1990 – Code of the supplementary Japanese character set for information interchange
JA	Unified Japanese IT Vendors Contemporary Ideographs, 1993
K0	KS C 5601-1987 – Code for information interchange (Hangul and Hanja) – (unique ideographs)
K1	KS C 5657-1991 – Code for information interchange, supplementary set
K2	PKS C 5700-1 1994 – Universal multiple-octet coded character set (UCS) – Part 1: architecture and basic multilingual plane
K3	PKS C 5700-2 1994
T1	CNS 11643-1992 – Chinese standard interchange code – plane 1
T2	CNS 11643-1992, plane 2
T3	CNS 11643-1992, plane 3 (with some additional characters)
T4	CNS 11643-1992, plane 4
T5	CNS 11643-1992, plane 5
T6	CNS 11643-1992, plane 6
T7	CNS 11643-1992, plane 7
TF	CNS 11643-1992, plane 15
V1	TCVN 5773:1993 – Nom 16-bit standard code set for information interchange
V2	TCVN 6056:1995 – Nom 16-bit standard code for information interchange – Han Nom character
	KS C 5601-1987 (duplicate ideographs)
	ANSI Z39.64-1989 – East Asian character code for bibliographic use
	Big-5 (Taiwan)
	CCCII – Chinese character code for information interchange – level 1

Name	Source
V2	GB 12052-89 – Korean character code set for information interchange
	JEF – Japanese processing extended feature (Fujitsu)
	PRC Telegraph Code
	Taiwan Telegraph Code (CCDC)
	Xerox Chinese
	Han Character Shapes Permitted for Personal Names (Japan)
	IBM Selected Japanese and Korean Ideographs

The Unicode Standard, Version 3.0, and ISO/IEC 10646-1:2000 do not list the number of characters in the source standards that were unified into their 27,484 ideographs. The Unicode Standard, Version 2.0, did list the number of characters in the majority of its source standards: In Unicode 2.0, over 110,000 characters were unified into the 20,902 ideographs encoded in the CJK Unified Ideographs block.

At the time of this writing, approximately 40,000 additional unified ideographs are under consideration for inclusion in Plane 2. Furthermore, the characters in the Ideographic Description block can be used to describe the appearance of any of the many thousands of rare ideographs that are not yet encoded by the Unicode Standard.

CJK (Han) Unification

Unification follows three rules that were developed by the Japanese delegation to the CJK-JRG (as it was then known):

1. *Source Separation Rule*: If two ideographs are distinct in a primary source standard, they are not unified. This ensures round-trip mapping between the source standard and the Unicode Standard. For example, Figure 7-1 shows five variants of the ideograph for "sword" that would have been unified except that they are all encoded in the primary source JIS X 0208-1990.

剣 劍 劔 剱 釼

Figure 7-1 *Variants preserved by "Source Separation Rule"*

2. *Non-Cognate Rule*: In general, if two ideographs do not share a common ancestor (non-cognate characters), they are not unified. For example, Figure 7-2 shows the characters for "earth" and "warrior." They look very similar (compare the lengths of the horizontal lines), but they were not unified since, as Ken Lunde, the Unicode Standard, and my old kanji textbook all note, they have different origins and, in fact, are unrelated.

earth   warrior

Figure 7-2 *Visually similar but historically different characters are not unified*

3. *Two-level Classification and Ideograph Component Structure*: Two ideographs with the same abstract shape are unified unless disallowed by the previous two rules. Determining the abstract shape involves breaking an ideograph down into its components, and the components and their arrangement are both taken into consideration. If any of the features are different, the ideographs are not unified.

In principle, unifying the CJK ideographs is no different from, say, unifying the French "a" and the English "a" or encoding a single abstract "a" to represent all of the multiple *a* characters that you saw in the Introduction. In practice, however, the different scripts have each had centuries in which to develop local variations on the abstract character, so perhaps the CJK unification is closer to unifying blackletter and sans serif forms of the same character. To illustrate this point, Figure 7-3 shows "knoll" written with three variants of the Lucida typeface. They all have a common root in the Lucida design, but if you are accustomed to reading one variant, the fact that they have a common root won't make you instantly comfortable with the other forms.

knoll *knoll* *knoll*

Figure 7-3 *"knoll" written with three variants of the Lucida typeface*

Table 7-2 shows how three ideographs rendered, where possible, in a Simplified Chinese, Traditional Chinese, Japanese and Korean font. Note how the characters are not all identical across scripts but nor are they all markedly different.

Table 7-2 *Similar and Dissimilar Ideographs*

Unicode character number	Definition	Simplified Chinese (MS Song) glyph	Traditional Chinese (MingLiU) glyph	Japanese (MS Mincho) glyph	Korean (GulimChe) glyph
U+5E73	Flat, level, even, peaceful	平	平	平	平
U+72AC	Dog	犬	犬	犬	犬
U+7DF4	Practice, drill, exercise, train		練	練	練

The prognosis is not universally bleak, however. A Japanese user, for example, is most likely to use a font or font set that incorporates Japanese-style glyphs for the CJK ideographs. Even when a pan-Unicode font is used, ideographs are generally readable as plain text. In addition, Unicode-encoded text containing CJK ideographs can have some locale or language indication so that the correct glyphs can be used. Unifying the ideographs has, therefore, made character handling easier, but in this case, at least, it has created additional requirements for the output system. Language indication can be part of the Unicode character stream using the Plane 14 language tags described in Chapter 6 or, preferably, can be specified in a higher-level protocol such as the xml:lang attribute in XML markup.

A benefit of the CJK ideograph unification is that the Unicode Standard incorporates characters for each of the characters in the primary sources, so, as discussed in Chapter 4, a Unicode encoding can be used as a "pivot" when transcoding from one source standard into another.

Ideograph Order

The sequence of the ideographs encoded in the CJK Unified Ideographs block is based upon their position in the four authoritative dictionaries listed in Table 7-3. The dictionaries were consulted in order. The character sequence follows that of *KangXi Zidian*. If a character is not found in *KangXi Zidian* but is found in *Dai Kan-Wa Jiten*, it is inserted into the sequence based on the position of the preceding character in *Dai Kan-Wa Jiten* that is also in *KangXi Zidian*. If the character is not found in either *KangXi Zidian* or *Dai Kan-Wa Jiten*, then *Hanyu Da Zidien* and *Dae Jaweon* are consulted in turn. Characters not found in any of the dictionaries are inserted into the sequence following the other characters with the same radical and stroke count. Additionally, ideographs with simplified radicals are placed following their corresponding traditional radicals.

Table 7-3 *Dictionaries Used to Determine Ideograph Sequence*

Priority	Dictionary	City	Publisher	Edition
1	*KangXi Zidian*	Beijing	Zhonghua Bookstore, 1989	7th
2	*Dai Kan-Wa Jiten*	Tokyo	Taisyuukan Syoten, 1986	Revised
3	*Hanyu Da Zidian*	Chengdu	Sichuan Cishu Publishing, 1986	1st
4	*Dae Jaweon*	Seoul	Samseong Publishing Co. Ltd, 1988	1st

Since *KangXi Zidian* is arranged by radical (standardized component) and by the number of strokes, the CJK Unified Ideographs block is also arranged by radical (in *KangXi Zidian* order) then by additional stroke count (excluding the radical).

Unihan Database

The work put into cataloging the ideographs in the source standards was not thrown out once the unification was complete. All of the information about the ideographs and the cross-references between standards is preserved in the Unihan.txt file that is part of the Unicode Character Database. UniHan.txt is explained here rather than in Chapter 3 with the rest of the database files since you need to know the background of the CJK Unified Ideographs to understand the contents of the file.

Each line in Unihan.txt contains information for an ideograph in the CJK Unified Ideograph or CJK Unified Ideograph Extension A block. Up to 57 data items (not including the character number) may be present for each character. Because of number of data items and because not every data item is present for every character, Unihan.txt lists its information one data item per line. Each line contains three fields: the Unicode character number, the tag indicating the type of data in the third field, and the data itself. Five sample lines of Unihan.txt are shown below.

```
U+4E01  kBigFive       A442
U+4E01  kDefinition    male adult; robust, vigorous;4th heaven stem;
U+4E01  kIRGDaeJaweon  0135.010
U+4E01  kJapaneseKun   HINOTO ATARU YOBORO
U+4E01  kRSKangXi      1.1
```

The tags and their definitions are listed in comments at the beginning of Unihan.txt. They are divided into six main types:

- Position. This includes position both in the dictionaries by which the ideographs are ordered and in other dictionaries.

- Definition in English.
- Mapping to source standards. This includes the primary source standards as well as numerous other national, industry, and company standards.
- Pronunciation in Cantonese, Japanese Kun and On, Korean, and/or Mandarin.
- Radical/stroke count as recorded in various dictionaries and standards.
- Variants identified in source standards, dictionaries, or in the Unicode Standard.

The identification of position within the source dictionaries is interesting. As you may recall, if an ideograph is not included in a higher-precedence dictionary, its position is inferred based on the position of the nearest preceding character that is in both the current list or dictionary and the higher-precedence dictionary. The Unihan.txt position fields record this by numbering characters in each dictionary and leaving gaps between the numbers assigned to the "real" dictionary characters so that the inferred character's place in the sequence can be recorded. For example, the value of the kIRGKangXi field is the character's position in the *KangXi* dictionary recorded as page.position. When the character really is in the *KangXi* dictionary, the last digit of its position is 0; when its position is inferred, its last digit is 1. When multiple characters have the same dictionary position field value (which only happens for inferred positions), the characters' order is determined by their respective position values in the lower-precedence dictionaries.

The following example shows the official IRG dictionary position fields for characters U+51E1 to U+51E3. I have modified the Unihan.txt data slightly by changing the starting column of the third field in each line based upon the precedence of the dictionaries: *KangXi, Dai Kan-wa Jiten, Hanyu Da Zidian,* and *Dae Jaweon*

```
U+51E1   kIRGKangXi          0134.020
U+51E1   kIRGDaiKanwaZiten     01739
```

```
U+51E1   kIRGHanyuDaZidian      10276.030
U+51E1   kIRGDaeJaweon           0299.100
U+51E2   kIRGKangXi             0134.021
U+51E2   kIRGDaiKanwaZiten       01740
U+51E2   kIRGHanyuDaZidian      10276.020
U+51E2   kIRGDaeJaweon           0299.110
U+51E3   kIRGKangXi             0134.021
U+51E3   kIRGHanyuDaZidian      10276.011
```

U+51E1 is the only one of these characters that occurs in the *KangXi* dictionary, so its kIRGKangXi value is 0134.020, and for the other two characters, their value is 0134.021. You can see why U+51E2 follows U+51E1 even though it does not appear in the *KangXi* dictionary: it follows the U+51E1 character in the *Dai Kan-Wa Ziten* dictionary. Their order is reversed in the *Hanyu Da Zidian* dictionary, but their positions in the *Dai Kan-Wa Ziten* dictionary have precedence. U+51E3 does not have a kIRGDaiKanwaZiten field, so it follows U+51E2, even though its kIRGHanyuDaZidian value is less than that of U+51E2.

Unihan Database Online

All the information in Unihan.txt, and more besides, is available online at http://charts.unicode.org/unihan.html. The information is available as a page for each character, and as summary pages showing 256 characters from which you can "click through" to view each individual character's page. You can also locate the radical for a character. The Web page warns, however, that the radical lookup is less reliable than the other method.

Page selection is based on a character's four-digit hexadecimal Unicode character number. Oddly, there is no input form at present for selecting a character to view, so the only way to get to a page is to construct the URL for the page yourself and enter it into your browser. For example, for U+51E1, the URL for the character's page is http://charts.unicode.org/unihan/unihan.acgi$0x51e1;

for its page of 256 ideographs, http://charts.unicode.org/unihan/ unihan.acgi$Grid/51e1; and for its radical, http://charts. unicode.org/unihan/unihan.acgi$RS/51e1. Note that the "0x" is only required for the page for the character itself.

In addition to all of the textual information contained in Unihan.txt, each character's Web page shows up to eight different glyphs. These include the "standard" glyph used by the Unicode Standard, the character as rendered by your Web browser, and glyphs for fonts designed for a subset of the source standards. When a source standard does not include the character, an empty box is shown.

Ideograph Code Charts

The code charts for the CJK Unified Ideographs in the Unicode Standard book have a different format from other code charts. These code charts are a compact format that packs definitions for 224 characters onto one page. Unlike with other code charts, the character names are not listed because they are simply CJK UNIFIED IDEOGRAPH- followed by a Unicode character number in the range 3400 to 9FA5 (except for the unassigned code values 4DB6 to 4DFF, inclusive, at the end of the CJK Unified Ideographs Extension A block).

Korean Hangul and Jamo

We have talked about Korean ideographs (*hanja*) as part of the CJK Unified Ideographs. Ideographs predominated in written Korean until the 1910s, but today the majority of written Korean uses Hangul. Although its overwhelming adoption is comparatively recent, Hangul was invented in the 15th century C.E. by King Seycong. However, it then spent its first five centuries being looked down upon as the writing system for the uneducated. Today, Hangul is viewed as the Korean writing system. Although South Korean students learn approximately 1800 hanja before leaving high school and hanja are still used in newspapers and some government publications, Hangul is the dominant script in both North and South Korea (although it is called "*cosenkul*" or "*wuli kulca*" in North Korea).

Hangul is written in syllable blocks, and the blocks are composed of primitives called Jamo. There are three types of Jamo: *choseong* (leading consonants), *jungseong* (vowels), and *jongseong* (trailing consonants). A common (English-language) shorthand for the three types is L, V, and T, for "leading consonant," "vowel," and "trailing consonant," respectively. A Hangul character has either an L+V or L+V+T format. Figure 7-4 shows how three Jamo are fitted into the block for the Hangul character. As an aside, the Jamo sequence exactly matches how I typed the three characters into a Korean IME that then selected the composed Hangul for me.

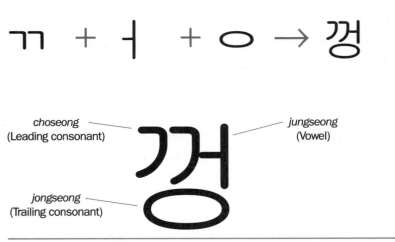

Figure 7-4 *Composing Jamo into Hangul*

The Unicode Standard includes both Jamo and modern Hangul characters. The syllables in the Hangul block (U+AC00 to U+D7A3) are the same as, and are in the same order as, the Hangul syllables in KSC 5601. This enables round-trip mapping between that standard and the Unicode Standard.

As you by now expect, these Hangul can be composed from the Jamo in the Jamo block (U+1100 to U+11FF). The Jamo are also sufficient to compose ancient syllable blocks that are no longer commonly used. Furthermore, the Unicode Standard defines an algorithm (which I won't go into) for composing a Hangul syllable from Jamo and determining the Unicode character number of the composed character. The Unicode Standard also defines the reverse mapping from a Hangul syllable into its component Jamo. For use in composition, the Unicode Standard also defines two invisible filler characters for handling Jamo sequences other than L+V+T, including, of course, the L+V pattern.

Not coincidentally, the character names for the Hangul syllables are derived from shortened forms of the Jamo from which they are composed. For example, the Hangul in Figure 7.4 is composed from HANGUL CHOSEONG SSANGKIYEOK (abbreviated as "GG"), HANGUL JUNGSEONG EO (abbreviated as "EO"), and HANGUL JONGSEONG IEUNG (abbreviated as "NG"). The name of the composed Hangul, therefore, is HANGUL SYLLABLE GGEONG.

Chapter 8

Standard Issues

The previous chapters have outlined the details of handling characters in Unicode as characters, as text, and as scripts. Now that you appreciate the details of the Unicode Standard, this chapter covers the conformance requirements of both the Unicode Standard and ISO/IEC 10646. It also covers the requirements for proposals for submitting new characters or scripts to the Unicode Technical Committee and WG2.

Conformance

Chapter 3 of the Unicode Standard, Version 3.0, formally specifies conformance requirements for applications of the standard. These requirements, summarized below, cover correct handling of Unicode Transformation Formats, invalid code values, interpretation of coded characters, and permissible modification of coded characters.

In addition to the Unicode Standard, Version 3.0 book, the following Unicode Technical Reports are also considered part of the Unicode Standard, Version 3.0:

- **UTR #9**, The Bidirectional Algorithm
- **UTR #11**, East Asian Width, Version 4
- **UTR #13**, Unicode Newline Guidelines, Version 4
- **UTR #14**, Line Breaking Properties, Version 5
- **UTR #15**, Unicode Normalization Forms, Version 16

At the time of this writing, the following Technical Reports are approved but are not considered part of the Unicode Standard, Version 3.0. These reports, however, do specify normative requirements for applications claiming conformance to each of them:

- **UTR #6**, A Standard Compression Scheme for Unicode
- **UTR #7**, Plane 14 Characters for Language Tags
- **UTR #10**, Unicode Collation Algorithm
- **UTR #16**, EBCDIC-friendly UCS Transformation Format
- **UTR #17**, Character Encoding Model
- **UTR #18**, Unicode Regular Expression Guidelines
- **UTR #21**, Case Mappings

You will recognize that the topics of all of these UTR have been covered to some extent in the previous chapters. For all of these topics, however, the definitive information source remains the reports themselves, which can be obtained from the Unicode Consortium's Web site at http://www.unicode.org/reports/techreports.html.

Cross-Reference

Descriptions of all the UTR and their status at the time of this writing are provided in Appendix B.

Unicode Transformation Formats

Conforming applications can support one or more Unicode Transformation Formats as well as other encoding formats, such as SCSU. Support includes interpretation of the Unicode code values as 16-bit or 32-bit quantities (or as byte sequences in the case of UTF-8). Support also includes correct handling of code values for surrogate pairs.

Cross-Reference

Encoding formats such as SCSU are described in Chapter 4.

The order of the bytes within a Unicode code value is not specified by the Unicode Standard. So, depending on the encoding used, a conforming application must be able to recognize and correctly interpret data with a different "endianness" from the application's native format.

Cross-Reference

See Chapter 4 for more on endianness.

In the absence of a higher-level protocol, including the use of ZERO WIDTH NO-BREAK SPACE as the Byte Order Mark (BOM), serializations of 16-bit and 32-bit encodings are to be interpreted as most-significant byte first. This allows interchange without the BOM between applications with the same "endianness" since they will interpret each other's native format as most-significant byte first. When dealing with the data as 16-bit chunks, only data with the opposite endianness (whether big-endian or little-endian) is interpreted by an application as least-significant byte first.

Invalid Code Values

Conforming applications do not:

- Interpret an unpaired high- or low-surrogate code value as a character.
- Interpret U+FFFE, U+FFFF, or the corresponding code values in planes 01 to 10 as characters.
- Interpret any unassigned code values as abstract characters.

Interpretation

Applications of the Unicode Standard are not required to recognize or interpret all of the code values for characters defined in the Standard. An application, for example, could provide complete support for characters in the Khmer block and, at the minimum, not mangle the code values for characters outside the Khmer block. When conforming applications do interpret a code value, however, they interpret the character with the full character semantics defined by the Unicode Standard. In particular, conforming applications must not have different interpretations for two canonically equivalent character sequences.

Note

The XML Recommendation does not claim conformance to the Unicode Standard, and it only references the Unicode Standard and ISO/IEC 10646 for their character repertoire. Most XML applications do not conform to the interpretation requirement since the Recommendation does not require that equivalent sequences be recognized as matching. Normalizing characters to a canonical form is mentioned in the Recommendation only as a "user option", and few, if any, XML processors implement this even as an option. Normalization in XML processors may become redundant anyway because of the "early normalization" requirements of the character model for the World Wide Web, described in Chapter 9.

Modification

Conforming applications do not change valid code values, except perhaps to replace character sequences with their canonical equivalents. The exception, of course, is an application designed to transcode or otherwise modify data. Changing the byte order of data in 16-bit or 32-bit encodings does not count, for these purposes, as modifying the data. Replacing or deleting an unrecognized or unsupported character sequence, however, is a non-conforming modification of the data.

ISO/IEC 10646 Conformance

ISO/IEC 10646 has a somewhat different idea of conformance when compared to the Unicode Standard. Since ISO/IEC 10646 is concerned with interchange of data between two devices, it divides conformance into two categories: information interchange, and devices.

A sequence of coded characters for information interchange is considered conformant when:

- The coded representation of the characters conforms to the structure defined by the standard and to an identified implementation level and defined encoding of ISO/IEC 10646.
- No undefined code values are used.
- The characters used are within the identified subset (see Chapter 3 and Appendix C).
- The use of control functions conforms to the standard.

An originating device is conformant when a user can supply characters from any identified subset, and the device transmits them with the chosen form and implementation level. A receiving device is conformant when it can receive characters with the chosen form and implementation level, and make them available to the user in a way that the user can identify the characters. In addition—and quite sensibly—conformant originating and receiving devices require a description of how the user will supply or receive the characters.

Submitting New Scripts

Submitting new characters or scripts for inclusion in the Unicode Standard and ISO/IEC 10646 is not for the faint of heart. A submission requires a lot of supporting information, including a sample TrueType or PostScript font for use in the published standards. In addition, the approval process can take years since, among other things, it requires revising an international standard, which involves drafts, balloting of national bodies, and a lot of committee work.

Cross-Reference

Information on the submission process is available at `http://www.unicode.org/pending/proposals.html`.

The first step in submitting a new character or script is ensuring that it is not already included by the Unicode Standard. You should check both the character tables in the Unicode Standard and the Unicode Consortium's Web pages detailing proposed new scripts and characters. The Consortium also suggests discussing a proposal on the Unicode mailing list before making a detailed submission.

Cross-Reference

Unicode Consortium Resources are discussed in Appendix B

For inclusion, characters must conform to the Unicode Standard's definition of a character. Glyph variants, ligatures, and other pre-composed variants of characters will not be considered for inclusion, although the Unicode Consortium remains interested in such variants for research purposes.

The standard form—which, of course, must be completed—is currently available at `http://www.dkuug.dk/JTC1/SC2/WG2/prot/form1.html`. Filling in the form provides sufficient information for both the Unicode Technical Committee and WG2 to be able to consider the proposal.

Information required when completing the form includes:

- Your contact information
- Details of the script name or the block to which to add the characters
- ISO/IEC 10646 implementation level (described in Chapter 3)
- Information on the user community for the characters and their current use of the characters

- Evaluation of whether the characters should be in the BMP, whether they should be kept together, whether they are presentation forms of existing characters, and other information about the characters' role in the character repertoire

The Unicode Consortium warns that ideographic characters especially require evidence that they are both unique and indispensable to users.

Part III

Use of Unicode

Chapter

9 Unicode on the Internet

10 Operating System Support

11 Programming Language Support

12 Unicode and Fonts

Chapter 9

Unicode on the Internet

Reliance upon and support for the Unicode Standard and ISO/IEC 10646 permeate the Internet. New standards from the W3C and IETF typically reference the character repertoire of the UCS, if not the complete character encoding standards. The proposed character model for the World Wide Web is being based upon the repertoire and normalization forms specified in the Unicode Standard. Names of character encodings for the UCS have been registered with the Internet Assigned Numbers Authority; and Internet software — including Web browsers and e-mail agents — is becoming increasingly more capable of supporting these encodings. This chapter covers the bare essentials of using the Unicode Standard — or, at least, the characters of the Unicode Standard — on the Internet.

Character Model for the World Wide Web

The Character Model for the World Wide Web is defined (or, more accurately, is being defined) in a Technical Recommendation of the same name available at http://www.w3.org/TR/WD-charmod. At the time of this writing, only the one working draft (WD) has been released, and it is very much a work in progress. As noted in its "Status of this document" section, the draft TR (like all drafts from the W3C) may be "updated, replaced, or obsoleted [sic] by other documents at any time."

Early versions of HTML and HTTP used the character set and character encoding of ISO 8859-1. In early 1997, the Internet Engineering Task Force (IETF, see `http://www.ietf.org/`) published a Request for Comments (RFC, which is the closest that the IETF comes to defining standards) that changed that. IETF document RFC 2070, Internationalization of the Hypertext Markup Language, expanded HTML's horizons when it redefined HTML's character set to be the Universal Character Set (UCS) of ISO/IEC 10646 and the Unicode Standard. However, blanket adoption of the UCS is not enough to ensure interoperability. RFC 2070 also gave specific guidelines for, for example, handling bidirectional text, language-dependent formatting, cursive joining behavior, and handling non-displayable characters; HTML 4.0 and later have included the same provisions.

The Changing Nature of the Web

The WD provides a more complete character model than that in RFC 2070 (which itself was more complete than any earlier descriptions). The rationale provided for specifying a character model for the Web is that the makeup of the Web is changing, and a more complete character model is required to ensure consistent behavior.

The WD notes that the nature of the Web is changing from the unidirectional model of servers sending data to browsers to a bidirectional or multidirectional model of proxies, multi-tier applications, and clients sending data back to the server. In addition, the Web is increasingly being used for machine-to-machine communication.

The TR is noted as applying to the following W3C activities or specifications:

- The Document Object Model (DOM)
- The XML activity, including XPointer and other specifications

- Extensible Style Language (XSL)
- Resource Description Framework (RDF) Model and Syntax
- Digital signatures

From my own observations, even as a first draft, the WD has influenced how people view the use of the Unicode Standard on the Web, particularly their approaches to normalization of equivalent sequences.

The fundamental aspect of the Character Model for the World Wide Web is that it is based on the Universal Character Set defined by ISO/IEC 10646 and the Unicode Standard. This isn't particularly surprising since, as noted above, recognition of the UCS has been official policy with regard to HTML since RFC 2070 was published in early 1997. In addition, the UCS is referenced in the specifications for HTML 4.0, XML 1.0, and CSS2. Notice, however, that it is often just the UCS that it being referenced, not the complete conformance requirements of the Unicode Standard, nor the subsets, implementation levels, or other features of ISO/IEC 10646. For example, the XML 1.0 Recommendation references ISO/IEC 10646 only for its definition of "character," its shared "legal graphic characters," and its definitions of UTF-8 and UTF-16. The XML Recommendation also references the Unicode Standard only for its shared "legal graphic characters," its definition of compatibility characters and surrogates, and its character classes in its guidelines for identifiers.

Other aspects of using the UCS are mentioned briefly in the current WD and are due for expansion in the next draft. Topics covered or to be covered include:

- The differences between characters and the bytes that represent the characters
- The identification of character encodings
- The use of the `charset` parameter
- An explanation of why the term "character set" is considered harmful

- The problems with defaults and heuristics
- The need for escapes for special characters
- The necessity of using only one form of escaping
- Handling of escaping and escaping of escaping

The Push for Early Normalization

The largest and best-developed section of the current WD covers "Webwide Early Uniform Normalization." This section calls for all "text data interchange using W3C protocols and formats" to be based on *early normalization*, where all data produced or sent is normalized to its Unicode Canonical Composition (Normalization Form C, see Chapter 5).

The rationale given for early normalization is largely the same as the rationale given earlier for defining the Character Model for the World Wide Web. The biggest problem that early normalization solves is *string identity matching*.

String identity matching is a problem for people using the UCS because Unicode and ISO/IEC 10646 support multiple encodings, variable-length encodings and, in some cases, duplicate encodings (uncomposed and precomposed) of characters. String identity matching is also a problem with many legacy encodings that will continue to be used on the Web.

There are many places and situations on the Web where strings are compared for equality or identity with other strings. These include:

- Data, e.g., people's names
- XML and HTML markup
- URIs
- Identifiers and other strings in scripts embedded within HTML pages

In these and other situations, communication fails or processing fails if strings that should be recognized as identical aren't recognized as such because of differences in encoding, use of precomposed characters, or different order of their combining marks. In addition, many protocols and programming languages — including XML and Java — support the UCS but don't support normalization of strings. Furthermore, many small, handheld, or low-level devices don't have the capacity or can't support the overhead of normalizing strings before checking for identity. Lastly, the number of devices or applications that are connected to the Web and that need to do string identity matching is going to increase, not decrease. However, there will always be more devices doing the matching than generating the data to be matched.

This all leads to the conclusion that early normalization — where the data is generated or transmitted in a normalized form — is preferable to late normalization — where every receiving device or application normalizes strings before checking for identity.

Early normalization has the following other advantages:

- It helps "future-proof" the Web, since only the applications producing data need to be updated when new, non-normalized characters are added to the UCS.

- It improves matching in strings, such as URIs, where the character encoding is partly undefined.

- It increases interoperability of APIs that expose string data.

- It allows you to be conservative in what you send.

- It is a prerequisite for canonicalization.

- It simplifies definition and implementation of string indexing.

Note

The last three advantages satisfy requirements expressed in another, earlier TR working draft, "Requirements for String Identity and Character Indexing Definitions for the WWW," which is available at http://www.w3.org/TR/WD-charreq.

Text data is normalized according to the WD when the following requirements have been met:

- The text data is in Unicode Canonical Composition form (Normalization Form C)
- The data does not include any of the following:
  - Alternate Format Characters (U+206A–U+206F), which comprise Symmetric Swapping, Character Shaping Selectors, and Numeric Shape Selector codes

Note

Use of Alternate Format Characters is strongly discouraged by the Unicode Standard and forbidden in W3C data.

  - U+FFFC, OBJECT REPLACEMENT CHARACTER
  - Plane 14 Language Tags (see Chapter 6). The WD notes that the `html:lang` or `xml:lang` attributes, as appropriate, should be used to indicate language

Text data in a legacy (i.e., non-Unicode, non-10646) encoding is also considered normalized when all of the following requirements have been met:

- References to UCS characters (e.g. numeric character references in XML and HTML) are normalized characters
- Data in a legacy encoding is allowed at that point
- The text is tagged with the appropriate "charset" or other label

Where and How to Use Early Normalization

The WD notes several guidelines for implementing early normalization:

- Applications or tools transcoding from a legacy encoding to an encoding based on UCS must output normalized text.

- Producers of text — for example, senders of data or tools producing data — must assure that data is sent out in a normalized form.

- Implementers are encouraged to delegate normalization to their data sources; e.g., the operating system, keyboard driver, etc.

- Intermediate recipients of text data must assure that the result after any operations have been applied to the text is also in a normalized form.

- Intermediate recipients that just pass data along without touching it do not have to normalize or check normalization of data.

- Recipients should assume that data is normalized but may provide normalization as an add-on or safety measure.

- Tools or operations doing string identity matching should do so by binary comparison.

The WD does not address compatibility equivalents and advises that applications should not use compatibility characters as delimiters or as markup characters. It also doesn't address other forms of equivalence such as case mapping, equivalence between hiragana and katakana, between accented and unaccented characters, or between spelling differences (e.g., color versus colour). Finally, the WD doesn't address handling control characters beyond noting that, "Control characters should be replaced by appropriate markup or style information wherever possible."

The WD also notes a requirement for at least three levels of string indexing of increasing complexity: physical representation; abstract code points; and indexing based on language, user preferences, etc. Note that these three levels are quite similar to what you would get by adding normalization to the three implementation levels for regular expression engines defined in UTR #18 (and described in Chapter 6).

Finally, the WD adds a requirement that all non-ASCII or specifically excluded characters in URIs must be represented by the bytes of their UTF-8 encoding converted to the form %*HH*, where *HH* is the byte value in hexadecimal.

Implications of Early Normalization

The specified normalization form is defined by UTR #15 and the Unicode Standard, Version 3.0, so there are no surprises involved in normalizing text data for the Web.

In Normalization Form C, a string is first *decomposed* to its canonical decomposition using the *latest* version of the Unicode Character Database, then *recomposed* using the *fixed* canonical mappings of the Unicode Character Database, version 3.0.0. As noted above, when new precomposed, or non-normalized, characters are added to the Unicode Standard, only the data generators need to be updated with the latest canonical decomposition data. Since the Unicode Character Database, version 3.0.0 is enshrined as the source for composition mappings, this does mean that implementations will need to maintain two tables: one fixed and one infrequently changing.

However, since early normalization does not include case mappings, etc., the data required for implementing early normalization is a fraction of the size of the complete Unicode Character Database. Furthermore, many characters — for example, CJK ideographs and Hangul syllables — do not have canonical decompositions, so careful design can save you from implementing mapping tables with too many identity mappings.

Finally, early normalization is, if anything, a disincentive to adding new precomposed characters after the Unicode Standard, Version 3.0, since they may not appear on the Web in their precomposed form. When you normalize data to Normalization Form C, any new precomposed characters, like all precomposed characters, will be decomposed before being recomposed according to the Version 3.0.0 canonical composition table. Since new precomposed characters won't be in the 3.0.0 table, they won't be recomposed, and instead will be included in the text data as the decomposed sequence of base plus combining characters.

IETF Policy on Character Sets and Languages

RFC 2277, IETF Policy on Character Sets and Languages, describes best current practices for use of character sets and specification of language on the Internet. Among its requirements and recommendations, it specifies that all protocols must support the UTF-8 character encoding of the ISO 10646 coded character set.

HTML

HyperText Markup Language (HTML) is the publishing language used on the World Wide Web. The version current at the time of this writing is HTML 4.01.

XHTML 1.0 is a reformulation of HTML 4.0 as an XML application that interoperates with XML tools and is easier to produce subsets of and to extend than HTML. It is another HTML-related Proposed Recommendation that should have reached Recommendation status by the time you read this.

HTML and XHTML are both part of the W3C's User Interface domain; see `http://www.w3.org/MarkUp/` and `http://www.w3.org/MarkUp/Activity.html`.

HTML 4.0, HTML 4.01, and the Unicode Standard

HTML 4.01 was published in December 1999, approximately 20 months after HTML 4.0. The two recommendations are very similar, which makes it easy to overlook their minor differences. For your reference, this section details the difference between how HTML 4.0 and HTML 4.01 refer to the Unicode Standard and ISO/IEC 10646.

- HTML 4.0 and HTML 4.01 both reference ISO/IEC 10646-1:1993 plus its first five amendments. HTML 4.01 additionally makes it clear that the reference includes future amendments and future parts of ISO/IEC 10646 (provided the amendments don't change any of the existing character assignments).

- HTML 4.0 references Unicode 2.0, and HTML 4.01 references Unicode 2.1.

- HTML 4.0 notes that ISO/IEC 10646 is equivalent to the Unicode Standard, Version 2.0, then thereafter refers to either ISO/IEC 10646 or the Unicode Standard as the source of the UCS. HTML 4.01 similarly notes that ISO/IEC 10646 is equivalent to Unicode 2.1, but thereafter it consistently refers to ISO/IEC 10646 as the source of the UCS.

Note that both HTML 4.0 and HTML 4.01 reference the Unicode Standard for its bidirectional algorithm.

Document Character Set

The HTML Recommendation specifies support for the Universal Character Set (UCS) defined by both ISO/IEC 10646-1:1993 (as amended) and the Unicode Standard, Version 2.1. HTML is an application of SGML (see the later section on SGML) and, as such, uses the UCS as its "document character set." HTML documents, however, do not need to be encoded in one of the encodings of the Unicode Standard or ISO/IEC 10646. It is sufficient if they use character encodings that can be mapped to those of the UCS.

As a practical measure, HTML documents may be in any character encoding for which there is an Internet Assigned Numbers Authority (IANA) identifier (see upcoming sidebar). However, the Recommendation does not specify which encodings a HTML user agent (e.g., a Web browser) must support, so you should not assume that every user agent supports every registered character encoding.

In addition, servers and proxies may transcode HTML documents on the fly to meet the `Accept-Charset` HTTP requests of user agents.

Numeric Character References

It is also possible to make numeric character references to any UCS character from within any HTML document, no matter what character encoding is used. Both decimal and hexadecimal numeric references are supported, and the reference format is common among HTML, XML, and SGML.

The decimal representation is `&#`*nnn*`;`, where *nnn* is a string using only the digits 0 to 9. There does not have to be a fixed number of digits, and leading zeroes are ignored. For example, `&#61;` and `&#0061;` are both valid references to the "=" character (U+003D, EQUALS SIGN), although the former is probably easier to read.

The hexadecimal representation is `&#x`*nnn*`;`, where *nnn* is a hexadecimal string using only the digits 0 to 9 and the letters "a" to "f" and "A" to "F". For example, `&#x61;` is a reference to the "a" character (U+0061, LATIN SMALL LETTER A).

Specifying Character Encoding

The three methods for determining the character encoding of an HTML document, listed in decreasing priority, are:

1. HTTP `charset` parameter in a `Content-Type` header
2. `<META>` element within the HTML document with `http-equiv` attribute set to `Content-Type` and with a value set for `charset`
3. `charset` attribute on the element referencing the resource

In the absence of other indicators, user agents may also use heuristics and user settings to determine a document's character encoding.

HTTP charset parameter

The HTTP/1.1 protocol, defined in RFC 2626 and described below, allows many headers that identify information about the message body or the resource identified by an HTTP request. When transferring an HTML document, the content-type header indicates the text/html media type, but may also indicate the character encoding of the document with a charset parameter. The parameter value should be an IANA-registered character encoding. The following example shows the content-type header for a document encoded in UTF-8:

```
Content-Type: text/html; charset=UTF-8
```

<META> element

When servers cannot or will not provide the charset parameter, a <META> element inside the <HEAD> element in HTML documents may provide the character encoding information. A <META> element may have a number of attributes, but the two of interest here are http-equiv and content. These have special significance when documents are retrieved via HTTP: The http-equiv attribute's value is interpreted as an HTTP property name, and the content attribute's value is interpreted as the property's value. The following example shows the top-level structure of one of the sample HTML files used in Chapter 11. It shows the sample document's <HEAD> element and its contents, including a <META> element indicating the character encoding.

```
<html>
<head>
<title>ECMAScript Unicode Demonstration</title>
<meta http-equiv="Content-Type"
      content="text/html; charset=UTF-8">
</head>
<body bgcolor="#FFFFFF">
...
</body>
</html>
```

Note that the HTML Recommendation advises that the `<META>` declaration should only be used when ASCII-valued bytes stand for themselves (at least until the `<META>` element is parsed), and that the `<META>` declarations should appear as early as possible in the `<HEAD>` element. The example above conforms to the first requirement, since UTF-8 is a superset of ASCII and only ASCII byte values were used up until that point. It doesn't conform to the second requirement, but to no ill effect.

charset attribute

The `<A>`, `<LINK>`, and `<SCRIPT>` elements each have a `charset` attribute that identifies the character encoding of the external resource identified in the element's `href` or `src` attribute, as appropriate. When the server doesn't indicate the resource's encoding and the resource doesn't indicate its own encoding, then this particular `charset` attribute may be used to determine the document's character encoding.

UTF-16 and UTF-1

The HTML Recommendation notes that HTML text sent in UTF-16 (i.e., `charset=UTF-16`) should be in "network byte order" (i.e., big-endian) and include the BOM as the first character.

The Recommendation also notes that UTF-1 should not be used. UTF-1 is a encoding that was dropped from ISO/IEC 10646 and that is not part of the Unicode Standard. Actually, UTF-1 should not be used anywhere and, as such, is not covered by this book.

Language Indication

Most elements have a `lang` attribute for indicating the base language of the element's attributes and text content. The value is a language code conforming to RFC 1766 (see sidebar). There is no default value if the attribute is not present.

The Recommendation doesn't define what use to make of the `lang` attribute, but it can, for example, be used to select glyph variants, control hyphenation, or select spelling dictionaries.

Language indication is inherited from the following elements, listed here in order of precedence:

1. The `lang` attribute of the element itself

2. The closest parent element that has a `lang` attribute

3. The HTTP `Content-Language` header

4. The default settings and user preferences for the current user agent

Directionality

Many elements also have a `dir` attribute for indicating the directionality of apparently directionally neutral text. The allowed values are `LTR` and `RTL`, indicating left-to-right and right-to-left directionality, respectively. The `dir` attribute is also used to determine the directionality of a table's structure.

In addition, HTML includes a `<BDO>` element that is used for overriding the effects of the bidirectional algorithm on a span of text.

The HTML Recommendation also references the bidirectional algorithm of the Unicode Standard, and there is an extensive discussion of the interaction between the effects of the `dir` attribute and the Unicode bidirectional algorithm. In summary, the Recommendation states that controlling directionality with HTML markup is preferable to using Unicode's directionality override characters.

Cross-Reference

HTML markup being preferable to using Unicode's directionality override characters is covered in Chapter 6.

Web Browsers

Since HTML 4.0 supports the UCS, it is not surprising that recent versions of the major Web browsers have steadily increased their support for the Unicode Standard. The two most visible areas of a Web browser's support are detection or selection of an HTML document's character encoding, and support for rendering the characters of the Unicode Standard. Other aspects that are not so immediately obvious are the browser's support for the lang attribute and bidirectionality.

The following examples and screen shots demonstrate the support by Internet Explorer 5 and Netscape Communicator 4.7 running on Windows 95, but you should expect comparable support from the current version of any GUI Web browser on any platform.

Internet Explorer 5

The examples and screen shots demonstrate the support by Internet Explorer 5 running on Windows 95.

Character encoding

The current default character encoding recognized by Internet Explorer 5 may be selected from the View ➪ Encoding submenu. Figure 9-1 shows the Encoding submenu. The HTML document is a UTF-8 file used in the examples in Chapter 11. Here you see that Internet Explorer correctly detected the document's encoding when the file was opened. Note that in IE5, the indication of text direction only appears when the HTML document contains right-to-left text.

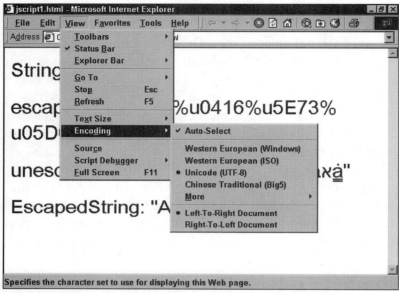

Figure 9-1 *Character encoding indication in Internet Explorer 5*

Font selection

To specify the default font that will be displayed on a Web page (unless the Web page specifies its own fonts — which it is now almost certain to do), select Tools ⇨ Internet Options, and then click on the Fonts button. This brings up the Fonts dialog box shown in Figure 9-2. The fonts here are shown in a drop-down list marked Language script. These fonts, for the most part, correspond to the blocks of the Unicode Standard. The exceptions are the multiple blocks containing Latin characters that (not inaccurately) are lumped together as "Latin based"; and the CJK Unified Ideographs, which are broken out as separate Simplified Chinese, Traditional Chinese, Japanese, and Korean fonts.

If you look closely at Figure 9-2, you'll notice that IE5 supports scripts that are new with Unicode 3.0, including Braille and Cherokee. For each script, you can select a proportionally spaced "Web page font" and a fixed-width "plain text font" from the installed fonts of each type that IE5 detects as including the script's characters.

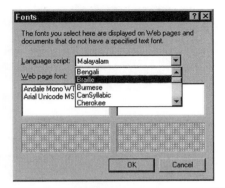

Figure 9-2 *Selecting fonts for scripts*

lang support

Listing 9-1 presents a page of HTML markup that demonstrates the effect of four different values of the `lang` attribute on the rendering of U+5E73, CJK UNIFIED IDEOGRAPH 5E73.

Listing 9-1 *How changing the lang attribute affects one glyph's rendering*

```
<html>
<head>
<title>Language detection</title>
</head>
<body>
<table border="1" style="font-size: 24pt">
<tr>
<th><tt>lang=</tt></th>
<th>Language</th>
<th>Country</th>
<th><tt>&amp;#x5e73;</tt></th>
</tr>
<tr>
<td><tt>zh-CN</tt></td>
<td>Chinese</td>
<td>China</td>
```

```
<td lang="zh-CN" style="font-size: 44pt">&#x5e73;</td>
</tr>
<tr>
<td><tt>zh-TW</tt></td>
<td>Chinese</td>
<td>Taiwan</td>
<td lang="zh-TW" style="font-size: 44pt">&#x5e73;</td>
</tr>
<tr>
<td><tt>ja</tt></td>
<td>Japanese</td>
<td>&#x2013;</td>
<td lang="ja" style="font-size: 44pt">&#x5e73;</td>
</tr>
<tr>
<td><tt>ko</tt></td>
<td>Korean</td>
<td>&#x2013;</td>
<td lang="ko" style="font-size: 44pt">&#x5e73;</td>
</tr>
</table>
</body>
</html>
```

Each row in the HTML table provides and explains a different
lang attribute value. The last cell in each row sets the lang attribute
to a specific value, and every row concludes with a numeric character reference to U+5E73. When a Web browser supports the lang
attribute and has the correct font for the specified language, it
should show a language-specific glyph for U+5E73.

Figure 9-3 shows the HTML markup viewed in IE5. Since I
have Simplified Chinese, Traditional Chinese, Japanese, and Korean
fonts on my system and, in the Fonts dialog box, have selected them
for their respective scripts, the U+5E73 character is displayed as a
different glyph for each value of the lang attribute.

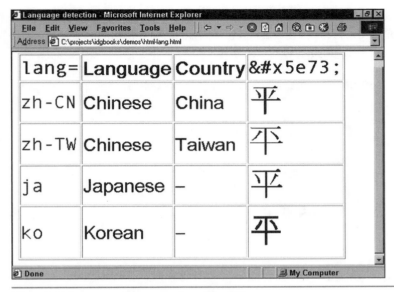

Figure 9-3 *lang attribute test viewed in IE5*

Netscape Communicator 4.7

The examples and screen shots demonstrate the support by Netscape Communicator 4.7 running on Windows 95, but you should expect comparable support from the current version of any GUI Web browser on any platform.

Character encoding

The current default character encoding recognized by Netscape Communicator 4.7 may be selected from its View➪ Character Set submenu. This sets the default character set selection that is used when the character encoding cannot be determined from the HTTP headers or the `<META>` element. Figure 9-4 shows the Character Set submenu when a UTF-16 text file is being viewed in the browser. Although the UTF-16 encoding was detected correctly, the selected character set is "Western (ISO-8859-1)" but the text being displayed is clearly not "Western." Note also that the Character Set submenu includes "UTF-8" and "UTF-7" but has no entry for UTF-16 even though the browser detects it correctly. This is probably because, at the time of this writing, UTF-16 is not an IANA-registered character set.

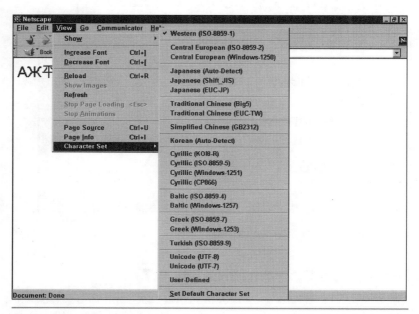

Figure 9-4 *Default character set selection in Netscape Communicator 4.7*

Font selection

To specify the default font that will be displayed on a Web page, select Preferences from the Edit menu. Then from the Category list at the left of the Preferences dialog box shown in Figure 9-5, choose the Appearance category, followed by Fonts. The fonts shown in the two drop-down lists marked "Font" are arranged by their "encodings," which correspond to the subgroups shown in the View ➪ Character Set submenu. For example, there is a single "Unicode" selection that will be used for the UTF-8 and UTF-7 "character sets" (and, incidentally, for UTF-16). For each "encoding," you can select a "variable width font" and a "fixed-width font" from the installed fonts.

lang support

For best results, the HTML markup to demonstrate lang support in Netscape Communicator 4.7 is different from that used with Internet Explorer 5, as demonstrated in Listing 9-2.

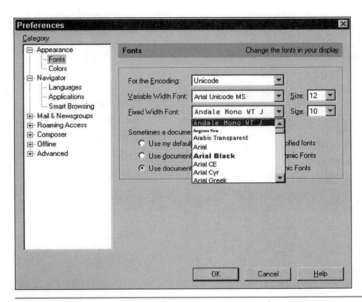

Figure 9-5 *Selecting fonts for an "encoding" in Netscape Communicator 4.7*

Listing 9-2 *Adjusting the character references for Netscape's sake*

```
<html>
<head>
<title>Language detection</title>
<meta http-equiv="Content-Type" content="text/html;
charset=UTF-8">
</head>
<body>
<table border="1" style="font-size: 24pt">
<tr>
```

```
<th><tt>lang=</tt></th>
<th>Language</th>
<th>Country</th>
<th><tt>&amp;#24179;</tt></th>
</tr>
<tr>
<td><tt>zh-CN</tt></td>
<td>Chinese</td>
<td>China</td>
<td lang="zh-CN" style="font-size: 44pt">&#24179;</td>
</tr>
<tr>
<td><tt>zh-TW</tt></td>
<td>Chinese</td>
<td>Taiwan</td>
<td lang="zh-TW" style="font-size: 44pt">&#24179;</td>
</tr>
<tr>
<td><tt>ja</tt></td>
<td>Japanese</td>
<td>&#8211;</td>
<td lang="ja" style="font-size: 44pt">&#24179;</td>
</tr>
<tr>
<td><tt>ko</tt></td>
<td>Korean</td>
<td>&#150;</td>
<td lang="ko" style="font-size: 44pt">&#24179;</td>
</tr>
</table>
</body>
</html>
```

Specifically, the 平 hexadecimal character references were changed to 平, which is their decimal equivalent. Even after that change was made, the decimal references were not recognized until the <meta> tag indicating the UTF-8 character encoding was added to the <head> element. The – references to the en-dash character were similarly changed to 舑. Note that – — the named reference to the en-dash character — should have also worked, but didn't. Note also that – — which is a reference to the code value for the en-dash character in the Windows CP 1252 variant of ISO 8859-1 — should *not* have worked, but *did* in both Communicator and IE5. As a reference to a Unicode code value, – refers to U+0096, which is a C1 control character with no graphical representation.

Figure 9-6 shows the HTML markup viewed in Communicator. Despite the different values of the lang attribute, all the U+5E73, CJK UNIFIED IDEOGRAPH 5E73, characters appear the same.

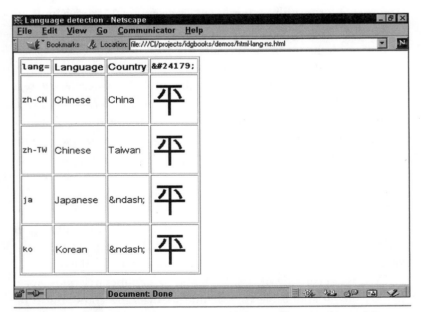

Figure 9-6 *lang attribute test viewed in Netscape Communicator 4.7*

XML

Extensible Markup Language (XML) is a W3C Recommendation for a subset of SGML (Standard Generalized Markup Language, see section later in this chapter) for use on the Web. The version current at the time of writing is 1.0. There are also many other W3C Recommendations under development that either add to the XML effort or rely upon it, and many industry initiatives are being based upon XML. For information on the W3C XML activity, see http://www.w3.org/XML. For broader information about XML and related efforts, see Robin Cover's SGML/XML web page at http://www.oasis-open.org/cover/sgml-xml.html.

The Appeal of Extensible Markup

XML has gained a lot of attention because it truly is extensible. Where HTML has a fixed set of tags — for example, <h1>, <p>, and <img> — and the only extensions between HTML revisions are proprietary extensions by the browser manufacturers, XML is designed so that you can define and use your own tags, and you can also define rules for what each tag may contain. This appeals to individuals and industry groups alike because they can now use tags that describe their data. Furthermore, when using an XML browser, the tags retain their meaning all the way to the user's desktop, instead of reducing them to HTML's *lingua franca* of paragraphs and headings. XML enables industry-specific markup, vendor-neutral data exchange, and the processing of Web documents by intelligent clients.

The XML Recommendation divides the behavior of computer programs that process XML into two parts: an XML processor that reads the XML data and provides access to its contents, and the application that controls the XML processor and uses the data.

XML is concerned with "documents" — a deliberately loose term that is equally applicable to machine-to-machine communication such as XML/EDI (Electronic Data Interchange) and to the works of Shakespeare (which are available as XML documents). The files (or other storage objects) making up an XML document are called *entities*. They may be *parsed entities* — which may contain tags and other XML markup — or *unparsed entities* that the XML processor just hands off to the application.

XML documents may be *well-formed* — conforming to the "well-formedness" constraints of the XML Recommendation — or *valid* — conforming also to a Document Type Definition (DTD) that specifies additional constraints on the structure of the document.

XML references both the Unicode Standard, Version 2.0, and ISO/IEC 10646-1:1993. At the time of this writing, the XML Recommendation has not been updated to match the Unicode Standard, Version 3.0 (nor has Version 3.0 been released). However, an unofficial proposal for changes to the XML Recommendation to match Version 3.0 was posted to the XML-Dev mailing list by John Cowan (see `http://www.lists.ic.ac.uk/hypermail/xml-dev/xml-dev-Sep-1999/0476.html` and related messages). It is not yet clear how the XML Recommendation (or many other standards, for that matter) will deal with revisions to the Unicode Standard, but the unofficial proposal indicates the extent of the changes required to align XML with the Unicode Standard, Version 3.0.

How XML Addresses the Issue of Characters

Section 2.2, Characters, of the XML Recommendation references ISO/IEC 10646 for its definition of *character*. It also states that legal characters include "tab, carriage return, and the legal graphic characters of Unicode and ISO/IEC 10646." The definition of "graphic character" is a bit hazy, since this encompasses characters that do not have any graphic representation. Examples include space characters (e.g., SPACE, NO-BREAK SPACE, EM SPACE, and IDEOGRAPHIC SPACE) and the layout and format control characters (e.g., ZERO WIDTH JOINER, LEFT-TO-RIGHT MARK, LINE SEPARATOR, and INHIBIT SYMMETRIC SWAPPING).

Numeric reference restrictions

The production from the XML Recommendation specifying the characters that are legal in XML documents is shown below. Note that the Recommendation uses #x to designate hexadecimal code values.

```
Char ::= #x9 | #xA | #xD | [#x20-#xD7FF] |
         [#xE000-#xFFFD] | [#x10000-#x10FFFF]
```

The production covers the range of code values that can be addressed with UTF-16 (and UTF-32). Outside of tags or other forms of XML markup, you can use nearly any defined character code. The exceptions are the C0 control characters (other than U+0009, U+000A, and U+000D), the code values from the Surrogates Area, and U+FFFE and U+FFFF, which are not Unicode characters anyway. Within tags and other XML markup, you should observe the recommended restrictions on characters in names and tokens, which will be described in due course.

Section 2.2 also states that "use of 'compatibility characters', as defined in section 6.8 of Unicode, is discouraged." Other than this warning, however, there has been no action taken to make XML "compatibility-free." Indeed, since the rules for XML names and name tokens are based on the Unicode 2.0 recommendations for identifiers, many compatibility characters are allowed in XML names and name tokens. Characters in the Compatibility area are excluded from names, but other compatibility characters, including many characters in the Latin-1 Supplement block, are allowed.

Like many programming languages, and like the Unicode recommendations for identifiers, XML distinguishes between characters allowed as the first character in a name and those allowed as the second and subsequent characters. Its resulting rules apply to element, attribute, entity, and notation names. They do not apply to enumerated attribute values or to the contents of attributes with attribute type NMTOKEN or NMTOKENS, which are all XML *name tokens* (like names but without the special restriction on their first characters).

Tag naming restrictions

XML names may begin with a letter, a colon (:), or an underscore
(_), and any following characters may be a letter, a digit, a combining character, an extender, a colon, an underscore, or a period (.).
The characters in the "letter" and "digit" character classes are listed
in the Recommendation's Appendix B, Character Classes.

Since, as noted above, the character classes are based on the
Unicode 2.0 recommendations for identifiers, the classification of
characters as letters or digits was based upon their properties in the
Unicode Character Database, Version 2.0.0. In Unicode terms,
XML's letters have a Ll, Lu, Lo, Lt, or Nl value in the General
Category field. The other characters allowed in XML names, but not
allowed as the first character, have a Mc, Me, Mn, Lm, or Nd value
in the General Category field. Note that the following modifier let-
ters (with "Lm" General Category value) are actually classified as
XML letters: U+02BB–U+02C1, U+0559, U+06E5, and U+06E6.

If that's not complicated enough, there are exceptions to the just-
mentioned rules. Characters in the compatibility area, characters
with a font or compatibility decomposition (i.e., with <font> or
<compat> tag in their Character Decomposition Mapping field),
and characters U+20DD–U+20E0 are not allowed in names.
U+00B7, MIDDLE DOT, is classified as an extender (as detailed in
section 5.14 of the Unicode Standard, Version 2.0). U+0387,
GREEK ANO TELEIA, is also classified as an extender since its
canonical equivalent is U+00B7, which is classified as an extender.

XML makes no other claims to or requirements for conformance
to the Unicode Standard. In particular, it does not require that XML
processors perform any canonical or compatibility decomposition or
canonical ordering. The XML Recommendation does state that "at
user option, processors may normalize such characters to some
canonical form," but the user option is not widely implemented, and
even less widely used.

For example, the canonical equivalent of U+00F6, LATIN SMALL LETTER O WITH DIAERESIS is the sequence of U+006F, LATIN SMALL LETTER O, and U+0308, COMBINING DIAERESIS. XML requires that the name in an element's start-tag match the name in its end-tag. If, as Figure 9-7 shows, the name in the start-tag includes U+00F6 and the name in the end-tag instead includes U+006F and U+0308, then they are not equivalent in XML. This is a error of proper formation that will stop the processing of your data.

Well-formed

```
<ö>some text</ö>
<ö̈>some text</ö̈>
```

Not well-formed

```
<ö>some text</ö̈>
<ö̈>some text</ö>
```

Figure 9-7 *Canonical equivalents are not normalized in XML*

This error is more likely to happen, however, when two occurrences of a name or string both appear in different types of documents. Suppose, for instance, a document and its own DTD were created using different editor applications. These applications could conceivably produce dissimilar character sequences for the same two strings, although both formations would be canonically equivalent under Unicode.

The presence of equivalent sequences has never been a problem for HTML markup, since the element and attribute names include only characters from the Basic Latin block, which don't have decompositions or canonical equivalents. It remains to be seen whether the early normalization requirement of the Character Model for the World Wide Web will save users from being caught out by equivalent sequences. Early normalization may help you with XML data sent over the Web, but it probably won't save you from causing yourself problems with different software on your own computer.

Incidentally, XML is case-sensitive, so the requirement for matching names extends to matching case as well. So, for example, <ö> and <ö> are different elements.

XML processors recognize U+000A and U+000D (in ISO 6429, line feed and carriage return, respectively) as spacing characters and ends of lines. In addition, to simplify end-of-line handling, XML processors pass a single U+000A character to the application for each occurrence of U+000A, U+000D, or the two-character sequence U+000D + U+000A. XML does not attach any importance to U+2028, LINE SEPARATOR, or U+2029, PARA-GRAPH SEPARATOR.

Supported Encodings

All XML processors must be able to read documents — more formally, document entities and externaly parsed entities — encoded in UTF-8 and UTF-16. A processor can support other encodings, but it doesn't have to.

Entities encoded in UTF-16 must begin with the Byte Order Mark (BOM), as XML processors use the BOM as an encoding signature to distinguish between UTF-8 and UTF-16 encodings. The UTF-16 BOM is not part of either the markup or the character data of the XML document.

Document entities encoded in UTF-8 or UTF-16 may begin with an XML Declaration, and document entities in any other encoding must begin with one. Figure 9-8 shows the XML Declaration format. In addition to identifying the file as being XML, the declaration identifies the version of XML being used and, most importantly for this discussion, it optionally indicates the encoding used in the file. The encoding declaration portion can be omitted for documents encoded in UTF-8 or UTF-16, but (like the XML Declaration itself) must be present for documents in any other encoding. (The optional standalone portion indicates whether any external markup declarations will affect what the XML processor passes to the application, but that's outside the scope of this book.)

```
<?xml version="1.0" encoding="UTF-8" standalone="no"?>
```

Version of	Name of	Standalone
XML being	encoding	declaration
used	being used,	
	e.g. UTF-8,	
	UTF-16, EUC-KR,	
	ISO-8859-1	

Figure 9-8 *XML Declaration format*

The XML recommendation provides several sample encoding names, including:

- Unicode and ISO/IEC encodings: "UTF-8", "UTF-16", "ISO-10646-UCS-2", and "ISO-10646-UCS-4"

- ISO 8859 encodings: "ISO-8859-1", "ISO-8859-2", ... "ISO-8859-9"

- JIS X-0208-1997 encodings: "ISO-2022-JP", "Shift_JIS", and "EUC-JP"

Other encodings may also be supported by an XML processor. The Recommendation notes that character encodings registered with the Internet Assigned Numbers Authority (IANA) should be referred to by their registered names. Since IANA-registered names are defined to be non-case-sensitive, matches against registered encoding names may also be non-case-sensitive.

It is an error if the document's encoding doesn't match the declared encoding, unless the encoding declaration is also overridden by the encoding information provided by a transport protocol such as HTTP or MIME. Note that the ASCII encoding is supported by all

XML processors and does not need an encoding declaration because ASCII is a subset of UTF-8.

Parsed entities may begin with a "text declaration," which is similar in appearance to an XML Declaration. Figure 9-9 shows the text declaration format. In contrast to the XML Declaration, the encoding declaration is required in the text declaration, and the version information is optional. Parsed entities that are not in either UTF-8 or UTF-16 are required to have a text declaration with its required encoding declaration. The format and requirements for the encoding declaration in the text declaration are the same as for the XML Declaration.

```
<?xml version="1.0" encoding="UTF-8">
```
        Version of   Name of
        XML being   encoding
        used   being used,
                              e.g. UTF-8,
                              UTF-16, EUC-KR,
                              ISO-8859-1

Figure 9-9 *Text declaration format*

No matter what character encoding is used, an XML processor should convert the characters to Unicode internally. When a document is made up of a document entity plus one or more external parsed entities, each entity may (but doesn't have to) use a different character encoding. Since your XML document could reference and incorporate multiple parsed entities located anywhere else on the Web that you didn't write and that you don't control, it is good that you don't have to use the same character encoding in all the entities.

Referencing Characters Not in the Current Encoding

XML supports the characters of the Unicode Standard but, as we've seen, a document doesn't have to use a character encoding that can represent all of the characters in Unicode. However, XML supports decimal and hexadecimal numeric references to the Unicode scalar value of any Unicode character. This is particularly useful for characters that you otherwise couldn't include in your document, but it works equally well for any character.

You can only make numeric character references to the characters in the production from the XML Recommendation shown earlier in this chapter. Characters outside the BMP can be referred to using a numeric character reference to the character's Unicode scalar value. They cannot be referred to by numeric character references to the High Surrogate and Low Surrogate character numbers. For example, 𐀀 is a valid reference, but &#xD800;&#xDC00; — which refers to its corresponding Surrogate Pair — is made up of two invalid character references, since the Surrogate Area code values are not legal XML characters.

Language Identification

The XML recommendation reserves a special attribute xml:lang for identifying the natural or formal language in which the content is written. This attribute may be used on any element, although, in valid documents, the attribute must be declared if it is used.

Using the xml:lang attribute is better than using the Plane 14 Language Tags described in Unicode Technical Report #7 (see Chapter 6). Using xml:lang to indicate the language means there's one markup mechanism — XML markup — for indicating both the structure and language of the document. The alternative — using XML markup for structure and Plane 14 tags for language identification — means parsing the document twice.

Values for xml:lang are language identifiers as defined by IETF RFC 1766, Tags for the Identification of Languages, (see sidebar). By convention, the language codes are given in lowercase and the country codes (if any) in uppercase but, in accordance with RFC 1766, the code values are non-case-sensitive. Any language identification made by an element with the xml:lang attribute applies to all content and other attributes of that element, unless overridden by another `xml:lang` attribute of a nested element.

How to make use of the `xml:lang` attribute isn't specified by the XML Recommendation any more than how to make use of the Plane 14 tags is specified by UTR #7. In the example shown in Figure 9-10, the `xml:lang` attribute is used to control the choice of glyphs for an ideograph, but the language identification could also be used to control spell checkers, hyphenation dictionaries, etc. Note that the element names in the example were chosen for their brevity, not for their meaning.

With `xml:lang`

```
<m>
Simplified Chinese: <n xml:lang="zh-CN">平</n>
Traditional Chinese: <n xml:lang="zh-TW">平</n>
Japanese: <n xml:lang="jp">平</n>
Korean: <n xml:lang="ko">平</n>
</m>
```

Simplified Chinese: 平
Traditional Chinese: 平
Japanese: 平
Korean: 平

Without `xml:lang`

```
<m>
Simplified Chinese: <n>平</n>
Traditional Chinese: <n>平</n>
Japanese: <n>平</n>
Korean: <n>平</n>
</m>
```

Simplified Chinese: 平
Traditional Chinese: 平
Japanese: 平
Korean: 平

Figure 9-10 *Example* `xml:lang` *usage*

RFC 1766 – Tags for the Identification of Languages

RFC 1766 defines a scheme for identifying the human language (not computer language) used in "an information object." Many other RFCs and other standards – including HTML, XML, and UTR #7 – refer to RFC 1766 for their language tags rather than define their own scheme. Similarly, RFC 1766 defines its language tags using values from ISO 639 language codes, IANA language codes, and ISO 3166 country codes.

Language tags are comprised of a primary tag and, optionally, one or more subtags. Tag length is limited to eight characters. The primary tag and the first subtag, and any two subtags, are separated by hyphens. An example language tag is:

`en-AU`

Two-letter primary tags are interpreted as two-letter ISO 639 language codes (see `http://www.oasis-open.org/cover/iso639a.html`). For example, en is the language code for English. The "`i`" primary tag is reserved for use with IANA-registered language codes, and the "`x`" primary tag is reserved for use with private-use language codes. No other prefixes are currently defined.

The first subtag has special constraints:

- Two-letter codes are interpreted as ISO 3166 alpha-2 country codes (see `http://www.oasis-open.org/cover/country3166.html`). For example, AU is the country code for Australia.

- Three-letter to eight-letter codes following an "`i`" primary code are interpreted as language codes registered with IANA, for example cherokee. Anyone may follow the rules in RFC 1766 and register an identifier with IANA.

Second and subsequent subtags of any length may also be registered with IANA.

Language tags are case-insensitive. However, the ISO convention is that ISO 639 language codes are written in lowercase letters, and ISO 3166 country codes in uppercase letters.

Some example tags and their meanings:

en – English

en-US – English spoken in the US

en-cockney – Cockney English

i-sami – Sami

i-sami-no – The north dialect of Sami

x-klingon – Private use tag for the Klingon language

Note that these subtags have not been registered and are used as examples only.

HTTP

The most current version of Hypertext Transfer Protocol (HTTP) at the time of this writing is HTTP/1.1, defined in RFC 2626 (see http://www.ietf.org/rfc/rfc2626.txt). HTTP is "an application-level protocol for distributed, collaborative, hypermedia information systems." It is the protocol that governs how files are requested and transferred between a Web server and your Web browser.

HTTP does not directly depend on the Unicode Standard, although it does reference RFC 2277, IETF Policy on Character Sets and Languages, which advises the adoption of UTF-8.

However, the body of the HTTP message has the same format as a MIME e-mail message, which probably has something to do with the fact that MIME is employed as the "envelope" for the HTTP message. An HTTP message is enclosed by a header that includes a `Content-Type:` attribute that specifies the character encoding. When present, one of these headers may look like the following:

```
Content-Type: text/html; charset=UTF-8
```

Note that `text/html` is not the only content type that can be used with HTML, nor is `charset` the only parameter that can be used with the `Content-Type` header.

The value of the `charset` parameter is a character set identifier defined in the IANA Character Set registry. Matches are non-case-sensitive.

HTTP supports content negotiation between the server and the client. In server content negotiation, the `Accept-Charset` request-header field sent from the client to the server indicates what character sets are acceptable in a response. Here's an example:

```
Accept-Charset: utf-8
```

As with the `charset` field in the `Content-Type` header, the character set must be registered with IANA.

Note

The character encoding names for those encodings of the Unicode Standard that are registered with IANA may be used in the charset parameter in MIME message and body part headers and in message headers. See RFC 2045, RFC 2047, and related RFCs.

IANA Character Set Registry

The Internet Assigned Numbers Authority (IANA) maintains a registry of character sets, which is available at `http://www.isi.edu/in-notes/iana/assignments/character-sets`. The registration procedure is defined in RFC 2278. Many RFCs and other standards use the IANA registry as the source for names of character sets that conforming applications may recognize.

At the time of this writing, the registry contains over 200 character set names and over 500 character set aliases. IANA does not maintain the definitions of the character sets; it merely names them or records a character set name defined in an RFC.

This registry exists so that different applications can use the same name for the same character set. This removes the guesswork in determining if one application really can handle data created by another application. However, nobody expects every application to recognize or do the right thing with all 700 names, nor are applications expected to be able to create data in over 700 character encodings.

The registry is a text file. Although the registry entries are organized consistently, the text file begins with introductory comments and ends with a list of references. The following example is the entry for UTF-8:

```
Name: UTF-8                                    [RFC2279]
MIBenum: 106
Source: RFC 2279
Alias:
```

The `Name` field lists the official name for the character set. Names (and aliases) comprise only characters from US-ASCII (ANSI_ X3.4-1968) and may be up to 40 characters. Names are non-case-sensitive.

The text in the right margin, when present, refers to a citation at the end of the text file. Citations are made both to other documents and to people who provided the information for entries.

The `MIBenum` field is a unique value by which a Simple Network Management Protocol (SNMP) Management Information Base (MIB) can unambiguously identify the character set. This is useful since, in an HTTP or other transfer, the message may be labeled with the official character set name or one of possibly several aliases for a character set, but all of the variants can map to a single numeric identifier. `MIBenum` values are divided into three ranges, as shown in Table 9-1.

Table 9-1 MIBenum *Value Ranges*

From	To	Description
3	9999	Coded character sets standardized by another standard-setting organization
1000	1999	Unicode and ISO/IEC 10646 coded character sets and their subsets
2000	–	Vendor-specific coded character sets

Each Alias field identifies an alternative name for the character set. Aliases are not - class names, and in some cases, an alias is the preferred name for a character set. For example, US-ASCII is an alias but it is also the preferred name for ANSI_X3.4-1968 (MIBenum: 3).

Not surprisingly, there are several registered names for Unicode and ISO/IEC 10646 and their variants. These are shown in Table 9-2. Note that not all of these are in the MIBenum range 1000–1999.

Table 9-2 *Unicode and ISO/IEC 10646 Registered Character Sets*

Name	MIBenum	Comment
ISO-10646-UTF-1	27	Universal Transfer Format (1). Although registered, it should not be used since UTF-1 has been dropped from ISO/IEC 10646 and is not part of the Unicode Standard. Where possible, use UTF-8 instead, or UTF-7 if necessary.
UNICODE-1-1-UTF-7	103	UTF-7, defined in RFC 1642 (see Chapter 4).
UTF-7	104	UTF-7, defined in RFC 2152 (see Chapter 4).
UTF-8	106	UTF-8, defined in RFC 2279 (see Chapter 4).
ISO-10646-UCS-2	1000	Two-octet Basic Multilingual Plane (BMP). The Source description notes that the byte order isn't specified.
ISO-10646-UCS-4	1001	Four-octet UCS. The same comment about byte order applies.

Name	MIBenum	Comment
`ISO-10646-UCS-Basic`	1002	BASIC LATIN subset of ISO/IEC 10646. See Chapter 3 and Appendix C for details on subsets of ISO/IEC 10646.
`ISO-10646-Unicode-Latin1`	1003	LATIN-1 SUPPLEMENT subset of ISO/IEC 10646, which, like all subsets, includes the characters from the BASIC LATIN block. See Chapter 3 and Appendix C.
`ISO-10646-J-1`	–	Japanese version of ISO 10646, defined in RFC 1815.
`ISO-8859-1`	1004	Encoding with alias `csUnicodeIBM2039`. The `Source` field contains "IBM Latin-1 SAA Core Coded Character Set. Extended ISO 8859-1 Presentation Set, GCSGID: 2039." Note that `ISO-8859-1` is also an alias and the preferred name for `ISO_8859-1:1987`, which is registered character set name for ISO 8859-1.
`ISO-Unicode-IBM-1261`	1005	IBM code page. The `Source` field contains "IBM Latin-2, -3, -5, Extended Presentation Set, GCSGID: 1261."
`ISO-Unicode-IBM-1268`	1006	IBM code page. The `Source` field contains "IBM Latin-4 Extended Presentation Set, GCSGID: 1268."
`ISO-Unicode-IBM-1276`	1007	IBM code page. The `Source` field contains "IBM Cyrillic Greek Extended Presentation Set, GCSGID: 1276."
`ISO-Unicode-IBM-1264`	1008	IBM code page. The `Source` field contains "IBM Arabic Presentation Set, GCSGID: 1264."
`ISO-Unicode-IBM-1265`	1009	IBM code page. The `Source` field contains "IBM Hebrew Presentation Set, GCSGID: 1265."
`UNICODE-1-1`	1010	The Unicode Standard, Version 1.1, defined in RFC 1641.

Inclusion of UTF-16 as a registered character set is being balloted at the time of this writing.

Although many character set names and aliases for Unicode and ISO/IEC 10646 and their subsets have been registered, you shouldn't expect that every Web browser, mail agent, or other piece of software handles all of these character sets. It remains safest to use the only the best known variants — UTF-8 and, to a lesser extent, UTF-7 — since most applications will understand at least those two.

SGML

The Standard Generalized Markup Language (SGML), defined in ISO 8879:1986 and its corrigenda, is not usually thought of as an Internet application, although XML and HTML are a subset and an application of SGML, respectively. SGML is presented here because much of how you use or reference the characters of the Unicode Standard in XML and HTML has its roots in how SGML handles characters, character sets, and character encodings.

SGML does not specify a fixed character set. If anything, it provides too much flexibility when specifying the character set used in SGML documents.

An SGML document contains tags and text, just like an HTML or XML document. (For the record, it's actually HTML and XML that are just like SGML.) In SGML terms, the tags and text are just a part of the document — the part called the *document instance*. The other part is the *prolog*, which is frequently just the document model or *document type definition*. Together they make an SGML document.

If you've looked at HTML or XML markup, you've seen tags like "<para>" that are delimited with "<" and ">" (sometimes referred to as "chicken lips"). In HTML and XML, these delimiters are always the same. SGML's dirty not-so-secret is that you can change the delimiters — and practically every other aspect of the SGML markup — in the *SGML declaration* that appears before the two parts of the SGML document. The SGML declaration sets up the conditions for processing the document. There's always an SGML declaration involved in SGML processing. If you don't provide one, the SGML system will infer one for you.

Note

The SGML declaration is significantly different from the XML declaration, since they serve different functions. There is also an SGML declaration for XML, which you only need to use when processing XML on an SGML system. As we'll see, however, the SGML declaration for XML makes a useful example of how to specify Unicode (actually, ISO/IEC 10646) in an SGML system.

The SGML Declaration

The parts of the SGML Declaration that interest us are the two places where you specify the character set to use in the markup. Two places? Isn't that redundant?

Character set specifications turn up twice in the SGML declaration. This is because SGML decouples the specification of those characters that are significant as delimiters or as element names, etc., from the description of how those characters are encoded in the SGML document. The significant characters are defined in terms of the *syntax reference character set*, and the characters in the SGML document are in the *document character set*.

The connection between the two is that all of the characters that are significant for markup (i.e., the "<" and ">" characters, etc.), which are specified in terms of the syntax reference character set, also have to be present in the document character set. Otherwise, the SGML system won't be able to recognize the markup characters. The characters don't have to have the same code value in both the syntax reference character set and the document character set. Both the syntax reference character set and the document character set are specified in terms of known "base" character sets. The document character set definition relies on the base character sets for the syntax reference character set and the document character set both including the same abstract character. The SGML declaration maps from a delimiter's character number in the syntax reference character set to the character number for the abstract character in a base character set. It also maps from the same abstract character's number in the document character set's base character set to a character number in the document character set. The character numbers don't have to be the same, just the abstract characters.

This is convoluted, I admit, but it does mean that you can change the encoding used in your document without having to change your definition of what constitutes a significant character. For example, you can change only the document character set portion of your SGML declaration when you change from using Shift-JIS encoded documents to using the Unicode Standard.

Listing 9-3 shows the first part of an SGML declaration — in this case, the SGML declaration for XML — that specifies ISO/IEC 10646 as the document character set. The full SGML declaration is available at http://www.w3.org/TR/NOTE-sgml-xml.

Listing 9-3 *The initial portion of the SGML declaration for XML*

```
<!SGML -- SGML Declaration for XML --
"ISO 8879:1986 (WWW)"


CHARSET
    BASESET
        "ISO Registration Number 176//CHARSET
        ISO/IEC 10646-1:1993 UCS-4 with implementation
        level 3//ESC 2/5 2/15 4/6"
    DESCSET
        0        9        UNUSED
        9        2        9
        11       2        UNUSED
        13       1        13
        14       18       UNUSED
        32       95       32
        127      1        UNUSED
        128      32       UNUSED
        160      55136    160
        55296    2048     UNUSED    -- surrogates --
        57344    8190     57344
```

```
65534    2        UNUSED   -- FFFE and FFFF --
65536    1048576 65536
```

The CHARSET keyword indicates the start of the description of the document character set. The BASESET keyword is followed by the identifier for a base character set, and the DESCSET keyword is followed by a description of the document character set in terms of character numbers of characters in the previous BASESET.

The string following the BASESET keyword is a *formal public identifier* for ISO/IEC 10646. For SGML, specifying ISO/IEC 10646 as a base character set is a better choice than specifying the Unicode Standard. Specifying the UCS-4 form of ISO/IEC 10646 is not a problem since, at this point, the SGML declaration is working with character numbers, and it's not important how many bits are used to represent the character numbers. Since this is the SGML declaration for XML, specifying the UCS-2 form of ISO/IEC 10646 isn't good enough because XML allows the use of characters outside the BMP. Specifying UTF-16 isn't an option, because we're only dealing with characters in a character set, not with their encoded representation.

The particular BASESET character set identifier shown in Listing 9-3 specifies UCS-4 with implementation level 3 since, as discussed in Chapter 3, the Unicode Standard conforms to implementation level 3. The last part of the identifier, ESC 2/5 2/15 4/6, is a human-readable form of the *designating sequence* that identifies UCS-4 with implementation level 3 when you change character sets in an ISO/IEC 2022 application. Some SGML systems pay more attention to the representation of the designating sequence when trying to recognize the character set than they do to the rest of the character set identifier.

The portion after the DESCSET keyword describes the document character set in terms of ISO/IEC 10646-1:1993. Each entry in the left column shows a character number in the document character set; the middle column shows the extent of a range of characters beginning with that left column's number; and the right column, when present, shows an associated character number in ISO/IEC 10646. For example, 9 2 9 indicates that the two characters in the document character set starting with character number 9 are the same as the two characters in ISO/IEC 10646 starting with its character number 9. (The character numbers are all in decimal, because that's all that's allowed in an SGML Declaration.) Because we're really just saying that the document character set uses the same character numbers as ISO/IEC 10646, the numbers in the left column and in the right column are the same. You can get fancy and move character numbers around, and more besides, but that's unnecessary for this application.

The control characters, code values in the Surrogate block, and character numbers 0xFFEF and 0xFFFF are declared UNUSED because they are not allowed in XML documents. The UCS-4 character numbers above 1,114,112 (2^{16} + 2^{20}, or 65,536 + 1,048,576) are also not allowed in XML documents, and the SGML parser will enforce this simply because the character numbers are not listed in this description of the document character set.

Following the DESCSET section of the SGML Declaration is a single line whose complete definition isn't important to this discussion, though it is shown below so you won't get confused when you look at a full SGML Declaration:

SCOPE DOCUMENT

The SCOPE DOCUMENT statement indicates that the concrete syntax we're about to define applies to the prolog — i.e., to the DTD — as well as to the document instance. The alternative, SCOPE INSTANCE, specifies that the concrete syntax applies only to the document instance.

Following SCOPE DOCUMENT, the next important part is the definition of the syntax reference character set as part of the declaration of the *concrete syntax* to be used for your documents. The concrete syntax is the mapping of delimiter roles, etc., to characters in the syntax reference character set. "Concrete syntax" is used in apposition to "abstract syntax," not because it's set, concrete-like, and will never change. In practice, however, people seldom need to change much from the *reference concrete syntax* defined in ISO 8879. The exception is the SGML Declaration for XML (which we've been discussing) which made sweeping changes from the reference concrete syntax, in part to support the characters of ISO/IEC 10646.

Below is the portion of the SGML declaration that follows SCOPE DOCUMENT. After the SYNTAX keyword, and the SHUNCHAR parameter (which we won't go into), the syntax reference character set is declared by the same combination of BASESET and DESCSET parameters that we used to describe the document character set. This time, we indicate that all of the characters in the first 17 planes (1,114,112 characters starting from character number 0 of ISO/IEC 10646-1:1993) can be used in the syntax reference character set.

```
SYNTAX
   SHUNCHAR NONE
   BASESET "ISO Registration Number 176//CHARSET
          ISO/IEC 10646-1:1993 UCS-4 with implementation
          level 3//ESC 2/5 2/15 4/6"
   DESCSET
       0 1114112 0
```

The next part is SGML "legalese" to assign roles to the carriage return, line feed, space, and tab characters:

```
FUNCTION
     RE       13
     RS       10
     SPACE   32
     TAB     SEPCHAR 9
```

Following the FUNCTION section, the NAMING section shown below assigns the characters — in addition to the built-in assignments — that may be used in element names. The character numbers and ranges following the NAMESTRT keyword indicate characters that may be used as the first letter in names. This example has been reduced for brevity, but you can see the full assignment in the W3C Note located at http://www.w3.org/TR/NOTE-sgml-xml:

```
NAMING
     LCNMSTRT  ""
```

```
UCNMSTRT ""
NAMESTRT
    58 95 192-214 216-246 248-305 308-318 321-328
    ...
    12449-12538 12549-12588 19968-40869 44032-55203
LCNMCHAR ""
UCNMCHAR ""
NAMECHAR
    45-46 183 720-721 768-837 864-865 903 1155-1158
    ...
    12337-12341 12441-12442 12445-12446 12540-12542
```

The character numbers and ranges following the NAMECHAR key-word indicate characters that, in addition to the built-in and NAMESTRT assignments, may be used as the second and subsequent characters in the names of XML tags. The distinction between characters that may start a name and those that may continue it has always been a part of SGML, but it is also in accordance with the identifier guidelines in the Unicode Standard. The editors of the XML Recommendation put considerable effort into assigning characters to these ranges based upon the identifier guidelines (not to mention considerable effort translating hexadecimal character numbers to decimal). The rationale, along with the hexadecimal character numbers, is presented in Appendix B, Character Classes, of the XML Recommendation.

The effect of the following NAMECASE section is to make names non-case-sensitive.

```
NAMECASE
    GENERAL NO
    ENTITY  NO
```

The remainder of the SGML declaration has been omitted since none of the remaining parameters are particularly relevant to speci-fying support for the Unicode Standard in an SGML system.

Numeric Character References

SGML — and, consequently, XML and HTML — allow you to make numeric references to characters in the document character set. The format is `&#`*nnn*`;`, where *nnn* is the character number in decimal, or `&#x`*nnnn*`;`, where *nnnn* is the character number in hexadecimal. (The hexadecimal format is a recent addition to SGML, and may not be supported by all SGML systems.)

The number of digits in a numeric reference isn't fixed, and recognition of hexadecimal digits is not case-sensitive, so `&#10;`, `&#000010;`, `&#xA;`, `&#x0a;`, and `&#x000A;` all represent character number 10 in the document character set. The character being referenced is determined by the description of the document character set in the SGML Declaration. In the SGML Declaration for XML, character number 10 maps to character number 10 in ISO/ IEC 10646-1:1993 — or, in Unicode 3.0 terminology, to U+000A, `<control>`.

The SGML character set discussion so far has been about the document character set and the syntax reference character set. A reformulation of SGML's character handling model in recent years has added another layer (or two) to the interpretation of a document's encoding, its document character set, and numeric character references.

If you consider that a document's encoding determines its document character set in such a way that the document character set describes the characters that you can represent with that encoding (a presumption that used to be made all the time), then numeric character references must be to characters in the current encoding. In that scenario, the numeric character reference `&#x4E00;` would represent a different character in an EUC-KR-encoded (multi-byte Korean encoding) document than it would in a UTF-16-encoded document.

However, EUC-KR, for example, doesn't even fit SGML's character model because SGML considers that characters are all represented with the same number of bits, and EUC-KR uses either one or two bytes to represent characters. An SGML system, therefore, should (conceptually, at least) map the EUC-KR-encoded characters onto some internal, fixed-length representation. The representation form isn't important, provided it can represent all of the characters in the document character set. The EUC-KR encoding, therefore, is not the document encoding, but a variable-length representation of the characters in the document character set. The various terms used to describe the EUC-KR encoding's role are: "character encoding," "storage representation of characters," and "data storage character set."

If a character encoding (to use the HTML 4.0 term) is a representation of the characters in the document character set, it becomes possible that more than one encoding can represent the characters in the document character set. Nevertheless, no matter which encoding is used, numeric character references must be to character numbers in the document character set. In this scenario, the same numeric character reference appearing in a Shift-JIS document and in an EUC-JP document refers to the same character, since Shift-JIS and EUC-JP both encode the same characters.

Next, consider that a character encoding doesn't necessarily have to represent all of the characters in a document character set. Consider an SGML system where the document character set matches the characters in ISO/IEC 8859-1 (probably by referencing ISO/IEC 8859-1 as a BASESET). An ISO/IEC 8859-1–encoded document can directly include the "ö" character, but an ASCII-only document cannot. The ASCII document can, however, include a ö numeric character reference to refer to the document character set character number for "ö". (Actually, the ISO/IEC 8859-1 document can include "ö", ö or ö to represent the character.)

So you have just seen how, in both XML and HTML, you can use any character encoding and make numeric character references to ISO/IEC 10646 character numbers.

SGML, UTF-16, and Unicode Scalar Values

Since SGML uses a fixed-width representation of characters, it follows that SGML works on the Unicode Scalar Value of a character, not the one code value of a BMP character or the two code values making up a Surrogate Pair in UTF-16.

Chapter 10

Operating System Support

Support for the Unicode Standard is not confined to Web applications. Unicode support is increasingly being built into the services provided by operating systems. Ubiquitous system-wide support for Unicode makes it possible for Unicode text handling to be consistent across applications. As a result, applications can shrink a little since they don't need to implement their own Unicode support independently.

This chapter surveys the level of Unicode support current at the time of this writing in the following operating systems:

- Windows 95/98
- Windows 2000
- Windows CE
- Solaris 7
- Linux
- FreeBSD
- MacOS

Windows

The different versions of Windows are not consistent in their support for the Unicode Standard. This reflects both the different ages of the operating systems and their different purposes, since the heavy duty operating systems — Windows NT and Windows 2000 — and the newest operating systems — Windows CE and Windows 2000 (again) — offer the best support.

Windows 95/98

The Windows 95 and Windows 98 operating systems count as partially Unicode-enabled, at best. As Chapter 11 will explain in greater detail, string-handling functions on Windows platforms come in three flavors: ANSI, MBCS, and Wide. These three types accept strings as one byte per character, a changeable number of bytes per character, and a fixed number of bytes per character, respectively. In principle, programs working with Unicode text should use the wide form of these functions. On Windows 95 and Windows 98, the majority of the wide versions of the string functions are just stubs that, when called, return an error.

There are exceptions. For example, the OLE interface requires that strings be Unicode characters, and TrueType fonts map Unicode code values to glyphs.

Windows NT

Windows NT is built from the ground up to use Unicode. Its kernel uses Unicode strings, as do resource strings. NTFS file names are in Unicode, and system information is stored as Unicode.

All of the Unicode string functions that don't work on Windows 95/98 do work under Windows NT.

Windows 2000

Windows 2000 is the most Unicode-enabled version of Windows. Rather than develop its many language-varied packages with adjusted

APIs (libraries of internal function calls) for each language, Windows 2000 will utilize a single API for all variations, and simply apply that API differently for each language package. This API will reportedly be compliant with the Unicode Standard, Version 2.0 (not 3.0).

As well as using Unicode in its internals, Windows 2000 takes advantage of Unicode in the user interface, utilizing Unicode-compliant character sets wherever possible. This does not necessarily mean that applications cannot continue to use the old code pages; as you might expect, "legacy applications" (those released prior to Windows 2000) will probably continue to utilize the old code page system. Windows 2000 must support that old system in order for those applications to continue to run, but Microsoft is actively encouraging developers and ISVs to switch over to Unicode text. For more information, see `http://support.microsoft.com/support/kb/articles/q227/4/83.asp`.

Windows CE

Windows CE, which is used with handheld PCs and other small devices, uses Unicode for all string functions. But CE is an odd beast in that, at the API level, it simultaneously supports an independent effort by Microsoft called National Language Support (NLS). The purpose of NLS is apparently to enable a CE application to determine which language is best to use for its own internal phraseology — such as what to say on its own menu bar. When processing characters at the binary level, however, CE claims to use Unicode (presumably 2.0). For more information, see `http://msdn.microsoft.com/library/wcedoc/wceglob/unicode.htm`.

Unix

There are multiple flavors of Unix, both free and commercial. This section summarizes Unicode support for what, at the time of this writing, are considered the top three: Solaris 7 from Sun Microsystems, Linux, and FreeBSD.

Solaris 7

The Solaris operating system uses a single binary image, but its interfaces are localized for different countries. For example, there are separate Japanese and Korean versions that each support regional characteristics and separate input methods for their respective languages.

Locales

Solaris makes great use of locales: When you set the LANG environment variable, the operating environment dynamically loads information about what date and time formats to use. It also swaps to using error messages and user interface component labels in the appropriate language for your locale. When you change your locale, any new applications that you launch will pick up the new locale.

Figure 10-1 shows the three parts of the LANG environment variable. The second and third portions are optional, but enabling Unicode support depends on their being present and with the standardized values.

en_US.utf-8

Language
ISO 639 language tag

Country
ISO 3166 country code

Character Set

Figure 10-1 *The three parts of the LANG environment variable*

Solaris 7 enables Unicode support in eight specific locales:

- en_US.UTF-8 (American English)
- fr.UTF-8 (French)
- de.UTF-8 (German)

- it.UTF-8 (Italian)
- es.UTF-8 (Spanish)
- sv.UTF-8 (Swedish)
- jp_JP.UTF-8 (Japanese)
- ko_KR.UTF-8 (Korean)

Note that you need to specify the UTF-8 character set as part of the locale setting to enable the Unicode support.

Every Unicode-enabled locale supports English/European, Cyrillic, Greek, Arabic, Hebrew, and Thai input modes. The Japanese and Korean locales also support hexadecimal code input and table lookup of characters, which are the only input methods that give access to the full Unicode character repertoire.

The non-English locales support regional definitions for national currency, date and time, numerical notation, and translated text messages. The European locales (`fr`, `de`, `it`, `es`, and `sv`) also support the euro ( ) symbol.

The Unicode-enabled locales provide a utility for printing plain text to a PostScript printer using bitmap fonts. The Japanese locale additionally provides new Japanese UCS-2/UTF-8 PostScript fonts.

It is obvious that the Unicode-enabled locales work with Unicode text encoded as UTF-8. Solaris uses UTF-8 for much the same reasons that UTF-8 was invented: compatibility with ASCII, no unexpected NUL (0x00) characters or other control codes, and interoperability with single-byte file I/O operations.

However, the Solaris operating environment also provides command-line, GUI, and programmatic interfaces — `iconv(1)`, `Sdtconvtool`, and `iconv(3)`, respectively — to a common conversion utility that can convert between UTF-8 and many other character sets. The supported target characters sets are:

- ISO 646 (ASCII)
- ISO 8859 parts 1–10 and part 15
- Taiwanese character sets — Big5, IBM code page 937, EUC-TW, and ISO-2022-TW

- Chinese character sets—EUC-CN and ISO-2022-CN
- Japanese character sets—EUC-JP, Shift JIS, and ISO-2022-JP
- Korean character sets—IBM code page 933, KS C 5601 Johab, EUC-KR, and ISO-2022-KR
- Cyrillic character set KOI8-R
- UTF-7, UTF-16, UCS-2, and UCS-4

However, data can be converted between any two supported encodings by using UTF-8 as a "pivot"; that is, by converting from the source character set to UTF-8, then converting from UTF-8 to the target character set. Of course, converting between two non-Unicode character sets, or from Unicode text to an existing character set, may cause loss of data. This is because the target character set may not be able to represent all of the characters in the source data.

The conversion utility can also convert from UTF-8-Java (the modified UTF-8 format that Java uses for its own data files) to the Japanese character encodings.

Cross-Reference

See Chapter 11 for more information on modified UTF-8 format that Java uses.

When using a Unicode-enabled locale, the Solaris e-mail application, DtMail, supports sending and receiving e-mail in a variety of character encodings, including (to use Solaris terminology) the Latin, Greek, Cyrillic, Complex Text Layout, and Asian character sets. .

The Solaris operating environment does not provide a monolithic Unicode font. Instead, it allows the definition of a font set that combines multiple existing fonts so they appear to be a large Unicode font. In addition, each locale incorporates a font table specifying which glyph in which font to use for each of the CJK unified ideographs. This default mapping from a unified character to a Simplified Chinese, Traditional Chinese, Japanese, or Korean glyph can be overridden by a local administrator. The administrator can set the priority among the fonts and specify fallbacks so that, for example, if a character is not present in any Simplified Chinese fonts, the system will use the matching glyph in a Traditional Chinese font.

Programming

The white paper describing Unicode support in the Solaris operating environment also cautions against "direct Unicode localization" when developing applications.

Applications should not directly manipulate Unicode characters, but instead use the POSIX multi-byte and wide character interfaces when dealing with text. These shield the application program from the details of the character encoding. In addition, applications should use the standard APIs for language and cultural-specific operations rather than writing their own.

Linux

Linux does not yet have pervasive Unicode support. However, adding Unicode support to Linux, and generally internationalizing Linux, has some active supporters.

One promising development is the September 1999 formation of the Linux Internationalisation Initiative (`http://www.li18nux.org/`). The group — which has approximately 50 member companies or organizations and an undisclosed number of individual members — is a collaborative effort to develop internationalized APIs for Linux systems. Unfortunately, at the time of this writing, it is still too soon to tell if the group will achieve its goals.

There is also a separate Linux UTF-8 mailing list for people working on adding UTF-8 support to common Linux applications. To subscribe, send a message to `majordomo@nl.linux.org` with `subscribe linux-utf8` in the body of your message.

One of the most active promoters of using Unicode for Unix is Markus Kuhn, who, besides developing Unicode BDF fonts for Linux, maintains the "UTF-8 and Unicode FAQ for Unix/Linux" at `http://www.cl.cam.ac.uk/~mgk25/unicode.html`. The FAQ provides many details about Unicode, UTF-8, and where and why UTF-8 can be used in a Linux system. It also lists software that has been modified to support UTF-8, and provides links to other sites with more information.

FreeBSD

FreeBSD (`http://www.freebsd.org/`) does not show any built-in Unicode support. However, there are several conversion utilities and Unicode-enabled editors in its list of ported software. In addition, FreeBSD systems can run Linux software (when the correct libraries are installed), so FreeBSD users can take advantage of any Linux Unicode applications that haven't yet been ported to FreeBSD.

Mac OS

Recent releases of the Macintosh Operating System — the current consumer-oriented version being 9.0 — have seen a major revamp of the text handling system to better support Unicode.

Mac OS, for a long time, has been able to support multiple scripts, including Japanese, Chinese, Korean, Hebrew, and Arabic. However, Apple's WorldScript I and WorldScript II language kits each supported a single encoding of a single script, and every kit had its own input method, fonts, and text utilities.

Hindsight shows that the one script/one encoding idea isn't optimal. But Apple had the foresight to realize this very early, and Apple was one of the original participants in the effort that later became the Unicode Consortium.

With Mac OS 8.5, released in October 1998, the Macintosh operating system finally had the pieces in place for Unicode support from input to output. The most visible Unicode-enabled component is the ATSUI (both "Apple Type Services for Unicode Imaging" and the Japanese word for "hot") display engine that draws the characters on the screen or on the printed page. Additional new features in recent releases include a character set conversion utility, an input manager, a text engine, and a string processing utility.

Another component, the Text Encoding Converter (TEC), supports conversion between Unicode and over 50 other encodings, and a third, the Text Services Manager (TSM), supports both legacy keyboards and keyboards and input methods that generate Unicode code values.

ATSUI draws the characters on the screen or page, but it does more than just use the same glyph for the same character every time. For example, ATSUI can draw Chinese and Japanese text both vertically and horizontally. In addition to representing punctuation characters using glyphs that have the correct orientation, ATSUI can rotate embedded text from other scripts so that it has the correct orientation for the writing direction.

Mac OS also provides several text utilities to, for example, sort Unicode text and parse Unicode text strings as dates, times, and measurements. In addition, Mac OS 8.1 introduced the new HFS Plus file system that supports Unicode filenames.

Mac OS X Server

This is the *other* Macintosh operating system. Its development followed a very different path from where Mac OS 9 stands now. Mac OS X is a fully object-oriented operating system based on a BSD Unix and Mach core, originally developed by NeXT Computer Inc. Apple bought NeXT to acquire the NeXT operating system (among other reasons). The operating system was renamed Rhapsody and the ability to run existing Mac OS applications was added. For a time, Rhapsody was to become replace Mac OS, but Apple's plans changed, and the operating system is now being marketed as Mac OS X Server.

The operating system represents text as Unicode characters, and it has good support for character code conversions. It also supports reading and writing files encoded as UTF-8 and UTF-16. Its extensive high-level libraries are accessible to developers through both Java and Objective-C interfaces. (Objective-C is an object-oriented interpretation of the C programming language that predates C++, but that made headway first on the Macintosh platform. Much of Mac OS' low-level code was written in Objective-C.)

This chapter has summarized the Unicode support in multiple operating systems. There are many differences in how the operating systems implement their Unicode support: some are built from the ground up to work with Unicode text, and others, such as Linux, have had UTF-8 support retrofitted to existing 8-bit software. The one consistent feature you'll find among all of these systems is that their level of Unicode support is increasing. The new releases of the Windows, Mac OS, and Solaris operating systems provide better and more comprehensive Unicode support than their predecessors.

Chapter 11

Programming Language Support

This chapter describes the level of support for the Unicode Standard from a handful of programming languages, which are representative of how many such languages are changing to support Unicode. The languages covered here are:

- C/C++
- DSSSL
- EcmaScript/JavaScript/Jscript
- Java (and Microsoft Visual J++)
- Perl
- Python
- Tcl
- Visual Basic
- VBScript

The information in this chapter is possibly the most volatile in the entire book, since the languages (and their implementations, where the two are not indistinguishable) are continually undergoing refinement and improvement. In fact, three of the descriptions note planned or expected improvements in a language's support for the Unicode Standard. The release of the Unicode Standard, Version 3.0, is likely to prompt more changes in future releases of some of these languages. This is because, at the time of this writing, the languages support the character repertoire of either Version 2.0 or Version 2.1. For up-to-date information on support of the Unicode Standard in programming languages, see the Web page for this book.

Common Example

As much as possible, the programming languages in this chapter have been tested with a simple sequence of characters encoded in a variety of ways. Figure 11-1 shows the characters and their code values. Note that the example includes two Hebrew characters and two combining marks. Figure 11-2 shows how these same characters should be represented when displayed or printed. Notice that the Hebrew characters are displayed right-to-left, and that the two combining marks combine with their base character.

Character								
Code value	0041	0416	5E73	05D0	05D1	0061	0333	0306

Figure 11-1 *Character sequence used in examples*

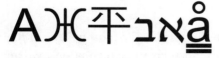

Figure 11-2 *Correct representation of characters used in the example*

Table 11-1 lists the code value and Unicode character name of each of the characters in the sample.

Table 11-1 *Characters Used in the Sample Files*

Code Value	Unicode Character Name
U+0041	LATIN CAPITAL LETTER A
U+0416	CYRILLIC CAPITAL LETTER ZHE
U+5E73	CJK UNIFIED IDEOGRAPH 5E73
U+05D0	HEBREW LETTER ALEF
U+05D1	HEBREW LETTER BET
U+0061	LATIN SMALL LETTER A
U+0333	COMBINING DOUBLE LOW LINE
U+0307	COMBINING DOT ABOVE

The programming languages with built-in support for reading, writing, or displaying Unicode characters were tested with files containing the sample characters encoded as each of the following:

- UTF-8
- UTF-16BE
- UTF-16BE with BOM
- UTF-16LE
- UTF-16LE with BOM

Note that "UTF-16BE with BOM" and "UTF-16LE with BOM" are both really "UTF-16" but the test programming languages differed in their ability to handle big-endian and little-endian encodings. Also, some of the parameters for each test differed, since the test machine was a little-endian Pentium computer, running either Windows 95 or FreeBSD 3.2.

Note

The files used in these examples are available on the Web site for this book.

C/C++

When working in C or C++, you have the option of using the encoding format that seems best to you: UTF-8, UTF-16, or UTF-32. There is no one-size-fits-all choice. Although there is little call to work in UTF-32 at this point, the question of whether to manipulate your string data as UTF-8 or UTF-16 is often the subject of heated discussion on the Unicode mailing list.

When working with UTF-8, you can use the familiar character-oriented functions and `char*` pointers. However, it's up to you to keep together the possibly multiple bytes of a UTF-8 character and not, for example, extract a substring that is not one or more complete characters.

When working with UTF-16, you can treat each character as a single 16-bit quantity—that is, until you need to manipulate Surrogate Pairs. ANSI/ISO C provides the `wchar_t` wide character type and wide versions of functions from `wmain()`, the wide-character enabled entry point to your program, down to `putwchar`, `wcscpy`, and `wprintf` versions of the familiar `putchar`, `scopy`, and `printf` functions, among others. The width of "wide," however, is compiler-specific: `wchar_t` may be as little as eight bits. In the interests of portable code, you can use a macro or `typedef` to define your own Unicode character type and, depending on the compiler and platform, map it to `unsigned short` or `wchar_t`, as appropriate.

If you're using Microsoft's Visual C++, you can define the symbol `_UNICODE` then use the predefined `_TCHAR` macros and related portable data types when dealing with characters and strings. When `_UNICODE` is declared, `_TCHAR` and friends evaluate to `wchar_t` and wide (aka "Unicode") versions of the string-handling functions. Additionally, when _MBCS is declared, the macros evaluate to the multibyte-enabled form of the string functions. When neither _UNICODE nor _MBCS is declared, the macros evaluate to the default char data type and single-byte ASCII string-handling functions.

Using _TCHAR, therefore, makes it easier to switch between single-byte and "Unicode" versions of the string-handling functions, but if you know you are programming for Unicode support, you can just as easily use the wide functions directly. On the plus side, using _TCHAR, etc., for all programs, whether single-byte, multibyte, or Unicode-enabled, will save you having to remember the different function names for the different types of character handling. It will also go partway toward future-proofing your single-byte applications for an eventual upgrade to supporting the Unicode Standard.

Note

I have used "Unicode" in quotes when referring to the wide-string handling functions and to the use of the _UNICODE symbol with _TCHAR and related macros. This is because there is more to handling the characters of the Unicode Standard than treating characters as 16-bit chunks. Supporting the Unicode Standard means supporting the conformance requirements, which means that some of your "characters" may be base characters followed by one or more combining characters, or characters represented by two 16-bit code values.

Class or Function Libraries

Several companies and individuals have released C++ class libraries and/or C function libraries for handling Unicode data. These libraries typically provide methods or functions for converting between Unicode and other character encodings, collating Unicode text, and finding word and character boundaries. Some also provide functions for supporting localization, including handling resource bundles and converting date, time, and number formats between different locales. The libraries in the following list include commercial products, libraries provided free of charge but without source code, and open-source products.

- *IBM Classes for Unicode* (`http://www10.software.ibm.com/developerworks/opensource/icu/project/index.html`) is an open-source C++ and C library that provides Unicode-compliant support for locale-sensitive string, date, time, number, currency, and message handling. It has been ported to multiple platforms, including Windows NT, Windows 95, Windows 98, Mac OS, RedHat Linux, Solaris, and OS/2.

- *Rosette C++ Library for Unicode* by Basis Technology (`http://unicode.basistech.com/`) is available under royalty-free source-code or object-code licenses for Windows, Solaris, Linux, and other platforms. The version current at the time of this writing is 2.1, which supports conversion between over 150 legacy encodings and the Unicode Standard, Version 1.1, 2.0, and 2.1 character repertoires and UTF-7, UTF-8, and UCS2 transformation formats. A command-line file conversion utility, uniconv, is a free demonstration application of the Rosette library available at `http://unicode.basistech.com/demo.html`.

- *Batam* by Alis Technologies (`http://www.alis.com/castil/batam.html`) is a Windows DLL and ancillary files that collectively provide an API. This API supplements and, in part, replaces the Windows APIs for display, GUI controls, keyboard input, and sorting. Batam provides APIs for Win32 SDK, Microsoft Foundation Classes (MFC), and Delphi. It also supports conversion between approximately 70 legacy encodings and UTF-8.

- *Unilib* by Sybase (http://www.sybase.com/products/ global/products/unilib.html) is a programming library for use with C++ and C (and any language that can call C functions). It is part of Sybase's Developer's Kit for Unicode (UDK) and Runtime Kit for Unicode (URK), and is included in multiple Sybase products. Unilib is available for Windows, Linux, Solaris, and other platforms, although the UDK is only available for Windows 95, Windows NT, and Solaris. Unilib provides functions for character and string handling, sorting, and character set conversion. The version current at the time of this writing supports the Unicode Standard, Version 2.1, and a future version will support Version 3.0.

- *libutf-8* by Whiz Kid Technomagic (http://www.whizkid tech.net/i18n/) is a free function library for converting strings and files between 16-bit Unicode characters and UTF-8. Other free programs available from Whiz Kid Technologies convert files between 159 legacy encodings and UTF-8.

- *UniAPI* by Bjondi International (http://www.bjondi.com/ products/uniapi/) is a free function library provided as a Windows DLL and a header file. It provides functions for accessing character properties, case conversion, and character composition and decomposition. It also implements a bidirectional algorithm, and provides functions for visual caret movement that take into account the bidirectional embedding level. Bjondi also provides Character Agent, a free utility for looking up the properties of any Unicode 2.1 character.

- *UCData* by Mark Leisher (http://crl.nmsu.edu/ ~mleisher/ucdata.html) is a free function library for determining character properties, case mappings, and decompositions. The version current at the time of this writing is 2.1, which added Pretty Good Bidi Algorithm (PGBA), a simple but non-standard implementation of the bidirectional algorithm.

This list is by no means complete, and products may become available, be withdrawn, or change their distribution model at any time (for example, the IBM Classes for Unicode only recently changed to being open-source). For up-to-date information, see the Web site for this book.

DSSSL

Document Style Semantics and Specification Language (DSSSL) is actually comprised of several interrelated languages. These inter-related languages are designed for specifying the transformation and formatting of SGML documents. However, DSSSL has increasingly become used for formatting XML documents. It is defined in ISO 10179:1996.

Conceptually, a DSSSL system does all of the following:

- Reads both an input SGML (or XML) document and a stylesheet

- Applies the transformation portion of the stylesheet to the input document to produce an intermediate form of the document

- Applies the style portion of the stylesheet to the intermediate form of the document to produce a result expressed in terms of DSSSL's formatting primitives, or *flow objects*

The resulting *flow object tree* is passed to a formatting backend that does the actual work of drawing the flow objects on the page or screen.

In practice, no one has implemented the transformation portion of the DSSSL standard, but users can still do very sophisticated transformations of the input using the *style language* component of DSSSL.

In addition, the most popular DSSSL engine, Jade (and its successor, OpenJade), has implemented an SGML backend with which you can transform your document directly to SGML, XML, or HTML.

DSSSL references ISO/IEC 10646 for its character repertoire. In addition to including characters directly in your stylesheet, you can use character references derived from the character's name in the English edition of ISO/IEC 10646. As a non-standard extension, Jade and OpenJade allow numeric character references. Table 11-2 shows these references as both character and string objects for U+0041, LATIN CAPITAL LETTER A.

Table 11-2 *DSSSL Character References for U+0061, LATIN CAPITAL LETTER A*

Object Type	Usage	Description
Character	#\A	#\ followed by the character. For example, although you can't see it, #\ represents the space character.
	#\latin-capital-letter-a	#\ followed by the lowercase form of the character name from the English version of ISO/IEC 10646, with spaces replaced by dashes. For example, #\space represents (and is the preferred form for) the space character.
		Jade and OpenJade implement this for a limited subset of the ISO/IEC 10646 character repertoire.
	#\U+0061	#\U+ followed by the four *uppercase* hexadecimal digits of the character's code value.
		This is a non-standard extension implemented by Jade and OpenJade.
String	"A"	The character itself.
	"\latin-capital-letter-a;"	\ followed by the lowercase form of the character name. The name should be terminated by a semicolon if the next character can be interpreted as part of the character name.
	"\U+0061"	\U+ followed by the four *uppercase* hexadecimal digits of the character's code value.

The DSSSL example to be presented shortly uses the following two-line XML file, utf8.xml:

```
<?xml version="1.0" encoding="UTF-8"?>
<demo>AÐ□$(He9³×□×'□(BaÌ³Ì‡</demo>
```

The text between the <demo> tags is our familiar sample string shown as Word's interpretation of UTF-8.

The following DSSSL stylesheet sets up the page size and margins plus the default font family and size to be used for the text in the output, then adds four paragraph flow objects to the output. The result is a page that illustrates creation of the sample string in the following forms:

- A string of characters contained in the stylesheet
- A string containing, as much as is supported by Jade, named character references; e.g., \latin-capital-letter-a
- A string created from a sequence of character objects specified using the non-standard numeric character reference extension
- The character data from the <demo> element in the input XML file

The stylesheet is presented in Listing 11-1.

Listing 11-1 *A DSSSL demonstration of four forms of the sample string.*

```
<!DOCTYPE style-sheet PUBLIC "-//James Clark//DTD DSSSL Style Sheet//EN">
<!-- Demonstration DSSSL stylesheet -->
<!-- $Id: demo.dsl,v 1.1 1999-09-06 14:15:42-04 tkg Exp $-->
(element demo
  (make simple-page-sequence
    page-width: 4in
    page-height: 4.5in
    top-margin: 0.25in
    bottom-margin: 0.25in
    left-margin: 0.25in
    right-margin: 0.25in
    font-family-name: "Arial Unicode MS"
    font-size: 24pt
    min-leading: 24pt
    (make paragraph
```

```
(literal "Characters:")
(make paragraph-break)
(literal
"AÐ$(He9³×□''(Baȉ³Ȉ‡"))
(make paragraph
(literal "Character names:")
(make paragraph-break)
(literal
(string-append
"\latin-capital-letter-a;\cyrillic-capital-letter-zhe;"
"\U-5E73;\U-05D0;\U-05D1;\latin-small-letter-a;\U-0333;\U-0307;")))
(make paragraph
(literal "Numeric references:")
(make paragraph-break)
(literal
(string
#\U-0041 #\U-0416 #\U-5E73 #\U-05D0 #\U-05D1 #\U-0061 #\U-0333
#\U-0307)))
(make paragraph
(literal "From file:")
(make paragraph-break)
(process-children))))
```

If you're using a non-default encoding as in Listing 11-1, you need to specify it in the SP_ENCODING environment variable before you run Jade. The first of the following MS-DOS commands sets the encoding to UTF-8, then the second one runs Jade:

```
demo>set SP_ENCODING=utf-8
demo>jade -d demo.dsl -wno-valid -t rtf utf8.xml
```

The -d parameter specifies the DSSSL stylesheet, the -wno-valid parameter turns off validation since utf8.xml doesn't have a DTD, and the -t parameter specifies which type of output we want — in this case, RTF to be viewed with Microsoft Word. The last parameter is the name of the XML file that we're processing.

Figure 11-3 shows a screen shot of the result viewed in Microsoft Word's Print Preview mode. Note that the Cyrillic character caused problems with Jade's specification of fonts in the RTF file, so the correct font was manually reapplied to the document before the screen shot was taken. When the characters appear correctly, you can see that the right-to-left Hebrew characters are not in the correct order, although that is more likely to be a problem with the American version of Word than with the DSSSL engine. The base and combining characters, however, do display correctly.

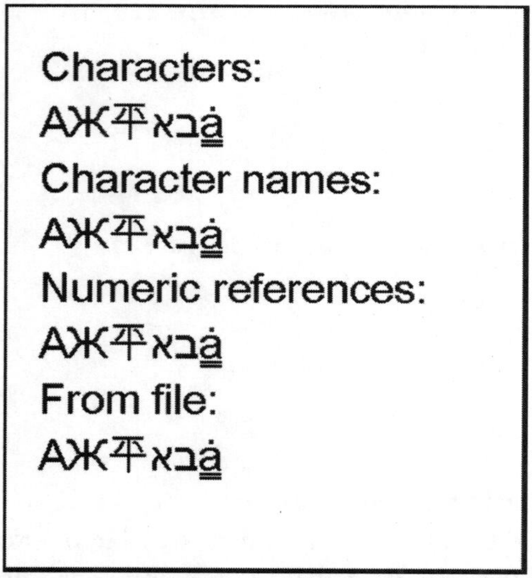

```
Characters:
АЖ꓿אבְ
Character names:
АЖ꓿אבְ
Numeric references:
АЖ꓿אבְ
From file:
АЖ꓿אבְ
```

Figure 11-3 *Screen shot of sample text formatted with DSSSL and Microsoft Word*

ECMAScript/JavaScript/JScript

ECMAScript is the standardized form of the scripting language implemented in Web browsers (and other applications). It is defined in ECMA-262, ECMAScript Language Specification, and has been adopted as ISO/IEC 16262. At the time of this writing, the current version of ECMA-262 is the second edition, dated August 1998. This describes the first version of the language, since the changes between the first and second editions were just editorial changes to keep ECMA-262 aligned with ISO/IEC 16262. ECMA-262 Version 3, which describes the second version of the language, was voted on at the end of 1999. At the time of this writing, the ECMA Web site lists Edition 2, and the final candidate draft is available at `http://www.mozilla.org/js/language/futures.htm`. Changes expected in Edition 3 include addition of language constructs that have been implemented in Web browsers for quite some time, plus improved internationalization support, including better definition of the language's support for the Unicode Standard.

What is ECMAScript Really?

ECMAScript is implemented in the Netscape Navigator browser as JavaScript, and in Microsoft's Internet Explorer browser as JScript. You'll also find ECMAScript—or one of its incarnations—as a macro or scripting language in non-browser applications such as SoftQuad's XMetaL editor.

In truth, ECMAScript is based on JavaScript and JScript, rather than the other way around. JavaScript was invented by Brendan Eich at Netscape, and was first implemented in Navigator 2.0. Not long afterwards, Microsoft implemented a similar but slightly different JScript in Internet Explorer. Rather than fragment the Web with similar but incompatible scripting languages, the major players agreed to standardize the core of the language under the auspices of ECMA, an international, Europe-based industry association for standardizing information and communication.

ECMA-262 defines a number of primitive object types: Null, Undefined, Boolean, and String. It also defines the ECMAScript syntax, plus core functions and operators for manipulating objects. Implementations can, and do, define additional object types, functions, and operators.

ECMAScript is designed for use inside a host, such as a Web browser, and the standard does not define an I/O interface. Implementations, therefore, must define their own I/O methods. Since ECMAScript is designed to run inside a browser or other host and not, for example, load programs from external files, I/O handling can be simple.

ECMAScript's Handling of Unicode

ECMA 262 Edition 2 begins well enough by defining everything in terms of characters defined in the Unicode Standard, Version 2.0, and requiring the UCS-2 encoding (one of many flip-flops between using Unicode terminology and ISO/IEC 10646 terminology). It then promptly limits all characters, except in comments and strings, to the Basic Latin block. Characters may be represented using a \u*nnnn* escape sequence, where *nnnn* is the four hexadecimal digits of a character's code value.

ECMAScript does not have a Character object type, so all text manipulation is done in terms of String objects. String comparisons are done on the bit values of the strings' characters, and ECMAScript does not support canonical equivalents, or locale-sensitive collation sequences. The standard does provide toLowerCase and toUpperCase functions, but these use the canonical, locale-insensitive case mapping defined in the Unicode Standard, Version 2.0. The standard also provides an escape function, and corresponding unescape, to convert non-ASCII characters into a 7-bit–safe form for transmission between computers. The escape function transforms a Latin-1 character into a three-character sequence %*nn*, where *nn* is the character's code value in hexadecimal. It transforms other non-ASCII, non-Latin-1 characters into %u*nnnn*, where *nnnn* is the four hexadecimal digits of the character's code value.

The next version of ECMAScript will support UTF-16 and the repertoire of the Unicode Standard, Version 2.1, *or later*, and will allow Unicode characters in identifiers. In addition, U+2028, LINE SEPARATOR, and U+2029, PARAGRAPH SEPARATOR, are to be recognized as line terminators, and all of the Unicode "whitespace" characters are to be recognized as whitespace in ECMAScript. However, formatting control characters, such as bidirectional overrides, etc., will be ignored by the ECMAScript parser. Also, only the European digits (0–9) will be recognized as numerals, only the ASCII quote characters (0x22) will be recognized as quotes, and only the ASCII minus sign (0x2D) will be recognized as minus.

It's fair to say that ECMA 262 Edition 3 plans to handle character normalization by not handling it. Since scripts execute inside a host application, such as a browser, and the host handles any I/O, Edition 3 of the standard simply assumes that all strings a program receives from the host will be normalized to their canonical composition (Normalization Form C). You can still write a program that produces non-normalized text, but if you do, it's your problem. The alternative — including the normalization tables in every implementation — was considered too much code and data to add to every ECMAScript implementation.

ECMA 262 Edition 3 also adds recognition of the default locale of the host program. It provides locale-sensitive string comparison and conversion functions that, for example, correctly handle the Turkish dotless i. The next version also improves ECMAScript's regular expressions and date and time handling.

Listing 11-2 presents some HTML markup that includes a `<script>` element. Inside this element is a short JScript program that demonstrates some of the string-handling features of ECMAScript. Although ECMA-262 specifies UCS-2, the HTML is encoded as UTF-8, and we can rely on the Web browser to make the conversion to its internal format. The program declares our now-familiar sequence of characters in two ways: as a UTF-8 string, and as a sequence of escaped numeric character references. The remainder of the program simply writes several things to the screen: the UTF-8–encoded string, the result of using **escape** on the string, the result of unescaping the escaped string, and the string resulting from the sequence of escaped numeric character references.

Listing 11-2 *A JScript interpretation (Internet Explorer) of our sample string*

```
<!-- Demonstrate some JScript features -->
<!-- $Id: jscript1.html,v 1.2 1999-09-05 17:17:50-04 tkg Exp $ -->
<html>
<head>
<title>ECMAScript Unicode Demonstration</title>
<meta http-equiv="Content-Type" content="text/html; charset=UTF-8">
</head>
<body bgcolor="#FFFFFF">
<script language="JScript">
var String = "AÐ□$(He9³x□× □(Baĺ³Ì‡";
var EscapedString = "\u0041\u0416\u5e73\u05d0\u05d1\u0061\u0333\u0307";

document.write("<body style='font-size: 24pt'>");
document.write("<p>String: \"" + String + "\"</p>");
document.write("<p>escape(String): \"" + escape(String) + "\"</p>");
document.write("<p>unescape(escape(String)): \"" + unescape(escape(String))
        + "\"</p>");
document.write("<p>EscapedString: \"" + EscapedString + "\"</p>");
document.write("</body>");
</script>
</body>
</html>
```

Figure 11-4 shows a screen shot of the strings that are written to the browser.

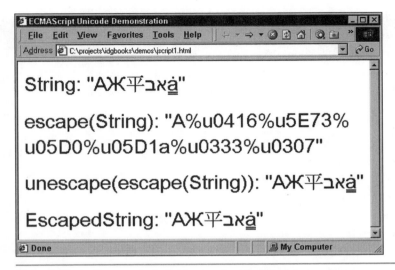

Figure 11-4 *Screen shot of strings output by JScript program*

Listing 11-3 presents another passage of HTML markup. This time it includes a `<script>` element containing a JScript program that demonstrates some of Microsoft's scripting extensions for file I/O. The program opens each of the sample files as "Unicode" text, indicated by the `TristateTrue` (-1) value of the fourth argument to each call to `OpenTextFile`, and writes the result to the screen.

Listing 11-3 *Using JScript to open four files as "Unicode."*

```
<!-- Demonstrate Microsoft's JScript file I/O extensions -->
<!-- $Id: jscript2.html,v 1.1 1999-09-05 17:37:30-04 tkg Exp $ -->
<html>
<head>
<title>JScript File Handling Demonstration</title>
<meta http-equiv="Content-Type" content="text/html; charset=UTF-8">
</head>
<body bgcolor="#FFFFFF">
<script language="JScript">
```

Continued

Listing 11-3 *Continued*

```
var String = "AÐ□$(He9³×□× □(Baİ_İ‡";

var ForReading = 1, ForWriting = 2, ForAppending = 8;

var TristateUseDefault = -2, TristateTrue = -1, TristateFalse = 0;

var FileSystem = new ActiveXObject("Scripting.FileSystemObject");

var File;


document.write("<body style='font-size: 24pt'>");
File = FileSystem.OpenTextFile(
        "c:\\projects\\idgbooks\\demos\\utf8.txt",
        ForReading, false, TristateTrue);
document.write("<p>UTF-8: \"" + File.ReadAll() + "\"</p>");
File.Close();


File = FileSystem.OpenTextFile(
        "c:\\projects\\idgbooks\\demos\\utf16le.txt",
        ForReading, false, TristateTrue);
document.write("<p>UTF-16LE: \"" + File.ReadAll() + "\"</p>");
File.Close();


File = FileSystem.OpenTextFile(
        "c:\\projects\\idgbooks\\demos\\utf16lebom.txt",
        ForReading, false, TristateTrue);
document.write("<p>UTF-16LE+BOM: \"" + File.ReadAll() + "\"</p>");
File.Close();


File = FileSystem.OpenTextFile(
        "c:\\projects\\idgbooks\\demos\\utf16be.txt",
        ForReading, false, TristateTrue);
document.write("<p>UTF-16BE: \"" + File.ReadAll() + "\"</p>");
File.Close();
```

```
File = FileSystem.OpenTextFile(
        "c:\\projects\\idgbooks\\demos\\utf16bebom.txt",
        ForReading, false, TristateTrue);
document.write("<p>UTF-16BE+BOM: \"" + File.ReadAll() + "\"</p>");
File.Close();

File = FileSystem.OpenTextFile(
        "c:\\projects\\idgbooks\\demos\\jscriptout.html",
        ForWriting, true, TristateTrue);
File.writeline(String);
File.Close();
</script>
</body>
</html>
```

You'll notice that several of the assignment expressions in Listing 11.3 make reference to complete filenames, such as c:\\projects\ idgbooks\\demos\\utf16bebom.txt. (As you may know, the double-backslashes are necessary for filename assignments to string variables and as passed string parameters even though they are not standard form within URIs.) Of course, the file utf16bebom.txt is located in this particular directory on the particular computer for which I wrote this script. The files themselves are available from the Web site for this book. For this script to be executed properly, you'll either need to re-create my own directory structure, or edit this script so that the filename parameters point to your own directories.

Figure 11-5 shows the result of running Listing 11-3 through Internet Explorer. As can be expected for a Unicode-aware program running on a little-endian processor, the UTF-16–encoded files with the BOM were interpreted correctly, as was the UTF-16LE file. The UTF-16BE file and the UTF-8 file produced unintelligible results.

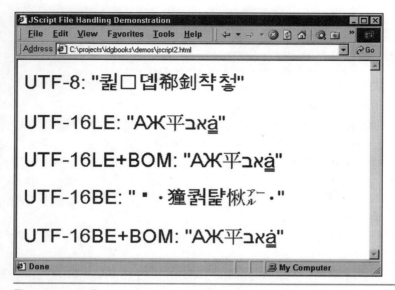

Figure 11-5 *Screen shot of output of strings read from sample files with different encodings*

The last part of the JScript program wrote out the same sample string as "Unicode" text to jscriptout.html. As the following hexadecimal dump of jscriptout.html shows, the text is written as big-endian UTF-16 (i.e. UTF-16BE with the BOM):

```
bash.exe-2.02$ od -h jscriptout.html
0000000 feff 0041 0416 5e73 05d0 05d1 0061 0333
0000020 0307 000d 000a
0000026
```

Figure 11-6 shows the result of viewing jscriptout.html in a Web browser: The presence of the BOM enabled the browser to correctly determine the file's encoding.

Figure 11-6 *Screen shot of jscriptout.html*

Java

Java is possibly the best-known example of a computer language with support for the characters of the Unicode Standard. Java has extensive internationalization support — the details of which are beyond the scope of this book — but as part of its support, all `char` and `String` types are represented internally as 16-bit Unicode characters. Comments and identifiers — variable, method, and class names — are also represented as Unicode text, and, therefore, include non-ASCII characters. Java supports I/O in a variety of locale-specific encodings (as well as UTF-8 and UTF-16), but no matter what encoding is used, the characters are converted to and from Unicode as they are read or written.

Your Java programs may themselves also be encoded as UTF-8 or UTF-16 (including the BOM). If, as is likely, UTF-8 or UTF-16 is not your default local encoding, you need to specify the encoding when you compile your program, as in the following examples:

```
javac -encoding UTF8 demo.java
javac -encoding Unicode demo16.java
```

Even if you don't encode the characters directly, you can represent any character using a \u*nnnn* escape sequence, where *nnnn* is the four hexadecimal digits of the character's code value. Java also supports C-style escape sequences — such as \n, \r, \t, and *nnn* to represent characters using three octal digits — but there are two major differences between the \u*nnnn* escape sequences and the C-style escape sequences:

- A \u*nnnn* escape sequence may be allowed *anywhere*, whereas the C-style escape sequences are only allowed in strings.
- A \u*nnnn* escape sequence is always evaluated *before* any other escape sequences. For example, \n in a string represents a newline, but so does \u005Cn and \u005C\u006E, since \u005C and \u006E are the escape sequences for REVERSE SOLIDUS and LATIN SMALL LETTER N, respectively. (The other combination, \\u006E, evaluates as the five characters \u006E because of the doubled \).

Identifiers in Java begin with a letter character or "_" or "$" (i.e., a character for which `Character.isJavaIdentifierStart()` returns true), and may continue with letters, "_", "$", or digits (for which `Character.isJavaIdentifierPart()` returns true). Java letters include A–Z, a–z, and many non-alphabetic characters. The list of allowed characters changes with Java versions: Java 1.0 assignments are based on Unicode 1.1.5, and Java 1.1 assignments are based on Unicode 2.0.14. Note that `Character.isJavaIdentifierStart()` and `Character.isJavaIdentifierPart()` were added in Java 1.1, and Java 1.0 uses the now deprecated `Character.isJavaLetter()` and `Character.isJavaLetterOrDigit()` methods.

The `java.lang.Character` class provides a number of additional class methods for determining properties of characters and finding uppercase, lowercase, and titlecase mappings of characters. These, of course, are based upon the properties defined in the Unicode Character Database (either version 2.0.14 or 1.1.5, depending on the Java version). The synopses are shown in the following code listing:

```
public static int getNumericValue(char ch);
public static int getType(char ch);
public static boolean isDefined(char ch);
public static boolean isDigit(char ch);
public static boolean isISOControl(char ch);
```

```
public static boolean isIdentifierIgnorable(char ch);
public static boolean isJavaIdentifierPart(char ch);
public static boolean isJavaIdentifierStart(char ch);
public static boolean isJavaLetter(char ch);
public static boolean isJavaLetterOrDigit(char ch);
public static boolean isLetter(char ch);
public static boolean isLetterOrDigit(char ch);
public static boolean isLowerCase(char ch);
public static boolean isSpace(char ch);
public static boolean isSpaceChar(char ch);
public static boolean isTitleCase(char ch);
public static boolean isUnicodeIdentifierPart(char ch);
public static boolean isUnicodeIdentifierStart(char ch);
public static boolean isUppercase(char ch);
public static boolean isWhitespace(char ch);
public static char toLowerCase(char ch);
public static char toTitleCase(char ch);
public static char toUpperCase(char ch);
```

Note that `Character.getType()` returns a value indicating the character's value in the General Category field in the Unicode Character Database. The class also defines a constant for each possible value—for example, `Character.UPPERCASE_LETTER`—so you can easily take action based on whether or not a character's type matches a defined constant.

`Character.getNumericValue()` returns the numeric value of the character as a non-negative integer. It returns -1 if the character does not have a numeric value, or -2 if the character has a numeric value that cannot be expressed as an integer. For example, the numeric character values of \u0030, \u0061, \u00BC, and \u2182 are 0, -1, -2, and 10,000, respectively.

Identifiers (and strings) are not normalized. For example, two identifiers ö and ö may look the same, although one may be U+00F6 (\u00F6), LATIN SMALL LETTER O WITH DIAERESIS, and the other may be the two-character sequence of U+004F (\u004F),

LATIN SMALL LETTER O, followed by U+0308 (\u0308), COMBINING DIAERSIS.
Java can read and write UTF-8 and UTF-16 files. It has separate methods for reading and writing a modified form of UTF-8 that is intended *only* for internal use in Java libraries. This data-only form of UTF-8 is read and written using the `DataInputStream.readUTF()` and `DataOutputStream.writeUTF()` methods, respectively. The UTF-8 data format encodes U+0000 as a two-byte sequence so that the UTF-8 data never contains null characters. This convention is well known, and conversion programs such as uniconv by Basis Technology Corp. support Java's UTF-8 data flavor among their encoding options.

In addition, the UTF-8 data begins with an unsigned short integer indicating the length of the UTF-8 string. Reading a conventional UTF-8 file using `DataInputStream.readUTF()`, therefore, results in a `UTFDataFormatException`, while a file written with `DataInputStream.writeUTF()` is similarly unintelligible to conventional UTF-8 systems. The following hexadecimal dumps of `utf8.txt`, one of the sample files used in this chapter, and `utf8data.txt`, the sample string written to a file using `DataInputStream.writeUTF()`, illustrate the difference. `utf8data.txt` begins with the zero-based offset of the end of the UTF-8 string. On my little-endian Pentium, the length is written least-significant byte first.

```
bash.exe-2.02$ od -h utf8.txt
0000000 d041 e596 b3b9 90d7 91d7 cc61 ccb3 0087
0000017
bash.exe-2.02$ od -h utf8data.txt
0000000 0f00 d041 e596 b3b9 90d7 91d7 cc61 ccb3
0000020 0087
0000021
bash.exe-2.02$
```

Standard Java

Listing 11-4 presents a Java program that demonstrates some of Java's support for the Unicode Standard. Like other sample programs in this chapter, it writes a UTF-8–encoded HTML file showing the results (or lack of results) from evaluating our sample string as a sequence of UTF-8 characters, as a sequence of character references, and as the result of reading the string from files with different encodings.

Listing 11-4 *Generating the sample string with Java code*

```
// Java program to illustrate support for UTF-16 and UTF-8 in Java
//
// Compile with "-encoding UTF-8" since it contains UTF-8 characters
//
// $Id: demo.java,v 1.1 1999-09-23 17:12:57-04 tkg Exp $


import java.io.*;


public class demo {
    public static void main(String[] args)
        throws FileNotFoundException, UnsupportedEncodingException, IOException {


        // Strings containing:
        // - U+0041, LATIN CAPITAL LETTER A
        // - U+0416, CYRILLIC CAPITAL LETTER ZHE
        // - U+5E73, CJK UNIFIED IDEOGRAPH 5E73
        // - U+05D0, HEBREW LETTER ALEF
        // - U+05D1, HEBREW LETTER BET
        // - U+0061, LATIN SMALL LETTER A
        // - U+0333, COMBINING DOUBLE LOW LINE
        // - U+0307, COMBINING DOT ABOVE


        // UTF-8 string
        String characters =
```

Continued

Listing 11-4 *Continued*

```
"AÐ□$(He9³x□x □(Baĺ³Ì‡";
// Sequence of escaped characters
String escapedCharacters =
    "\u0041\u0416\u5E73\u05D0\u05D1\u0061\u0333\u0307";


// Strings that will be read from files
String utf8;
String utf16be;
String utf16bebom;
String utf16le;
String utf16lebom;
String utf8Data;
String utf8DataRedux;


try { // Read UTF-8 file
    InputStream utf8File;
    utf8File = new FileInputStream("utf8.txt");
    BufferedReader utf8r =
        new BufferedReader(new InputStreamReader(utf8File, "UTF8"));
    utf8 = utf8r.readLine();
    utf8r.close();
} catch (Exception err) {
    utf8 = err.getMessage();
}



try { // Read UTF-8 file using DataInputStream.readUTF()
    InputStream utf8File;
    utf8File = new FileInputStream("utf8.txt");
    DataInputStream utf8datar =
        new DataInputStream(utf8File);
    utf8Data = utf8datar.readUTF();
    utf8datar.close();
} catch (Exception err) {
```

```
    utf8Data = "Couldn't read UTF-8 file as data";

}


try { // Write UTF-8 file using DataOutputStream.writeUTF()

    OutputStream utf8DataFile = new FileOutputStream("utf8data.txt");

    DataOutputStream utf8dataw =

        new DataOutputStream(utf8DataFile);

    utf8dataw.writeUTF(utf8);

    utf8dataw.close();

} catch (Exception err) {

    utf8Data = "Couldn't write UTF-8 as data";

}


try { // Using DataInputStream.readUTF(), read the file we wrote

    InputStream utf8DataFile = new FileInputStream("utf8data.txt");

    DataInputStream utf8datar =

        new DataInputStream(utf8DataFile);

    utf8DataRedux = utf8datar.readUTF();

    utf8datar.close();

} catch (Exception err) {

    utf8DataRedux = "Couldn't read UTF-8 file as data";

}


try { // Read UTF-16BE file

    InputStream utf16beFile;

    utf16beFile = new FileInputStream("utf16be.txt");

    BufferedReader utf16ber =

        new BufferedReader(new InputStreamReader(utf16beFile,

                                        "Unicode"));

    utf16be = utf16ber.readLine();

} catch (Exception err) {

    utf16be = err.getMessage();

}
```

Continued

Listing 11-4 *Continued*

```
try { // Read UTF-16BE+BOM file
    InputStream utf16bebomFile;
    utf16bebomFile = new FileInputStream("utf16bebom.txt");
    BufferedReader utf16bebomr =
        new BufferedReader(new InputStreamReader(utf16bebomFile,
                                                  "Unicode"));
    utf16bebom = utf16bebomr.readLine();
} catch (Exception err) {
    utf16bebom = err.getMessage();
}


try { // Read UTF-16LE file
    InputStream utf16leFile;
    utf16leFile = new FileInputStream("utf16le.txt");
    BufferedReader utf16ler =
        new BufferedReader(new InputStreamReader(utf16leFile,
                                                  "Unicode"));
    utf16le = utf16ler.readLine();
} catch (Exception err) {
    utf16le = err.getMessage();
}


try { // Read UTF-16LE+BOM file
    InputStream utf16lebomFile;
    utf16lebomFile = new FileInputStream("utf16lebom.txt");
    BufferedReader utf16lebomr =
        new BufferedReader(new InputStreamReader(utf16lebomFile,
                                                  "Unicode"));
    utf16lebom = utf16lebomr.readLine();
} catch (Exception err) {
    utf16lebom = err.getMessage();
}


// Write HTML file encoded as UTF-8
```

```
OutputStream javaout;

javaout = new FileOutputStream("javaout.html");

Writer w = new BufferedWriter(new OutputStreamWriter(javaout, "UTF8"));


w.write("<html>\n<head>\n");

w.write("<title>Java Unicode Demonstration</title>\n");

w.write("<meta http-equiv='Content-Type' ");

w.write("content='text/html; charset=UTF-8'>");

w.write("</head>\n<body bgcolor='#FFFFFF'>\n");

w.write("<p>UTF-8 string: \"");

w.write(characters);

w.write("\"</p>\n");

w.write("<p>Escaped characters: \"");

w.write(escapedCharacters);

w.write("\"</p>\n");

w.write("<p>UTF-8 from file: \"");

w.write(utf8);

w.write("\"</p>\n");

w.write("<p>UTF-8 DataInputStream: \"");

w.write(utf8Data);

w.write("\"</p>\n");

w.write("<p>UTF-8 from written file: \"");

w.write(utf8DataRedux);

w.write("\"</p>\n");

w.write("<p>UTF-16BE from file: \"");

w.write(utf16be);

w.write("\"</p>\n");

w.write("<p>UTF-16BE+BOM from file: \"");

w.write(utf16bebom);

w.write("\"</p>\n");

w.write("<p>UTF-16LE from file: \"");

w.write(utf16le);

w.write("\"</p>\n");
```

Continued

Listing 11-4 *Continued*

```
w.write("<p>UTF-16LE+BOM from file: \"");

w.write(utf16lebom);

w.write("\"</p>\n");

w.write("</body>\n</html>\n");


w.flush();

w.close();

    }

}
```

Figure 11-7 shows the resulting HTML file, `javaout.html`, viewed in a Web browser. As the screenshot shows, the Java program was able to read the UTF-8 file and the two UTF-16 files, but not the UTF-16BE or UTF-16LE files. It also shows that the sample UTF-8 file was not acceptable as a data file, but the Java program could read back the UTF-8–encoded data file that it wrote.

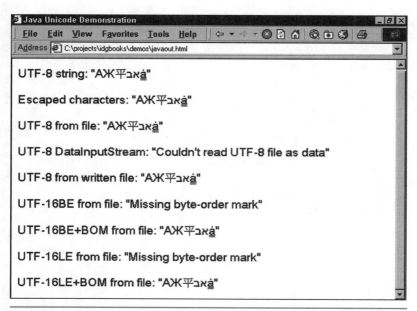

Figure 11-7 *Screen shot of javaout.html*

Java programs can also present a GUI using either the AWT or
Swing classes. Listing 11-5 is a Java applet that demonstrates the
sample string being drawn on the screen.

Listing 11-5 *Producing the sample string through Java using
escape sequences*

```
// Java applet to illustrate display of Unicode text with Java
//
// $Id: DemoApplet.java,v 1.1 1999-10-03 15:13:03-04 tkg Exp $
//
import java.applet.*;
import java.awt.*;


public class DemoApplet extends Applet {
    private Font font;


    // Strings containing:
    //  - U+0041, LATIN CAPITAL LETTER A
    //  - U+0416, CYRILLIC CAPITAL LETTER ZHE
    //  - U+5E73, CJK UNIFIED IDEOGRAPH 5E73
    //  - U+05D0, HEBREW LETTER ALEF
    //  - U+05D1, HEBREW LETTER BET
    //  - U+0061, LATIN SMALL LETTER A
    //  - U+0333, COMBINING DOUBLE LOW LINE
    //  - U+0307, COMBINING DOT ABOVE
    String escapedCharacters =
        "\u0041\u0416\u5E73\u05D0\u05D1\u0061\u0333\u0307";


    // Initialize the applet
    public void init() {
        font = new Font("serif", Font.PLAIN, 48);
    }


    // Paint the applet
```

Continued

Listing 11-5 *Continued*

```
public void paint(Graphics g) {

    g.setColor(Color.black);

    g.setFont(font);

    g.drawString(escapedCharacters, 40, 75);

}

}
```

The following HTML markup can be used within an HTML document to reference the applet:

```
<applet code="DemoApplet.class" width="450" height="100"></applet>
```

Microsoft Visual J++

Visual J++ is the Java component of Microsoft's Visual Studio development environment. The version current at the time of this writing is 6.0; see `http://msdn.microsoft.com/vstudio/`.

Visual J++ 6.0 implements Java 1.1. It also includes several additional, Microsoft-specific class libraries that provide close integration with the Windows environment and with Microsoft technologies such as ActiveX, Component Object Model (COM), Remote Data Objects (RDO), and Active Data Objects (ADO). The Microsoft Java compiler also recognizes several Microsoft-specific compiler directives that aid the integration of Java programs and Windows DLLs.

There are two aspects to the use of the characters of the Unicode Standard with these Microsoft extensions: additional classes and methods for handling Unicode text, and passing Unicode characters from a Java program to the rest of Windows.

For handling text, the `com.ms.lang.SystemX` class provides methods for converting between local code pages and Unicode. In addition, the `com.ms.wfc.app.Locale.Sort` class provides some sort IDs for local-specific sorting of Unicode text.

The details of passing Unicode characters to the rest of Windows vary with the interface being used to pass data between program components. For example, OLE interfaces require Unicode characters, whereas other interfaces may or may not require Unicode characters depending on whether the program is running on Windows NT or Windows 95/98. A developer also has the choice of using J/Direct to make direct calls to system and third-party DLLs or using the Raw Native Interface (RNI) or Java Native Interface (JNI). J/Direct handles most data type translations, including changing encodings, for you, at the cost of being non-standard. However, the two native interface formats still require platform-specific code (that's why they're called "native" interfaces). The RNI, on the other hand, is a high-performance interface, but it requires that you do more work; for example, to deal with Java's garbage collection. The low-level details include choosing between using `makeJavaString()`, `makeJavaStringW()`, or `makeJavaStringFromUtf8()` when converting strings between your native code and your Java code.

Visual J++ also includes Microsoft-specific classes for creating forms and other user-interface components. The Visual J++ IDE, just like the Visual C++ and Visual Basic IDEs, automatically generates the code for the form as you lay out the components in the "Designer" window and set their properties in the "Properties" window. Listing 11-6 presents a Visual J++ program that builds a form containing two labeled text boxes and an "Exit" button. The two text boxes display our familiar string derived from two sources: from the file "utf8.txt" and from a String object created from multiple character escape sequences.

Listing 11-6 *A partly Wizard-generated form including Unicode text*

```
// Visual J++ program to demonstrate Unicode support in
// com.ms.wfc.ui classes
//
import java.io.*;

import com.ms.wfc.app.*;
import com.ms.wfc.core.*;
import com.ms.wfc.ui.*;
```

Continued

Listing 11-6 *Continued*

```
/**

 * @author: Application Wizard

 * @version: 1.0

 * This class can take a variable number of parameters on the command

 * line. Program execution begins with the main() method. The class

 * constructor is not invoked unless an object of type 'Project1'

 * created in the main() method.

 */


public class demo extends Form

{


    BufferedReader in;


    // String containing:

    //  - U+0041, LATIN CAPITAL LETTER A

    //  - U+0416, CYRILLIC CAPITAL LETTER ZHE

    //  - U+5E73, CJK UNIFIED IDEOGRAPH 5E73

    //  - U+05D0, HEBREW LETTER ALEF

    //  - U+05D1, HEBREW LETTER BET

    //  - U+0061, LATIN SMALL LETTER A

    //  - U+0333, COMBINING DOUBLE LOW LINE

    //  - U+0307, COMBINING DOT ABOVE

    String EscapedString =

            "\u0041\u0416\u5E73\u05D0\u05D1\u0061\u0333\u0337";


    public demo()

    {

            super();


            //Required for Visual J++ Form Designer support

            initForm();


            try {
```

```
    // Read "utf8.txt" and display its contents
    in = new BufferedReader(new InputStreamReader(new
FileInputStream("../utf8.txt"), "UTF8"));
    edit1.setText(in.readLine());
    // Display the string built from character escape sequences
    edit2.setText(EscapedString);
    } catch (Throwable t) {
        t.printStackTrace ();
    }
}


/**
 * Project1 overrides dispose so it can clean up the
 * component list.
 */
public void dispose()
{
    super.dispose();
    components.dispose();
}


// The "Exit" button's "onClick" handler
private void exitClick(Object source, Event e)
{
    super.dispose();
    components.dispose();
}


/**
 * NOTE: The following code is required by the Visual J++ form
 * designer.  It can be modified using the form editor.  Do not
 * modify it using the code editor.
 */
```

Continued

Listing 11-6 *Continued*

```
Container components = new Container();

Label label1 = new Label();

Label label2 = new Label();

Edit edit1 = new Edit();

Edit edit2 = new Edit();

Button ExitButton = new Button();


private void initForm()

{

    this.setAnchor(ControlAnchor.ALL);

    this.setFont(new Font("Arial Unicode MS", 9.0f, FontSize.POINTS,
FontWeight.NORMAL, false, false, false, CharacterSet.DEFAULT, 0));

    this.setLocation(new Point(298, 88));

    this.setText("J++ Unicode Demo");

    this.setAutoScaleBaseSize(new Point(5, 16));

    this.setClientSize(new Point(226, 114));


    label1.setLocation(new Point(8, 16));

    label1.setSize(new Point(88, 16));

    label1.setTabIndex(1);

    label1.setTabStop(false);

    label1.setText("String:");

    label1.setTextAlign(HorizontalAlignment.RIGHT);


    label2.setLocation(new Point(0, 40));

    label2.setSize(new Point(96, 16));

    label2.setTabIndex(0);

    label2.setTabStop(false);

    label2.setText("Escaped string:");

    label2.setTextAlign(HorizontalAlignment.RIGHT);


    edit1.setFont(new Font("Arial Unicode MS", 8.0f, FontSize.POINTS,
FontWeight.NORMAL, false, false, false, CharacterSet.DEFAULT, 0));

    edit1.setLocation(new Point(112, 8));
```

```
      edit1.setSize(new Point(104, 21));

      edit1.setTabIndex(2);

      edit1.setText("");


      edit2.setEnabled(false);

      edit2.setFont(new Font("Arial Unicode MS", 8.0f, FontSize.POINTS,

FontWeight.NORMAL, false, false, false, CharacterSet.DEFAULT, 0));

      edit2.setLocation(new Point(112, 40));

      edit2.setSize(new Point(104, 21));

      edit2.setTabIndex(3);

      edit2.setText("");


      ExitButton.setLocation(new Point(112, 80));

      ExitButton.setSize(new Point(80, 24));

      ExitButton.setTabIndex(4);

      ExitButton.setText("Exit");

      ExitButton.addOnClick(new EventHandler(this.exitClick));


      this.setNewControls(new Control[] {

                    ExitButton,

                    edit2,

                    edit1,

                    label2,

                    label1});

   }

   // End of code generated by J++ IDE


   /**

    * The main entry point for the application.

    *

    * @param args Array of parameters passed to the application

    * via the command line.

    */

   public static void main(String args[])
```

Continued

Listing 11-6 *Continued*

```
{
    Application.run(new demo());
}


}
```

Figure 11-8 shows a screenshot of the form created by the program. Even though the font is specified as "Arial Unicode MS," which is the same font as is used in the Web browser screenshots, the non-ASCII characters display as "?"

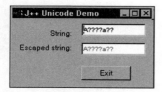

Figure 11-8 *Screen shot of Visual J++ program*

Perl

Perl is a scripting language created by Larry Wall. It is available from http://www.perl.com.

The version of Perl current at the time of this writing is 5.005. It supports UTF-8 characters in strings. The next version — which will be 5.6 due to a change in the numbering scheme — will provide much more support for the Unicode Standard. This section describes the Unicode support implemented in version 5.6 based upon the features of the experimental 5.005_60 release, which was noted as being very close to the 5.6 release.

In both Perl 5.005 and the forthcoming Perl 5.6, the `utf-8` pragma controls whether or not strings are interpreted as UTF-8 characters. The following program statement:

```
use utf8;
```

switches to representing strings as UTF-8 characters for the rest of the enclosing block. The corresponding statement:

```
no utf8;
```

turns off the `utf8` pragma for the rest of the enclosing block. The scoping of the effect of the pragma statement to the enclosing block allows you to use UTF-8 string processing in parts of your program, and ordinary byte-oriented processing in other parts. Of course, including `pragma utf8` at the top level near the beginning of your program enables UTF-8 string processing for the remainder of your program (unless explicitly overridden by a later no `utf8` pragma).

Strings, however, are not annotated with the pragma in effect when they were created or modified. When the `utf8` pragma is in effect, *all* strings are interpreted as UTF-8, and when it is not in effect, *all* strings are interpreted as byte sequences. You have to keep track of whether or not you're using a string as UTF-8 characters or as bytes.

Perl, including version 5.6, does not support reading and writing files as anything other than UTF-8. You cannot, for example, specify a file to be encoded with UTF-16 and read a sequence of UTF-16 characters that are automatically converted into the UTF-8 internal representation. Support for this sort of coercing of input and output encoding is planned for the "near future" but at the time of this writing, it has yet to be specified which version number will be the first to support it.

As of version 5.6, the `utf8` pragma has a number of effects on string functions and regular expressions. In addition, version 5.6 introduces some additions and extensions to regular expression patterns, the `tr///` operator, and the `pack()` and `unpack()` functions.

Table 11-3 shows the new regular expression extensions. Note that the \L, \l, \u, and \U regular expression notations were introduced along with the `locale` pragma in version 5.004, and so are not documented here.

Table 11-3 *Perl Version 5.6 Regular Expression Extensions*

Notation	Description
\x{abcd}	Unicode character U+ABCD. The curly brackets distinguish Unicode character references from hexadecimal numbers. Distinguishing between the two is necessary because the UTF-8 representations of characters are a variable number of bytes and, except for the ASCII characters, are different from the corresponding binary representation of the hexadecimal number. For example, \xa and \x{a} evaluate to 0x61, but \xab and \x{ab} evaluate to the byte value 0xAB and the byte sequence 0xC2AB, respectively. Similarly, \x{abcd} evaluates to 0xEAAF8D, which is the UTF-8 representation of U+ABCD.
	If you use the \xab form when you're running Perl with the -w command line switch and the utf8 pragma, the Perl interpreter warns you that you may be generating invalid UTF-8 characters.
\C	Match a single C (i.e., the C computer language) char, even when the utf8 pragma is in effect.
\pP, \p{Prop}	Match named property P. Use the second form with the curly brackets for longer property names. The property names (e.g., IsDigit, IsM, IsKannada) and the lists of characters with each property are either contained in mktables.pl or generated from a copy of the Unicode Character Database in the Perl sources. At the time of this writing, version 5.005_60 uses the Unicode 2.0 version of the Unicode Character Database, but it can be expected that later versions will use the Unicode 3.0 version of the Unicode Character Database.
	The properties are not all "pure" Unicode, however. For example, the IsXDigit property derives from the POSIX xdigit character class, not from the Unicode Standard.
\PP	Match any characters without named property P.
\X	Matches any sequence of a base character plus any combining characters. It is equivalent to (?:\PM\pM*), which is Perl-speak for a sequence consisting of a non-mark character (one without the Mn or Mc property) followed by zero or more characters with either the Mn or Mc property.
.	When the utf8 pragma is in effect, matches any character, otherwise it matches any byte value.

As noted in Table 11.4, some of the properties specified with the \p and \P notations were derived from the POSIX (IEEE Std 1003.1) standard. However, the utf8 pragma also affects interpretation of some of the POSIX character classes. When the pragma is in effect, several character classes — alpha, alnum, ascii, cntrl, digit, graph, lower, print, punct, space, upper, word, and xdigit — are treated as equivalent to the IsAlpha, etc. named properties, and the alpha, etc. character classes are calculated from the data in the Unicode Character Database.

Other character classes, such as \w, match on characters instead of bytes when the utf8 pragma is in effect, plus the definition of the character classes derives, like the POSIX character classes, from the data in the Unicode Character Database.

The tr/// operator has new U and C options that override the current utf8 state and translate to (or from) UTF-8 and to (or from) 8-bit characters, respectively. They are used in pairs: the first of the pair applies to the left side of the translation, and the second to the right side, as shown in the following code fragment:

```
tr/\0-\xFF//CU;      # change Latin-1 to Unicode
tr/\0-\x{FF}//UC;    # change Unicode to Latin-1
```

Translation functions uc(), ucfirst(), and lc() (and their corresponding backslash sequences) use the Unicode Character Database case mappings when the utf8 pragma is in effect.

The following operators dealing with strings, string position, or string length automatically switch to operating on characters instead of bytes when the utf8 pragma is in effect:

```
chop()
chr()
index()
length()
```

```
ord()
pos()
rindex()
scalar reverse()
sprintf()
substr()
write()
```

The vec(), pack(), and unpack() operators do not change behavior with the change in pragma, but pack() and unpack() have a new U specifier that converts between UTF-8 characters and integers.

Other operators, including chomp(), sort(), and operators dealing with filenames, don't care about the utf8 pragma. The fact that chomp() doesn't change implies that chomp() doesn't chomp U+2028, LINE SEPARATOR, or U+2029, PARAGRAPH SEPARATOR.

Last but not least, identifiers, such as variable names, may contain non-Latin-1 characters, including ideographs. Based on my reading of the Perl source code, it appears that any character with a UnicodeData.txt General Category value of Lu, Ll, Lo, or Nd (plus U+005F, LOW LINE) is acceptable in an identifier.

Listing 11-7 presents a Perl script that demonstrates some of the features of Perl's UTF-8 support. The first part of the program enables the utf8 pragma then initializes three identical strings in three different ways: from a sequence of UTF-8 characters, from a sequence of \x escape sequences, and from a file containing UTF-8 text. Note that the declaration for $cCharacters below looks like gibberish because the UTF-8 characters are being interpreted as a sequence of one-byte characters.

Listing 11-7 *A Perl script that initializes three strings in three forms each*

```
#
# Perl script to demonstrate support for UTF-8 in Perl 5.6
```

```perl
#
# $Id: demo.pl,v 1.2 1999-09-04 21:43:51-04 tkg Exp $


# Use the utf8 pragma so strings are UTF-8
use utf8;


# String containing:
#   - U+0041, LATIN CAPITAL LETTER A
#   - U+0416, CYRILLIC CAPITAL LETTER ZHE
#   - U+5E73, CJK UNIFIED IDEOGRAPH 5E73
#   - U+05D0, HEBREW LETTER ALEF
#   - U+05D1, HEBREW LETTER BET
#   - U+0061, LATIN SMALL LETTER A
#   - U+0333, COMBINING DOUBLE LOW LINE
#   - U+0307, COMBINING DOT ABOVE
#


# String of UTF-8 characters
$cCharacters = "AĐ□$(He9³x□x □(Baȋ³ȋ‡";


# Same string using \x notation
$cEscapedCharacters =
    "\x{41}\x{416}\x{5e73}\x{5d0}\x{5d1}\x{61}\x{333}\x{307}";


# Get the same string from a file
open(UTF8, "utf8.txt");
$gFileCharacters = <UTF8>;
```

The program output is written as an HTML file since, for many people, the easiest way to view UTF-8 text is with their Web browser. The second part of the program, shown in Listing 11-8, outputs the start of the HTML wrapper, including the `<meta>` element specifying the UTF-8 charset. As part of printing the same line-oriented quoted string, the program outputs each of the three strings preceded by an explanation of its source.

Listing 11-8 *Initiating the HTML file output*

```
# Print HTML since viewing UTF-8 in web browser is easy and common.
print<<EndOfHTML;
<html>
<head>
<title>Perl Unicode Demonstration</title>
<meta http-equiv="Content-Type" content="text/html; charset=UTF-8">
</head>
<body bgcolor="#FFFFFF">
<h1>UTF-8 Strings</h1>
<p>UTF-8 string: "$cCharacters"</p>
<p>Escaped characters: "$cEscapedCharacters"</p>
<p>UTF-8 from file: "$gFileCharacters"</p>
EndOfHTML
```

Figure 11-9 shows a screen shot of a portion of the HTML page. The Hebrew characters appear in their correct right-to-left presentation order, and the combining marks appear correctly over and under the a character. This can be attributed to the Web browser doing the right thing, not to any magic on the part of the Perl print statement.

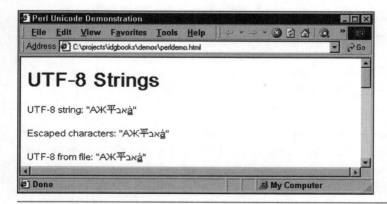

Figure 11-9 *Screen shot of three Perl strings displayed in browser*

To illustrate Perl's support for character properties, Listing 11.9 prints the HTML markup for a table of the characters in the sample string and, for each character, an indication of whether or not it has a handful of properties. The column titles indicate the property being tested. Note that the `InCJKUnifiedIdeographs` property name has been shortened to "InCJK" in the column title. The code for the table cell containing the character from the example outputs a   entity (i.e., non-breaking space) when the character has the `Mn` property. This is because the combining marks were not printing correctly without a previous base character.

Listing 11-9 *An HTML page that evaluates the sample string*

```
# Make a table demonstrating a few of the properties of characters
print "<h1>Character Properties</h1>\n";

print "<table border=\"1\">\n";

# Headrow with label for each column
print "<tr>";
print "<th>Character</th>\n";
print "<th>IsAlpha</th>\n";
print "<th>IsBidiL</th>\n";
print "<th>IsBidiR</th>\n";
print "<th>InHebrew</th>\n";
print "<th>InCyrillic</th>\n";
print "<th>InCJK</th>\n";
print "<th>IsM</th>\n";
print "</tr>\n";

# For each character, if has property, print a check mark, otherwise
# print   so the table cell is rendered
foreach $lChar (split('', $cCharacters)) {
    print "<tr>";
```

Continued

Listing 11-9 *Continued*

```
print "<td>";

# Print a no-break space if $lChar is a non-spacing mark

$lChar =~ m/\p{IsMn}/ ? print " " : print "" ;

print "$lChar</td>\n";

print "<td>";

$lChar =~ m/\p{IsAlpha}/ ? print "\x{2714}" : print " " ;

print "</td>\n";

print "<td>";

$lChar =~ m/\p{IsBidiL}/ ? print "\x{2714}" : print " " ;

print "</td>\n";

print "<td>";

$lChar =~ m/\p{IsBidiR}/ ? print "\x{2714}" : print " " ;

print "</td>\n";

print "<td>";

$lChar =~ m/\p{InHebrew}/ ? print "\x{2714}" : print " " ;

print "</td>\n";

print "<td>";

$lChar =~ m/\p{InCyrillic}/ ? print "\x{2714}" : print " " ;

print "</td>\n";

print "<td>";

$lChar =~ m/\p{InCJKUnifiedIdeographs}/ ?
    print "\x{2714}" : print " " ;

print "</td>\n";

print "<td>";

$lChar =~ m/\p{IsM}/ ? print "\x{2714}" : print " " ;

print "</td>\n";

print "</tr>\n";

}


print "</table>\n";
```

Figure 11-10 shows a screen shot of the resulting table. A check mark (U+2714, HEAVY CHECK MARK) indicates that a character has a specified property.

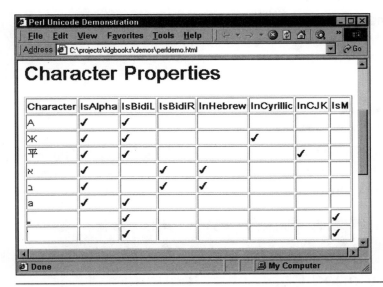

Figure 11-10 *Screen shot of table of sample properties of characters*

The last part of the program in Listing 11-10 illustrates how the \X regular expression notation matches a base character and any following combining characters. The `while` block prints a separate paragraph for each character or character sequence matching the \X regular expression. This portion also prints the closing </body> and </html> tags for the HTML page.

Listing 11-10 *A function that matches extended sequences, followed by the close*

```
# Find the extended character sequences in the string
print "<h1>Extended Character Sequence</h1>\n";


# Match on an extended character sequence
while ($gFileCharacters =~ m/\X/) {
    # Set the string to everything after the match
    $gFileCharacters = $';
```

Continued

Listing 11-10 *Continued*

```
# Print the matched character sequence
print "<p>Extended character sequence: $&</p>\n";

}


# End the HTML page
print "</body>\n</html>\n";
```

Figure 11-11 shows a screen shot of this portion of the page. Note how the a character and its two combining marks matched the single \X pattern.

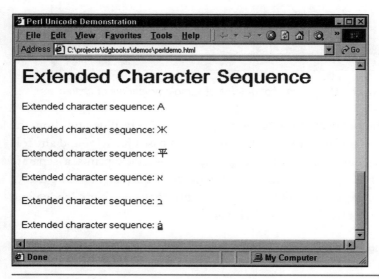

Figure 11-11 *Screen shot of breakdown of extended character sequences in sample string*

Python

Python is a scripting language invented by Guido van Rossum. The version current at the time of this writing is 1.5.2. For information on Python, see http://www.python.org and the comp.lang.python newsgroup.

Python does not currently support the Unicode Standard, but the Python String-SIG Activities page at http://starship.python.net/crew/amk/python/string.html reports of preliminary work on a Unicode type in the Windows port of Python. It also raises the possibility that Python 1.6 will support the Unicode Standard.

Tcl

Tcl is a scripting language invented by John Ousterhout. Its current home is http://www.scriptics.com/. The version current at the time of this writing is 8.2.

Beginning with Tcl/Tk 8.1, Tcl supports the characters of the Unicode Standard. All strings are represented internally as UTF-8. Tcl does not, however, bill itself as an application of the Unicode Standard. UTF-8 support was added under the "internationalization" banner, and the newest versions of Tcl support reading and writing files in a number of encodings, numeric references to Unicode characters in strings and regular expressions, and "message catalogs" for localizing user interfaces (which are beyond the scope of this book).

Tcl scripts and files that you open within a script are interpreted as being in the system encoding—in other words, the one used by the operating system. Tcl attempts to determine the system encoding at startup, and defaults to ISO 8859-1 if it can't work it out. You can, however, read and write files in other encodings using the fconfigure -encoding command, as the following code fragment shows:

```
set file1 [open "utf8.txt" r]
fconfigure $file1 -encoding utf-8
```

In the first line of this example, the file utf8.txt is opened for reading (indicated by the "r"). The open command returns a *channel identifier*, which is assigned to the file1 variable. In the second line, the encoding of the newly opened channel is configured to UTF-8.

Tcl interpreters have built-in recognition for about 30 common encodings, including UTF-8 and "unicode." You can define additional encodings by creating additional .enc encoding files in the encoding directory in your Tcl distribution. The encoding file format is defined in the Tcl_GetEncoding.3 man page, but Tcl's encoding details are beyond the scope of this book. Discovering what encodings are supported by your Tcl interpreter, however, is easy. The following one-line Tcl script prints the supported encodings, one per line, in alphabetical order:

```
puts stdout [join [lsort [encoding names]] "\n"]
```

The "unicode" encoding—at least on my little-endian Pentium processor running Windows 95—correctly interprets UTF-16LE–encoded text, but does not recognize big-endian UTF-16 text, either with or without the BOM, nor does it strip the leading BOM from UTF-16LE with the BOM.

Listing 11-11 presents a script that demonstrates Tcl's Unicode support. For a UTF-8 string internal to the program that designates the Unicode characters with \u*nnnn* escape sequences, and for each of the different encodings of the sample text, this script displays a description of the encoding, the number of characters that the Tcl interpreter counts in the string or file, and the string itself.

Listing 11-11 *A Tcl script that interprets the sample string*

```
#
# Tcl/Tk script to demonstrate support for the Unicode Standard
#
# $Id: demo.tcl,v 1.1 1999-09-03 03:43:09-04 tkg Exp $

# Set the window title
wm title . "Tcl/Tk Unicode Demonstration"

# Make an overall frame
frame .demo -bg white
```

```
# String containing:

#  - U+0041, LATIN CAPITAL LETTER A

#  - U+0416, CYRILLIC CAPITAL LETTER ZHE

#  - U+5E73, CJK UNIFIED IDEOGRAPH 5E73

#  - U+05D0, HEBREW LETTER ALEF

#  - U+05D1, HEBREW LETTER BET

#  - U+0061, LATIN SMALL LETTER A

#  - U+0333, COMBINING DOUBLE LOW LINE

#  - U+0307, COMBINING DOT ABOVE

#

set BuiltIn "\u0041\u0416\u5E73\u05D0\u05D1\u0061\u0333\u0307"


label .demo.builtin -font {"Arial Unicode MS" 18} -bg white \
    -text "Built-in String ([string length $BuiltIn]): $BuiltIn"
pack .demo.builtin -fill x -side top


# Open a UTF-8-encoded file
set file1 [open "utf8.txt" r]
fconfigure $file1 -encoding utf-8
gets $file1 UTF8


label .demo.utf8 -font {"Arial Unicode MS" 18} -bg white \
    -text "UTF-8 ([string length $UTF8]): $UTF8"
pack .demo.utf8 -fill x -side top


# Open UTF-16BE-encoded file
set file1 [open "utf16be.txt" r]
fconfigure $file1 -encoding unicode
gets $file1 UTF16BE


label .demo.utf16be -font {"Arial Unicode MS" 18} -bg white \
    -text "UTF-16BE ([string length $UTF16BE]): $UTF16BE"
pack .demo.utf16be -fill x -side top
```

Continued

Listing 11-11 *Continued*

```
# Open UTF-16BE-BOM-encoded file
set file1 [open "utf16bebom.txt" r]
fconfigure $file1 -encoding unicode
gets $file1 UTF16BEBOM


label .demo.utf16bebom -font {"Arial Unicode MS" 18} -bg white \
    -text "UTF-16BE+BOM ([string length $UTF16BEBOM]): $UTF16BEBOM"
pack .demo.utf16bebom -fill x -side top


# Open UTF-16LE-encoded file
set file1 [open "utf16le.txt" r]
fconfigure $file1 -encoding unicode
gets $file1 UTF16LE


label .demo.utf16le -font {"Arial Unicode MS" 18} -bg white \
    -text "UTF-16LE ([string length $UTF16LE]): $UTF16LE"
pack .demo.utf16le -fill x -side top


# Open UTF-16LE-BOME-encoded file
set file1 [open "utf16lebom.txt" r]
fconfigure $file1 -encoding unicode
gets $file1 UTF16LEBOM


label .demo.utf16lebom -font {"Arial Unicode MS" 18} -bg white \
    -text "UTF-16LE+BOM ([string length $UTF16LEBOM]): $UTF16LEBOM"
pack .demo.utf16lebom -fill x -side top


# Add a button so we can exit gracefully
button .demo.dismiss -text Exit -command "exit"
pack .demo.dismiss -pady 2m


# Pack the entire window
pack .demo
```

The same operation is repeated for each encoding: A file is opened, its encoding is set, and the file contents are read into a variable. Next, a label widget is created to display the encoding name, the number of characters (within parentheses), and then the string itself, and then added to the contents of the displayed .demo window. Figure 11-12 shows the result. Note that only the internal string, the UTF-8–encoded file, and the UTF-16LE file show the correct number of characters. The two encodings with the BOM have the BOM counted along with the other characters, and the two UTF-16–encoded samples are unintelligible because their big-endian code values are being interpreted as little-endian. Note also that the Hebrew characters are not in right-to-left order, but the combining characters are rendered correctly. I think this can be attributed more to the font than to Tcl doing the right thing.

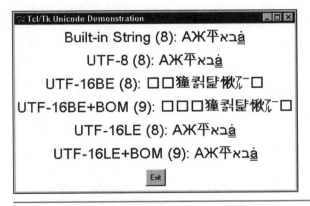

Figure 11-12 *Screen shot of sample Tcl application*

The previous code sample illustrated Unicode characters in strings and in file I/O. You can also use Unicode characters in the new regular expression implementation introduced with Tcl 8.1. You can reference BMP characters with the four-digit escape sequence \u*nnnn*, and reference characters outside the BMP with an eight-digit escape sequence beginning with an uppercase "U": \U*nnnnnnnn*. The new regular expressions also support POSIX character classes, such as

[[:digit:]] or [[:alpha:]]. Interestingly, [[:digit:]] matches only 0–9, but [[:alpha:]] matches non-ASCII alphabetic characters such as å.

The regular expression syntax also includes "collating symbols" and "equivalence classes" for improved collation of text. The current Tcl version, however, only supports single-character collating symbol, and does not support equivalence classes at all.

Visual Basic

"Visual Basic" is both the name of the Visual Basic programming language — which is a highly evolved form of the BASIC programming language — and the name of the Visual Basic development environment, which is part of Microsoft's Visual Studio development suite. The versions current at the time of this writing are both 6.0. See http://msdn.microsoft.com/vstudio/.

Visual Basic represents strings as Unicode characters, but under American Windows 95, the development environment only supports characters in the default 8-bit code page. The language includes these functions: AscW(), which returns a character's code value; ChrW(), which returns a string containing the character for a specified character number; and StrConv(), which, in part, converts strings between "Unicode" encoding and the default code page of the system. Visual Basic programs can read and write "Unicode" text using the same "Scripting Run-Time Library" as JScript and VBScript.

Listing 11-12 presents a combination listing for a Visual Basic "form" (dialog box) plus the source code pertaining to the form and its constituent objects. This code demonstrates the support for the characters of the Unicode Standard that is implemented in Visual Basic 6.0. The form listed here contains two text boxes and an MSFlexGrid control. The contents of the two text boxes is the familiar sample string initialized from a Visual Basic string and from the concatenation of a sequence of numeric character references that were turned into one-character strings using the ChrW() intrinsic function. The catch is that you cannot represent non-Latin characters — such as the Hebrew and ideograph characters in the example — in the American version of the Visual Basic programming environment running on Windows 95, so the "string" is represented as A????a??, where ? represents a character that the programming environment can't display.

Listing 11-12 *Visual Basic form listing and source code testing the sample string*

```
VERSION 5.00

Object = "{5E9E78A0-531B-11CF-91F6-C2863C385E30}#1.0#0"; "MSFLXGRD.OCX"

Begin VB.Form OutputForm

    Caption         =  "Visual Basic Unicode Demonstration"

    ClientHeight    =  4290

    ClientLeft      =  60

    ClientTop       =  345

    ClientWidth     =  4275

    BeginProperty Font

        Name          =  "Arial Unicode MS"

        Size          =  8.25

        Charset       =  0

        Weight        =  400

        Underline     =  0    'False

        Italic        =  0    'False

        Strikethrough =  0    'False

    EndProperty

    LinkTopic       =  "Form1"

    ScaleHeight     =  4290

    ScaleWidth      =  4275

    StartUpPosition =  3    'Windows Default

    Begin MSFlexGridLib.MSFlexGrid CharacterGrid

        Height        =  2535

        Left          =  1560
```

Continued

Listing 11-12 *Continued*

```
    TabIndex        =   6

    Top             =   1080

    Width           =   2295

    _ExtentX        =   4048

    _ExtentY        =   4471

    _Version        =   393216

    Rows            =   9

    FixedCols       =   0

    Enabled         =   0      'False

    ScrollBars      =   0

    AllowUserResizing=  1
End

Begin VB.TextBox EscapedText

    Enabled         =   0      'False

    Height          =   330

    Left            =   1560

    Locked          =   -1     'True

    TabIndex        =   4

    Top             =   442

    Width           =   2295
End

Begin VB.TextBox StringText

    Enabled         =   0      'False

    Height          =   330

    Left            =   1560

    Locked          =   -1     'True

    TabIndex        =   2

    Top             =   82

    Width           =   2295
End

Begin VB.CommandButton ExitButton

    Caption         =   "Exit"

    Height          =   375
```

```
    Left            =   1560

    TabIndex        =   1

    Top             =   3840

    Width           =   1335

End

Begin VB.Label CharacterGridLabel

    Alignment       =   1  'Right Justify

    Caption         =   "Character info"

    Height          =   255

    Left            =   120

    TabIndex        =   5

    Top             =   1080

    Width           =   1215

End

Begin VB.Label EscapedStringLabel

    Alignment       =   1  'Right Justify

    Caption         =   "Escaped String:"

    Height          =   255

    Left            =   120

    TabIndex        =   3

    Top             =   480

    Width           =   1215

End

Begin VB.Label StringLabel

    Alignment       =   1  'Right Justify

    Caption         =   "String:"

    Height          =   255

    Left            =   120

    TabIndex        =   0

    Top             =   120

    Width           =   1215

    End

End

Attribute VB_Name = "OutputForm"
```

Continued

Listing 11-12 *Continued*

```
Attribute VB_GlobalNameSpace = False

Attribute VB_Creatable = False

Attribute VB_PredeclaredId = True

Attribute VB_Exposed = False

' Sample string contains:

'   - U+0041, LATIN CAPITAL LETTER A

'   - U+0416, CYRILLIC CAPITAL LETTER ZHE

'   - U+5E73, CJK UNIFIED IDEOGRAPH 5E73

'   - U+05D0, HEBREW LETTER ALEF

'   - U+05D1, HEBREW LETTER BET

'   - U+0061, LATIN SMALL LETTER A

'   - U+0333, COMBINING DOUBLE LOW LINE

'   - U+0307, COMBINING DOT ABOVE

'

' Sample string as UTF-8 text

Private CharacterString As String

' Sample string constructed from code values

Private EscapedString


Private Sub ExitButton_Click()

    Unload OutputForm

    End                     ' Ends application.

End Sub


Private Sub Form_Initialize()

    ' Constants used when opening files

    ForReading = 1

    ForWriting = 2

    ' Used to indicate "Open as Unicode"

    TristateTrue = -1

    ' The file system

    Set FileSys = CreateObject("Scripting.FileSystemObject")

    ' Object to use and re-use as input text stream
```

```
Dim File
' Our sample string made from numeric references
EscapedString = ChrW(&H41) & ChrW(&H416) & ChrW(&H5E73) & ChrW(&H5D0) _
    & ChrW(&H5D1) & ChrW(&H61) & ChrW(&H333) & ChrW(&H307)


' We can't insert UTF-8 text into a VB file!
StringText.Text = "A????a??"
EscapedText.Text = EscapedString


' Set up the grid that will show the "characters" and their hex values
CharacterGrid.Row = 0
CharacterGrid.Col = 0
CharacterGrid.Text = "Character"
CharacterGrid.Col = 1
CharacterGrid.Text = "Value (Hex)"


' For each character in EscapedString, add its data to the grid
For i = 1 To Len(EscapedString)
    Char = Mid(EscapedString, i, 1)
    CharacterGrid.Row = i
    CharacterGrid.Col = 0

    CharacterGrid.Text = Char
    CharacterGrid.Col = 1
    CharacterGrid.Text = Hex(AscW(Char))
Next


' We've finished with the visual stuff
' Write a HTML file using what we find in the sample text files


' Create the output file and output the initial tags
Set VBOut = FileSys.CreateTextFile("vbout.html", True, True)
VBOut.write ("<html>" & vbCrLf)
VBOut.write ("<head>" & vbCrLf)
```

Continued

Listing 11-12 *Continued*

```
VBOut.write ("<title>Visual Basic Unicode Demonstration</title>" & vbCrLf)

VBOut.write ("<!-- Rely on Visual Basic to use UTF-16 for 'Unicode' files so
don't set encoding-->" & vbCrLf)

VBOut.write ("</head>" & vbCrLf)

VBOut.write ("<body bgcolor='#FFFFFF' style='font-size: 24pt'>")


' For each of the sample files, check if it exists, open it, and add its
contents to the output


' UTF-8
If FileSys.FileExists("utf8.txt") Then
    Set File = FileSys.OpenTextFile( _
        "utf8.txt", _
        ForReading, False, TristateTrue)
    VBOut.write ("<p>UTF-8: '" + File.ReadAll() + "'</p>")
    File.Close
End If


' UTF-16LE
If FileSys.FileExists("utf16le.txt") Then
    Set File = FileSys.OpenTextFile( _
        "utf16le.txt", _
        ForReading, False, TristateTrue)
    VBOut.write ("<p>UTF-16LE: '" + File.ReadAll() + "'</p>")
    File.Close
End If


' UTF16-LE+BOM (Little-endian UTF-16)
If FileSys.FileExists("utf16lebom.txt") Then
    Set File = FileSys.OpenTextFile( _
        "utf16lebom.txt", _
```

```
        ForReading, False, TristateTrue)

        VBOut.write ("<p>UTF-16LE+BOM: '" + File.ReadAll() + "'</p>")

        File.Close

    End If


    ' UTF-16BE

    If FileSys.FileExists("utf16be.txt") Then

        Set File = FileSys.OpenTextFile( _

            "utf16be.txt", _

            ForReading, False, TristateTrue)

        VBOut.write ("<p>UTF-16BE: '" + File.ReadAll() + "'</p>")

        File.Close

    End If


    ' UTF-16BE+BOM (Big-endian UTF-16)

    If FileSys.FileExists("utf16bebom.txt") Then

        Set File = FileSys.OpenTextFile( _

            "utf16bebom.txt", _

            ForReading, False, TristateTrue)

        VBOut.write ("<p>UTF-16BE+BOM: '" + File.ReadAll() + "'</p>")

        File.Close

    End If


    ' Output the end tags for open HTML elements, then close output file

    VBOut.write ("</body>" & vbCrLf)

    VBOut.write ("</html>")

    VBOut.Close

End Sub
```

The two-column grid produced by the MSFlexGrid control is populated with the characters in the sample string and their hexadecimal code values.

The program also reads the sample text files in each of the sample encodings and, like other sample programs, writes an HTML file containing the text from each of the sample files.

Figure 11-13 shows a screen shot of the form created by the program. Even though the font is specified as Arial Unicode MS, the non-ASCII characters only appear as ? characters.

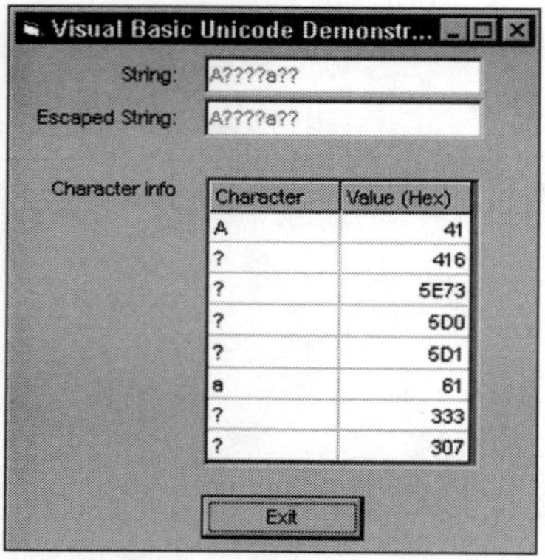

Figure 11-13 *Screen shot of Visual Basic form*

Figure 11-14 shows a screen shot of the vbout.html HTML file written from the Visual Basic program. Although the form couldn't correctly display non-ASCII characters, the HTML file shows that the Unicode characters were being handled correctly by the program, at least for the encodings that the program would interpret as "Unicode." The program, like the JScript and VBScript programs, could correctly interpret files in UTF-16 (both big-endian and little-endian) and UTF-16LE. This is not surprising for a program running on a little-endian processor like the Pentium. The UTF-8 and UTF-16BE files, however, came out as gibberish.

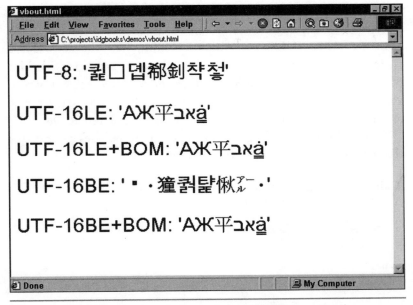

Figure 11-14 *Screen shot of* `vbout.html` *HTML file written from Visual Basic program*

VBScript

VBScript—more properly "Microsoft Visual Basic Scripting Edition"—is a subset of Visual Basic implemented as a scripting language interpreter, in contrast to Visual Basic, where programs may be compiled into stand-alone executables. VBScript 1.0 was introduced with Microsoft's Internet Explorer 3.0. The version current at the time of this writing is 5.0, and it is implemented in Internet Explorer 5.0 and Microsoft Internet Information Server 5.0. With the release of the Windows Script Host, you can also run VBScript programs as stand-alone programs on your computer. For more information on VBScript and related technologies, see `http://msdn.microsoft.com/scripting/`.

VBScript uses the same "Scripting Run-Time Library" as
Microsoft's JScript (covered earlier with ECMAScript), so it has the
same file I/O capabilities as JScript, including the ability to read and
write text files as "Unicode" text. The only other functions that hint
of support for the Unicode Standard are chrW() and ascW(), which
are the "wide" forms of the chr() and asc() functions that return a
character given its character number and vice versa, respectively.

Listing 11-13 presents HTML markup that includes a <script>
element containing a VBScript program.

Listing 11-13 *VBScript code embedded in an HTML page,
using the sample string*

```
<!-- Demonstrate some VBScript features -->
<!-- $Id: vbscript1.html,v 1.2 1999-09-06 20:17:27-04 tkg Exp $ -->
<html>
<head>
<title>VBScript Unicode Demonstration</title>
<meta http-equiv="Content-Type" content="text/html; charset=UTF-8">
</head>
<body bgcolor="#FFFFFF">
<script language="VBScript">
<!--
Dim String, EscapedString
' Sample string contains:
'   - U+0041, LATIN CAPITAL LETTER A
'   - U+0416, CYRILLIC CAPITAL LETTER ZHE
'   - U+5E73, CJK UNIFIED IDEOGRAPH 5E73
'   - U+05D0, HEBREW LETTER ALEF
'   - U+05D1, HEBREW LETTER BET
'   - U+0061, LATIN SMALL LETTER A
'   - U+0333, COMBINING DOUBLE LOW LINE
'   - U+0307, COMBINING DOT ABOVE
'
' Sample string as UTF-8 text
String = "AÐ$(He9³x□³'(Baï³Ì‡"
```

```
' Sample string constructed from code values
EscapedString = chrW(&H0041) & chrW(&H0416) & chrW(&H5e73) & chrW(&H05d0) _
        & chrW(&H05d1) & chrW(&H0061) & chrW(&H0333) & chrW(&H0307)


document.write("<body style='font-size: 16pt'>")
' Write out the strings
document.write("<p>String: '" & String & "'</p>")
document.write("<p>EscapedString: '" & EscapedString & "'</p>")


' Make a table showing each character and its character number
' found using AscW.
document.write("<table style='font-size: 16pt' border='1'>")
For pos = 1 to len(String)
        char = mid(String, pos, 1)
        document.write("<tr align='right'><td>" & char & "</td><td>" _
                & Hex(AscW(char)) & "</td></tr>")
Next
document.write("</table>")


document.write("</body>")
-->
</script>
</body>
</html>
```

The first part of the program declares and initializes two variables. The `String` variable is assigned to our familiar character sequence, which is expressed as a string of UTF-8 characters. The `EscapedString` variable is assigned the same value expressed as the concatenation of the results of multiple `chrW()` functions, one for each character in our string. The `&H` prefix on the character numbers indicates that they are in hexadecimal. The second part of the program writes the two strings (and some HTML markup) to the browser window so we can verify that the assignments worked. The last part of the program writes to the browser window a table of the characters in String and their character numbers returned by chrW(). The Hex() function converts the decimal number returned by chrW() into hexadecimal. Note that the table cells are right-aligned so that the combining marks appear correctly. Figure 11-15 shows a screen shot of the output of the VBScript program.

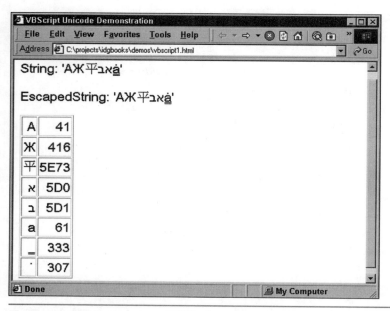

Figure 11-15 *Screen shot of VBScript program output*

Listing 11-14 shows HTML markup that contains a VBScript program that reads and displays the sample files in each encoding. Since VBScript and JScript share the same file I/O library, this example is the same as the previous JScript file I/O example, except that it is expressed in VBScript syntax. Figure 11-16 shows the results. Not surprisingly, these results are also the same as with JScript: the UTF-16 encoded files (i.e., those with the BOM) and the UTF-16LE encoded file (which matches the endianness of the processor) were interpreted correctly. The other encodings produced unintelligible results.

Listing 11-14 *A reiteration of the JScript example in VBScript*

```
<!-- Demonstrate Microsoft's VBScript file I/O -->

<!-- $Id: vbscript2.html,v 1.1 1999-09-06 20:30:50-04 tkg Exp $ -->

<html>

<head>

<title>VBScript File Handling Demonstration</title>

<meta http-equiv="Content-Type" content="text/html; charset=UTF-8">

</head>

<body bgcolor="#FFFFFF">

<script language="VBScript">

<!--

dim String, ForReading, ForWriting, TristateTrue

' Sample string contains:

'    - U+0041, LATIN CAPITAL LETTER A

'    - U+0416, CYRILLIC CAPITAL LETTER ZHE

'    - U+5E73, CJK UNIFIED IDEOGRAPH 5E73

'    - U+05D0, HEBREW LETTER ALEF

'    - U+05D1, HEBREW LETTER BET

'    - U+0061, LATIN SMALL LETTER A

'    - U+0333, COMBINING DOUBLE LOW LINE

'    - U+0307, COMBINING DOT ABOVE

'

' Sample string as UTF-8 text

String = "AÐ□$(He9³x□x □(BaÌ³Ì‡"

ForReading = 1

ForWriting = 2

TristateTrue = -1

Set FileSystem = CreateObject("Scripting.FileSystemObject")

dim File


document.write("<body style='font-size: 24pt'>")

Set File = FileSystem.OpenTextFile( _

        "c:\projects\idgbooks\demos\utf8.txt", _
```

Continued

Listing 11-14 *Continued*

```
        ForReading, false, TristateTrue)
document.write("<p>UTF-8: '" + File.ReadAll() + "'</p>")
File.Close()


Set File = FileSystem.OpenTextFile( _
        "c:\projects\idgbooks\demos\utf16le.txt", _
        ForReading, false, TristateTrue)
document.write("<p>UTF-16LE: '" + File.ReadAll() + "'</p>")
File.Close()


Set File = FileSystem.OpenTextFile( _
        "c:\projects\idgbooks\demos\utf16lebom.txt", _
        ForReading, false, TristateTrue)
document.write("<p>UTF-16LE+BOM: '" + File.ReadAll() + "'</p>")
File.Close()


Set File = FileSystem.OpenTextFile( _
        "c:\projects\idgbooks\demos\utf16be.txt", _
        ForReading, false, TristateTrue)
document.write("<p>UTF-16BE: '" + File.ReadAll() + "'</p>")
File.Close()


Set File = FileSystem.OpenTextFile( _
        "c:\projects\idgbooks\demos\utf16bebom.txt", _
        ForReading, false, TristateTrue)
document.write("<p>UTF-16BE+BOM: '" + File.ReadAll() + "'</p>")
File.Close()


Set File = FileSystem.OpenTextFile( _
        "c:\projects\idgbooks\demos\vbscriptout.html", _
        ForWriting, true, TristateTrue)
File.writeline(String)
File.Close()
-->
```

```
</script>
</body>
</html>
```

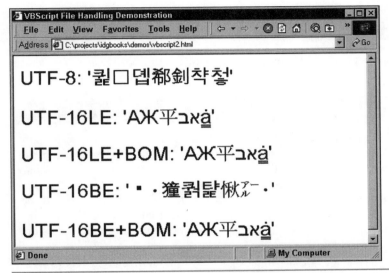

Figure 11-16 *Screen shot of results of VBScript file I/O demonstration*

The last portion of the VBScript program in Listing 11.14 wrote the sample string to a file as "Unicode" text (specified by the `TristateTrue` value of the fourth parameter to `OpenTextFile()`). As the following hexadecimal dump of `vbscriptout.html` shows, the "Unicode" text is big-endian UTF-16 (i.e. UTF-16BE with the BOM).

```
bash.exe-2.02$ od -h vbscriptout.html
0000000 feff 0041 0416 5e73 05d0 05d1 0061 0333
0000020 0307 000d 000a
0000026
```

Figure 11-17 shows `vbscriptout.html` opened in a Web browser; the browser correctly determines the encoding based on the presence of the BOM.

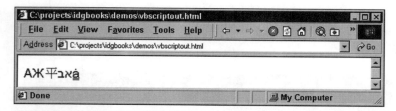

Figure 11-17 *HTML page* `vbscriptout.html` *opened in a Web browser*

Database Support

There is growing support for databases that handle Unicode data. As an indication of the level of interest, both Oracle and Sybase are full members of the Unicode Consortium, and both have been full or associate members for the last several years. For the purposes of this primer, there are a few things to consider when using Unicode with a database. Perhaps most importantly, there is the matter of how the database manager encodes its data. Consider the following:

- For a database manager to simply state that it "supports Unicode" does not tell you everything you need to know. As you well know, there are multiple encodings for the Unicode Standard: UTF-8, UTF-16, UTF-16BE, UTF-16LE, UTF-32, and also UTF-EBCDIC on some systems. You need to find a match between the Unicode encoding that you want to use and the Unicode encodings supported by your database.

- When you have UTF-16 data, drop the BOM from the data – and know that you've dropped the BOM – to save two bytes per field, not just per record.

- When you convert an existing database to Unicode, you need to know the encoding of the original data.

- Database vendors typically provide conversion utilities to convert an existing database to Unicode.

- The Unicode Consortium's byline is, "When the world wants to talk, it speaks Unicode;" when database vendors want to talk Unicode, they most commonly speak UTF-8.

When you're administering a network application whose DBMS ("back end") supports Unicode – or at least claims to – you should make certain you do the following:

- Ensure that your database client supports the input methods required to enter your data into the database.

- Similarly, ensure that your clients support the font or fonts necessary to display the data. If the client only supports a single font at a time, you'll need one of the comprehensive Unicode fonts described in the next chapter.

- You should also check that the client has the level of support that you need for right-to-left scripts, Indic scripts, etc.

- You may need to use a special Unicode-enabled application to access your Unicode database.

- The Unicode-enabled application may not support all of the features of the plain English version of the same application.

The programming languages featured in this chapter demonstrate a variety of levels of support for the Unicode Standard. This ranges from C and C++ — which provide a data type for wide characters that you can use but probably don't want to — to Java and Perl — which support Unicode characters in strings and also provide methods for testing the properties of Unicode characters.

One factor to consider is whether and how well a language supports the inclusion of Unicode characters in a program or script. Only some of the languages shown here allow non-ASCII characters in programs or scripts, and of those, some only allow Unicode characters in strings or, possibly, in comments. However, all of the languages provide a mechanism for referencing a Unicode character by its code value, but the languages vary in the verbosity and readability of strings made up of numeric character references.

The languages also differ in what they consider to be a "Unicode" encoding. Table 11-4 shows which encodings each programming language will read or write as "Unicode." Note that C and C++ can read and write all listed encodings because their standard libraries provide functions for reading and writing files, but you (or your third-party library) have to take care of the details of the character encoding. DSSSL is listed as reading all encodings but writing none because a DSSSL engine passes its "flow object tree" to a backend formatter, and the mechanics of the engine-to-formatter transfer isn't detailed by the DSSSL standard. JScript is listed instead of ECMAScript because ECMAScript does not define any I/O functions and the JScript implementation of ECMAScript was featured in this chapter. The results for JScript, Visual Basic, and VBScript are identical because they all use the same I/O library.

Table 11-4 *Unicode Encodings Read and Written by Programming Languages*

Programming language	UTF-8	UTF-16LE	UTF-16LE + BOM	UTF-16BE	UTF-16BE + BOM
C/C++	R/W	R/W	R/W	R/W	R/W
DSSSL	R/–	R/–	R/–	R/–	R/–
Java	R/W	–/–	R/–	–/–	R/W
JScript	–/–	R/–	R/–	–/–	R/W
Perl	R/W	–/–	–/–	–/–	–/–
Tcl	R/W	R/W	–/–	–/–	–/–
Visual Basic	–/–	R/–	R/–	–/–	R/W
VBScript	–/–	R/–	R/–	–/–	R/W

As the table shows, there is no single encoding supported by all programming languages. However, if you're prepared to do all the work yourself, you can write the required I/O routines using any of these languages. When you want to take advantage of the Unicode encoding support built into these languages, the factors to consider are your familiarity with a particular language, the level of Unicode support that you need from a programming language, and whether or not a language can read and write the same character encoding as your other tools.

Chapter 12

Unicode and Fonts

This chapter discusses details of displaying Unicode text. In particular, it describes fonts and techniques for managing fonts designed for use with Unicode text. Techniques and technologies like those described here are useful for optimal viewing or printing of Unicode text, but, it should be emphasized, they are not prerequisites for viewing plain text.

Displaying text is often both the first and the last requirement of a software system. When you type your text into the computer, you want to see what you are entering as you are type it. When your data is processed, your database report is run, or (oh, happy day) your book is finally printed, you want to see the result on the screen or on the page. Using Unicode for your text doesn't change that page's appearance — at least it shouldn't. But it may make the process of rendering that page harder, although any inconvenience due to increasing complexity is offset by the increase in the range of characters that you can potentially use.

The most obvious, but not the most important, requirement when developing an application that displays Unicode text is finding a font that covers all of the characters in the Unicode Standard. Pan-Unicode fonts — described in the third section that follows — are fonts covering large portions of the Unicode character repertoire. Large fonts like these are useful, but usually only as a fallback, since a single font covering many scripts and many languages has to compromise among multiple type styles. This is contrary to the more important requirement that fonts reflect the typographic conventions of the language or script being displayed or printed.

Handling Typographic Conventions

Different languages have different typographic conventions. High-quality font handling for a given language takes into account the conventions for shaping a character's glyph, the range of type styles used within the language, and the necessity for different glyphs based on a character's context.

The most obvious and overworked example of language-dependent glyphs concerns the differences between Chinese, Japanese, and Korean ideographs, although it is seldom mentioned anywhere that the styles of the glyphs for Chinese, Japanese, and Korean punctuation characters differ. Figure 12-1 shows the ideographic full stop and comma characters from sample Simplified Chinese, Traditional Chinese, Japanese, and Korean fonts. Even for these simple characters, the size and position of the glyphs vary with the script. Note that punctuation characters like these can also be written vertically, requiring a second set of glyphs (or different font metrics) for the same encoded characters.

Glyph variations are not restricted to Asian languages, no matter how much I or anyone else may make it seem so. It is widely acknowledged that different European languages have different typographic conventions for their accented characters, and the description of the Combining Diacritical Marks block in Section 7.9 of the Unicode Standard, Version 3.0, lists some of the variations. For example, font.org (http://www.font.org/) has an article on Polish diacritics detailing the differences between Polish typography and the accepted conventions for "European" characters.

Figure 12-2, reproduced from the font.org article, shows the difference between a conventional acute accent and the Polish *kreska* (stroke).

Different languages use different glyphs for the same character, but within a single language, there are usually several common type styles for what, in Unicode, is a single character. High-quality typesetting of English, for example, uses monospaced, proportionally spaced, and old-style variants of the numbers 0–9, small capitals versions of letters A–Z, and numerous variants of the humble dash character (-).

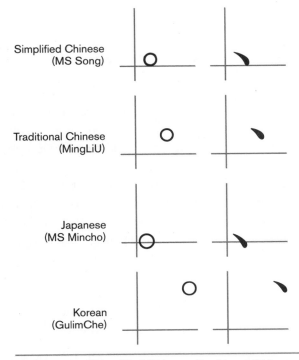

Figure 12-1 *Simplified Chinese, Traditional Chinese, Japanese, and Korean ideographic full stop and comma characters*

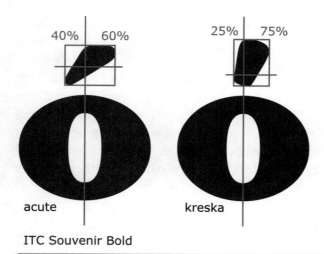

acute   kreska

ITC Souvenir Bold

Figure 12-2 *Comparison of acute accent and Polish* kreska

A singe font for some scripts — such as Mongolian, Tibetan, and the Indic scripts such as Devanagari and Tamil — requires more glyph variants for everyday typesetting than are used for all glyph permutations in the finest English-language typesetting. For example, Mongolian can routinely use ten glyph variants for a single character, and scripts such as Devanagari use dependent and independent vowel form glyphs, half-consonant form glyphs, and ligature glyphs. Tamil goes beyond Devanagari's level of difficulty since it adds vowel splitting and reordering plus ligating vowel signs. There are good reasons why the Unicode Standard emphasizes that "in a font capable of rendering Tamil, the set of glyphs is greater than the number of Tamil characters."

Ideally, then, a font should support language-specific glyphs, stylistic variants of glyphs, and contextual glyph variants.

Font Techniques

There are several ways to solve some or all of the requirements outlined above, including:

- *Modular fonts*, such as WorldType by Monotype. When you make such a font, you individually choose the font module — and therefore the glyph style — for each script or character block.

- *Font subsetting*, such as those used in the Solaris operating environment. Here, you configure your software to use available fonts as if they were part of a larger Unicode font.

- *Fonts and/or software* that chooses among available glyphs in available fonts based on the locale or the indicated language.

- *Monolithic pan-Unicode fonts*, such as those described in the following section.

The following segments provide more detail about some of the more prominent font technologies in current use. Note that some of these technologies rely on the ability of a display engine — such as Apple's ATSUI, Microsoft's Uniscribe, or the Solaris layout engine — to use the information provided in a font.

OpenType

Adobe and Microsoft are jointly developing the OpenType font format as the next generation of the TrueType font format. The OpenType format supports:

- Mapping between characters and glyphs, including ligatures, positional forms, alternates, and other substitutions

- Two-dimensional positioning and glyph attachment

- Language and script indication

Apple Advanced Typography

Apple Advanced Typography (AAT), in combination with the ATSUI display engine, supports comparable features to OpenType, including arbitrary or automatic ligature generation, or *overriding*.

Solaris

The Solaris layout engine performs three types of mapping from characters to glyphs:

- For European scripts, the layout engine maps each character code to a single glyph
- For Arabic, Hebrew, and Thai, the layout engine performs right-to-left swapping and selects glyphs by a character's context
- For East Asian scripts, it maps character codes to glyphs based on the locale-specific font map

The layout engine builds font sets from 15 separate fonts that cover European, Greek, Cyrillic, Turkish, Simplified Chinese, Traditional Chinese, Japanese, Korean, Arabic and Hebrew character sets. For example, Listing 12-1 shows a sample font set definition. Notice the variety of character sets in the last field in each line.

Listing 12-1 *Sample Solaris font set definition*

```
fs = XCreateFontSet(display,
"-dt-interface system-medium-r-normal-s*utf*-*-*-*-*-*-*-*-iso8859-1,
-dt-interface system-medium-r-normal-s*utf*-*-*-*-*-*-*-*-iso8859-2,
-dt-interface system-medium-r-normal-s*utf*-*-*-*-*-*-*-*-iso8859-4,
-dt-interface system-medium-r-normal-s*utf*-*-*-*-*-*-*-*-iso8859-5,
-dt-interface system-medium-r-normal-s*utf*-*-*-*-*-*-*-*-iso8859-6,
-dt-interface system-medium-r-normal-s*utf*-*-*-*-*-*-*-*-iso8859-7,
-dt-interface system-medium-r-normal-s*utf*-*-*-*-*-*-*-*-iso8859-8,
-dt-interface system-medium-r-normal-s*utf*-*-*-*-*-*-*-*-iso8859-9,
-dt-interface system-medium-r-normal-s*utf*-*-*-*-*-*-*-*-iso8859-15,
```

```
-dt-interface system-medium-r-normal-s*utf*-*-*-*-*-*-*-big5-1,

-dt-interface system-medium-r-normal-s*utf*-*-*-*-*-*-*-gb2312.1980-0,

-dt-interface system-medium-r-normal-s*utf*-*-*-*-*-*-*-jisx0201.1976-0,

-dt-interface system-medium-r-normal-s*utf*-*-*-*-*-*-*-jisx0208.1983-0,

-dt-interface system-medium-r-normal-s*utf*-*-*-*-*-*-*-ksc5601.1992-3,

-dt-interface system-medium-r-normal-s*utf*-*-*-*-*-*-*-tis620.2533-0",

&missing_ptr, &missing_count, &def_string);
```

Java AWT

Java's Abstract Windowing Toolkit (AWT) also supports composite fonts. Very simply, each locale has a font.properties file that contains the definition of the fonts to use for each variant of each font family name that Java will use at a given time. The example in Listing 12-2 shows the font properties definition for Java's sanserif font on Windows. The base font and bold, italic, and bolditalic variants are shown in the listing. When Java has a character to display in the sanserif font, it searches the font named as sanserif.0; if sanserif.0 does not contain the character, Java searches sanserif.1, and so on. In this case, the sanserif.0 font that is searched first is Arial. The second and possibly third parameters on each line tell Java how to translate between Unicode and the encoding of glyphs in the font.

Listing 12-2 *Sample Java font properties definition*
```
sansserif.0=Arial,ANSI_CHARSET
sansserif.1=WingDings,SYMBOL_CHARSET,NEED_CONVERTED
sansserif.2=Symbol,SYMBOL_CHARSET,NEED_CONVERTED

sansserif.bold.0=Arial Bold,ANSI_CHARSET
sansserif.bold.1=WingDings,SYMBOL_CHARSET,NEED_CONVERTED
sansserif.bold.2=Symbol,SYMBOL_CHARSET,NEED_CONVERTED

sansserif.italic.0=Arial Italic,ANSI_CHARSET
```

Continued

Listing 12-2 *Continued*

```
sansserif.italic.1=WingDings,SYMBOL_CHARSET,NEED_CONVERTED
sansserif.italic.2=Symbol,SYMBOL_CHARSET,NEED_CONVERTED

sansserif.bolditalic.0=Arial Bold Italic,ANSI_CHARSET
sansserif.bolditalic.1=WingDings,SYMBOL_CHARSET,NEED_CONVERTED
sansserif.bolditalic.2=Symbol,SYMBOL_CHARSET,NEED_CONVERTED
```

Wide-Coverage Fonts

Several available fonts cover large portions of the Unicode character repertoire. As noted above, large monolithic fonts make a useful, but not always aesthetic, backup. You can use one of these fonts as the sole typeface provided for an application. Alternately, when your system supports font subsetting, you can use a pan-Unicode font as the last alternative when none of the language-specific fonts matches a character. However, for low resolution displays where the finer details will be lost anyway, a single wide-coverage font may be all that you need.

Wide-coverage Unicode fonts are *big*! For example, the file for Arial Unicode MS — which includes glyphs for all of the characters in Unicode 2.1 — is 23MB. These fonts take up a lot of system resources and can slow down your machine. When I was developing the examples for Chapter 11, I used two large Unicode fonts with my Web browser — one for proportionally spaced text and the other for monospaced text. The load on my system wasn't bad when I was simply viewing the examples — which involved only a handful of characters — but when I viewed a Web page with a lot of text, scrolling became a real chore.

Wide-coverage Unicode fonts also typically include glyphs for thousands of characters that you will never use and that, if you did view them, you probably could not read. More than half of the characters in Unicode 3.0 are Han ideographs, and much of the rest are Hangul syllables. If the extra glyphs in your pan-Unicode font are ones that you can't read, you are loading your system for no good purpose.

Note

The utility of showing a character that you can't read compared to showing, for example, a black box for an unsupported character, is sometimes debated on the Unicode mailing list. An alternative is to show a generic glyph indicating the *type* of the character; for example, a glyph indicating the character's block within the standard. Apple, for example, ships a *Last Resort* font with its operating system (see `http://fonts.apple.com/LastResort/LastResort.html`).

There are only a handful of wide-coverage Unicode fonts available at the time of this writing. Few fonts implement all of Unicode 2.1, and I have yet to see any that support all of Unicode 3.0. The only support that I have seen for the scripts currently proposed for inclusion in the Unicode Standard was on T-shirts at the 15th Unicode conference.

Not every font with "Unicode" in its name has wide coverage of the repertoire. For example, the "DynaFont Premium 85 Pack" CD contains 85 "Japanese" fonts plus 10 "Unicode" fonts. The "Japanese" fonts can represent the characters in the Shift-JIS encoding of the characters in JIS X 0208:1997. The "Unicode" fonts can represent both the characters in JIS X 0208:1997 and the additional 5,801 kanji in JIS X 0212-1990 for which there is no room in the Shift-JIS encoding. Both font types represent standardized Japanese character repertoires (using Japanese-style glyphs), so the "Unicode" fonts earn their name from their encoding, not their coverage.

Table 12-1 shows some of the TrueType Unicode fonts that are available at the time of this writing. Alan Wood actively maintains a list of Unicode fonts, including those that cover only subsets of the repertoire, at `http://www.hclrss.demon.co.uk/unicode/fonts.html`.

Table 12-1 *TrueType Pan-Unicode Fonts*

Font	Description
Bitstream Cyberbit	An OEM font that was initially available as a free download. See `http://www.bitstream.com/products/world/custom/`, and for the current status of Cyberbit, `http://www.bitstream.com/news/press/1997/pr-mar10.html`.
Monotype WorldType	A modular font system available as an OEM font. Depending on the modules chosen, a WorldType font can include glyphs for a greater or lesser portion of the Unicode repertoire. The modular design allows a choice of font styles for different portions of the repertoire. See `http://www.monotype.com/`.
Arial Unicode MS	A font distributed with Microsoft Office 2000 that covers all of Unicode 2.1.
Lucida Sans Unicode	A font initially distributed with Windows NT 3.5. An upgraded version is said to ship with the Java JDK.
DynaLab Unicode font	A font covering 37,506 characters from Unicode 2.0 blocks. Includes Latin, Greek, Cyrillic, Hebrew, Arabic, Thai, and Hangul characters plus 20,902 Han ideographs. See `http://dynalab.com.hk/font/UniSpec.htm`.

Several wide-coverage BDF Unicode fonts for X Window System terminals and Unix systems are available, including the following:

- Several fonts at different sizes by Markus Kuhn, available at `http://www.cl.cam.ac.uk/~mgk25/ucs-fonts.html`

- The ClearlyU BDF font from Mark Leisher, available at `http://crl.nmsu.edu/~mleisher/cu.html`, which contains over 4,000 glyphs

- The Unicode font proposed by Roman Czyborra at `http://czyborra.com/unifont/`

The Transition to Unicode

Font developers and operating system vendors are making the transition to using Unicode fonts, and are also defining the glyphs in their existing fonts in terms of characters in the Unicode Standard. Adobe, Apple, and Microsoft, for example, have published supported subsets of the Unicode Standard, including standard assignments for code values in the Private Use area.

Adobe's conventions for Postscript names for Unicode characters are defined in the "Unicode and Glyph Names" document at `http://partners.adobe.com/asn/developer/typeforum/unicodegn.html`. The document includes:

- Rules for glyph name length and allowed characters
- Conventions for naming a glyph based on its Unicode code value
- The algorithm for determining which glyph name to use for a given character
- The algorithm for determining a character's Unicode semantics from its glyph name
- A summary of the character sets and code pages covered by the standard Adobe glyph list

The Adobe glyph list is a semicolon-delimited text file available at `http://partners.adobe.com/asn/developer/typeforum/glyphlist.txt`. The 1,071 glyphs in the Adobe list can represent the characters in the following:

- Many standard Adobe character sets
- Windows code pages 1250–1258
- The standard Windows WGL4 glyphs (see below)
- Ten Macintosh character encodings (with the exception of the Apple logo character)
- ISO 8859 Parts 1–10

Of course, there is a lot of overlap between the different character sets and encodings, especially since the Basic Latin characters are included in so many other character sets.

The Adobe list includes 171 assignments in the Corporate Use subarea of the Private Use area for glyph variants such as small capitals, cursive forms, precomposed characters, and other variants of Latin, Central European, and Cyrillic characters. The Web address `http://partners.adobe.com/asn/developer/typeforum/ corporateuse.txt` is a semicolon-delimited text file containing the mappings between Unicode code values in the Private Use area, standard Adobe glyph names, Unicode character names, and character decompositions for the characters represented by each glyph.

Cross-Reference

See Chapter 5 and Appendix A for more on the Private Use areas.

To Adobe, the Corporate Use subarea assignments are an interim measure until the OpenType font technology that is being jointly promoted by Adobe and Microsoft is widely adopted.

The OpenType specification at `http://www.microsoft.com/ typography/tt/tt.htm` includes the specification of a standard Pan-European character set known as Windows Glyph List 4 (WGL4). WGL4 comprises 652 characters that form a superset of the characters in Windows code pages 1250–1254. For each glyph, the specification at `http://www.microsoft.com/typography/ OTSPEC/WGL4.htm` lists its Unicode code value, PostScript character name, and descriptive name plus `MacChar` and `MacIndex` values, where applicable.

Apple has also specified a list of approved glyph names for TrueType fonts.

Appendix A

Character Blocks

This appendix presents descriptions of each of the character blocks in the Unicode Standard, Version 3.0. In these descriptions, I've tried to hit the high points about each character block and its origins. Each description also references the appropriate section in Chapters 6 to 13 of the Unicode Standard, Version 3.0, that describes the character block. The descriptions in the Unicode Standard, Version 3.0, frequently contain more detailed descriptions about the character blocks, and often about individual characters, than I have provided here. However, I have frequently included information that is not in the descriptions in the Standard, so this appendix complements rather than paraphrases the material in the Standard. In addition, several of the books listed in the Bibliography can provide more information about the scripts, languages, and writing systems of both the present and the proposed character blocks.

The block descriptions are listed alphabetically by block name. There are numerous ways to organize the list—the Unicode Standard, Version 2.0, organizes block descriptions by code value. Version 3.0 groups them mostly by geography. However, if all you have is the block name and you want to know more, an alphabetic lookup will get you there fastest.

When dates are used, C.E. denotes "Common Era," which is a non-sectarian year designation equivalent to A.D. (*anno domini*, "in the year of the Lord"). Similarly, B.C.E. denotes "Before Common Era," which is equivalent to B.C. ("Before Christ").

Figures A-1 to A-7 show the first ten printing characters from selected character blocks (or the entire contents of the block, when the block contains fewer than ten characters). The characters are separated by spaces so the glyphs do not run together, even when the usual style for a script joins adjacent letters.

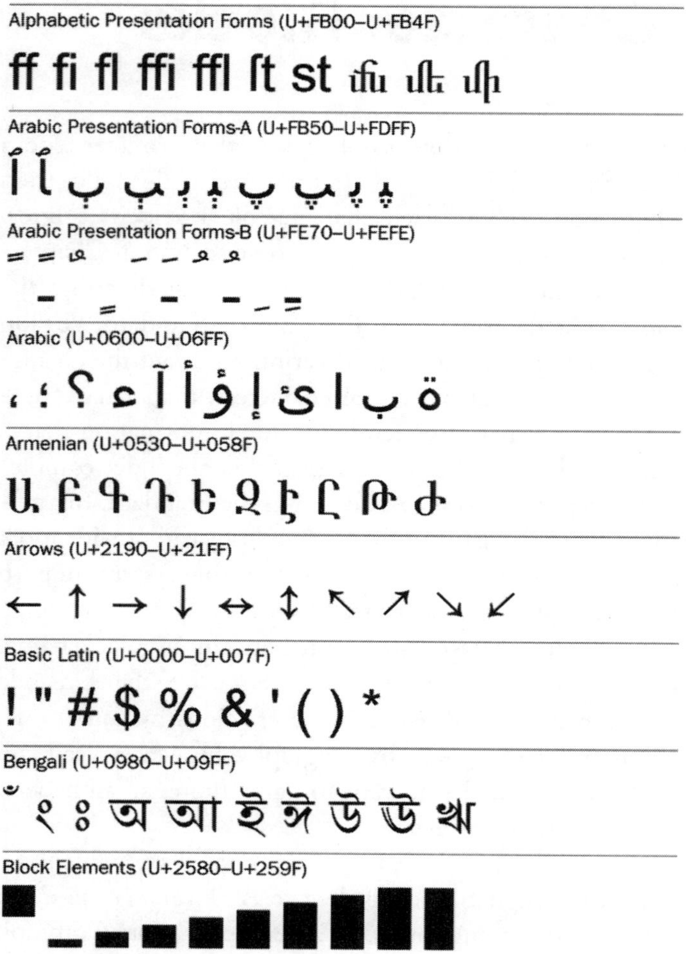
Alphabetic Presentation Forms (U+FB00–U+FB4F)
ﬀ ﬁ ﬂ ﬃ ﬄ ﬅ ﬆ ﬓ ﬔ ﬕ
Arabic Presentation Forms-A (U+FB50–U+FDFF)
Arabic Presentation Forms-B (U+FE70–U+FEFE)
Arabic (U+0600–U+06FF)
Armenian (U+0530–U+058F)
Ա Բ Գ Դ Ե Զ Է Ը Թ Ժ
Arrows (U+2190–U+21FF)
← ↑ → ↓ ↔ ↕ ↖ ↗ ↘ ↙
Basic Latin (U+0000–U+007F)
! " # $ % & ' ( ) *
Bengali (U+0980–U+09FF)
ঁ ং ঃ অ আ ই ঈ উ ঊ ঋ
Block Elements (U+2580–U+259F)

Figure A-1

Sample characters from selected blocks

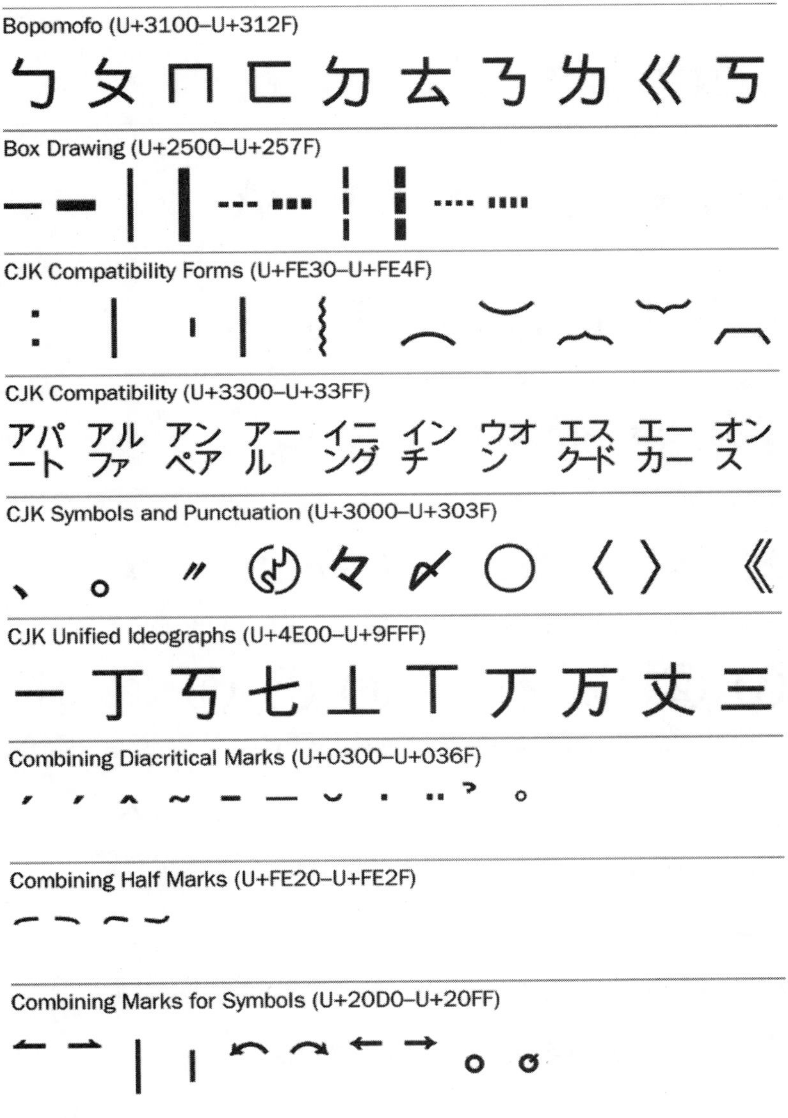

Bopomofo (U+3100–U+312F)

ㄅ ㄆ ㄇ ㄈ ㄉ ㄊ ㄋ ㄌ ㄍ ㄎ

Box Drawing (U+2500–U+257F)

─ ━ │ ┃ ┄ ┅ ┆ ┇ ┈ ┉

CJK Compatibility Forms (U+FE30–U+FE4F)

︰ ︱ ︳ ︴ ﹁ ﹂ ﹃ ﹄ ﹅

CJK Compatibility (U+3300–U+33FF)

㌀ ㌁ ㌂ ㌃ ㌄ ㌅ ㌆ ㌇ ㌈ ㌉

CJK Symbols and Punctuation (U+3000–U+303F)

、 。 〃 ㊞ 々 〆 〇 〈 〉 《

CJK Unified Ideographs (U+4E00–U+9FFF)

一 丁 丂 七 丄 丅 丆 万 丈 三

Combining Diacritical Marks (U+0300–U+036F)

̀ ́ ̂ ̃ ̄ ̅ ̆ ̇ ̈ ̉ ̊

Combining Half Marks (U+FE20–U+FE2F)

︠ ︡ ︢ ︣

Combining Marks for Symbols (U+20D0–U+20FF)

⃐ ⃑ ⃒ ⃓ ⃔ ⃕ ⃖ ⃗ ⃘ ⃙

Figure A-2

Sample characters from selected blocks

Control Pictures (U+2400–U+243F)

␀ ␁ ␂ ␃ ␄ ␅ ␆ ␇ ␈ ␉

Currency Symbols (U+20A0–U+20CF)

₠ ₡ ₢ ₣ ₤ ₥ ₦ ₧ ₨ ₩

Cyrillic (U+0400–U+04FF)

Ё Ђ Ѓ Є Ѕ І Ї Ј Љ Њ

Devanagari (U+0900–U+097F)

ँ ं ः अ आ इ ई उ ऊ ऋ

Dingbats (U+2700–U+27BF)

✁ ✂ ✃ ✄ ✆ ✇ ✈ ✉ ✌ ✍

Enclosed Alphanumerics (U+2460–U+24FF)

① ② ③ ④ ⑤ ⑥ ⑦ ⑧ ⑨ ⑩

Enclosed CJK Letters and Months (U+3200–U+32FF)

㈀ ㈁ ㈂ ㈃ ㈄ ㈅ ㈆ ㈇ ㈈ ㈉

General Punctuation (U+2000–U+206F)

‐ ‑ ‒ – — ― ‖ ‗ ‘ ’

Geometric Shapes (U+25A0–U+25FF)

■ □ ▢ ▣ ▤ ▥ ▦ ▧ ▨ ▩

Figure A-3

Sample characters from selected blocks

Georgian (U+10A0–U+10FF)

ა ბ გ დ ე ვ ზ თ ი კ

Greek Extended (U+1F00–U+1FFF)

ἀ ἁ ἂ ἃ ἄ ἅ ἆ ἇ Ἀ Ἁ

Greek (U+0370–U+03FF)

ʹ ͵ ͺ ; ΄ ΅ Ά · Έ Ή

Gujarati (U+0A80–U+0AFF)

ઁ ં ઃ અ આ ઇ ઈ ઉ ઊ ઋ

Gurmukhi (U+0A00–U+0A7F)

ਂ ਅ ਆ ਇ ਈ ਉ ਊ ਏ ਐ ਓ

Halfwidth and Fullwidth Forms (U+FF00–U+FFEF)

！ ＂ ＃ ＄ ％ ＆ ＇ （ ） ＊

Hangul Compatibility Jamo (U+3130–U+318F)

ㄱ ㄲ ㄳ ㄴ ㄵ ㄶ ㄷ ㄸ ㄹ ㄺ

Hangul Jamo (U+1100–U+11FF)

ᄀ ᄁ ᄂ ᄃ ᄄ ᄅ ᄆ ᄇ ᄈ ᄉ

Hangul Syllables (U+AC00–U+D7A3)

가 각 갂 갃 간 갅 갆 갇 갈 갉

Figure A-4

Sample characters from selected blocks

Hebrew (U+0590–U+05FF)

ּ... ֣ ׃ ׃׃   ֽ ֝ ֿ

ֿ   ֿ   ֿ

Hiragana (U+3040–U+309F)

ぁ あ ぃ い ぅ う ぇ え ぉ お

IPA Extensions (U+0250–U+02AF)

ɐ ɑ ɒ ɓ ɔ ɕ ɖ ɗ ɘ ə

Kannada (U+0C80–U+0CFF)

ಀ ಃ ಅ ಆ ಇ ಈ ಉ ಊ ಋ ಌ

Katakana (U+30A0–U+30FF)

ア ア イ イ ウ ウ エ エ オ オ

Lao (U+0E80–U+0EFF)

ກ ຂ ຄ ງ ຈ ຊ ຍ ດ

Latin Extended Additional (U+1E00–U+1EFF)

Ḁ ḁ Ḃ ḃ Ḅ ḅ Ḇ ḇ Ç ç

Latin Extended-A (U+0100–U+017F)

Ā ā Ă ă Ą ą Ć ć Ĉ ĉ

Latin Extended-B (U+0180–U+024F)

ƀ Ɓ Ƃ ƃ ƅ Ɔ Ƈ Đ

Figure A-5

Sample characters from selected blocks

Latin-1 Supplement (U+0080–U+00FF)

¡ ¢ £ ¤ ¥ ¦ § ¨ © ª

Letterlike Symbols (U+2100–U+214F)

℀ ℁ ℂ ℃ ℄ ℅ ℆ ℇ ℈ ℉

Malayalam (U+0D00–U+0D7F)

ഃ ം അ ആ ഇ ഈ ഉ ഊ ഋ ണ

Mathematical Operators (U+2200–U+22FF)

∀ ∁ ∂ ∃ ∄ ∅ ∆ ∇ ∈ ∉

Miscellaneous Symbols (U+2600–U+26FF)

☀ ☁ ☂ ☃ ☄ ★ ☆ ☇ ☈ ☉

Miscellaneous Technical (U+2300–U+23FF)

⌀ ⌂ ⌃ ⌄ ⌅ ⌆ ⌇ ⌈ ⌉ ⌊

Number Forms (U+2150–U+218F)

⅓ ⅔ ⅕ ⅖ ⅗ ⅘ ⅙ ⅚ ⅛ ⅜

Optical Character Recognition (U+2440–U+245F)

⑀ ⑁ ⑂ ⑃ ⑄ ⑅ ⑆ ⑇ ⑈ ⑉

Oriya (U+0B00–U+0B7F)

ँ ం ః ଅ ଆ ଇ ଈ ଉ ଊ ଋ

Figure A-6

Sample characters from selected blocks

Small Form Variants (U+FE50–U+FE6F)

, ` . ; : ? ! — ( )

Spacing Modifier Letters (U+02B0–U+02FF)

h ɦ j ɾ ɹ ɻ ʁ ʍ y ′

Specials (U+FFF0–U+FFFD)

⌊OBJ⌋ ◆?

Superscripts and Subscripts (U+2070–U+209F)

0 4 5 6 7 8 9 + − =

Tamil (U+0B80–U+0BFF)

° ஂஃ அ ஆ இ ஈ உ ஊ எ ஏ

Telugu (U+0C00–U+0C7F)

ఁ ం ః అ ఆ ఇ ఌఄ ఉ ఊఄ ఋ

Thai (U+0E00–U+0E7F)

ก ข ฃ ค ฅ ฆ ง จ ฉ ช

Figure A-7

Sample characters from selected blocks

These samples do not include every block. The Unicode Standard, Version 3.0, does include a sample glyph for every character in the standard, but it also credits nine companies and more than ten individuals with providing the fonts that were used. That I could produce these samples using freely available fonts and commercial software is a credit to the increasingly widespread implementation of Unicode support in off-the-shelf software.

Alphabetic Presentation Forms (U+FB00–U+FB4F)

This block contains ligatures and other presentation forms from Latin, Armenian, and Hebrew scripts. The Latin ligatures are described in Section 7.1 of the Unicode Standard, Version 3.0, the Armenian ligatures in Section 7.4, and the Hebrew presentation forms in Section 8.1.

All of these characters have compatibility or canonical decompositions into one or more other characters.

Arabic (U+0600–U+06FF)

The Arabic block encodes 206 Arabic script characters. The Unicode Standard encodes the basic Arabic characters in the same relative positions as ISO 8859-6, Latin/Arabic. This was based on ECMA-114, which was based on ASMO 449. The block is described in Section 8.2 of the Unicode Standard, Version 3.0.

The Arabic script developed in the 6th century AD as a derivative of an early Aramaic script, which in turn derived from Phoenician. Arabic script is used today for the Arabic language and, with slight variations, for other languages such as Persian, Urdu, Pashto, and Sindi. The Arabic language is the official language of nearly 20 countries, and there are an estimated 165,000,000 speakers.

Arabic is a cursive script, and most letters connect with their neighbors. It is written from right to left. Characters have different forms depending on whether they stand alone or, if they do not, to their position in relation to other characters. In addition, because of the importance of Arabic calligraphy, there are several well-known calligraphic styles for Arabic, including Diwani, Kufi, Maghribi, Naskh, Natstaliq, Ruqaa, and Thuluth.

The Arabic block, however, encodes only the basic set of Arabic letters, and implementations require a much larger glyph set for rendering characters in different joining contexts and, in some cases, as ligatures of sequences of characters. Section 8.2 of the Unicode Standard defines a minimum set of rules for cursive joining and ligature substitution. Because Unicode text is stored in logical rather than visual order, implementations supporting Arabic should support the bidirectional algorithm described in Section 3.12 of the Unicode Standard.

Arabic Presentation Forms-A (U+FB50–U+FDFF)

These are mostly presentation forms (i.e. glyph variants) of Arabic letters. Arabic can and should be written by using the characters of the Arabic block, and these presentation forms are only encoded in the Unicode Standard for compatibility with existing standards. The exceptions are the ornate parentheses at U+FD3E and U+FD3F, which are not compatibility characters. The block is described in Section 8.2 of the Unicode Standard, Version 3.0.

The presentation forms include contextual variants of characters and of multi-character ligatures, plus spacing forms of Arabic diacritic combinations and some contextual variants of letter/diacritic combinations. This is not the complete set of contextual forms, nor do all fonts include all of these variants or only variants from this list. As noted above, these characters are included for compatibility, not for completeness.

Arabic Presentation Forms-B (U+FE70–U+FEFE)

These are presentation forms of Arabic diacritics (used both as spacing characters and combined with the *tatweel* joining connector) plus contextual variants of Arabic letters, and the LEM-ALEF ligature. As with the Arabic Presentation Forms-A block, these characters are encoded for compatibility with existing standards.

This block is described in Section 8.2 of the Unicode Standard, Version 3.0.

Armenian (U+0530–U+058F)

The Armenian alphabet, or *aybuben*, is used for writing the Armenian language. The Armenian block is described in Section 7.4 of the Unicode Standard, Version 3.0. Armenian is written from left to right, and characters have uppercase and lowercase forms.

The Armenian script was invented in 405, 406, or 407 C.E. (estimates vary) by the cleric Mesrop Maštoc' so that Christian texts could be translated into the local language. Recorded Armenian history extends back to 500 B.C.E., but until this time, Armenians had written using Greek or Aramaic languages, not their own.

The script that Maštoc' invented contained 36 characters — 30 consonants and 6 vowels — where each letter represented one sound in the language, and each sound was represented by only one letter. The script is generally considered to be modeled on Greek, and the sounds that are common between the Greek and Armenian alphabets appear in the Armenian alphabet in the same order as in the Greek alphabet. Additional symbols that Maštoc' invented or borrowed for sounds that are not in Greek are interspersed among the other symbols. Except for the 12th century addition of two extra characters, the script remains the same today.

There are at least four styles of Armenian script. Listed in order of age, they are *erkat'agir* (iron-forged letters), *bologir* (cursive), *notrgir* (miniscule), and *šelagir* (slanted writing), which is currently the most popular form.

The Armenian block includes several modifier and punctuation letters; in addition, punctuation letters from other blocks are used with Armenian. Note that U+0559, ARMENIAN MODIFIER LETTER LEFT HALF RING, is stated to have no recorded usage, and the Unicode Standard, Version 3.0, concludes that "its presence in this block is thus probably spurious."

Ligatures have been used with Armenian since the 7th century, and the Unicode Standard encodes five Armenian ligatures in the Alphabetic Presentation Forms block.

Arrows (U+2190–U+21FF)

These are generic arrow shapes, not every stylistic variation. This block is described in Section 12.4 of the Unicode Standard, Version 3.0.

Basic Latin (U+0041–U+007A)

The Basic Latin block encodes the characters of ASCII (ANSI X3.4). This block encodes the basic 26 uppercase and 26 lowercase Latin letters, the European digits, and some basic mathematical and punctuation characters. It is described in Section 7.1 of the Unicode Standard, Version 3.0.

The Latin script is written from left to right. Latin letters have uppercase and lowercase forms.

Many languages are written using some or all of the letter forms in the Basic Latin block plus accented characters or other letter forms from other Latin-related blocks. Other blocks containing Latin letters are Latin-1 Supplement, Latin Extended-A, Latin Extended-B, IPA Extensions, Latin Extended Additional, and Latin Ligatures. Blocks containing other Latin or Latin-derived characters are Letterlike Symbols, Currency Symbols, Miscellaneous Symbols, Enclosed Alphanumerics, and Fullwidth Forms.

Additional mathematical and punctuation characters are encoded in the Latin-1 Supplement block and in the General Punctuation and subsequent blocks.

The unaccented letters in the Basic Latin block are frequently part or all of the canonical or compatibility decompositions of the Latin characters that have decompositions.

Many of the Basic Latin characters have glyph variants that are encoded in the Unicode Standard as separate characters included for compatibility with existing standards. Since the Basic Latin characters were originally in the ASCII character set, these characters were all you had. Some of the punctuation characters, especially, have overloaded meanings, and it is often better to use one of the variants instead of the Basic Latin character. For example, U+002D, HYPHEN MINUS, has, as its name suggests, double use as the hyphen character and the minus sign. The Unicode Standard also encodes separate hyphen and minus characters, plus several hyphen variants including U+2011, NON-BREAKING HYPHEN, and U+2013, EN DASH, etc. When you are using a hyphen, dash, or minus sign for a particular purpose, it is best to use the specific variant that conveys your meaning rather than relying on the overloaded character from the Basic Latin block.

Bengali (U+0980–U+09FF)

Bengali is used to write the Bengali language, spoken in the West Bengal state in India and the national language of Bangladesh, as well as Assamese, Manipuri, and several minority languages. This block is described in Section 9.2 of the Unicode Standard, Version 3.0, although that section refers to Section 9.1, Devanagari, for the rules for rendering Bengali.

Bengali, like Devanagari, is derived from Brahmi. Brahmi dates from the third century B.C.E., and development of Bengali and Devanagari began diverging between the seventh century and twelfth century C.E. (depending on which reference source you read). Bengali and Devanagari have essentially the same makeup, although the characters, and the sounds for each character, differ between the two scripts. Assamese, likewise, differs from Bengali in just one or two consonant characters; in addition, some of the Assamese pronunciation differs from Bengali.

Reflecting the similarities between Bengali and Devanagari, the structure of the Bengali encoding in the Unicode Standard parallels the encoding structure of Devanagari, with some Bengali characters for currency and fractions added.

Block Elements (U+2580-U+259F)

These are included for compatibility with existing standards. This block is described in Section 12.6 of the Unicode Standard, Version 3.0.

Bopomofo (U+3100-U+312F)

Bopomofo is a phonetic alphabet for representing spoken Chinese. It was developed for Mandarin but has since been extended to also represent sounds of some other Chinese dialects. The Unicode Standard encodes both the standard Mandarin Bopomofo letters and some extension characters for other dialects.

This block is described in Section 10.5 of the Unicode Standard, Version 3.0.

Box Drawing (U+2500-U+257F)

These are included for compatibility with existing standards and support of legacy applications such as terminal emulation. This block is described in Section 12.6 of the Unicode Standard, Version 3.0.

Braille Patterns (U+2800-U+28FF)

These are 256 8-dot Braille patterns arranged in the same sequence as in ISO 11548-1. They are sufficient to represent the dot combinations of both 6-dot Braille and 8-dot Braille systems. This block is described in Section 12.9 of the Unicode Standard, Version 3.0.

The dots are numbered 1 to 8, and the Unicode name of a Braille pattern character indicates the dots that are set (tangible). For example, U+28FF, which has all dots set, is named BRAILLE PATTERN DOTS-12345678. The exception, of course, is U+2800, which has no dots set and which is named BRAILLE PATTERN BLANK.

The Braille patterns are encoded in the Unicode Standard to allow input and output software to work with character codes representing Braille patterns. There is no set correspondence between a Braille pattern character and any character in any language or script.

Cherokee (U+13A0–U+13FF)

The Cherokee syllabary for the Cherokee language was invented by Sequoyah, a monolingual Cherokee speaker, between 1815 and 1821. He had observed that marks on paper were used to represent English, so he invented marks for representing Cherokee.

Sequoyah's invention was adopted by Dr. Samuel Worcester, a missionary (some say the first missionary) to the Cherokee, but he also adapted it to symbols that he could print on a printing press. Dr. Worcester also developed a commonly used transliteration for Cherokee.

Today, Cherokee script is read more than it is written. It is still used in traditional Cherokee medicine and in Cherokee Christian church services.

This block is described in Section 11.2 of the Unicode Standard, Version 3.0.

CJK Compatibility (U+3300–U+33FF)

These represent words, symbols, and abbreviations that are sized to fill the same display space as a single ideographic character. They include words spelled out in katakana, telegraphic symbols for hours and days, Latin abbreviations, and the Japanese ideographs for "corporation" and for four recent Japanese eras. They are included for compatibility with existing standards, and the Unicode Standard notes that modern software can create this sort of character on the fly.

This block is described in Section 12.8 of the Unicode Standard, Version 3.0.

CJK Compatibility Forms (U+FE30–U+FE4F)

This block encodes vertical variants of CJK punctuation characters plus variant forms of overscores and underscores. They are included for round-trip mapping with Taiwan's CNS 11643. It is, of course, preferable to use the nominal character in your text and to leave the choice of vertical or horizontal presentation form to the display software.

This block is described in Section 6.1 of the Unicode Standard, Version 3.0.

CJK Compatibility Ideographs (U+F900–U+FAFF)

This block contains ideographs that are included in the Unicode Standard largely for compatibility with existing standards. It includes 268 characters from KS C 5601-1987 that were included in that standard merely to mark alternate pronunciations of some standards. The block also includes 34 ideographs from other standards. Note that 12 of these ideographs are not duplicates of characters in the CJK Unified Ideographs block, and, despite their placement in this block, they should be treated as part of the set of unified ideographs.

This block is described in Section 10.1 of the Unicode Standard, Version 3.0.

CJK Radicals Supplement (U+2E80–U+2EFF)

These are alternative forms of the radicals in the KangXi Radicals block. They can be variants that represent the appearance of the radicals, as they are used as part of an ideograph. They can also be simplified forms for use with simplified Chinese. Only some of the KangXi radicals have alternative forms to be encoded here, and some have multiple forms that are each encoded as a separate character.

These characters represent radicals, and they should not be used as ideograph characters. Similarly, any ideograph character with the same form should not be used to represent the radical.

This block is described in Section 10.1 of the Unicode Standard, Version 3.0.

CJK Symbols and Punctuation (U+3000–U+303F)

This block encodes punctuation characters, numerals, and other symbols that are principally used in association with Han ideographs. This block is described in Section 6.1 of the Unicode Standard, Version 3.0.

Many of the characters are included for round-trip mapping with existing East Asian character sets, although only U+3000, IDEO-GRAPHIC SPACE, and three Hangzhou-style numerals have decomposition mappings to characters outside this block.

The block includes U+303E, IDEOGRAPHIC VARIATION INDICATOR, and U+303F, IDEOGRAPHIC HALF FILL SPACE, which are graphic characters that indicate something about the text.

CJK Unified Ideographs (U+4E00–U+9FFF)

These are common ideographs from Chinese, Japanese, and Korean standards and other sources.

Cross-Reference

For more information, see the CJK Unified Ideographs section in Chapter 7.

This block is described in Section 10.1 of the Unicode Standard, Version 3.0.

CJK Unified Ideographs Extension A (U+3400–U+4DB5)

These are rare ideographs from Chinese, Japanese, Korean, and Vietnamese standards and other sources.

Cross-Reference

For more information on rare ideographs, see the CJK Unified Ideographs section in Chapter 7.

This block is described in Section 10.1 of the Unicode Standard, Version 3.0.

Combining Diacritical Marks (U+0300–U+036F)

This block contains combining diacritical marks that are not specific to any particular script — script-specific combining marks are encoded with the alphabet for that script. Additionally, combining marks (to be used with symbols) are encoded in the Diacritical Marks for Symbols block. The Combining Diacritical Marks block is described in Section 7.9 of the Unicode Standard, Version 3.0.

In keeping with the Unicode design principles described in Chapter 2, these combining marks may be combined with any base character. Also as illustrated in Chapter 2, the combining marks follow the base character to which they apply.

This block also includes two double diacritics that apply to the side-by-side combination of "their" base character and the following base character. Since the double diacritics have a very high combining class, they stack above every other combining character except the iota subscript.

Cross-Reference

For more on double diacritics having a very high combining class, see Chapter 5.

Many combining marks represent the unification of similar or identical combining marks from multiple scripts. When the script or language is known — for example, when Plane 14 language tags or the `xml:lang` attributes are used — the mark or the combined character should, if possible, be displayed with the correct stylistic variation for the script or language.

Combining Half Marks (U+FE20–U+FE2F)

For compatibility with existing standards, this block encodes two pairs of combining half marks. Unlike other combining marks, these characters are used in pairs — one on each of two adjacent base characters — to build up the appearance of a double diacritic, such as those encoded in the Combining Diacritical Marks block. The characters in this block are glyph variants that are really only useful when a display system can't display a double diacritic as a single character. As you might expect, using the double diacritics is preferred to using these characters.

This block is described in Section 7.9 of the Unicode Standard, Version 3.0.

Combining Marks for Symbols (U+20D0–U+20FF)

This block contains combining marks that are predominately used with mathematical and technical symbols. However, note that these characters, like the combining diacritical marks, can be used with any base character. Furthermore, combining marks from other blocks may likewise be used with any mathematical or technical symbol base character. For example, this block contains U+20DB, COMBINING THREE DOTS ABOVE, and U+20DC, COMBINING FOUR DOTS ABOVE, which are used to indicate third and fourth derivatives, respectively. In contrast, U+0307, COM-BINING DOT ABOVE, and U+0308, COMBINING DIAERI-SIS, from the Combining Diacritical Marks block, are used to indicate first and second derivatives, respectively.

For compatibility with existing standards, the block includes several enclosing diacritics that may each enclose a single character (or base plus combining character sequence).

This block is described in Section 7.9 of the Unicode Standard, Version 3.0.

Control Pictures (U+2400–U+243F)

These are graphic symbols for representing the C0 control codes and the space character plus symbols for computer-related actions, such as "undoable delete," for which there is no control code. This block is described in Section 12.5 of the Unicode Standard, Version 3.0.

The space character is usually represented by a blank space, but there are times when you need to show the space characters in a sequence of characters. The Unicode Standard encodes specific glyphs for two of the conventions used in computer communications and programming for representing the space character: " b" and " ⌴ ".

Other existing standards also have encoded symbols for representing the C0 control codes and the other characters encoded in this block. The Unicode Standard provides sample glyphs for the other control pictures, but, unlike the control pictures for the space character, it explicitly encodes only the semantic of each C0 character. It leaves the actual representation up to each application that uses the characters.

Currency Symbols (U+20A0–U+20CF)

These are the currency symbols not encoded in other blocks. Script-specific currency symbols are encoded in the block with their script. This includes currency symbols, such as the dollar sign in ASCII, included when the Unicode Standard replicates the layout of an entire standard.

Note that the euro character is encoded as U+20AC, EURO SIGN. This block is described in Section 12.1 of the Unicode Standard, Version 3.0.

Cyrillic (U+0400–U+04FF)

The Cyrillic script is based on uncial (capital) Greek with additional characters representing sounds that are not found in Greek. It is traditionally used for the Slavic languages: Russian, Belarussian, Ukrainian, Bulgarian, and Serbo-Croatian (which may also be written in Latin characters). Cyrillic is also used for over 50 non-Slavic languages of the former Soviet Union, including Moldovan, Tajik, Komi, Azeri, Turkmen, Tatar, and Uzbek. The Cyrillic block is described in Section 7.3 of the Unicode Standard, Version 3.0.

Cyrillic is written left to right, and has uppercase and lowercase letter pairs. The characters in the Cyrillic block, and their sequence, are based on ISO 8859-5. The block includes extended Cyrillic characters that are only used in the scripts for the minority languages of the former Soviet Union to represent sounds that are not part of Russian.

Cyrillic has a historic form that, for many characters, is quite close to the modern form. This block includes the historic Cyrillic characters that do not have modern forms, but an Old Cyrillic font should represent all of its Cyrillic characters in the historic form.

Devanagari (U+0900–U+097F)

Simply put, Devanagari is used to write Sanskrit, Hindi, and a variety of other related languages.

In more detail, Sanskrit is the classical language of India and the sacred language of Hindu; Hindi, which is one of the principal languages of India, is just one of the many languages that derives from Sanskrit. Both Sanskrit and Hindi (and over 20 other languages listed in Section 9.1 of the Unicode Standard, Version 3.0) are conventionally written in Devanagari, but they could be written in almost any southern or southeastern Asian script. Sanskrit still is written in a variety of scripts, but Devanagari has become most common. Hindi, likewise, is primarily associated with Devanagari. However, *Dictionary of Languages* notes that when the Kannada-speaking Indian Prime Minister H. D. Deve Gowda gave the Independence Day speech in 1996 in Hindi, he is said to have read from a text in the Kannada script.

Vedic Sanskrit, the oldest known form of Sanskrit, dates from approximately 1000 B.C.E., and a grammar for "classical Sanskrit" was written about 400 B.C.E. The "classical Sanskrit" was the language of learning in India, and even today, Sanskrit is used for plays and technical writings as well as its use in Hindu religious rituals. Sanskrit also became the language of communication of India and countries under Indian influence, and Sanskrit inscriptions from the first millennium C.E. are found in Sri Lanka, Burma, Thailand, Cambodia, Vietnam, Malaya, Sumatra, Java, and Borneo.

Sanskrit is sometimes described as the perfect language (or Devanagari as the perfect script) because the complexity and flexibility of one or the other has been reduced to simple rules. However, any compendium of languages or writing systems turns up numerous examples that are said to be perfect in some respect. English, however, is never among them.

Hindi dates from the 12th century, at least. Estimates of the current number of Hindi speakers range from 180 million to 275 million. In India, it is spoken in Delhi, Uttar Pradesh, Bihar, Madhya

Pradesh, Rajasthan, Hayana, and Himachal Pradesh, and, along with English, it is an official language in all regions of India.

Colloquial Hindi is almost the same language as Urdu, but Hindi is written in Devanagari, and Urdu is written in a Perso-Arabic script. With additions to Devanagari to represent Perso-Arabic sounds, the same spoken text can be written in both Devanagari and Urdu script.

Other languages written in Devanagari include Nepali, Marathi, and Bhojpuri plus many minority languages. Sources differ as to whether Hindi or Bhojpuri is the language spoken by portions of the populations of Mauritius, Fiji, Guyana, Suriname, and Trinidad.

The Unicode Standard encodes the Devanagari characters in the same sequence as ISCII-1988 (Indian Standard Code for Information Interchange). ISCII-1991 (IS 13194:1991), published in November 1991, modified the layout and added new Vedic (oldest form of Sanskrit) extension characters. Except for some Vedic extension characters, the Unicode Standard encodes a superset of the ISCII-1991 repertoire and supports round-trip mapping of modern, non-Vedic text.

The Devanagari script, like many South Asian scripts, derives from Brahmi. Closely related scripts encoded by the Unicode Standard include Bengali, Gurmukhi, Gujarati, Oriya, Tamil, Telugu, Kannada, and Malayalam. To emphasize the similarities in their structural patterns, these scripts are encoded with the same layout as Devanagari. Other related scripts encoded by the Unicode Standard that differ from the Devanagari structural pattern include Sinhala, Thai, Lao, Khmer, and Myanmar.

Devanagari, like its related scripts, is variously described as an *alphasyllabary*, an *abugida*, an *alphabet*, a *syllabic alphabet*, and "a cross between syllabic writing systems and phonemic writing systems [alphabets]." The experts providing these descriptions (besides proving that they can't agree) are trying to express how Devanagari is made up of consonant–vowel sequences, called *aksara*. Each consonant has an inherent short vowel *a* sound, and any vowel other than *a* is written as a diacritic that combines with the base character and overrides the inherent vowel sound. There are also independent vowel letters (the consonant is null), consonants not followed by a vowel (the vowel is "killed" by a *virama* sign), and consonant clusters (the initial consonants do not have inherent vowels and are rendered as *half-forms*). Furthermore, some characters have different presentation forms depending on their adjacent consonants. Rendering Devanagari, therefore, is not exactly easy. The full details—including fourteen rules for rendering Devanagari plus sample half-forms, ligatures, and half-form ligatures—are contained in Section 9.1 of the Unicode Standard, Version 3.0.

Consonants are written with a horizontal headstroke. When characters are joined together, this headstroke makes the text appear suspended as if by clothespins from an imaginary washline. In fact, when writing on ruled paper, people really do "hang" the characters from the line. However, when writing rapidly on unlined paper, the headstroke may be omitted.

Devanagari was traditionally written without spaces between words and with a single or double vertical line, or *danda*, marking the ends of phrases or sentences. Modern practice uses Latin punctuation characters, adds spaces between words, and uses European numbers instead of the Devanagari digits.

Dingbats (U+2700–U+27BF)

Dingbats are typographic symbols or ornaments, and they don't correspond to any human language. The characters in this block represent specific glyphs from the industry standard "Zapf Dingbat" font. The characters are in the same order as in the Postscript encoding of the font. The exceptions are dingbats that would be encoded in the Unicode Standard anyway because of inclusion in other standards and that have glyph shapes that are normally indistinguishable from the Zapf Dingbat glyph shape. Those dingbats are encoded in other blocks, and their positions in the Dingbats block have been left unassigned. For example, the generic symbols for the four playing card suits — "♠", "♣", "♥", and "♦" — appear in other existing standards, so they are encoded in the Miscellaneous Symbols block. Their positions in the Dingbats block (based on the Postscript encoding sequence) have been left unassigned but with a cross-reference to the code values in the Miscellaneous Symbols block.

This block is described in Section 12.7 of the Unicode Standard, Version 3.0.

Enclosed Alphanumerics (U+2460–U+24FF)

These are precomposed symbols for numbers and Latin letters, which are enclosed by circles, surrounded by parentheses, or, in the case of numbers, followed by a period. They are included for compatibility with existing standards, principally East Asian standards. All of these characters have compatibility decompositions into sequences of other characters. This block is described in Section 12.8 of the Unicode Standard, Version 3.0.

Enclosed CJK Letters and Months (U+3200–U+32FF)

These are enclosed, parenthesized, or compound symbols from Korean Standard KS C 5601, Japanese Standard JIS X 0208-1990, Taiwan Standard CNS 11643, and industry standards. All of these characters (except U+327F, KOREAN STANDARD SYMBOL) have compatibility decompositions into sequences of other characters.

This block is described in Section 12.8 of the Unicode Standard, Version 3.0.

Ethiopic (U+1200–U+137F)

The Ethiopic syllabary was developed for the Ethiopic language, also called Ge'ez. Ge'ez dates from the fourth century C.E., and it was widely used in Ethiopia for literature and official documents as recently as the 19th century, but is now limited to liturgical use. The writing system, however, has also been adopted by some of the languages that supplanted Ge'ez. Modern languages using the Ethiopic syllabary include Tigre, Oromo, and Amharic, which is the official language of Ethiopia.

Conceptually, the Ethiopic syllabary combines 43 consonants with eight vowel sounds, but not all combinations are used. The Unicode Standard encodes the syllabary in the traditional alphabetic order, and unused consonant/vowel combinations in the sequence are marked by unassigned code points. Note that the traditional alphabetic sort order doesn't necessarily match the sort order of the languages that now use the script.

This block is described in Section 11.1 of the Unicode Standard, Version 3.0.

General Punctuation (U+2000–U+206F)

This block encodes punctuation and text-layout characters that are not specific to a single script; script-specific punctuation is generally encoded in the block for that script. This block is described in Section 6.1 of the Unicode Standard, Version 3.0.

Other punctuation characters are encoded in the Basic Latin and Latin-1 Supplement blocks, but many of them are overloaded with multiple meanings since, for a long time, they were the only punctuation characters you could use on your computer. For example, U+002D, HYPHEN-MINUS, traditionally functions as both the hyphen sign and the minus sign because there is just one dash character in ASCII.

In contrast, quality typesetting has long used a variety of dashes for different purposes, and many of these are encoded in the General Punctuation block, including hyphen, non-breaking hyphen, figure dash, en dash, em dash, and horizontal bar characters. Similarly, a minus sign that is only a minus sign is encoded as U+2212, MINUS SIGN, in the Mathematical Operators block. The complete list of characters with the "Dash" property is contained in PropList.txt in the Unicode Character Database.

The same is true for space characters: U+0020, SPACE, has ambiguous width, but the General Punctuation block contains multiple space characters with precisely defined widths, and the complete list of characters with the "Space" property is in PropList.txt.

This block contains other characters from Western or European typography, including quotation marks and apostrophes. Note, however, that which quotation marks are used depends heavily upon the language of the text. See the Unicode Standard for details.

This block, however, does include characters from other typographic traditions. This includes U+203B, REFERENCE MARK ("※"), which unifies the Japanese Kome mark and the Urdu paragraph separator. It also includes U+203C, DOUBLE EXCLAMATION MARK, U+2048, QUESTION EXCLAMATION MARK, and U+2049, EXCLAMATION QUESTION MARK, specifically for the convenience of rendering vertical East Asian and Mongolian text.

Finally, the block includes several formatting characters with no visible representation, including U+200C, ZERO WIDTH NON-JOINER, U+200D, ZERO WIDTH JOINER, line and paragraph separator characters, and formatting characters for use with bidirectional text. It also includes formatting characters in the range U+206A to U+206F whose use is now deprecated.

Cross-Reference

For more information on formatting characters for use with bidirectional text, see Chapter 6.

Geometric Shapes (U+25A0–U+25FF)

These are prototypical geometric shapes derived from existing national and vendor standards. This block is described in Section 12.6 of the Unicode Standard, Version 3.0.

Georgian

Georgian script is used to write the Modern Georgian language that is based on the Kartli dialect, and other Georgian dialects. As part of script reform in the former Soviet Union, the Georgian script was also used from the late 1930s to the mid 1950s to write Abkhaz and Ossetic. Georgian script is written from left to right. There are no diacritical marks. The Georgian block is described in Section 7.5 of the Unicode Standard, Version 3.0.

Modern Georgian is written with the *mkhedruli* (or *mxedruli*, depending on your transliteration) script that is comprised of 33 lowercase characters. The alphabet begins with the sound equivalent of a Greek *alpha*, and ends with the equivalent of a Greek *omega*, although the last letter is now obsolete. The other characters follow the order of Greek, except that eleven characters for the additional consonant sounds of Georgian have been added before the final character.

Georgian characters can have ascenders and descenders, but it is common practice to make the characters the same height in titles and headlines.

The earliest forms of Georgian writing were *asomtavruli* (capital letter) and *nusxa-xucuri* (angular) scripts that, when used in combination, are collectively referred to as *xucuri* (priest) script. *Mkhedruli* (soldier's) script first appeared in the 10th century as a derivative of *nusxa-xucuri*. It was initially restricted to secular text while *xucuri* was used for religious writings, but eventually *mkhedruli* was used for both secular and religious writings. The form of *mkhedruli* text has changed little since the 11th century, although five characters that no longer corresponded to sounds in Modern Georgian were dropped from the alphabet in the 1860s.

The Unicode Standard encodes uppercase and lowercase forms of the Georgian alphabet to accommodate both the lowercase *mkhedruli* and the uppercase and lowercase pairs in *xucuri*. The standard also includes the Georgian paragraph separator in the Georgian block, but U+0589, ARMENIAN FULL STOP, should be used for the Georgian full stop. Other punctuation characters from the Basic Latin block may also be used.

Greek (U+0370–U+3FF)

The Greek block encodes Greek characters for writing both ancient and modern Greek plus the additional characters that are also used when writing Coptic. The block is described in Section 7.2 of the Unicode Standard, Version 3.0.

The characters in this block and their sequence are based on ISO 8859-7, which is based in turn upon ELOT 928. This block also includes characters, including archaic variants, from ISO 5428. In addition, non-spacing marks used with Greek are encoded in the Combining Diacritical Marks block, and precomposed Greek letters with diacritical marks are encoded in the Greek Extended block. Variant forms of Greek characters for use as math symbols are encoded in the Mathematical Operators block.

The earliest recorded Greek was written on clay tablets in the Linear B script (see later section) at about 1300 B.C.E. The earliest Greek texts in the Greek alphabet are dated at about 700 B.C.E. The Greek alphabet, which developed from Phoenician, was the first alphabet with letters for vowels as well as consonants.

The Greek language has a long history of dialects emerging and combining. Ancient Greek, dating from 700 B.C.E. to 500 C.E., initially had several dialects, but the Attic dialect of Athens became dominant by about 400 B.C.E. It formed the basis for the *koiné* (common) dialect that was spoken in Greek and Roman times. Greek was also the language of the Byzantine Empire in the 4th to 15th centuries. As the Byzantine Empire declined, it left behind Greek-speaking communities that developed their own dialects. Modern Greek was standardized in the 19th century, and it is based on the dialect of Athens. Today, Greek is spoken in Greece and Cyprus, and by minorities in Albania, Egypt, Georgia, Italy, and Turkey. There are also sizable Greek-speaking communities in major cities around the world, including Chicago, London, and Melbourne.

Coptic developed in Egypt following the conquest of Egypt by Alexander the Great. It originated as spoken Egyptian with many Greek loanwords, and it is written with Greek characters instead of hieroglyphics. Coptic script also borrows seven characters from the Demotic form of Egyptian script to represent sounds that are not in Greek. The script is usually written with a different style from Greek, and text mixing Greek and Coptic should use the appropriate font for each language.

Once the everyday speech of Christians in Egypt, its use declined in favor of Arabic following the Arab conquest of Egypt in the 642 C.E. Although not spoken today, it remains the liturgical language of the Coptic Church, which has approximately six million members.

Greek Extended (U+1F00–U+1FFF)

This block contains precomposed Greek characters with one or more diacritical marks plus spacing variants of the diacritical marks used with Greek. All of these characters have canonical decompositions to one or more characters. The precomposed forms, however, are useful for representing Polytonic (ancient) Greek without using combining marks. The block is described in Section 7.2 of the Unicode Standard, Version 3.0.

Gujarati (U+0A80–U+0AFF)

Gujurati is used to write Gujurati and Kacchi, and, with a few additions, it can be used to write Sanskrit. It is closely related to Devanagari, but consonants do not have the characteristic horizontal headstroke of Devanagari. The script also has a strong resemblance to the extinct Kaithi script.

Gujarati is described in Section 9.4 of the Unicode Standard, Version 3.0, although that section refers to Section 9.1, Devanagari, for the rules for rendering Gujurati.

As with other scripts that are closely related to Devanagari, the encoding structure of Gujurati in the Unicode Standard closely parallels that of Devanagari.

Gurmukhi (U+0A00–U+0A7F)

Gurmukhi (literally "from the mouth of the Guru") was invented in the 16th century by Guru Angad, the second Guru of the Sikhs. It is used to write the Punjabi language in the Indian state of Punjab, although Punjabi is written in Persian script in the Punjab region of Pakistan. This block is described in Section 9.3 of the Unicode Standard, Version 3.0, although that section refers to Section 9.1, Devanagari, for the rules for rendering Gurmukhi.

Gurmukhi is derived from the older Lahnda (or Landa) script, but is also similar to Devanagari. For example, its consonants have the same horizontal headstroke as in Devanagari.

As with other scripts that are similar to Devanagari, the encoding structure for Gurmukhi in the Unicode Standard parallels that of Devanagari.

Halfwidth and Fullwidth Forms (U+FF00-U+FFEF)

The halfwidth forms are variants of Katakana and Hangul characters plus some symbols that are all conventionally displayed as fullwidth characters. The fullwidth forms are variants of the ASCII characters (except SPACE) plus a handful of symbols that are all conventionally displayed as halfwidth characters. Not surprisingly, these character forms are encoded in the Unicode Standard for compatibility with existing standards.

This block is described in Section 10.3 of the Unicode Standard, Version 3.0.

Hangul Compatibility Jamo (U+3130-U+318F)

These are spacing, non-conjoining forms of the Hangul Jamo that are encoded for compatibility with KS C 5601.

Cross-Reference

See the Korean Hangul and Jamo section in Chapter 7.

This block is described in Section 10.4 of the Unicode Standard, Version 3.0.

Hangul Jamo (U+1100-U+11FF)

Jamo are the building blocks of Korean Hangul characters.

Cross-Reference

See the Korean Hangul and Jamo section in Chapter 7.

This block is described in Section 10.4 of the Unicode Standard, Version 3.0.

Hangul Syllables (U+AC00–U+D7A3)

These are the full set of 11,172 modern Hangul syllables, known as the *Johab* set, from KS C 5601-1992. These characters can be decomposed into Jamo from the Hangul Jamo block, and the Jamo can be composed into these modern syllables along with many more ancient Hangul syllables that are not directly encoded in the Unicode Standard.

Cross-Reference

See the Korean Hangul and Jamo section in Chapter 7.

This block is described in Section 10.4 of the Unicode Standard, Version 3.0.

Hebrew (U+0590–U+05FF)

Hebrew is used to write the Hebrew, Yiddish, and Judezmo languages, among others. The script is comprises consonantal letters written from right to left plus small dots and dashes, called *points*, that are written above, inside, and below the base letters to indicate vowels and pronunciation changes. Points, which where developed in about the 8th century, are only used, however, in liturgical texts, school books, and textbooks for foreigners. Hebrew is described in Section 8.1 of the Unicode Standard, Version 3.0.

The characters are not joined, and five base letters have different forms when used at the end of words. Use of the final forms, however, is merely a convention, and software should not automatically substitute the final form glyphs at the ends of words.

The Unicode Standard encodes the Hebrew alphabetic characters in the same sequence as ISO 8859-8, Latin/Hebrew Alphabet. It also encodes the points and Hebrew punctuation characters that are not included in ISO 8859-8, additional digraphs that are considered independent characters in Yiddish, and the *cantillation marks* for liturgical texts that are defined in Israeli standard SI 1311.2.

Conforming implementations need to support the Unicode Bidirectional Algorithm and, because of points, need to support combining marks and canonical ordering.

Additional Hebrew compatibility characters, including variants, precomposed characters, and wide letterforms of the consonantal letters, are included in the Alphabetic Presentation Forms block. In addition, U+20AA, NEW SHEKEL SIGN, is encoded in the Currency block.

High Private Use Surrogates (U+DB80–U+DBFF)

These 128 code values, in combination with a Low Surrogate code value in the range U+DC00–U+DFFF, form a Surrogate Pair that addresses a private use character in Planes 15 and 16.

Cross-Reference

For more information, see the Private Use Areas section in Chapter 3, the UTF-16 section in Chapter 4, and the Unicode Scalar Value and Private Use Characters sections in Chapter 5.

This block is described in Section 13.4 of the Unicode Standard, Version 3.0.

High Surrogates (U+D800–U+DB7F)

These code values, in combination with a Low Surrogate code value in the range U+DC00–U+DFFF, form a Surrogate Pair that addresses a character in Planes 1 to 14.

Cross-Reference

See the UTF-16 section in Chapter 4 and the Unicode Scalar Value section in Chapter 5.

This block is described in Section 13.4 of the Unicode Standard, Version 3.0.

Hiragana (U+3040–U+309F)

Hiragana is one of the two syllabaries that can be used to write all the sounds in the Japanese language (the other is Katakana). Anything that can be said in Japanese can be written in Hiragana.

Hiragana developed as a simplification of a set of kanji (Japanese ideographs) that were used phonetically to write Japanese words. (Some Katakana characters derive from some of the same kanji.) The current hiragana forms were standardized in 1900 by the Japanese Ministry of Education.

Hiragana characters are used for particles, auxiliary verbs, and to add inflections after kanji. In short, they bridge the gap between the Japanese language and the ideographic writing system that Japan borrowed from China. Hiragana characters are still used phonetically to indicate pronunciation of Japanese words as well.

This block is described in Section 10.2 of the Unicode Standard, Version 3.0.

Ideographic Description Characters (U+2FF0–U+2FFF)

The Ideographic Description Characters provide a means of representing the many thousands of rare ideographs that are not encoded (or not yet) by the Unicode Standard. This block is described in Section 10.1 of the Unicode Standard, Version 3.0.

The glyphs of almost all ideographs can be graphically divided into subparts that have representations as separate ideographs.

Quite often, the subparts can be further divided as well. The Ideographic Description Characters, in combination with the ideographs for an unencoded ideograph's subparts, describe the relationship of the graphic components of the unencoded ideograph. From this description, the reader can get an idea of the composition of the unencoded ideograph or, with sufficiently advanced software, see an approximation of the ideograph.

IPA Extensions (U+0250-U+02AF)

This block encodes symbols of the International Phonetic Alphabet (IPA) that are not encoded elsewhere in the Unicode Standard. It also includes some IPA symbols that are no longer in common use and additional symbols used by Sinologists, Americanists, and other linguists. The block is described in Section 7.1 of the Unicode Standard, Version 3.0.

The IPA is published by the International Phonetic Association (http://www2.arts.gla.ac.uk/IPA/ipa.html). The association was founded by a group of language teachers in Paris in 1886 as the Phonetic Teachers' Association, and it changed to its present name in 1897. Today, the Association is truly international, and the alphabet is used worldwide in dictionaries and textbooks. In addition, IPA symbols have been incorporated into scripts invented for previously unwritten languages, principally African languages.

The first edition of the IPA was published in 1888, and it has been revised several times since then. The current revision is dated 1993 (although updated in 1996). Each revision is slightly different from the preceding one. *The World's Writing Systems* notes that there have been slight changes to the typeface, name changes of some phonetic categories, and additions to and deletions from the alphabet.

The Unicode Standard covers all the single symbols and diacritics in the 1989 revision of the IPA, plus some that are no longer included in the IPA. Since many of the IPA symbols are directly or partially derived from the Latin alphabet, the Unicode Standard unifies many of the IPA symbols with the Latin lowercase letters and other Greek and Latin letters. However, the IPA includes typographic variants of some Latin and Greek letters that are encoded as separate characters because they have distinct semantics in plain text. Additionally, the Unicode Standard encodes six digraph ligatures for transcription of coronal affricatives (combinations of a plosive followed by a fricative sound). This is because the ligatures have a distinct meaning and because their design differs from similar ligatures found in old-style fonts.

The IPA-specific diacritical marks are encoded in the Combining Diacritical Marks block, not in this block.

Kanbun (U+3190–U+319F)

These are marks used in Japanese text to provide hints about how to read Chinese text. This block is described in Section 10.1 of the Unicode Standard, Version 3.0.

KangXi Radicals (U+2F00–U+2FDF)

These are the 214 radicals that are used in the KangXi dictionary, an authoritative eighteenth century Chinese dictionary that is also one of the sources for determining the order of the ideographs in the CJK Unified Ideographs blocks. *Radicals* are traditionally used for indexing ideographs and, while there is no universal set of radicals, the 214 used by the KangXi dictionary are widely recognized.

These characters represent the form of the radicals when they are used when an ideograph comprises just the one radical. Many of the radicals have one or more alternative forms that are used in simplified Chinese (or as one part of an ideograph), and they are encoded in the CJK Radicals Extension block.

The KangXi radicals (and the characters in the CJK Radicals Extension block) should be used only to represent radicals, and not used to represent ideographs. All of these radicals have compatibility decompositions to ideographs in the CJK Unified Ideographs blocks. Those ideographs, similarly, should not be used to represent radicals.

This block is described in Section 10.1 of the Unicode Standard, Version 3.0.

Note that *KangXi* is a Chinese reign name, not an alternative name for "Han character."

Kannada (U+0C80–U+0CFF)

Kannada is used to write the Kannada (or Kanarese or Canarese) language of Kanataka state in India. It is a South Indian script that is most closely related to Telugu, but as a descendant of Brahmi, it shares features with Tamil and other North Indian scripts.

The block is described in Section 9.8 of the Unicode Standard, Version 3.0.

Katakana (U+30A0–U+30FF)

Katakana is one of the two syllabaries that can be used to write all the sounds in the Japanese language (the other is hiragana). Anything that can be said in Japanese can be written in katakana.

Katakana developed as a simplification of a set of kanji (Japanese ideographs) that were used phonetically to write Japanese words. (Some hiragana characters derive from some of the same kanji.) The current katakana forms were standardized in 1900 by the Japanese Ministry of Education.

Katakana is mostly used for emphasis and, especially, for foreign loan words. For example, my name in katakana is トニー グラハム (to-ni gu-ra-ha-mu, with "ー" indicating a long vowel on "ni").

This block is described in Section 10.3 of the Unicode Standard, Version 3.0.

Khmer (U+1780–U+17FF)

Khmer is used to write the Khmer language, the official language of Cambodia. The script is described in Section 9.15 of the Unicode Standard, Version 3.0.

Lao (U+0E80–U+0EFF)

Lao is used to write the Lao language. The language is closely related to Thai, and the Lao script is similarly closely related to the Thai script, including the use of tone marks. The Unicode Standard encodes Lao in the same relative order as Thai.

This block is described in Section 9.12 of the Unicode Standard, Version 3.0.

Latin-1 Supplement (U+00C0–U+00FF)

The characters in this block are equivalent to the ISO 8859-1 characters with the same code values. They are comprised of uppercase and lowercase letter pairs plus some mathematical and punctuation characters. The block is described in Section 7.1 of the Unicode Standard, Version 3.0.

The letters in the Latin-1 Supplement, when combined with the letters in the Basic Latin block, support the characters for the following languages: Albanian, Basque, Breton, Catalan, Cornish, Danish, Dutch, English, Faroese, Frisian, Galician, German, Greenlandic, Icelandic, Irish Gaelic (new orthography), Italian, Latin, Luxemburgish, Norwegian, Portuguese, Rhaeto-Romanic, Scottish Gaelic, Spanish, and Swedish.

ISO 8859-1 includes several diacritic characters that are sometimes treated as spacing marks and sometimes treated as non-spacing marks. The Unicode Standard unambiguously treats the corresponding diacritic characters in this block as spacing marks, and it provides alternative, non-spacing marks in the Combining Diacritical Marks block.

Latin Extended-A (U+0100–U+017F)

This block encodes additional Latin letters that, in combination with the letters of the Basic Latin and Latin-1 Supplement blocks, adds support for additional languages. These include Afrikaans, Croatian, Czech, Esperanto, Estonian, French, Hungarian, Latvian, Maltese, Polish, Provençal, Romanian, Romany, Sami, Slovak, Slovenian, Sorbian, Turkish, Welsh, and others. The block is described in Section 7.1 of the Unicode Standard, Version 3.0.

The letters in this block are unique characters from multiple parts of ISO 8859, including: Part 2 – *Latin Alphabet No. 2*; Part 3 – *Latin Alphabet No. 3*; Part 4 – *Latin Alphabet No. 4*; and Part 9 – *Latin Alphabet No. 5*. The other letters from these standards that are not encoded in the Latin Extended-A block are already encoded in the Basic Latin and Latin-1 Supplement blocks. Other characters from these standards are encoded in the Spacing Modifier Letters block and in the General Punctuation and subsequent blocks.

Latin Extended-B (U+0180–U+024F)

The characters in this block, in combination with characters in the other Latin blocks, extend the Unicode Standard's coverage of Latin languages. This block is described in Section 7.1 of the Unicode Standard, Version 3.0.

This block includes the characters in ISO 6438, *Documentation – African coded character set for bibliographic information interchange*, and the 16 Pinyin characters from GB 2312 and JIS X 0212 that are not already encoded in other blocks. It also includes the Sami characters from ISO 8859-10, *Latin alphabet No. 6*, and some Croatian digraphs that are used for one-to-one transliteration of Serbian Cyrillic script. For compatibility with existing standards, two uppercase forms of each digraph are encoded: an uppercase form where both characters in the digraph are in uppercase, and a titlecase form where only the first of the two characters is in uppercase.

Latin Extended Additional (U+1E00–U+1EFF)

This block contains precomposed combinations of Latin letters with one or more diacritical marks. Each of these characters has a canonical equivalent comprising a base letter plus one or more non-spacing marks from the Combining Diacritical Marks block. The block is described in Section 7.1 of the Unicode Standard, Version 3.0.

Letterlike Symbols (U+2100–U+214F)

These are symbols derived from letters of an alphabetic script. This currently includes, but is not necessarily limited to, symbols based on Latin, Greek, and Hebrew letters. This block is described in Section 12.2 of the Unicode Standard, Version 3.0.

The block includes many symbols from national and corporate standards, including many that are encoded for compatibility.

Many symbols are simply stylistic variants—such as black letter, double-struck, or script versions—of "conventional" letters. They are encoded here as separate characters because, in these particular styles, they have particular meaning in certain fields, such as mathematics. Taking two examples from my own former field of endeavor, electrical engineering, this block includes U+2126, OHM SIGN

(Ω), and U+2127, INVERTED OHM SIGN ($\mho$). The ohm sign is essentially a capital omega (and U+2126 does have a canonical decomposition to U+03A9, GREEK CAPITAL LETTER OMEGA), but in electrical engineering, the symbols represent resistance, which is measured in ohms. It may look like Greek to you, but to an electrical engineer, a number followed by a capital omega-like symbol looks like a resistance value. There may be stylistic differences between U+2126 and U+03A9 (and in the bad old days before Unicode, I would have used the capital omega from the Symbol font, not a Greek font). However, at heart, they also have completely different meanings. U+2127, to an electrical engineer, represents conductance, which, appropriately enough, is the inverse of resistance.

Not all of the symbols have technical meanings. For example, the block also includes ᔆᴹ and ™ for the service mark and the trademark sign, respectively.

Note that the Unicode Standard discourages using letter-like symbols in place of other characters or sequences of characters when the symbol is just a stylistic variation.

Low Surrogates (U+DC00–U+DFFF)

These code values, in combination with a High Surrogates or High Private Use Surrogates code value in the range U+D800–U+DBFF, form a Surrogate Pair that addresses a character in Planes 1 to 16.

Cross-Reference

See the UTF-16 section in Chapter 4 and the Unicode Scalar Value section in Chapter 5.

This block is described in Section 13.4 of the Unicode Standard, Version 3.0.

Malayalam (U+0D00–U+0D7F)

Malayalam is used to write the Malayalam language of the Kerala state in India plus some other minority languages. Malayalam is also spoken by communities in Singapore and Malaysia, but they, and the Moslems in Kerala, write it using the Arabic script.

Malayalam is a South Indian script that is related to Tamil, Kannada, and Telugu, but it also shares features with Northern Indian scripts such as Devanagari. For example, Malayalam uses many conjunct consonant forms, which are also present in Devanagari but absent in Tamil. Because of their similarities, the structure of the Malayalam block parallels the structure of the Devanagari block.

This block is described in Section 9.9 of the Unicode Standard, Version 3.0.

Mathematical Operators (U+2200–U+22FF)

These are operators, relations, geometric symbols, and other symbols that are used for the most part only in mathematics. This block is described in Section 12.4 of the Unicode Standard, Version 3.0.

Other mathematical operators are encoded in the Basic Latin and Latin-1 Supplement blocks, plus some symbols from the Miscellaneous Technical, General Punctuation, and Letterlike Symbols blocks are also used, sometimes exclusively, in mathematical contexts.

All characters recognized as used in mathematics have the Mathematical property and are listed in PropList.txt from the Unicode Character Database.

Cross-Reference

The Mathematical property is discussed in Chapter 5.

Miscellaneous Symbols (U+2600–U+26FF)

This miscellany of symbols from various national and vendor standards includes weather and astrological symbols, pointing hands, warning signs, chess symbols, and others. They are frequently used for text decoration, although specific applications, such as a chess book, may use them as significant characters. The Unicode Standard explicitly does not attempt to encode every possible text decoration symbol. This block is described in Section 12.7 of the Unicode Standard, Version 3.0.

These characters do not have specific glyphs. Besides font or style variations, some characters have alternative glyphs in common use. For example, both "♁" and "⊕" are commonly used to represent U+2641, EARTH.

Miscellaneous Technical (U+2300–U+23FF)

These are, as the name says, miscellaneous technical symbols from a variety of sources. This block explicitly excludes symbols that are not normally used in one-dimensional text, such as the symbols used in electronic circuits. The block is described in Section 12.5 of the Unicode Standard, Version 3.0.

Mongolian (U+1800–U+18AF)

The traditional Mongolian script has been used since the time of Genghis Khan. However, in the early 1940's, the Mongolian People's Republic adopted Cyrillic characters for writing Mongolian. In 1992, the traditional script was restored as the official script, with an ambitious schedule to replace all use of the Cyrillic script within five years. In practice, because so many people have grown up using only the Cyrillic script, the idea didn't work and was since shelved, at least for now.

This block is described in Section 11.4 of the Unicode Standard, Version 3.0.

Myanmar (U+1000–U+109F)

Myanmar is the script used to write Burmese, which is the majority language of Myanmar, which was formerly called Burma. Note, however, that "Burma" and "Myanmar" are both English approximations of the same word.

This block is described in Section 9.14 of the Unicode Standard, Version 3.0.

Number Forms (U+2150–U+218F)

This block encodes symbols for some fractions and Roman numerals. They are included for compatibility with existing standards, since these fractions (and many more besides) can be composed using numerals and U+2044, FRACTION SLASH, and the Roman numerals can be composed using sequences of Latin letters. This block is described in Section 12.3 of the Unicode Standard, Version 3.0.

Three other fractions are encoded in the Latin-1 Supplement block, and the Hangzhou numerals, which are also number forms of other characters, are encoded in the CJK Symbols and Punctuation block.

Ogham (U+1680–U+169F)

Ogham ("Ogam" in Old Irish) script was used to write Irish and, according to some sources, Pictish. Ogham was used in monumental inscriptions found in Ireland, Devon, Cornwall, Wales, Scotland, and the Isle of Man dating from the fifth to seventh centuries, and, after the seventh century, was used in Irish manuscripts. The Ogham block is described in Section 7.7 of the Unicode Standard, Version 3.0.

The Ogham alphabet is comprised of twenty tally-like symbols grouped into four groups of five plus six *forfeda* (additional) symbols. The *forfeda* were used in the manuscripts, but only the first *forfeda* character was regularly used in the monumental inscriptions.

When written in stone, Ogham was written across the edge of the stone, usually beginning at the bottom-left corner and proceeding upward, across the top, and down the right edge of the monument. Some Ogham inscriptions are accompanied by Latin equivalents, and some are inscribed in lines of left-to-right text in the manner of the Latin translation. Sources differ in describing whether or not the left-to-right Ogham text with Latin translations appeared in Britain, or Ireland, or both.

In the manuscript (or "scholastic") tradition, Ogham was usually written horizontally from left-to-right. The text conventionally has a center stemline representing the edge of the stone, but the Unicode Standard notes that this is not necessary.

Monumental Ogham was written without punctuation or word division, but Scholastic Ohgams sometimes used a word separator. The Unicode Standard includes an Ogham space mark, an Ogham feather mark, and reversed feather mark that may be used to indicate the direction of the text.

Optical Character Recognition (U+2440–U+245F)

These are characters from ISO 2033 that are used in optical character recognition (specifically, the OCR-A character set) and in magnetic ink character recognition (MICR) that cannot be unified with characters from the Basic Latin block. This block is described in Section 12.5 of the Unicode Standard, Version 3.0.

Oriya (U+0B00–U+0B7F)

Oriya is principally used to write the Oriya language from the Orissa state in India. It is also used for some minority languages, and can be used to write Sanskrit. Oriya is related to Bengali and therefore is also related to Devanagari. However, Oriya does not have the horizontal headstroke of Bengali and Devanagari, since it was traditionally written using a stylus on palm leaves, and the long horizontal stroke would have split the leaves.

This block is described in Section 9.5 of the Unicode Standard, Version 3.0, although that section references Section 9.1, Devanagari, for details on rendering Oriya.

Like other scripts related to Devanagari, the structure of the Oriya block parallels the structure of the Devanagari block.

Private Use (U+E000–U+F8FF)

These code values are not assigned characters by the Unicode Standard, and are reserved for use by software developers and end users.

Cross-Reference

See the Private Use Characters section in Chapter 5.

This block is described in Section 13.5 of the Unicode Standard, Version 3.0.

Runic (U+16A0–U+16F0)

Different forms of German, Scandinavian, and Anglo-Saxon runes were used from the first century until modern times. They are now "historical" or "extinct" scripts that are mainly of use to scholars. The Runic block encodes 75 Runic letters from the original *futhark* and its derivatives plus three punctuation marks and three Runic symbols. The block is described in Section 7.6 of the Unicode Standard, Version 3.0.

There are conflicting theories about the origin and derivation of Runes, but it is generally agreed that their angular shapes developed or derived from the initial scratching of runes into wood. The German *furthark* (named for its first six symbols) was comprised of 24 symbols, but different forms of 16-letter furtharks were later used in Scandinavia from the eighth to eleventh century. In contrast, the Anglo-Saxon version of the Germanic furthark expanded over time to versions with twenty-eight, thirty-one, or thirty-three runes. Even the Scandinavian rune script eventually added "dotted" or "pointed" runes to better represent the sounds of Scandinavian language until, by the thirteenth century, the script resembled a runic alphabet.

Runes were mostly written from left to right, but they could also be written from right to left, or in alternate directions on alternate lines (boustrophedon), or following the outline of the object. Ligatures did occur, and runes could be written reversed, upside down, or both.

The different forms and different numbers of runes used over time in various places present problems to someone encoding runes in the Unicode Standard. The standard unifies runes where possible, but different graphic forms that developed over time are not unified, and neither are runes with the same graphic form but different origin. The standard provides a reference glyph for each rune, but it also notes that inscriptions can have considerable variations in rune shape so that it generally requires specialized knowledge when transcribing runes into Unicode text.

Sinhala (U+0D80–+0DFF)

Sinhala is used to write Sinhala (or Sinhalese), one of the two national languages of Sri Lanka, as well as Pali (the classical language of Buddhist literature) and Sanskrit (see Devanagari). It has many features in common with other South Indian scripts. The script is described in Section 9.10 of the Unicode Standard, Version 3.0.

Printed Sinhala combines heavy and dark strokes in a way that handwritten Sinhala does not.

Use of Western punctuation and European digits is replacing traditional Sinhala punctuation and digits.

Small Form Variants (U+FE50–U+FE6F)

These are presentation forms of ASCII punctuation characters that are encoded for round-trip mapping with Taiwan's CNS 11643 standard. These are fullwidth characters containing the glyphs for the halfwidth (small form) ASCII characters. That is, the conventional glyphs are rendered in the same space as that for a Han ideograph.

These characters are included for compatibility only, and it is preferable to use the conventional characters and to leave the presentation up to the formatting software.

Note that two small form variants from CNS 11643 were unified with U+00B7, MIDDLE DOT, and U+2215, DIVISION SLASH, respectively.

Spacing Modifier Letters (U+02B0–U+02FF)

This block is comprised of a collection of small signs. Most of these characters modify some aspect of their preceding letter, typically its pronunciation, but some modify their following letter, and a few are independent letters. These characters are spacing marks, unlike the marks in the Combining Diacritical Marks block, and they function as letter characters (and have the "letter" property), unlike any similar or identical punctuation characters in other blocks. This block is described in Section 7.8 of the Unicode Standard, Version 3.0.

Specials (U+FEFF, U+FFF0–U+FFFF)

U+FEFF, ZERO WIDTH NO-BREAK SPACE, has a special role as an encoding signature.

Cross-Reference

See the discussion of "endianness" in Chapter 4. Characters in the Specials block (U+FFF0–U+FFFF) are described in the Special Characters section in Chapter 5.

This block is described in Section 13.6 of the Unicode Standard, Version 3.0.

Superscripts and Subscripts (U+2070–U+209F)

These are superscript and subscript forms of "0" to "9", "+", "-", "=", and "n" (except for superscript digits one, two and three, which are encoded in the Latin-1 Supplement block) that are included for compatibility with existing standards. This block is described in Section 12.3 of the Unicode Standard, Version 3.0.

Syriac (U+0700–U+74F)

Syriac is the most important descendant of the Aramaic script. Four reference works provided four dates spanning four centuries for the earliest Syriac manuscripts. Section 8.3 of the Unicode Standard, Version 3.0, provides the earliest date at 6 C.E. Syriac was once widespread through the Middle East and Southeast India, but it was largely displaced by Arabic following the spread of Islam.

Today, Syriac is used as the liturgical language of the Maronite and Syrian Catholic Churches and the Syrian Jacobite Church, among others. Modern dialects of Aramaic are still spoken by small communities in Iran, Iraq, Syria and Turkey. Another variant, Gharshuni, is Syriac script with the addition of Arabic vowels and overstrike marks that is used by Syriac-speaking Christians to write liturgical texts in Arabic.

There are four forms of Syriac, with slightly different styles. The oldest is *Estrangela* (or *Estrangelo*). It was used exclusively up until a schism in the church in the 5th century, and still has some uses today. When the Church split into the East or Nestorian Christians and the West Monophysite or Jacobean Christians, the two communities gradually developed their own *East Syriac* and *Serto* (simple) styles, respectively. The fourth style, *Christian Palestinian Aramaic*, is a very square style that is sometimes considered a subcategory of Estrangela.

The variants all use the same Syriac characters, despite the stylistic differences. The Unicode Standard, therefore, encodes each character once, plus it includes the letters and diacritics particular to the Neo-Aramaic (or Neo-Syriac, depending again on your source) languages, Christian Palestinian Aramaic, and Garshuni. The character names follow the East Syriac convention.

Syriac is read from right to left, but *The World's Writing Systems* notes that Syriac was written by rotating the page 90° then writing down the page in columns progressing from left to right. Implementations of Syriac don't need to rotate anything, but they do need to support the Unicode Bidirectional Algorithm.

Syriac uses the same 22 consonants as Hebrew, although its style is more cursive. Most letters are connected, although eight do not connect to the following letter. The script also uses diacritics to indicate vowels, and to denote plural or feminine verbs, or guide pronunciation. The East Syriac and Serto styles use different diacritic marks, since, following the 7th century proposal of Jacob of Edessa, the Serto style sometimes uses the vowel letters of Greek to indicate pronunciation.

Tamil (U+0B80-U+0BFF)

Tamil is used to write the Tamil language, which is used in the Tamil Nadu state in India and also in portions of Sri Lanka, Malaysia, Singapore, Fiji, Mauritius, Guyana, Zanzibar, and parts of East Africa. It is described in Section 9.6 of the Unicode Standard, Version 3.0.

Tamil, like Devanagari, is descended from Brahmi, but Tamil is a South Indian script, whereas Devanagari is a North Indian script. The structure of the Tamil block in the Unicode Standard parallels the structure of Devanagari block, but Tamil has fewer consonants than other Indic scripts. Tamil also does not have the conjunct consonant forms—ligatures for consonant clusters—of Devanagari and related scripts.

Tamil characters are more rounded than, for example, Devanagari characters, because Tamil was traditionally written using a stylus on palm leaves, and angular lines would have ripped the leaves.

Tamil also has its own rules for rendering glyphs. The script supports vowel splitting and reordering, ligating vowel signs, and special spacing forms of vowels, so a Tamil font requires many more glyphs than there are Tamil characters.

The script includes numeric symbols—including symbols for 10, 100, and 1000, but none for zero—but European digits are now commonly used. Tamil also uses European punctuation.

Telugu (U+0C00-U+0C7F)

Telugu is used to write the Telugu language of Andhra Pradesh state in India. It is a South Indian script that is most closely related to Kannada, but as a descendant of Brahmi, it shares features with Devanagari and other North Indian scripts.

The block is described in Section 9.7 of the Unicode Standard, Version 3.0. This section refers to Section 9.6, Tamil, for rules for rendering Telugu, but also notes some differences between Tamil and Telugu.

Thaana (U+0780–U+07BF)

Thaana is the script used for Dhivehi (a.k.a., Maldivian), which is the official language of the approximately 230,000 people in the Republic of the Maldives. Under the name Mahl (or Mahal), the same language is also spoken by about 10,000 people on the Indian island of Minicoy. The script is described in Section 8.4 of the Unicode Standard, Version 3.0.

Written from right to left, Thaana has been used since the early 17th century, and it supplanted an earlier script that was written from left to right. Thaana borrows more than its directionality from Arabic, but it is not Arabic. It has 24 consonantal characters: nine are derived from Arabic numerals 1–9 and another nine from an older, local set of numbers, and most of the remaining six are also adaptations or borrowings. Thaana writes vowels as diacritics, but unlike other scripts, the consonants do not have an inherent vowel sound, so all vowels are marked.

Twelve variants of existing Thaana characters with added dots are used for Arabic loanwords. Less commonly, loanwords may also be written in Arabic.

Thaana uses both European and Arabic digits along with Arabic numeric punctuation. European digits are written left to right in Thaana. Not surprisingly, conforming implementations of Thaana need to support the Unicode Bidirectional Algorithm.

Thaana is not cursive — so adjacent characters are not linked — and it uses spaces between words. It also uses a mixture of European and Arabic punctuation; see Section 8.4 of the Unicode Standard for details.

Thai (U+0E00–U+0E7F)

Thai is used to write the Thai language plus Lao, Kuy, Lavna, and Pali. It is a descendant of Brahmi, but a nearer ancestor is Old Khmer. Invention of the Thai script is traditionally attributed to King Ramkhamhaeng of Sukhothai in 1283 C.E.

This block is described in Section 9.11 of the Unicode Standard, Version 3.0. The block's layout follows Thai Industrial Standard 620-2533.

Like Indic scripts (such as Devanagari), Thai consonants have an inherent vowel sound that one can overwrite by adding a vowel sign. However, the Thai language is tonal, so the script includes tone marks that similarly modify the tone of the base consonant. Both vowel signs and tone marks are encoded after the letter that they modify.

Thai also includes some full-size vowel signs that, unlike other Indic scripts, are encoded *before* their base consonantal letter.

Tibetan (U+0F00–U+0FBF)

Tibetan is used to write the Tibetan language, both in Tibet itself and in Ladakh, Nepal, Sikkim, Bhutan, and areas of northern India. The script is described in detail in Section 9.13 of the Unicode Standard, Version 3.0.

Invention of the Tibetan script is usually attributed to Thumi Sambhota, a minister under the first Buddhist king of Tibet, Songtsen Gampo. The king sent sixteen men (or one, or seventeen, depending on the source) to India to study Buddhist language and writing. On his return, Thumi Sambhota invented the Tibetan writing system to represent both Tibetan — which previously had no script — and Sanskrit, the classical language of India (see the explanation under Devanagari). *The World's Writing Systems* notes the conflicting view of the Bon po religious tradition that suggests different origins.

There are several different styles of Tibetan script, principally *uchen* ("with head"), which is a formal style usually used for printing, and variants of *u-mey* ("headless"), which are more cursive.

Tibetan contains 30 consonants that, as in Indic languages, have an inherent vowel sound, and four vowels. Tibetan words have a base consonant to which other consonants may combine as a subscript, prescript, superscript, postscript, or post-postscript symbol. Vowel marks also attach to the cluster. The elements alter the glyph shape or the sound of the cluster. The end of a syllable is marked by a *tsek* character. See the Unicode Standard for further details.

Unified Canadian Aboriginal Syllabics (U+1400–U+167F)

These are a unification of the syllabic symbols from multiple scripts that are in use by several aboriginal groups in Canada. This block is described in Section 11.3 of the Unicode Standard, Version 3.0.

The first Canadian aboriginal syllabaries were devised in 1840 by James Evans, a Wesleyan missionary, for the Ojibwe and Cree languages. The Cree syllabary used simple geometric shapes that were derived from symbols in British shorthand. Each basic shape represented a consonant, and the syllabary encoded five variants of each basic shape that represented the consonant combined with each of four vowels as well as standing alone. The consonant/vowel combinations were typically the same symbol with a different orientation, and the stand-alone consonant was typically a superscript form of the same symbol.

The Cree syllabary caught on among the Cree people, and the symbols were also borrowed for use in representing other aboriginal languages. Additional symbols were invented when people adapted the syllabary to languages with more sounds. In all, the symbols—originals and later additions—have been used to represent languages from the Algonquian, Inuktitut, and Athapascan language families.

Yi (U+A000–A48F)

This block contains 1,165 Yi syllables from GB 13134-91. The Yi syllabary, often referred to as "modern Yi" but also known as Cuan or Wei, is used to write the Yi language. This block is described in Section 10.6 of the Unicode Standard, Version 3.0.

Appendix B

Unicode Consortium Resources

This appendix lists useful information about the Unicode Consortium, versions of the Unicode Standard, Unicode Technical Reports, and International Unicode Conferences.

Contacting the Unicode Consortium

This section contains contact information for the Unicode Consortium.

The Unicode Consortium
P.O. Box 391476
Mountain View, CA 94039-1476 USA

Phone:	(650) 693-3921
	(650) 693-2958
Fax:	(650) 693-3010
E-mail:	info@unicode.org
Web:	http://www.unicode.org
FTP:	ftp://ftp.unicode.org

Unicode Mailing List

The Unicode Consortium operates multiple mailing lists, including one that is open to members and non-members alike. The mailing list at unicode@unicode.org is a forum for discussing implementing the Unicode Standard and proposals to modify it. To subscribe to unicode@unicode.org, send mail to unicode-request@unicode.org with the subject line "subscribe" and "subscribe *your-address* unicode" in the body of the message.

The unicode@unicode.org mailing list is not moderated, but only subscribers can post to the list, and it has strictly enforced rules against job postings and recruitment campaigns. See http://www.unicode.org/unicode/consortium/distlist.html for further information.

Frequently Asked Questions

The Unicode FAQ (Frequently Asked Questions) page is at http://www.unicode.org/unicode/faq/.

Versions of the Unicode Standard

The common timeline of the Unicode Consortium activities and the ISO/IEC 10646 developments is described in Chapter 1. During that time, there have been multiple versions of the Unicode Standard. The version current at the time of writing is 3.0.

Despite how this book has addressed them, version numbers for the Unicode Standard are made up of three parts, as shown in Figure B-1. I have used "Version 3.0" instead of "Version 3.0.0" throughout this book because there are currently no updates to Version 3.0, and because any updates that may follow probably won't affect the information provided here.

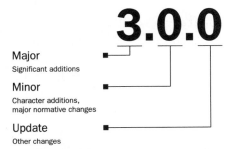

Figure B-1 *Version numbering fields*

Every new version of the Unicode Standard — even the updates such as 3.0.1 — has a separate directory on the Unicode Consortium's FTP site (`ftp://ftp.unicode.org/Public/`) that contains the Unicode Character Database files for that version. As noted in Chapter 3, all of the Unicode Character Database files have a version number as part of their filename. Some files include the current Unicode version number in their filename, and some that change infrequently include their own revision number in their filename. Whether or not a file has changed, a copy is placed in the database version's directory on the FTP site. In addition, the current Unicode Character Database files are always available at `ftp://ftp.unicode.org/Public/UNIDATA/`.

There are three places where you may locate the changes between successive versions of the Unicode Standard:

1. Appendix D of the Unicode Standard, Version 3.0

2. The `UnicodeData.html` file in the Unicode Character Database

3. The Web page at `http://www.unicode.org/unicode/standard/versions/enumeratedversions.html`.

The appendix in the standard provides the most detail, but it only lists the changes from Unicode 2.0 to 2.1 and from Unicode 2.1 to 3.0. (However, changes from Unicode 1.0 to 1.1 and 1.1 to 2.0 are listed in Appendix D of the Unicode Standard, Version 2.0.)

UnicodeData.html provides some details of the changes from Version 2.0.0 onwards, and enumeratedversions.html lists the files and books comprising each version of the Unicode Standard from 1.0 onwards. The two HTML files have the advantage of being updated for each version change, while the appendix in the standard is frozen at Version 3.0.

Table B-1 lists selected details of the significant versions of the Unicode Standard at the time of this writing. Complete details on these and other versions are available at the resources listed above.

Table B-1 *Significant Versions of the Unicode Standard*

Version	Date	Total Assigned Characters	Private Use, Surrogates, Controls, and Non-characters	Total Assigned Code Values	Unassigned Code Values
1.0	October 1991	28,302	5,699	34,001	31,535
1.1	June 1993	34,169	6,467	40,636	24,900
2.0	July 1996	38,885	8,515	47,400	18,136
2.1.9	December 1998	38,887	8,515	47,402	18,134
3.0	September 1999	49,194	8,515	57,709	7,827

Books of the Unicode Standard

Major versions of the Unicode Standard have been published as books:

- The Unicode Consortium. *The Unicode Standard, Version 1.0, Volume 1*. Reading, MA, Addison-Wesley Developers Press, 1991. ISBN 0-201-56788-1

- The Unicode Consortium. *The Unicode Standard, Version 1.0, Volume 2*. Reading, MA, Addison-Wesley Developers Press, 1992. ISBN 0-201-60845-6

- The Unicode Consortium. *The Unicode Standard, Version 2.0.* Reading, MA, Addison-Wesley Developers Press, 1996. ISBN 0-201-48345-9
- The Unicode Consortium. *The Unicode Standard, Version 3.0.* Reading, MA, Addison Wesley Longman, 2000. ISBN 0-201-61633-5

The Unicode Standard, Version 3.0, book is published as a hardback book, and all previous versions were published as paperbacks.

The books of the Unicode Standard, Version 2.0, and the Unicode Standard, Version 3.0, have both included a CD-ROM containing the current Unicode Character Database files, mappings to existing encodings, and so on. These are useful resources, but the same information is available from the Unicode Consortium's FTP site. The FTP site has the added advantage that it is kept up to date with changes to the Unicode Character Database and new or changed technical reports, and so on.

You should not copy and distribute the Unicode Character Database or other files from the Unicode Consortium. You should instead direct people to the Consortium's Web and FTP sites for the latest versions of the files.

Technical Reports

The Unicode Technical Committee (UTC) produces Unicode Technical Reports (UTR) that contain normative or informative information about the structure of the Unicode Standard and its use.

Cross-Reference

The UTC and the role of the UTR were introduced in Chapter 1.

The technical reports have both a number and a title. When reports are referred to by number, the usual format is "UTR #*n*", where *n* is the report number.

Table B.2 shows the Unicode Technical Reports that have been released at the time of this writing and their status as of January 2000—approved, draft, proposed draft, or superseded. Note that draft and proposed draft reports are subject to change without notice. See the Unicode Technical Report page at http://www.unicode.org/unicode/reports/techreports.html for links to the reports and up to date indications of their status.

The table also indicates the reports that are normative for implementations of the Unicode Standard, Version 3.0. In several areas, the text of the Unicode Standard, Version 3.0, both covers the same material as one of these reports and refers the reader to the appropriate technical report for the latest version of the information.

Finally, Table B-2 shows the chapter number of this book that covers the subject of each current technical report. A summary of each report follows the table. There is no UTR #12.

Table B-2 *Unicode Technical Reports*

No.	Title	Status (Jan. 2000)	Unicode 3.0	Chapter
1	Proposals for Burmese (Myanmar), Khmer, and Ethiopian	Superseded		–
2	Proposals for Sinhala, Mongolian, and Tibetan	Superseded		–
3	Proposals for Less Common Scripts	Superseded		–
4	The Unicode Standard, Version 1.1	Superseded		–
5	Handling Non-Spacing Marks	Superseded		–
6	A Standard Compression Scheme for Unicode	Approved		4
7	Plane 14 Characters for Language Tags	Approved		6
8	The Unicode Standard, Version 2.1	Superseded		–

No.	Title	Status (Jan. 2000)	Unicode 3.0	Chapter
9	The Bidirectional Algorithm	Approved	✓	5
10	Unicode Collation Algorithm	Approved		6
11	East Asian Width	Approved	✓	5
13	Unicode Newline Guidelines	Approved	✓	5
14	Line Breaking Properties	Approved	✓	5
15	Unicode Normalization Forms	Approved	✓	5
16	UTF-EBCDIC	Approved		4
17	Character Encoding Model	Approved		5
18	Unicode Regular Expression Guidelines	Approved		6
19	UTF-32	Draft		4
20	Unicode in XML and other Markup Languages	Proposed Draft		9
21	Case Mappings	Approved		5
22	Character Mapping Tables	Proposed Draft		4

UTR #1: Proposals for Burmese (Myanmar), Khmer, and Ethiopian

This report contains the proposals for three scripts that are now included in the Unicode Standard. This report has been superseded. It also succeeded: Myanmar, Khmer, and Ethiopian are all included in Unicode 3.0.

UTR #2: Proposals for Sinhala, Mongolian, and Tibetan

This report contains the proposals for three scripts that are now included in the Unicode Standard. This report has been superseded. It also succeeded: Sinhala, Mongolian, and Tibetan are all included in Unicode 3.0.

UTR #3: Proposals for Less Common Scripts

This report contains proposals for multiple scripts. Some, such as Cherokee and Ogham, are now included in Unicode 3.0. Others, such as Etruscan and Linear B, are in the pipeline for inclusion in Plane 1.

This report has been superseded.

UTR #4: The Unicode Standard, Version 1.1

The changes between Unicode 1.0.1 and Unicode 1.1 were detailed in this report. Since the current version is Unicode 3.0, it's not surprising that this report has been superseded.

UTR #5: Handling Non-Spacing Marks

This report has been superseded because its details have since been incorporated into the text of the Unicode Standard.

UTR #6: A Standard Compression Scheme for Unicode

This report covers the Standard Compression Scheme for Unicode (SCSU), which is an efficient compression scheme for compressing Unicode text.

Cross-Reference

SCSU is described in Chapter 4.

UTR #7: Plane 14 Characters for Language Tags

This technical report defines a simple protocol for specifying language that uses characters from Plane 14. Actually, it describes a general mechanism for annotating Unicode text with tags comprising Plane 14 characters, and the language tags are currently the only defined use for the mechanism.

Cross-Reference

Language identification, including using the Plane 14 characters for Language Tags, is described in Chapter 6.

UTR #8: The Unicode Standard, Version 2.1

This report, which details the changes between Unicode 2.0 and Unicode 2.1, has been superseded by the release of the Unicode Standard, Version 3.0.

UTR #9: The Bidirectional Algorithm

This describes both the conformance requirements for supporting bidirectional text and the Unicode Bidirectional Algorithm. The current version is identical to the text contained in the Unicode Standard, Version 3.0, book. It shouldn't surprise you, therefore, that this report is normative for implementations of the Unicode Standard, Version 3.0.

If there are changes or corrections made to the Bidirectional Algorithm, they will be made here first, so the book refers its readers to this technical report as the most up-to-date reference.

Cross-Reference

Bidirectional behavior is discussed in Chapter 6.

UTR #10: Unicode Collation Algorithm

This describes how to compare two Unicode strings. The discussion of sorting and searching in Chapter 5 directs you to the Unicode Standard and to this technical report.

UTR #11: East Asian Width

In the context of East Asian scripts, characters can be represented as fullwidth or halfwidth forms. Some characters have both fullwidth and halfwidth forms.

With the exception of some compatibility characters, the Unicode Standard does not distinguish between fullwidth and halfwidth characters. However, when displaying Unicode text in an East Asian context or when converting to an East Asian encoding, it is necessary for an application to use the representation with the appropriate width.

This technical report describes the problem and presents recommendations on when and how to map characters to fullwidth and halfwidth forms. The report is normative for implementations of the Unicode Standard, Version 3.0.

Cross-Reference

East Asian Width is discussed in Chapter 3.

UTR #13: Unicode Newline Guidelines

This report describes how to cope with the different conventions in use for indicating the ends of lines and the breaks between paragraphs.

This report is normative for implementations of the Unicode Standard, Version 3.0.

UTR #14: Line Breaking Properties

This describes the meaning of the Line Breaking property values and the breakdown of the values into normative and informative. The discussion of the line breaking property in Chapter 5 directs you to this report.

This report is normative for implementations of the Unicode Standard, Version 3.0.

UTR #15: Unicode Normalization Forms

This describes the four standard normalization forms for Unicode text.

Cross-Reference

The normalization forms are discussed in Chapter 5.

This report is normative for implementations of the Unicode Standard, Version 3.0.

UTR #16: UTF-EBCDIC

UTF-EBCDIC, or "EBCDIC-Friendly Unicode (or UCS) Transformation Format," describes a byte-oriented transformation format (i.e. an encoding) for EBCDIC systems.

The encoding is meant for use within EBCDIC systems and networks, and is not intended for use as an open interchange format. It allows the use of Unicode characters with existing EBCDIC systems, much as UTF-8 allows the use of Unicode characters with 8-bit ASCII systems.

Cross-Reference

UTF-EBCDIC is discussed in Chapter 4.

UTR #17: Character Encoding Model

This defines the five layers of the Unicode view of the relationship between characters and their encodings.

UTR #18: Unicode Regular Expression Guidelines

This defines three implementations for regular expression engines.

Cross-Reference

Regular expressions are discussed in Chapter 6.

UTR #19: UTF-32

UTF-32 is a 32-bit encoding of the characters in the first 17 planes. It covers the same code values as UTF-16. Over that range, a UTF-32 representation is identical to the UCS-4 representation of the same character. However, UTF-32 characters have additional semantics and restrictions that don't apply if they are labeled as UCS-4.

Cross-Reference

UTF-32 is described in Chapter 4.

UTR #20: Unicode in XML and other Markup Languages

This is a joint Unicode/W3C report describing technical considerations (and "gotchas") when using Unicode with markup languages such as XML.

Cross-Reference

Using Unicode with XML, HTML, and SGML is discussed in Chapter 9.

UTR #21: Case Mappings

This provides implementation guidelines for case mapping and case conversion.

Cross-Reference

The implementation guidelines are discussed in Chapter 5.

UTR #22: Character Mapping Tables

This defines an XML format for specifying the mapping (and alternative mappings for special purposes) between the Unicode Standard and other encodings.

Cross-Reference

Character mapping is discussed in Chapter 4.

Unicode Consortium Members

Tables B-3 to B-5 show the Full, Associate, and Liaison members of the Unicode Consortium as of January 2000. In addition, the Consortium had nine Specialist members (myself included) and 45 Individual members at that time.

Cross-Reference

The membership categories and their benefits are discussed in Chapter 1.

Table B-3 *Full Members*

Apple Computer, Inc.	Oracle Corporation
Basis Technology Corporation	PeopleSoft, Inc.
Booz, Allen, & Hamilton, Inc.	Progress Software Corporation
Compaq Computer Corporation	The Research Libraries Group, Inc. (RLG)
Hewlett-Packard Company	Reuters, Ltd.
Hyperion Solutions Corporation	SAP AG
IBM Corporation	Sun Microsystems, Inc.
Justsystem Corporation	Sybase, Inc.
Microsoft Corporation	Unisys Corporation
NCR Corporation	Xerox Corporation

Table B-4 *Associate Members*

Adobe Systems, Inc.	Logos Research Systems, Inc.
Agfa Monotype Corporation	Lycos, Inc.
ASMUS, Inc.	Netscape Communications Corporation
Automated Wagering International, Inc.	Novell, Inc.
Beijing Zhong Yi Electronics Co.	OCLC, Inc.
Bitstream, Inc.	OneRealm, Inc.
BMC Software, Inc.	Optio Software
Church of Jesus Christ of Latter-day Saints	Production First Software
Columbia University	QUALCOMM, Inc.
Data Research Associates	Quark, Inc.
DecoType, Inc.	Rogue Wave Software
Endeavor Information Systems, Inc.	Royal Library, Sweden
Ericsson Mobile Communications	RWS Group, LLC
eTranslate, Inc.	SHARE
Ex Libris, Inc.	Siebel Systems, Inc.
GE Information Services, Inc.	Software AG
Government of Tamil Dadu, India	Software Engineering Australia, Ltd.
iDNS	StarTV – Satellite Television Asia Region Ltd.
Innovative Interfaces, Inc.	Symbian, Ltd.
Internet Mail Consortium	Tegic Communications
Language Analysis Systems, Inc.	VTLS, Inc.
Libronix Corporation	

Table B-5 *Liaison Members*

China, Center of Computer and Information Development (CCID), Beijing ISO/IEC JTC1 SC22/WG20	The Internet Engineering Task Force (IETF) Korea, Kongju National Library, Chung-nam
Viet Nam, Technical Committee on Information Technology (TCVN/TC1), Hanoi	World Wide Web Consortium (W3C) – W3C I18N Working Group

International Unicode Conferences

International Unicode Conferences, held semiannually, are organized by Global Meeting Services under an exclusive license granted by the Unicode Consortium. Details of both past and future conferences are available at `http://www.unicode.org/unicode/conference/about-conf.html`. The conference organizer can be contacted at:

Global Meeting Services, Inc.
4360 Benhurst Avenue
San Diego, CA 92122 USA
Telephone: (858) 638-0206
Fax: (858) 638-0504
E-mail: `info@global-conference.com`
               `conference@unicode.org`

Appendix C

ISO/IEC 10646 Resources

This appendix lists some ISO/IEC 10646 resources. It tells you how to purchase the standard and how to join the mailing list. It also provides information about the available resources on the Web, ISO/IEC 10646-1:1993 amendments, ISO/IEC 10646-1 block names, and the collections of graphic characters for subsets.

Purchasing the Standard

ISO's catalog information for ISO/IEC 10646-1:1993 is available on the Web at http://www.iso.ch/cate/d18741.html.

You can buy a copy of ISO/IEC 10646-1:1993 and, separately, copies of all of its published amendments from ISO or from your national standards body. Be warned, however, that ISO/IEC 10646-1:1993 costs US$370 at the time of this writing.

ISO/IEC 10646-1:2000 is not available at the time of this writing. In the US, the national standards body is:

American National Standards Institute
11 West 42nd Street
13th floor
New York, N.Y. 10036
Phone: (212) 642-4900

Fax: (212) 398-0023
E-mail: info@ansi.org
Web: http://www.ansi.org

In Canada, the national standards body is:

Standards Council of Canada
45 O'Connor Street, Suite 1200
Ottawa, Ontario K1P 6N7
Phone: (613) 238-3222
Fax: (613) 995-4564
E-mail: info@scc.ca
Web: http://www.scc.ca/

Mailing list

The mailing list is `iso10646@jhuvm.hcf.jhu.edu`. To subscribe, send mail to `listproc@listproc.hcf.jhu.edu` with "`sub iso10646 firstname lastname`" in the body of the message.

This list is usually *very quiet*. Do not be surprised if you receive only a handful of messages per month.

On the Web

This section describes the ISO/IEC 10646 resources available on the Web.

WG2 Homepage

The homepage for JTC1/SC2/WG2 — ISO/IEC 10646 — UCS is `http://anubis.dkuug.dk/jtc1/sc2/wg2`. From that page, you can get a flavor of the operation of the ISO/IEC working group.

ISO International Register of Coded Character Sets

Another interesting resource is the ISO International Register of Coded Character Sets at `http://www.itscj.ipsj.or.jp/ISO-IR/`.

ISO/IEC 10646-1:1993 Amendments

Table C-1 lists the amendments to ISO/IEC 10646-1:1993. Note that the Unicode Standard, Version 2.0, is character-for-character identical with ISO/IEC 10646-1:1993 plus the first seven amendments. Two corrigenda for ISO/IEC 10646-1:1993 have also been published.

Table C-1 *ISO/IEC 10646-1:1993 Amendments*

No.	Description
1	UTF-16
2	UTF-8
3	Coding of C1 Controls
4	Removing Annex G: UTF-1
5	Hangul
6	Tibetan
7	33 additional characters
8	New annex on CJK ideographs
9	Unique identifiers
10	Ethiopic Script
11	Unified Canadian Aboriginal syllabics
12	Cherokee
13	CJK unified ideographs with supplementary sources
14	Yi

Continued

Table C-1 *Contiunued*

No.	Description
15	Kang Xi radicals and numerals
16	Braille
17	CJK vertical extensions
18	Symbols and other characters such as the Euro sign
19	Runic
20	Ogham
21	Sinhala
22	Keyboard symbols
23	Bopomofo, Romani, and others
24	Thaana
25	Khmer
26	Myanmar (Burmese)
27	Syriac
28	Ideographic description sequence
29	Mongolian
30	Additional Latin and other characters
31	Tibetan extensions

ISO/IEC 10646-1 Block Names

Table C-2 lists the blocks defined in ISO/IEC 10646-1:1993 (Corrigendum 2), ISO/IEC 10646-1:2000, and the Unicode Standard, Version 3.0. There is not always a 1:1 correspondence between the ISO/IEC 10646 blocks and the Unicode blocks. So that the differences stand out, names of Unicode blocks are shown in italic text when the blocks differ from their corresponding ISO/IEC 10646-1:2000 blocks by more than just capitalization of their names. The ISO/IEC 10646 names appear in capital letters because they appear that way, and only that way, in that standard. The Unicode Standard block names appear in mixed case because they appear in mixed case in that standard.

Table C-2 *ISO/IEC 10646 Block Names*

From	To	ISO/IEC 10646-1:1993 Block Name	ISO/IEC 10646-1:2000 Block Name	Unicode Block Name
0000	001F	–	–	*Basic Latin*
0020	007E	BASIC LATIN	BASIC LATIN	*Basic Latin*
0080	009F	–	–	*Latin-1 Supplement*
00A0	00FF	LATIN-1 SUPPLEMENT	LATIN-1 SUPPLEMENT	*Latin-1 Supplement*
0100	017F	LATIN EXTENDED-A	LATIN EXTENDED-A	Latin Extended-A
0180	024F	LATIN EXTENDED-B	LATIN EXTENDED-B	Latin Extended-B
0250	02AF	IPA EXTENSIONS	IPA (INTERNATIONAL PHONETIC ALPHABET) EXTENSIONS	*IPA Extensions*
02B0	02FF	SPACING MODIFIER LETTERS	SPACING MODIFIER LETTERS	Spacing Modifier Letters
0300	036F	COMBINING DIACRITICAL MARKS	COMBINING DIACRITICAL MARKS	Combining Diacritical Marks
0370	03CF	BASIC GREEK	GREEK AND COPTIC	*Greek*
03D0	03FF	GREEK SYMBOLS AND COPTIC	GREEK AND COPTIC	*Greek*
0400	04FF	CYRILLIC	CYRILLIC	Cyrillic
0530	058F	ARMENIAN	ARMENIAN	Armenian
0590	05CF	HEBEW EXTENDED-A	HEBREW	Hebrew
05D0	05EA	BASIC HEBREW	HEBREW	Hebrew
05EB	05FF	HEBREW EXTENDED-B	HEBREW	Hebrew
0600	065F	BASIC ARABIC	ARABIC	Arabic
0660	06FF	ARABIC EXTENDED	ARABIC	Arabic
0700	074F	–	SYRIAC	Syriac
0780	07BF	–	THAANA	Thaana

Continued

Table C-2 *Continued*

From	To	ISO/IEC 10646-1:1993 Block Name	ISO/IEC 10646-1:2000 Block Name	Unicode Block Name
0900	097F	DEVANAGARI	DEVANAGARI	Devangari
0980	09FF	BENGALI	BENGALI	Bengali
0A00	0A7F	GURMUKHI	GURMUKHI	Gurmukhi
0A80	0AFF	GUJARATI	GUJARATI	Gujarati
0B00	0B7F	ORIYA	ORIYA	Oriya
0B80	0BFF	TAMIL	TAMIL	Tamil
0C00	0C7F	TELUGU	TELUGU	Telugu
0C80	0CFF	KANNADA	KANNADA	Kannada
0D00	0D7F	MALAYALAM	MALAYALAM	Malayalam
0D80	0DFF	–	SINHALA	Sinhala
0E00	0E7F	THAI	THAI	Thai
0E80	0EFF	LAO	LAO	Lao
0F00	0FFF	–	TIBETAN	Tibetan
1000	109F	–	MYANMAR	Myanmar
10A0	10CF	GEORGIAN EXTENDED	GEORGIAN	Georgian
10D0	10FF	BASIC GEORGIAN	GEORGIAN	Georgian
1100	11FF	HANGUL JAMO	HANGUL JAMO	Hangul Jamo
1200	137F	–	ETHIOPIC	Ethiopic
13A0	13FF	–	CHEROKEE	Cherokee
1400	167F	–	UNIFIED CANADIAN ABORIGINAL SYLLABICS	Unified Canadian Aboriginal Syllabics
1680	169F	–	OGHAM	Ogham
16A0	16FF	–	RUNIC	Runic
1780	17FF	–	KHMER	Khmer
1800	18AF	–	MONGOLIAN	Mongolian
1E00	1EFF	LATIN EXTENDED ADDITIONAL	LATIN EXTENDED ADDITIONAL	Latin Extended Additional

From	To	ISO/IEC 10646-1:1993 Block Name	ISO/IEC 10646-1:2000 Block Name	Unicode Block Name
1F00	1FFF	GREEK EXTENDED	GREEK EXTENDED	Greek Extended
2000	206F	GENERAL PUNCTUATION	GENERAL PUNCTUATION	General Punctuation
2070	209F	SUPERSCRIPTS AND SUBSCRIPTS	SUPERSCRIPTS AND SUBSCRIPTS	Superscripts and Subscripts
20A0	20CF	CURRENCY SYMBOLS	CURRENCY SYMBOLS	Currency Symbols
20D0	20FF	COMBINING DIACRITICAL MARKS FOR SYMBOLS	COMBINING DIACRITICAL MARKS FOR SYMBOLS	Combining Marks for Symbols
2100	214F	LETTERLIKE SYMBOLS	LETTERLIKE SYMBOLS	Letterlike Symbols
2150	218F	NUMBER FORMS	NUMBER FORMS	Number Forms
2190	21FF	ARROWS	ARROWS	Arrows
2200	22FF	MATHEMATICAL OPERATORS	MATHEMATICAL OPERATORS	Mathematical Operators
2300	23FF	MISCELLANEOUS TECHNICAL	MISCELLANEOUS TECHNICAL	Miscellaneous Technical
2400	243F	CONTROL PICTURES	CONTROL PICTURES	Control Pictures
2440	245F	OPTICAL CHARACTER RECOGNITION	OPTICAL CHARACTER RECOGNITION	Optical Character Recognition
2460	24FF	ENCLOSED ALPHANUMERICS	ENCLOSED ALPHANUMERICS	Enclosed Alphanumerics
2500	257F	BOX DRAWING	BOX DRAWING	Box Drawing
2580	259F	BLOCK ELEMENTS	BLOCK ELEMENTS	Block Elements
25A0	25FF	GEOMETRIC SHAPES	GEOMETRIC SHAPES	Geometric Shapes
2600	26FF	MISCELLANEOUS SYMBOLS	MISCELLANEOUS SYMBOLS	Miscellaneous Symbols
2700	27BF	DINGBATS	DINGBATS	Dingbats

Continued

Table C-2 *Continued*

From	To	ISO/IEC 10646-1:1993 Block Name	ISO/IEC 10646-1:2000 Block Name	Unicode Block Name
2800	28FF	–	BRAILLE PATTERNS	Braille Patterns
2E80	2EFF	–	CJK RADICALS SUPPLEMENT	CJK Radicals Supplement
2F00	2FDF	–	KANGXI RADICALS	Kangxi Radicals
2FF0	2FFF	–	IDEOGRAPHIC DESCRIPTION CHARACTERS	Ideographic Description Characters
3000	303F	CJK SYMBOLS AND PUNCTUATION	CJK SYMBOLS AND PUNCTUATION	CJK Symbols and Punctuation
3040	309F	HIRAGANA	HIRAGANA	Hiragana
30A0	30FF	KATAKANA	KATAKANA	Katakana
3100	312F	BOPOMOFO	BOPOMOFO	Bopomofo
3130	318F	HANGUL COMPATIBILITY JAMO	HANGUL COMPATIBILITY JAMO	Hangul Compatibility Jamo
3190	319F	CJK MISCELLANEOUS	KANBUN (CJK miscellaneous)	*Kanbun*
31A0	31BF	–	BOPOMOFO EXTENDED	Bopomofo Extended
3200	32FF	ENCLOSED CJK LETTERS AND MONTHS	ENCLOSED CJK LETTERS AND MONTHS	Enclosed CJK Letters and Months
3300	33FF	CJK COMPATIBILITY	CJK COMPATIBILITY	CJK Compatibility
3400	3D2D	HANGUL	CJK UNIFIED IDEOGRAPHS EXTENSION A	CJK Unified Ideographs Extension A
3D2E	44B7	HANGUL SUPPLEMENTARY-A	CJK UNIFIED IDEOGRAPHS EXTENSION A	CJK Unified Ideographs Extension A

From	To	ISO/IEC 10646-1:1993 Block Name	ISO/IEC 10646-1:2000 Block Name	Unicode Block Name
44B8	4DBF	HANGUL SUPPLEMENTARY-B		
4DC0	4DFF	HANGUL SUPPLEMENTARY-B		
4E00	9FFF	CJK UNIFIED IDEOGRAPHS	CJK UNIFIED IDEOGRAPHS	CJK Unified Ideographs
A000	A48F	–	YI SYLLABLES	Yi Syllables
A490	A4CF	–	YI RADICALS	Yi Radicals
AC00	D7A3	–	HANGUL SYLLABLES	Hangul Syllables
D800	DB7F	–	–	*High Surrogates*
DB80	DBFF	–	–	*High Private Use Surrogates*
DC00	DFFF	–	–	*Low Surrogates*
E000	F8FF	PRIVATE USE AREA	PRIVATE USE AREA	*Private Use*
F900	FAFF	CJK COMPATIBILITY IDEOGRAPHS	CJK COMPATIBILITY IDEOGRAPHS	CJK Compatibility Ideographs
FB00	FB4F	ALPHABETIC PRESENTATION FORMS	ALPHABETIC PRESENTATION FORMS	Alphabetic Presentation Forms
FB50	FDFF	ARABIC PRESENTATION FORMS-A	ARABIC PRESENTATION FORMS-A	Arabic Presentation Forms-A
FE20	FE2F	COMBINING HALF MARKS	COMBINING HALF MARKS	Combining Half Marks
FE30	FE4F	CJK COMPATIBILITY FORMS	CJK COMPATIBILITY FORMS	CJK Compatibility Forms
FE50	FE6F	SMALL FORM VARIANTS	SMALL FORM VARIANTS	Small Form Variants

Continued

Table C-2 *Continued*

From	To	ISO/IEC 10646-1:1993 Block Name	ISO/IEC 10646-1:2000 Block Name	Unicode Block Name
FE70	FEFE	ARABIC PRESENTATION FORMS-B	ARABIC PRESENTATION FORMS-B	Arabic Presentation Forms-B
FEFF	FEFF	–	–	*Specials*
FF00	FFEF	HALFWIDTH AND FULLWIDTH FORMS	HALFWIDTH AND FULLWIDTH FORMS	Halfwidth and Fullwidth Forms
FFF0	FFFD	SPECIALS	SPECIALS	Specials

Not all of the differences between the two ISO/IEC 10646-1 columns in Table C-2 can be attributed to the development of ISO/IEC 10646-1:2000. Corrigendum 2 represents a 1996 snapshot of ISO/IEC 10646-1:1993. Amendments to the standard after Corrigendum 2 added many new blocks and also, for example, deleted the existing Hangul blocks. ISO/IEC 10646-1:2000 incorporates both new material and the amendments made to ISO/IEC 10646-1:1993 after 1996.

Note

The ISO/IEC 10646-1:2000 blocks shown here are based on preliminary information. Changes may occur before ISO/IEC 10646-1:2000 passes its ballot.

Collections of Graphic Characters for Subsets

Table C-3 shows the collections defined in Annex A of ISO/IEC 10646-1:2000 for use as selected subsets of the full character repertoire. Note that all subsets automatically include the characters from the BASIC LATIN block, (i.e., character positions 0020–007F of the BMP).

Table C-3 *ISO/IEC 10646-1:2000 Collections of Graphic Characters for Subsets*

Collection Number	Collection Name	Positions	Comment
1	BASIC LATIN	0020–007E	
2	LATIN-1 SUPPLEMENT	00A0–00FF	
3	LATIN EXTENDED-A	0100–017F	
4	LATIN EXTENDED-B	0180–024F	
5	IPA EXTENSIONS	0250–02AF	
6	SPACING MODIFIER LETTERS	02B0–02FF	
7	COMBINING DIACRITICAL MARKS	0300–036F	
8	BASIC GREEK	0370–03CF	
9	GREEK SYMBOLS AND COPTIC	03D0–03FF	
10	CYRILLIC	0400–04FF	
11	ARMENIAN	0530–058F	
12	BASIC HEBREW	05D0–05EA	
13	HEBREW EXTENDED	0590–05CF, 05EB–05FF	
14	BASIC ARABIC	0600–065F	
15	ARABIC EXTENDED	0660–06FF	
16	DEVANAGARI	0900–097F, 200C, 200D	200C and 200D are ZERO WIDTH NON-JOINER and ZERO WIDTH JOINER, respectively.
17	BENGALI	0980–09FF, 200C, 200D	
18	GURMUKHI	0A00–0A7F, 200C, 200D	
19	GUJARATI	0A80–0AFF, 200C, 200D	
20	ORIYA	0B00–0B7F, 200C, 200D	

Continued

Table C-3 *Continued*

Collection Number	Collection Name	Positions	Comment
21	TAMIL	0B80–0BFF, 200C, 200D	
22	TELUGU	0C00–0C7F, 200C, 200D	
23	KANNADA	0C80–0CFF, 200C, 200D	
24	MALAYALAM	0D00–0D7F, 200C, 200D	
25	THAI	0E00–0E7F	
26	LAO	0E80–0EFF	
27	BASIC GEORGIAN	10D0–10FF	
28	GEORGIAN EXTENDED	10A0–10CF	
29	HANGUL JAMO	1100–11FF	
30	LATIN EXTENDED ADDITIONAL	1E00–1EFF	
31	GREEK EXTENDED	1F00–1FFF	
32	GENERAL PUNCTUATION	2000–206F	
33	SUPERSCRIPTS AND SUBSCRIPTS	2070–209F	
34	CURRENCY SYMBOLS	20A0–20CF	
35	COMBINING DIACRITICAL MARKS FOR SYMBOLS	20D0–20FF	
36	LETTERLIKE SYMBOLS	2100–214F	
37	NUMBER FORMS	2150–218F	
38	ARROWS	2190–21FF	
39	MATHEMATICAL OPERATORS	2200–22FF	
40	MISCELLANEOUS TECHNICAL	2300–23FF	
41	CONTROL PICTURES	2400–243F	
42	OPTICAL CHARACTER RECOGNITION	2440–245F	
43	ENCLOSED ALPHANUMERICS	2460–24FF	
44	BOX DRAWING	2500–257F	
45	BLOCK ELEMENTS	2580–259F	
46	GEOMETRIC SHAPES	25A0–25FF	
47	MISCELLANEOUS SYMBOLS	2600–26FF	
48	DINGBATS	2700–27BF	

Collection Number	Collection Name	Positions	Comment
49	CJK SYMBOLS AND PUNCTUATION	3000–303F	
50	HIRAGANA	3040–309F	
51	KATAKANA	30A0–30FF	
52	BOPOMOFO	3100–312F, 31A0–31BF	
53	HANGUL COMPATIBILITY JAMO	3130–318F	
54	CJK MISCELLANEOUS	3190–319F	
55	ENCLOSED CJK LETTERS AND MONTHS	3200–32FF	
56	CJK COMPATIBILITY	3300–33FF	
57-59	–	–	Collections 57–59 deleted by ISO/IEC 10646-1:1993 Amendment 5.
60	CJK UNIFIED IDEOGRAPHS	4E00–9FFF	
61	PRIVATE USE AREA	E000–F8FF	
62	CJK COMPATIBILITY IDEOGRAPHS	F900–FAFF	
63	ALPHABETIC PRESENTATION FORMS	FB00–FB4F	
64	ARABIC PRESENTATION FORMS-A	FB50–FDFF	
65	COMBINING HALF MARKS	FE20–FE2F	
66	CJK COMPATIBILITY FORMS	FE30–FE4F	
67	SMALL FORM VARIANTS	FE50–FE6F	
68	ARABIC PRESENTATION FORMS-B	FE70–FEFE	
69	HALFWIDTH AND FULLWIDTH FORMS	FF00–FFEF	
70	SPECIALS	FFF0–FFFD	
71	HANGUL SYLLABLES	AC00–D7A3	
72	BASIC TIBETAN	0F00–0FBF	
73	ETHIOPIC	1200–137F	
74	UNIFIED CANADIAN ABORIGINAL SYLLABICS	1400–167F	
75	CHEROKEE	13A0–13FF	

Continued

Table C-3 *Continued*

Collection Number	Collection Name	Positions	Comment
76	YI SYLLABLES	A000–A48F	
77	YI RADICALS	A490–A4CF	
78	KANGXI RADICALS	2F00–2FDF	
79	CJK RADICALS SUPPLEMENT	2E80–2EFF	
80	BRAILLE PATTERNS	2800–28FF	
81	CJK UNIFIED IDEOGRAPHS EXTENSION A	3400–4DBF	
82	OGHAM	1680–169F	
83	RUNIC	16A0–16FF	
84	SINHALA	0D80–0DFF	
85	SYRIAC	0700–074F	
86	THAANA	0780–07BF	
87	BASIC MYANMAR	1000–104F, 200C, 200D	
88	KHMER	1780–17FF, 200C, 200D	
89	MONGOLIAN	1800–18AF	
90	EXTENDED MYANMAR	1050–109F	
91	TIBETAN	0F00–0FFF	
200	ZERO-WIDTH BOUNDARY INDICATORS	200B–200D, FEFF	
201	FORMAT SEPARATORS	2028–2029	
202	BI-DIRECTIONAL FORMAT MARKS	200E–200F	
203	BI-DIRECTIONAL FORMAT EMBEDDINGS	202A–202E	
204	HANGUL FILL CHARACTERS	3164, FFA0	
205	CHARACTER SHAPING SELECTORS	206A–206D	
206	NUMERIC SHAPE SELECTORS	206E–206F	
207	IDEOGRAPHIC DESCRIPTION CHARACTERS		2FF0–2FFF
250	GENERAL FORMAT CHARACTERS		Collections 200–203

Collection Number	Collection Name	Positions	Comment
251	SCRIPT-SPECIFIC FORMAT CHARACTERS		Collections 204–207
270	COMBINING CHARACTERS		Characters specified in Annex B.1 of ISO/IEC 10646-1:2000.
271	COMBINING CHARACTERS B-2		Characters specified in Annex B.1 of ISO/IEC 10646-1:2000.
299	BMP FIRST EDITION		BMP characters defined by the ISO/IEC 10646-1:1993 (with no amendments applied).
300	BMP	0000–D7FF, E000–FFFD	Does not include the S-zone.
301	BMP-AMD.7		BMP characters defined by ISO/IEC 10646-1:1993 with amendments 1–7 applied. This is identical to the repertoire of the Unicode Standard, Version 2.0.

Continued

Table C-3 *Continued*

Collection Number	Collection Name	Positions	Comment
302	BMP SECOND EDITION		BMP characters defined by the ISO/IEC 10646-1:2000 (with no amendments applied).
400	PRIVATE USE PLANES	G=00, P=0F, 10, & E0–FF	
500	PRIVATE USE GROUPS	G=60–7F	

Note

The ISO/IEC 10646-1:2000 collections shown here are based on preliminary information, and there may be minor differences between these and the collections in the balloted standard.

In the majority of cases, each of the collections defined in ISO/IEC 10646-1:2000 corresponds to a single block. The exceptions are merged or partial blocks, such as the HEBREW EXTENDED subset that includes parts of the HEBREW block (that corresponds to the ISO/IEC 10646-1:1993 HEBREW EXTENDED-A and HEBREW EXTENDED-B blocks); subdivisions of other blocks, such as format separators; and other collections, such as combining characters.

Appendix D

Other Resources

This appendix provides links to material on the Web that is not provided by either the Unicode Consortium or WG2. The references are arranged in alphabetical order by topic.

Bibliographies

BibTeX bibliography
Bibliography, in BibTeX format, of books, articles, and other materials that are related to Unicode. `http://www.math.utah.edu/pub/tex/bib/unicode.html`.

C/C++ Libraries

IBM Classes for Unicode
Open source C and C++ library. `http://www10.software.ibm.com/developerworks/opensource/icu/project/index.html`.

Rosette C++ Library for Unicode by Basis Technology
Royalty-free source code or object code. `http://unicode.basistech.com/`.

Batam by Alis Technologies
Windows DLL and ancillary files. `http://www.alis.com/castil/batam.html`.

Unilib by Sybase
Part of the Sybase Developer's Kit for Unicode (UDK). http://www.sybase.com/products/global/products/unilib.html.

libutf-8 by Whiz Kid Technomagic
Free function library. http://www.whizkidtech.net/i18n/.

UniAPI by Bjondi International
Free function library. http://www.bjondi.com/products/uniapi/.

UCData by Mark Leisher
Free function library. http://crl.nmsu.edu/~mleisher/ucdata.html.

Character Sets and Encodings

ConScript Unicode Registry
Coordinated assignment of blocks within the Private Use areas. http://www.ccil.org/~cowan/csur/index.html and http://www.egt.ie/standards/csur/index.html.

Good Ole' ASCII
Discussion of ASCII, EBCDIC, ISO 646, and Unicode. http://czyborra.com/charsets/iso646.html.

Non-Unicode Character Encodings
Broad overview of character encoding structures. http://developer.apple.com/techpubs/mac/TextEncodingCMgr/TECRefBook-142.html.

The ISO 8859 Alphabet Soup
Character charts and discussion of the numerous parts of ISO 8859. http://czyborra.com/charsets/iso8859.html.

UTF-7
RFC defining UTF-7. ftp://ftp.isi.edu/in-notes/rfc2152.txt.

UTF-8
RFC defining UTF-8 for the Internet. ftp://ftp.isi.edu/in-notes/rfc2279.txt.

DSSSL

DSSSList mailing list
http://www.mulberrytech.com/dsssl/dssslist/.

James Clark's DSSSL page
http://www.jclark.com/dsssl/.

Fonts

Unicode Corporate Use Subarea as used by Adobe Systems
http://partners.adobe.com/asn/developer/typeforum/
corporateuse.txt.

Microsoft Character Design Standards
General rules for character shapes in Latin fonts. Includes discussion of different diacritic shapes for different languages. http://www.
microsoft.com/typography/developers/fdsspec/.

Character sets and codepages
Discusses relationship of characters, glyphs, and fonts. http://www.
microsoft.com/typography/unicode/cscp.htm.

Character sets
Yet another discussion of characters, glyphs, and fonts. http://www.
microsoft.com/typography/unicode/cs.htm.

Polish diacritics: how to?
Typographic properties of Polish diacritics. http://www.font.org/.

Fonts for the Unicode Character Set
What Unicode is, who uses it, and lists of fonts and other resources.
http://www.math.utah.edu/~beebe/fonts/unicode.html.

Fonts that support Unicode
Comprehensive list of fonts arranged by coverage. http://www.
hclrss.demon.co.uk/unicode/fonts.html.

Unicode and glyph names

Adobe Postscript glyph naming conventions in the context of Unicode.
`http://partners.adobe.com/asn/developer/typeforum/`
`unicodegn.html`.

WGL4.01 character set

Specification of Microsoft's standardized Pan-European character set.
`http://www.microsoft.com/typography/OTSPEC/WGL4.htm`.

HTML

HTML 3.2 Recommendation

`http://www.w3.org/TR/REC-html32.html`.

HTML 4.0 Recommendation

`http://www.w3.org/TR/html401/`.

Internationalization of the Hypertext Markup Language

The RFC that put the UCS in HTML. `ftp://ftp.isi.edu/`
`in-notes/rfc2070.txt`.

Ruby

Proposal for XHTML markup for ruby text. `http://www.w3.org/`
`TR/WD-ruby`.

Web History

Historical documents about the development of HTML and the World
Wide Web. `http://www.w3.org/History/`.

XHTML 1.0 Recommendation

A reformulation of HTML as an XML application. This is the successor
to HTML 4. `http://www.w3.org/TR/xhtml1/`.

Internet

Character model for the World Wide Web

How the W3C wants to handle text on the Web. `http://www.w3.`
`org/TR/charmod/`.

HTTP/1.1

Definition of the Hypertext Transfer Protocol, including definition of the `content-type` header and the `charset` parameter. `ftp://ftp.isi.edu/in-notes/rfc2616.txt`.

IANA Character Set Registry

`http://www.isi.edu/in-notes/iana/assignments/character-sets`.

IANA Charset Registration Procedures

The RFC that sets up the IANA Character Set Registry. `ftp://ftp.isi.edu/in-notes/rfc2278.txt`.

IETF Policy on Character Sets and Languages

Policies for coping with the international nature of the Internet. `ftp://ftp.isi.edu/in-notes/rfc2277.txt`.

Requirements for String Identity and Character Indexing Definitions for the World Wide Web

`http://www.w3.org/TR/WD-charreq`.

RFC Search Page

A useful page when you don't know the RFC number. `http://www.rfc-editor.org/rfcsearch.html`.

The Multilingual World Wide Web

Opinion piece that, among other things, views the Web as a single, very large application. `http://www.mind-to-mind.com/documents/i18n/multilingual-www.html`.

Unicode support in browsers

Test pages for Unicode character ranges. `http://www.hclrss.demon.co.uk/unicode/`.

ISO

ISO 639 Language Codes

`http://www.oasis-open.org/cover/iso639a.html`.

ISO 3166 Country Codes
http://www.oasis-open.org/cover/country3166.html.

Linux

Linux Internationalisation Initiative
Working group established on October 1, 1999, to develop and promote interoperable internationalized APIs for Linux. http://www.li18nux.org/.

UTF-8 and Unicode FAQ for Unix/Linux
What you need to know to use Unicode and, specifically, UTF-8 on Unix/Linux systems. http://www.cl.cam.ac.uk/~mgk25/unicode.html.

Mac OS

Apple Type Services for Unicode Imaging (ATSUI)
Definition of the ATSUI API. http://developer.apple.com/techpubs/macos8/TextIntlSvcs/ATSUI/atsui.html.

Unicode Utilities
Documentation on Unicode utilities and Unicode input support in Mac OS 9. http://developer.apple.com/techpubs/macos8/TextIntlSvcs/UnicodeUtilities/unicodeutil.html.

Magazines

Multilingual Computing & Technology
Bimonthly magazine and associated Web site. The name says it all. http://www.multilingual.com.

Programming Languages

Perl
http://www.perl.com/.

Perl 5.6
Article describing Perl 5.6's features. http://www.perl.com/pub/1999/06/perl5-6.html.

Python
http://www.python.org/

Python String SIG Activities
http://starship.python.net/crew/amk/python/string.html.

Tcl
http://www.scriptics.com/.

VBScript
http://msdn.microsoft.com/scripting/.

Visual J++, Visual Basic
http://msdn.microsoft.com/vstudio/.

Solaris

Unicode Support in the Solaris 7 Operating Environment
White paper on Unicode support. http://www.sun.com/software/white-papers/wp-unicode/.

SGML

Comparison of SGML and XML, World Wide Web Consortium Note 15-December-1997, James Clark, http://www.w3.org/TR/ NOTE-sgml-xml.
Detailed description of similarities and differences between SGML and XML. Source of the SGML declaration for XML, which is an example of how to specify ISO/IEC 10646-1 as the character set for your SGML documents.

Robin Cover's SGML/XML Web Page
Definitive bibliography of all things related to SGML. http://www. oasis-open.org/cover/sgml-xml.html.

XML and Certain XML Applications

All of the major applications of XML are too numerous to mention here, so this section lists only those that have been mentioned in the book.

MathML Recommendation
http://www.w3.org/TR/REC-MathML/.

Changes to XML to match Unicode 3.0
Unofficial proposal listing changes to XML 1.0 so it uses the Unicode 3.0 repertoire. http://www.lists.ic.ac.uk/hypermail/xml-dev/ xml-dev-Sep-1999/0476.html and related messages.

Robin Cover's SGML/XML Web Page
Definitive bibliography of all things related to XML. http://www. oasis-open.org/cover/sgml-xml.html.

XML Recommendation
http://www.w3.org/TR/REC-xml.

Glossary

Abugida

A particular writing system where basic characters denote consonants with an inherent vowel, and where other vowel symbols modify the vowel sound of the consonant.

AFII

Association for Font Information Interchange. AFII is now defunct: the Association was dissolved after it had completed the final draft of the second edition of ISO/IEC 10646:1. Glyph registrations under ISO/IEC 10036:1996 that were handled by AFII are now handled by the Unicode Consortium.

Alphabet

Any writing system that includes both vowels and consonants.

Alphasyllabary

A writing system where vowels are indicated by subsidiary or diacritic symbols on or near the consonants.

Allocation Area

A group of character blocks; for example, "General Scripts." An allocation area is basically just a convenient label.

B.C.E.

Before Common Era. A non-sectarian year designation equivalent to B.C. ("Before Christ").

BMP

Basic Multilingual Plane. Conceptually, the *UCS* is comprised of 128 three-dimensional groups. Each group contains 256 planes, and each plane contains 256 rows, each of which contains 256 cells. Plane 00 of Group 00 is the BMP.

Boustrophedon

Writing organized in alternate lines of right-to-left and left-to-right text (or vice versa). The name is from the Greek for "ox turns," referring to the way an ox plows a field in strips running in alternate directions. While many scripts have used this style, none have retained it up to the present.

C.E.

Common Era. A non-sectarian year designation equivalent to A.D. (*anno domini*, "in the year of the Lord").

Conjoin

(v.) To combine.

Conjoining Jamo

Hangul characters that combine with each other, and not with other combining characters, to form Hangul syllables.

Digraph

A pair of letters denoting a single sound; for example, *ph*, *ch*.

EBCDIC

Extended Binary Coded Decimal Interchange Code. See the IBM publication, *IBM Character Data Representation Architecture, Reference and Registry, SC09:2190:00, December 1996.*

ECMA

An international Europe-based industry association. Originally known as "European Computer Manufacturers' Association," the organization changed its name in 1994 to "ECMA – an international Europe-based industry association for standardizing information and communication." In ECMA publications, the "international" is frequently made bold to remind you of the association's current focus. Many ECMA standards have been adopted as ISO standards.

FSS-UTF

File System Safe UTF. An earlier name for UTF-8. See *UTF-8*.

GL

Graphic Left, i.e., the graphic character set with the code point range 0x20–0x7F. These particular code points are in the left half of a 16(16 grid.

Here, the columns correspond to the most significant four bits of a code point value (the "2" in "0x20") and the rows correspond to the least significant four bits of a code point value (the "0" digit at the end of "0x20").

GMS
Global Meeting Services, Inc. The corporation licensed by the Unicode Consortium to organize the semi-annual International Unicode Conferences (IUC).

GR
Graphic Right, i.e., the graphic character set with the code point range 0xA0–0xFF. These particular code points are in the right half of a 16(16 grid. Here, the columns correspond to the most significant four bits of a code point value (the "" in "0xA0") and the rows correspond to the least significant four bits of a code point value (the "0" digit at the end of "0xA0").

Group
The term for a collection of 128 planes in the *ISO/IEC 10646* model of the *UCS*.

Group-octet
The most significant octet of the four octets of a UCS-4 code value. Identifies the group of a character. See *octet*.

Hangul
The script used for the Korean language.

HTML
HyperText Markup Language.

IANA
Internet Assigned Numbers Authority. See http://www.iana.org/.

IEC
International Electrotechnical Commission. See http://www.iec.ch/ and http://www.hike.te.chiba-u.ac.jp/ikeda/IEC/home.html.

IETF
Internet Engineering Task Force. See http://www.ietf.org/.

Informative

A portion of a standard that is provided for information only. Compliance or non-compliance with an informative section does not affect an application's conformance with the standard.

Input method

Any scheme by which a program or application translates keyboard input (generally from the user) into characters in a different script. Input methods become necessary when a script contains more characters than can be represented on a conventional computer keyboard. To give a simplistic example, Japanese kanji is often entered by typing the Roman transliteration, e.g., nihongo, which is automatically transliterated to hiragana, にほんご, and, at user option, the hiragana is then converted to kanji, e.g., 日本語.

Input method editor

Software (for example, Microsoft Global IME) that captures keyboard input and converts it to characters in a different script.

IRG

Ideographic Rapporteur Group or Ideographic character Rapporteur Group. See http://www.cse.cuhk.edu.hk/~irg/.

ISO

International Organization for Standardization. Note that "ISO" is not an acronym, but instead is derived from the Greek word "isos," meaning, "equal." "Isos" also gives us the prefix "iso-", meaning equal (as in "isobar" and "isosceles," etc.). With a bit of effort, "iso-" can be construed to mean "uniform" or even "standardized," so "ISO" becomes a play upon the meaning of the "iso-" prefix. "ISO" is used in place of "IOS" because the acronym would be different in different languages whereas the term "ISO" is, well, standardized. See http://www.iso.ch/.

ISO 8879:1986

Information processing – Text and Office Systems – Standard Generalized Markup Language (SGML).

ISO/IEC 10646

Information technology – Universal Multiple Octet Coded Character Set.

ISO/IEC 2022:1994
Information Technology – Character code structure and extension techniques.

ISO/IEC JTC1
ISO and IEC joint technical committee on Information Technology.

ISO/IEC JTC1/SC2
Subcommittee of ISO/IEC JTC1 that is responsible for WG2.

ISO/IEC JTC1/SC2/WG2
Working group responsible for *ISO/IEC 10646*.

IUC
International Unicode Conference. Held semi-annually in San Jose each September and at a different location each March.

Jamo
The Korean name for the characters that may be combined, or *conjoined*, to compose a Hangul syllable.

Katakana
カタカナ. One of the two syllabaries used in writing Japanese. Typically used for loan words from other languages. Was also used for the address on my electricity bills, as I recall.

Half-width Katakana
半角カタカナ. Katakana written in half the width of a kanji. For example, this is full-width katana: カタカナ, and this is the same text written with half-width katakana: ｶﾀｶﾅ.

L2
Technical committee L2 of NCITS is responsible for the creation and maintenance of US standards for the coding of graphic and control characters. See http://www.ncits.org/tc_home/l2.htm. Unicode Inc. is a member of L2, and L2 meetings are held concurrently with UTC meetings.

Limited Subset
Refers to the subset of the ISO/IEC 10646 character repertoire where each character in the subset is listed by name or code position.

NCITS

(Pronounced "insights.") National Committee for Information Technology Standards. NCITS develops national standards in information technology (for example, SCSI-2 interface, MPEG/JPEG, OCR characters), and its technical experts represent the United States to ISO/IEC JTC1. See http://www.ncits.org/.

Normative

A portion of a standard to which conforming applications must comply.

Octet

A collection of eight binary digits used to encode data. Not quite synonymous with "byte," the term is generally used in telecommunications and encoding, and does not relate to memory or data processing.

Plane

A block of 65,536 (2^{16}) code values in the *ISO/IEC 10646* model of the *UCS*.

Plane-octet

One of the four octets of a *UCS-4* character number. The Plane-octet (or P-octet) identifies the plane of a character. See *octet*.

Presentation Form

An alternative glyph or ligature for a character or characters that is included in a character set or, more often, in a font for the convenience of rendering multiple different representations of the character(s). The Unicode Standard encodes some presentation forms of characters as compatibility characters included for round-trip mapping between the Unicode Standard and existing standards.

RCSU

Reuters Compression Scheme for Unicode.

SCSU

Standard Compression Scheme for Unicode.

Selected Subset

Refers to the subset of the ISO/IEC 10646 character repertoire consisting of one or more of the collections listed in Annex A of each part of ISO/IEC 10646.

SGML

Standard Generalized Markup Language. See ISO 8879:1986.

Subset

Refers to the portion of the ISO/IEC 10646 character repertoire that an originating or receiving device supports. Subsets may be *limited subsets*, *selected subsets*, or a combination of the two. The Unicode Standard does not define subsets, and applications conforming to that standard are expected to handle all characters.

Surrogate

A code value from the surrogate area of the *BMP*. In the UTF-16 encoding, a code value from the High Surrogates block (U+D800–U+DB7F) or High Private Use Surrogates block (U+DB80–U+DBFF) followed by a code value from the Low Surrogates block (U+DC00–U+DFFF) represents an encoded character from planes 1 to 16.

Syllabary

A writing system where each sign represents a syllable.

Transcode

(v.) To translate from one character encoding to another. Transcoding can sometimes be algorithmic, such as the conversion between Shift-JIS and EUC-JP or between *UTF-8* and *UCS-2*. Many transcodings, such as those between existing character encodings and the Unicode Standard, require mapping tables when there is no consistent relationship between character numbers in the two encodings.

UCS

Universal Character Set.

UCS-2

Two-octet form of the *UCS*. Encodes characters in the Basic Multilingual Plane (*BMP*) only.

UCS-4

Four-octet form of the *UCS*. In the 128 three-dimensional group model of the UCS, the four octets of a UCS-4 code value, from most-significant to least-significant, identify a character's Group, Plane, Row, and Column, respectively.

Unicode Character Database
A set of text files collectively containing all the information about the normative and informative properties of the characters in the Unicode Standard. Most files are comprised of lines of semicolon-delimited data fields.

Unicode Consortium
The organization that publishes and promotes the Unicode Standard and related Technical Reports.

Unicode, Inc.
The Unicode Consortium's California-based non-profit company.

UTC
Unicode Technical Committee.

UTF
Unicode Transformation Format or UCS Transformation Format.

UTF-2
An earlier name for UTF-8. See UTF-8.

UTF-7
Unicode (or UCS) Transformation Format, 7-bit form.

UTF-8
Unicode (or UCS) Transformation Format, 8-bit form.

UTF-16
Unicode (or UCS) Transformation Format, 16-bit form.

UTR
Unicode Technical Report.

XML
Extensible Markup Language. See http://www.w3.org/TR/1998/
REC-xml-19980210.

Bibliography

Clark, James. *Comparison of SGML and XML*, World Wide Web Consortium Note 15 December 1997, http://www.w3.org/TR/NOTE-sgml-xml.

Crystal, David. *The Cambridge Encyclopedia of Language*. Second ed. Cambridge [etc.], Cambridge University Press, 1997. ISBN 0-521-5596-7.

Dalby, Andrew. *Dictionary of Languages*. New York, Columbia University Press, 1998. ISBN 0-231-11568-7.

De Roo, Joseph R. *2001 Kanji*. Second ed. Tokyo, Bonjinsha, 1982.

Extensible Markup Language (XML), 1.0. (W3C Recommendation 10 February 1998). (REC-XML-19980210). Editors: Tim Bray, Jean Paoli, and C. M. Sperberg-McQueen. http://www.w3.org/TR/1998/REC-xml-19980210.

Flanagan, David. *Java in a Nutshell*. Second ed. Cambridge [etc.], O'Reilly, 1997. ISBN 1-56592-262-X.

Gillam, Richard. *Internationalization in ECMAScript*. 15th International Unicode Conference, San Jose, California, September 1-2, 1999.

Goosens, Michel, Sebastian Rahtz, Eitan M. Gurari, Ross Moore, and Robert S. Sutor. *The LaTeX Web Companion*. Reading [etc.], Addison-Wesley, 1999. ISBN 0-201-43311-7.

Goldfarb, Charles F. *The SGML Handbook*. Oxford, Oxford University Press, 1990. ISBN 0-19-853737-9.

Graham, Tony. *XML and Internet Internationalization*. Multilingual Computing & Technology, Volume 9, Issue 4, June 1998, 32–33.

Huang, Kai-tung. *An Introduction to Chinese, Japanese, and Korean Computing*, by Jack K. T. Huang and Timothy D. Huang. Singapore, Teaneck, NJ, World Scientific, 1989. ISBN 9971-50-664-5.

Internet Mail Consortium. *Using International Characters in Internet Mail*. Internet Mail Consortium Report: MAIL-I18N, IMCR-010, August 1, 1998. http://www.imc.org/mail-i18.html.

Jenkins, John J. *New Ideographs in Unicode 3.0 and Beyond*. 15th International Unicode Conference, San Jose, California, September 1-2, 1999.

Kano, Nadine. *Developing International Software for Windows 95 and Windows NT*. Redmond, Microsoft Press, 1995. ISBN 1-55615-840-8.

Katzner, Kenneth. *The Languages of the World*. New ed. London, Routledge, 1995. ISBN 0-415-11809-3.

Lehey, Greg. *The Complete FreeBSD*. Walnut Creek, Walnut Creek CDROM, 1999. ISBN 1-57176-246-9.

Lunde, Ken. *CJKV Information Processing*. Beijing [etc.], O'Reilly, 1999. ISBN 1-56592-224-7.

Lunde, Ken. *Understanding Japanese Information Processing*. Sebastapol, O'Reilly, 1993. ISBN 1-56592-043-0.

Microsoft. *Microsoft Global IME 5.0 (Korean)*. Microsoft, 1998.

Microsoft. *MSDN Library – Visual Studio 6.0*. Microsoft, 1998. (X03-55262).

Monotype Typography. *WorldType Solutions Catalogue*. Elk Grove Village, IL, The Monotype Group; Surrey, Monotype Typography, 1998.

O'Conner, John. *Displaying Unicode with Java's Composite Fonts*. 15th International Unicode Conference, San Jose, California, September 1-2, 1999.

Sun Microsystems. *Unicode Support in the Solaris 7 Operating Environment.* http://www.sun.com/software/white-papers/wp-unicode/.

Tenney, Merle. *Unicode Applications for the Macintosh,* Multilingual Computing & Technology, Volume 10, Issue 3, April 1999, 46–49.

Turley, James. *Computing in Mongolian,* Multilingual Computing & Technology, Volume 10, Issue 1, December 1998, 29–31.

Turley, James. *Computing in Tibetan,* Multilingual Computing & Technology, Volume 9, Issue 6, October 1998, 30–33.

The Unicode Consortium. *The Unicode Standard, Version 2.0.* Reading [etc.], Addison-Wesley Developers Press, 1996. ISBN 0-201-48345-9.

The Unicode Consortium. *The Unicode Standard, Version 3.0.* Reading [etc.], Addison-Wesley Longman, 2000. ISBN 0-201-61633-5.

The World's Writing Systems. Edited by Peter T. Daniels and William Bright. New York, Oxford University Press, 1996. ISBN 0-19-507993-0.

Yergeau, F.,G. Nicol, G. Adams, M. Dürst. RFC 2070, *Internationalization of the Hypertext Markup Language,* http://www.ietf.org/rfc/rfc2070.txt.

Index

8-bit character sequences, trans-
  forming Unicode charac-
  ters to, 21
8-bit clean e-mail systems, 85
16-bit character sequences. *See
  also* UCS-2
  available vs. used code posi-
    tions, 22
  character numbers for, 79
  default character encoding
    form, 79
  enlarging using UTF-16
    encoding, 21
  needed code positions, 22
  UCS-2 character set (16-bit)
    for, 82
  as Unicode Standard, 21
32-bit character sequences. *See*
  UCS-4

A

A-zone (ISO/IEC
  10646-1:1993), 73
  Unicode standard equivalents,
    74
AAT (Apple Advanced
  Typography), 316
Abstract Windowing Toolkit
  (AWT), font-definitions
  using, 317–318
accented characters
  creating, 26

typographical conventions,
  312, 314
Accept-Charset, request-header
  field, 216
Afrikaans, Latin Extended-A
  character block, 34–35
Alias field (character set registry
  files), 217–218
allocation areas, 32
  CJK Ideographs, 33, 42
  CJK Phonetics and Symbols,
    33, 40–41
  Compatibility and Specials,
    33, 45–46
  General Scripts, 32, 34–38
  Hangul Syllables, 33, 43
  Private Use, 33, 45
  Surrogates, 33, 44
  Symbols, 33, 38–40
  Yi Syllables, 33, 43
Alphabet Presentation Forms
  character block, 45
Alphabetic property, 113, 117
Amharic, Ethiopic character
  block, 34, 37
Annex A (ISO/IEC 10646), 69
ANSI/ISO C, 242
ANSI single-character string-
  handling, 230
API, Windows 2000, Unicode
  Standard 2.0 compliance,
    231

apostrophe (ISO 8859-1 standard), mapping to Unicode characters, 105
Apple Advanced Typography (AAT), 316
Apple LastResort font, 319
applications, ISO/IEC 10646-conforming, 175
applications, Unicode-conforming. *See also* Unicode support
allowed modifications, 174
code value interpretations, 174
invalid code values, 173
surrogate pair support, 173
Unicode Standard components, 171–172
Unicode Transformation Formats support, 172–173
Arabic
Arabic-Indic digits, 126
Arabic Presentation Forms-A character block, 45, 46
Arabic Presentation Forms-B character block, 45, 46
character block, 34, 36
glyphs for, 55
joining/shaping guides, 55–56
in Macintosh systems, 236
right-to-left script, 145
ArabicShaping.txt (Unicode Character Database), 52, 55–56
architecture
ISO/IEC standard overview, 61–63
Unicode Standard overview, 20–21
Arial Unicode MS, 320
Armenian
character block, 34–35

presentation forms, 45
Arrows character block, 38, 39
ASCII-based systems, transferring data to EBCDIC-based systems, 87
ASCII characters
Basic Latin character block, 34–35
for HTML tags, 156
for language-identifier tags, 143
numeric character references, 228
Small Form Variants character block, 45, 46
UTF-7 encoding format, 85, 86
UTF-8 encoding format, 80, 93
UTF-16 encoding format, 85, 89–90
for XML declarations, 156
AscW() function
VBScript scripting language, 302
Visual Basic programming language, 292
Assamese, Bengali character block, 34, 36
Athabaskan, Unified Canadian Aboriginal Syllabics character block, 34, 37
ATSUI component (Apple Type Services for Unicode Imaging), 236–237
AWT (Java Abstract Windowing Toolkit), 317–318
Azerbaijani, Latin Extended-B character block, 34–35

B

base characters, defined, 119
Base64 encoding format
    applications for, 87
    definition (RFC 1521), 86,
        88
    maximum line length, 88
    using, 87
    with UTF-7, 85–86
BASESET keyword (SGML
    declaration), 222–223
Basic Latin character block,
    34–35
BASIC LATIN collection
    (ISO/IEC 10646), 69
Basic Multilingual Plane. *See*
    BMP (Basic Multilingual
    Plane)
Basic Unicode Support (regular
    expression engines), 152
Batam Unicode conversion API
    (Alis Technologies), 244
BDF Unicode fonts (X Window
    systems), 320
Beebe, Nelson, Unicode bibliog-
    raphy, 6
Bengali
    character block, 34, 36
    currency numerations, 127
    digits, 126
bidirectional algorithm, 145–150
    bidirectional category values,
        147–150
    HTML Recommendation ref-
        erences, 189–190, 194
    overriding, 146–149, 194
    UTR #9 definition, 124,
        145–146, 171
Bidirectional category
    descriptions, sources for, 124
    values, 147–150

bidirectionality in Web commu-
    nications, 182
Bidirectonal mapping field
    (Unicode Character
    Database), 124, 131
    properties in, 114
big-endian computers, 68, 97,
    193
    BOM (Byte Order Mark)
        character, 98–99
    byte order, 173
    encoding formats, 66
    network byte order for, 193
Bitsteam Cyberbit font, 320
Block Elements character block,
    38, 40
blocks (ISO/IEC 10646), 31,
    68
    relationship of ISO/IEC
        10646 collections to, 70
    Unicode Standard equivalent,
        74
Blocks.txt, 52, 56–57
BMP (Basic Multilingual Plane),
    8, 62–63
    G-octet/P-octet values, 81
    handling characters outside of,
        79–80
    RC-elements, 62
    Unicode Standard support
        limitations, 69
    zones, 71–74
BOM (Byte Order Mark) char-
    acter, 89, 132. *See also*
    directionality; endianness
    applications that use, 68
    as encoding signature, 98
    in Java applications, 259–260
    Special character block, 45, 46
    in Tcl applications, 288
                        Continued

BOM *(continued)*
in Unicode-conforming applications, 173
with UTF-16 encoded applications, 209
with Web browser applications, 258–259
Bopomofo
character block, 40, 41
extended character block, 40, 41
Box Drawing character block, 38, 40
Braille Patterns
character block, 38, 40
character-naming conventions, 130
Burmese, Myanmar character block, 34, 37
Byte Order Mark. *See* BOM (Byte Order Mark)
byte order, 97–98; 132, 172–174. *See also* bidirectional algorithm; BOM (Byte Order Mark); endianness; signatures
bytes. *See also* UCS-2 character set; UCS-4 character set
in Base64-encoding format, 88–89
in C/C++ programs using UTF-8, 242
differences from characters, 183
in EUC-KR encoding, 227
in Java applications, 262
MBCS (multi-byte character strings), 183, 242
mixing in character sets in, 20
network byte order, 193

non-ASCII characters in Web documents, 187
versus octets, 10, 61
one-byte-per-character strings (ANSI), 230
in Perl utf8 pragma, 277
in POSIX interfaces, 235
recognizing, in XML documents, 156
in SCSU compression, 100–102
and Unicode conformance, 96
in UTF-7 encoding format, 84, 86
in UTF-8 encoding format, 90–95

C
C/C++ programming language
bidirectional algorithm source code, 146
string handling, 241–242
Unicode support, 242–246
C normalization form, 135, 138
C-octet (UCS-2), 82
C-style escape sequences (Java), 259–260
C0/C1 control characters, naming, 130
CANCEL TAG character, with language tags, 142
Canonical combining class field (Unicode Character Database), 113, 121
canonical composition/decomposition, 123, 135
canonical mappings, 51, 122–123
canonical ordering, 27, 119–121
capitalization, Case property values, 117–118

CARRIAGE RETURN character
Base64 encoding format, 88
UTF-7 encoding format, 86
case conversion guidelines, 118
case detection guidelines, 118
Case mapping property, 113, 118
case mappings
fields for, 53–54
specialized, 54–55
Case Mappings (UTR #21), 172
implementation guidelines, 118
case matching (XML documents), 209
Case property, 113, 117–118
case sensitivity/insensitivity
in language tags, 214
in XML documents, 209
caseless matching guidelines, 118
CC-data-element (ISO/IEC 10646), Unicode Standard equivalent, 74
Cell-octets. *See* C-octet
cells
C-octet representation (UCS-2), 82
in UCS architecture, 62–63
character addresses, Planes 1-16, 79
character blocks (Unicode Standard)
applicability to multiple scripts, 47
General Scripts allocation area, 35–38
ISO/IEC 10646 standard equivalent, 74
listing of (Blocks.txt), 56–57
Character class (Java), class methods, 260–261

character code conversions
Mac OS X Server support for, 237
Macintosh OS 8.5 support for, 236–237
Character decomposition mapping field (Unicode Character Database), 114, 122, 207
character encoding
default, 79
forms for, 79
identifying in HTML documents, 191–193
IE5 (Internet Explorer 5) options, 195
Netscape Communicator 4.7 options, 199–200
Character Encoding Model (UTR #17), 172
character mapping
encoding forms, 79
round-trip, glyphs for, 58
Solaris 7 systems, 316–317
Character Model for the World Wide Web, 181–182
Character name field (Unicode Character Database), 114, 129–130
character names (ISO/IEC 10646), 11
character numbers, 79
character properties, Perl support for, 283
character references
adjusting for Netscape (HTML code listing), 201–202
in DSSSL applications, 246–247

Continued

character references *(continued)*
in ECMAScript applications,
limitations in, 252–253
in Java applications, 260–261
in XML Recommendation,
205
character sets/sequences
aliases, 218
allocation areas, 32
bidirectional algorithm,
145–150
decomposition versus canonical ordering, 121
defining in SGML declara-
tions, 221–224
IANA registry files for,
216–220
in CJK ideographs, authorities
for, 164–165
language identification, 139
language tagging, 139
Perl support for, 285–286
precomposed, 121
registration procedures (IETC
RFC 2278), 216
16-bit, 21
Solaris 7 supported, 233–234
storing in logical order, 24
variants among, 19–20
character strings
8-bit, sorting/searching,
152–153
generating in Java, sample
code, 263–268
handling in Perl applications,
277
parsing, in higher-level protocols, 155–156
parsing in Macintosh systems,
237

regular expressions, guidelines
for, 151–152
rendering, difficulties of,
150–151
string identity matching problems, 184–185
in Visual Basic applications,
292
in Windows systems, 230
characters
affecting directionality, listing,
147
Alphabetic property, 113, 117
basic information about
(UnicodeData.txt file),
53–54
byte order signatures, characters for, 132
canonical ordering, 119–121
Case mapping, 113, 118
Case property, 113, 117–118
character-naming conventions,
129–130
CJK Unified Ideographs, unification principles, 157–157
combining, canonical ordering
sequences, 119–121
Combining Class, 113, 121
Combining Jamo, 113, 122
combining using canonical
ordering, 27
control characters, 134
Dashes, 113, 122
Decomposition, 114, 122–123
Directionality, 114, 124
East Asian Width, 114, 124
forbidden, in Web applications, 186
versus glyphs, 22–23, intro
identifiers, rules for, 154–155
Ideographic, 114, 124

Jamo Short Name, 114, 125
Letter, 114, 125
Line Breaking, 114, 125
Mathematical, 114, 125
Mirrored, 114, 125–126
new, submitting to Unicode or ISO/IEC, 175–177
Numeric, 114, 126–128
precomposed forms, 26–27
Private Use, 114, 128
properties, listing of, 60–61
PropList.txt properties, 130–131
representing using Surrogate Pairs, 109–110
semantics, 23
Space, 114, 129
special characters, 131–134
storing, logical order for, 145
Surrogate, 114, 129
undefined, 110
Unicode 1.0 Name, 114, 129
Unicode Character Name, 114, 129–130
Unicode Scalar Value (N), 108–109
Unicode Standard definition of, 176
unification across languages, 25–26
unrecognized, handling, 111–112
user-defined assignments, 110–111
charset attribute (HTML documents)
with HTTP Content-Type headers, 215–216
identifying character encoding using, 191, 193

CHARSET keyword (SGML declaration), 222–223
charset parameter (HTTP documents), 191
check-cashing symbols (MICR), Optical Character Resolution character block, 38, 39
Cherokee character block, 34, 37
Chinese. *See also* CJK
Han, CJK Unified Ideographs, 158
Kanbun character block, 40, 41
in Macintosh systems, 236
similar/dissimilar ideographs, 163
in Solaris 7 systems, 234
text display conventions, 312, 313
unifying characters, rules for, 25
Chinese/Japanese/Korean characters. *See* CJK
choseong (Jamo leading consonants/L), 169
ChrW() function
VBScript scripting language, 302–304
Visual Basic programming language, 292
chu Han characters, 158
circled numbers, Numeric property values, 127
CJK Compatibility character block, 40, 41
CJK Compatibility Forms character block, 45, 46
CJK Compatibility Ideographs character block, 45

CJK (Han) Unification, rules for, 161–164

CJK Ideographs area, 33
  block layout, 42
  code value ranges/character block names, 42
  ISO/IEC 10646 standard equivalent, 74

CJK-JRG (CJK Joint Research Group), 159

CJK Phonetics and Symbols area, 33
  block layout, 40
  code value ranges/character block names, 41

CJK Radicals Supplement character block, 40, 41

CJK Symbols and Punctuation character block, 40, 41

CJK Unified Ideographs
  canonical decomposition forms, lack of, 188
  character-naming conventions, 130
  CJK Unified Ideographs character block, 42
  CJK Unified Ideographs Extension A character block, 42
  code charts, 168
  ideograph sequencing, 164–166
  lang attrib with, 197–199
  locale/language indicators, 163–164, 197–199
  output requirements, 164
  source standards, 159–161
  unification principles/rules, 157–158, 161–164

Unihan database, online version (Unihan.html), 167

Unihan database (Unihan.txt), 165–167

CJKV ideographs. *See* CJK Unified Ideographs

class libraries, Unicode-handling (C/C++)
  C/C++ programming language, 243–246
  Visual J++, 270–271

Classes for Unicode (IBM),244

CO control characters, Control Pictures character block, 38, 39

Co value (Private Use property), 128

code charts (CJK Unified Ideographs), 168

Code point (Unicode Standard), ISO/IEC 10646 standard equivalent, 74

Code position (ISO/IEC 10646), Unicode Standard equivalent, 74

code values
  generating using TSM (Text Services Manager), 236
  interpreting, 174
  invalid code values, 173
  ranges, General Scripts allocation area, 35–38
  relationship to UTF-8 bytes, 92
  unrecognized, handling, 111–112

Collection (ISO/IEC 10646), 69–70
  Unicode Standard equivalent, 74

combining characters
canonical ordering sequence, 119–120
combinination properties for Unicode characters, 23
defined, 119
locating combining marks, 25
COMBINING CHARAC-TERS collection, 70
Combining Class property, 113, 121
and canonical ordering, 119–120
Combining Diacritical Marks character block, 34–35
COMBINING DIAERESIS character, 25
COMBINING DOUBLE TILDE character, 119
COMBINING ENCLOSING CIRCLE character, 119
COMBINING GREEK YPOGEGRAMMENI character, 120
Combining Half Marks character block, 45, 46
Combining Jamo property, 113, 122
Combining Marks for Symbols character block, 38, 39
Compatibility and Specials area, 33, 105
block layout, 45
locating combining marks, 25
code value ranges/character block names, 45–46
compatibility characters (XML documents), 206
compatibility decomposition, 123

normalization forms for, 135
Compatibility Han characters, Ideographic property, 124
compatibility mapping, 122–123
composed character sequences, decomposition versus canonical ordering, 121
composition process, 59
composition mappings, 188
exclusions from (CompositionExclusions. txt), 59–60
composition types, normalization forms for, 135
CompositionExclusions.txt, 52, 59–60
single decompositions, 135–136
compression, 100–103
concrete syntax, 224–225
conformance requirements
ISO/IEC 10646-conforming applications, 175
Unicode-conforming applications, 9, 171–174
Content-Type: attribute (HTTP), 215–216
Content-Type header (HTML documents), charset field, 216
control characters, 134
Control Pictures character block, 38, 39
convertibility to pre-existing standards, 27–28
Coptic, Greek character block, 34–35
Corporate Use Subarea (Private Use area), 111
Adobe assignments in, 322

cosenkul. *See* Hangul
country codes (ISO 3166 alpha 2),
214
Cree, Unified Canadian
Aboriginal Syllabics char-
acter block, 34, 37
Cs value (Surrogate property),
129
CSS2 specification, inclusion of
UCS (Universal Character
Set), 183
Currency Symbols character
block, 38, 39, 105
CYRILLIC CAPITAL LET-
TER IE WITH BREVE,
code for, 53–54
CYRILLIC CAPITAL LET-
TER SCHWA, code for,
54
CYRILLIC CAPITAL LIGA-
TURE A IE, code for, 53
Cyrillic character block, 34–35
CYRILLIC SMALL LETTER
IE WITH BREVE, code
for, 54
CYRILLIC SMALL LIGA-
TURE A IE, code for, 53

D
D normalization form, 135, 138
Dae Jaweon dictionary, 164
Dai Kan-Wa Jiten dictionary, 164
Dashes property, 113, 122
data transfers
from ASCII-based to
EBCDIC-based systems,
87
endianness encoding signatures, 98

ISO/IEC 10646 standards
and, 10
databases, Unicode support in,
308–309. *See also* Unicode
Character Database
DataInputStream.readUTF()
(Java), 262
DataInputStream.writeUTF()
(Java), 262
decimal character representations. *See also* numeric
character representations
conversions in VBScript,
302–304
Decimal digit value field
(UnicodeData.txt), 53,
115
groupings for, 126–127
HTML support for, 191
Nd specification for, 126
XML support for, 211–212
decomposition
versus canonical ordering, 121
compatibility versus canonical
mapping, 123
normalization forms for, 135,
188
of precomposed characters,
26–27
process of, 59
singleton characters, 60,
135–136
Decomposition property, 114,
122–123
Default Unicode Collation
Element Table, 153–154
defaults, character encoding
form, 79
DESCSET keyword (SGML
declaration), 222–223

design principles, 20

designation sequences (ISO/IEC 10646)

  in SGML declarations, 223

  Unicode Standard support limitations, 71

Devangari

  character block, 34, 36

  digits, 126

  fonts, 314

diacritic marks

  Combining Marks for Symbols character block, 38, 39

  handling typographic conventions, 312

dictionary authorities, Unihan ideograph sequencing, 164–165

digit values, relationship to numeric values. *See also* zero

DIGIT ZERO, with Tamil digits, 126

digital signatures, WD applicability to, 183

Dingbats character block, 38, 40

dir attributes, using in HTML documents, 194

directionality properties, 145–146

  Directionality property, 114, 124

  high-level protocol controls over, 149–150

  indicating in HTML documents, 194

  logical order for, 24, 145

  Mirrored property, 125–126

  overriding, 146–149, 194

  for Unicode characters, 23

document character set (SGML), 221–224

Document Style and Semantic Specification Language. *See* DSSSL

DOM (Document Object Model), 183

double diacritics, canonical ordering for, 119

DSSSL (Document Style and Semantic Specification Language)

  character/numeric references, 246–248

  definition, 246

  example output, 250

  flow objects/flow object trees, 246

  ISO/IEC 10646 standard reference, 246–247

  sample style sheet, code listing, 248–249

DTD (Document Type Definition), 205

dtmail (Solaris 7), 234

dual-joining, in Arabic/Syriac characters, 55–56

DynaFont Premium 85 Pack, 319

DynaLab Unicode font, 320

dynamic composition, 26

dynamic windows, with SCSU compression, 100–101

E

early normalization

  guidelines for implementing, 186–187

Continued

early normalization *(continued)*
  handling new characters, 188
  string identity matching problems, 184–185
  in Web applications, 184–188
East Asian languages, full-width characters, 57–58
East Asian Width property, 58–59, 114, 124
EastAsianWidth.txt, 52, 57–59
  East Asian Width property, 114, 124
  Ideographic property, 114, 124
Eastern Arabic-Indic digits, 126
EBCDIC-based systems
  EBCDIC-friendly UCS Transformation Format (UTR #16), 172
  transferring data to ASCII-based systems, 87
  UTF-EBCDIC encoding format, 80
ECMAScript
  definition, 250–251
  ECMAScript Language Specification (ECMA-262), 250–253
  JScript example code, 254–257
  relationship to JavaScript/JScript, 251
  Unicode support, 252–259
efficiency, in Unicode design, 20
e-mail
  8-bit clean, 85
  Japanese/Chinese formats, 10
  RFC 1521 guidelines, 85
  "Unicode" list, 13

UTC discussions, 16
UTF-7 formats for, 85–88
Enclosed Alphanumerics character block, 38, 39
Enclosed CKJ Letters and Months character block, 40, 41
encoding formats
  Base64, 86–88
  changing among (transcoding), 103–106
  endianness, 97
  modified Base64, 88–90
  USC-2, 82
  USC-4, 81–82
  UTF-7, 84–86
  UTF-8, 90–96
  UTF-16, 82–84
  UTF-32, 96–97
  UTF-EBCDIC, 96
encoding signatures, 98, 132. *See also* **BOM (Byte Order Mark); endianness; signatures**
Encoding submenu (Internet Explorer 5), 195–196
End User subarea (Private Use area), 111
endianness, 47, 67–68, 97, 173. *See also* **BOM (Byte Order Mark); signatures**
  and byte order signature, 98, 132
  effects on output, IE5 example, 257–258
  Unicode Standard variants, 99–100
ZERO WIDTH NO-BREAK SPACE character
  signatures, 66, 133

entities (XML), parsed versus
  unparsed, 205
EQUALS SIGN character, representations of, 85, 88,
  191
equivalent sequences, in XML
  versus HTML documents,
  208–209
escape sequences (ISO/IEC
  10646)
  ISO/IEC 2022-compatible,
  71
  in Java applications, 259–260
Ethiopic
  character block, 34, 37
  digits, 127
EUC-JP encoding format,
  numeric character references, 228
EUC-KR encoding format,
  numeric character references, 227–228
European languages
  accented forms, typographical
  conventions, 312
  digits, 126
Ewe, Latin Extended-B character block, 34–35
Exclamation/Interrogation (EX)
  line-breaking properties,
  57
EXCLAMATION MARK
  character, EX
  Exclamation/Interrogation
  property, 57
extended character sequences,
  Perl support for, 285–286
Extended Unicode Support (regular expression engines),
  152

F
FEED character, UTF-7 encod-
  ing format, 86
FEFF. *See* BOM (Byte Order
  Mark)
FFEF code values, 84
FFFC code values, 132–133
FFFE character, code values, 47.
  See also ZERO-WIDTH
  NO-BREAK SPACE
FFFF code values, 47, 84,
  132–133
fields, 86
  Accept-Charset request-
  header field, 216
  ArabicShaping.txt, 55–56
  Character decomposition
  mapping field, 207
  CompositionExclusions.txt, 59
  in databases, 308
  EastAsianWidth.txt, 58
  General Category field, 61,
  112–113, 115–117, 149,
  155, 207, 261
  in IANA character set registry
  files, 217–220
  inapplicable properties, representation for, 54
  LineBreaking.text, 57
  normative, 53
  Solaris 7 font set definitions,
  316
  SpecialCasing.txt, 54
  in Unicode Character
  Database files, 51
  in UnicodeData.txt file, 53–54
  in Unihan.txt database file,
  165–167
file format, Unicode Character
  Database, 51

FileReader class (Java),
   transcoding using, 105
files, entities (XML), 204
flow object trees (DSSSL), 246
flow objects (DSSSL), 246
font selection
   in IE5 (Internet Explorer 5),
      196–197
   in Netscape Communicator
      4.7, 200
font software, 315
fonts
   AAT (Apple Advanced
      Typography), 316
   AWT (Java Abstract
      Windowing Toolkit) for,
      317–318
   font subsetting, 315
   modular, 315
   monolithic pan-Unicode
      fonts, 315
   OpenType font format, 315
   requirements for, 312–314
   Solaris character-to-glyph
      mapping, 316–317
   with Surrogate Pairs, 110
   transition to Unicode,
      321–322
   wide-coverage Unicode fonts,
      318–320
Fonts dialog box (Internet
   Explorer 5), 196–197
form signatures, encoding,
   Specials character block,
   45, 46
formal public identifier, for
   ISO/IEC 10646 standard,
   223
four-octet BMP. *See* UCS-4
fractions, Numeric property values, 127

FreeBSD systems, Unicode support limitations, 236
French, sorting accented keys,
   154
Fulani, Latin Extended-B character block, 34–35
full encoding, 22
full-width characters, 57–58
Fullwidth digits, 127
FUNCTION section (SGML
   Declaration), 225

G
G-octet, in UCS-4, 81
General Category field (Unicode
   Character Database), 61,
   112–113, 115–117, 149,
   155, 207, 261
General Punctuation character
   block, 38, 39, 105
General Scripts area (Unicode
   Standard), 32
   block layout, 34
   code value ranges/character
      block names, 35–38
   encoding in UTF-8, 93
   ISO/IEC 10646 standard
      equivalent, 74
Geometric Shapes character
   block, 38, 40
Georgian character block, 34,
   37
German characters, unifying
   umlaut character, 25
glyphs, 51
   Adobe glyph list, 321–322
   for Arabic characters, 55
   characters versus, 22–23
   debates about, 77
   directionality, 125–126
   effect of position on, 151

Hangul Jamo character block, 125
ISO/IEC 10646 character names and, 11
Japanese-style, 163
language/locale identification, 139, 143, 194, 197–198, 213
in Macintosh systems, 237
mapping TrueType fonts to, 230
representative, 64, 65
round-trip character mapping, 58
similar/dissimilar ideographs, 163
in Solaris 7 systems, 234
with Surrogate Pairs, 110
in Unicode Standard 3.0, 8
unification of, 25–26
in Unihan.txt file, 168
for unrecognized characters/code values, 112, 144
variations, handling typographic conventions, 312–314
Gondi, Telugu character block, 34, 36
Greek
character block, 34–35
extended character block, 34, 38
groups, in UCS architecture, 62–63, 81
Gujarati
character block, 34, 36
digits, 126
Gurmukhi
character block, 34, 36
digits, 126

H
half-width characters, 58
Halfwidth and Fullwidth Forms character block, 45, 46
Han character set
development of, 6
encoding of, 94, 156
Han unification, 31–32
Han ideographs, Kangxi Radicals character block, 40, 41
Hangul character set, 94, 169–170
Hangul Compatibility Jamo character block, 40, 41
Hangul Jamo character block, 34, 37
Hangul syllable blocks (Korean), 168
canonical decomposition forms, lack of, 188
composed character sequences, naming, 170
formats for, 169
Jamo components, 169
HANGUL SYLLABLE GGEONG, naming of, 170
Hangul Syllables area, 33
block layout, 43
code value ranges/character block names, 44
ISO/IEC 10646 standard equivalent, 74
Hangul Syllables character set, 43, 44
Hangzhou-style numerals
Ideographic property, 124
Numeric property values, 127
hanja characters (Korean ideographs), 158, 168

hankaku (half-width) characters, 58

Hanyu Da Zidien dictionary, 164

hanzi characters, 158

Hausa, Latin Extended-B character block, 34–35

Hawaiian, Latin-1 Supplement character block, 47

Hebrew

biblical, 77

character block, 34–35

in Macintosh systems, 236

presentation forms, 45

right-to-left script, 145

HEBREW LETTER BET

converting from UTF-16 to ASCII, 89–90

Modified Base64 encoding format, 88–89

UCS-4 representation, 81

USC-2 representation, 82

Hex Digit property, 131

hexadecimal character representations

conversions from, 302–304

DSSSL support for, 247

ECMAScript support for, 252

in Japanese/Korean locales, 233

in JScript, 258

Plane 14-tag characters, 141

RC-elements, 62

XML support for, 211–212

High-half zone (ISO/IEC 10646), 83

Unicode Standard equivalent, 74

High Private Use Surrogates character block, 44, 83–84

Surrogate property, 129

High Surrogates character block, 44, 83

encoding in UTF-8, 91

ISO/IEC 10646 standard equivalent, 74

Surrogate property, 129

Hindu, Devangari character block, 34, 36

Hiragana character block, 40, 41

HTML (Hypertext Markup Language) documents

adjusting character references for Netscape, 201–202

avoiding Plane 14 language tags with, 24

combining Unicode with other standards, 22

comparison with XML, 204

directionality controls, 149–150

early use of ISO 8859-1 standard, 182

equivalent sequences, 208

language tagging in, 140

modifying lang attribute, effects on glyphs, 197–198

numeric character references, 191

as output from Perl applications, 281

UCS character references, 189–191

use of ISO/IEC 10646 UCS, 182

HTML Recommendation

bidirectional algorithm reference, 194

inclusion of UCS (Universal Character Set), 183

language identification, 193–193
numeric character references, 22
<META> element, use of, 193
UTF-16 encoding format, use of, 193
versions 4.0 and 4.01 compared, 189–190
html:lang attribute (HTML documents), 144
HTTP charset parameter, identifying character encoding using, 191–192
HTTP (Hypertext Transfer Protocol) applications
  definition (RFC 2626), 215
  early use of ISO 8859-1 standard, 182
  message format, 215
  version 1.1, 214
Hypertext Transfer Protocol. *See* HTTP

I

I-zone (ISO/IEC 10646-1:1993), 73
  Unicode Standard equivalent, 74
IANA (Internet Assigned Numbers Authority) identifiers
  character set registry, 216–217
  for characters in HTML documents, 190
  with HTTP Content-Type headers, 216
  in XML documents, 211

Identification characters (Plane 14), 140
identifiers
  guidelines/rules for, 154–155
  identifier start/extend characters, 155
  IANA, 190, 211, 216–217
  for Java characters, 260–262
Ideograph Component Structure (CJK Unification), 162–164
IDEOGRAPHIC CLOSING MARK property, 124
Ideographic Description Characters character block, 40, 41
IDEOGRAPHIC NUMBER ZERO property, 124
ideographs, 158. *See also* CJK Unified Ideographs
  Ideographic property, 114, 124
IE5 (Internet Explorer 5)
  JScript, 251
  Unicode Standard support, 195–199
IEC (International Electrotechnical Commission), 9
IETF (Internet Engineering Task Force)
  character set registration procedures (RFC 2278), 189, 216
  HTTP/1.1 definition (RFC 2626), 215
  Policy on Character Sets and Languages (RTF 2277), 189, 213

Continued

IETF *(continued)*
  text-handling guidelines (RFC
    2070), 182
  Tags for the Identification of
    Language (RFC 1766),
    213, 214–215
implementation levels (ISO/IEC
    10646)
  Unicode Standard equivalent,
    74
  Unicode Standard support
    limitations, 70–71
Indic (Devanagari) digits, 126
Indonesian, Latin-1 Supplement
    character block, 47
information interchange,
    ISO/IEC 10646 standards
    and, 10
informative properties, 112
  Alphabetic, 113, 117
  Case mapping, 113, 118
  Dashes, 113, 122
  East Asian Width, 114, 124
  Ideographic, 114, 124
  Letter, 114, 125
  Line Breaking, 114, 125
  Mathematical, 114, 125
  Space, 114, 129
  Unicode 1.0 Name, 114, 129
  Unicode Character Name,
    114, 129–130
integrity of pairs, 110
interfaces (Windows systems),
    Unicode characters with,
    270–271
International Phonetic Alphabet
    (IPA). *See* IPA
    (International Phonetic
    Alphabet)

International Unicode
    Conferences, 15–16
Internet Assigned Numbers
    Authority. *See* IANA
Internet Explorer 5. *See* IE5
    (Internet Explorer 5)
Internet Society, Unicode
    Consortium liaison with,
    16
Inuit, Unified Canadian
    Aboriginal Syllabics char-
    acter block, 34, 37
IPA (International Phonetic
    Alphabet), 47
  IPA Extensions character
    block, 34–35
  multiple character sets for,
    47
IRG dictionary position fields
    (Unihan database),
    166–167
Irish, archaic, Ogham character
    block, 34, 37
ISO 10179:1996, DSSSL defini-
    tion, 246–250
ISO-10646-J-1, 219
ISO-10646-UCS-2. *See* UCS-2
    character set
ISO-10646-UCS-4. *See* UCS-4
    character set
ISO-10646-Unicode-Latin1,
    219
ISO 3166, country IDs, 142
ISO 639, language IDs, 142
ISO 6429 control codes, 80, 130
ISO 646 variants, Base64 encod-
    ing, 87
ISO 8859-1 standard, 219
  with early Web applications,
    182

as Tcl scripting language
default, 287
transcoding into Unicode
Standard, 104–105
XML support for, 210
**ISO 8879, reference concrete
syntax, 225**
ISO/IEC 10646 standard
absence of character properties, 23
application conformance
requirements, 175
basic architecture, 61–63
character names, 11
character names, guideline for
composing, 129
character set aliases, 218–219
collections in, listing, 70
comparison with Unicode
Standard, 5, 10–11, 32
development of, 3–5
development of, timeline
showing, 4
DSSSL referencing of,
246–247
endianness, support for, 98
features not in Unicode
Standard, 69–74
formal public identifier, 223
identifiers, defined, 9
IEC 2022 compatibility, 71
implementation levels, 70–71
interoperability with ISO/IEC
2022, 10
ISO/IEC 10646-1:1993, 6, 8,
61–63, 83, 205
ISO/IEC 10646-1:2000, 4, 8,
50, 70, 74, 75
ISO/IEC 10646-2:2000, 50

LATIN-1 SUPPLEMENT,
219
Planes 1-16 character
addresses, 79
relationship to XML
Recommendation, 174
reserved planes, 71
terminology, Unicode
Standard equivalents, 74
Unicode Standard-supported
features, 63–68
in Web applications, limited
application of, 183–184
**ISO/IEC 10651, default string
ordering, 153**
**ISO/IEC 16262, ECMAScript
Language Specification,
250–251**
ISO/IEC 2022 applications
advantages/disadvantages, 20
ISO/IEC 10646-compatible
escape sequences, 71
using designating sequences
with, 223
**ISO (International Organization
for Standardization), 9**
**ISO-Unicode-IBM code pages,
219**
**ITC Zapf dingbats, Dingbats
character block, 38, 40**

J
J/Direct, 271
Jamo. *See also* **Hangul**
character block, 170
composing Hangul syllables
from, 170
leading consonants
(choseong), 169

Jamo Short Name property, 114, 125

Jamo.txt (Unicode Character Database), 52

Combining Jamo property, 113, 122

Jamo Short Name property, 114, 125

Japanese. *See also* CJK Unified Ideographs

displaying Japanese-style glyphs (language tagging), 143–145

Hiragana character block, 40, 41

Kanbun character block, 40, 41

Katakana character block, 40, 41

in Macintosh systems, 236

similar/dissimilar ideographs, 163

in Solaris 7 systems, 234

text display conventions, 312, 313

unifying characters, rules for, 25

Java Native Interface (JNI), 271

Java programming language

AWT (Abstract Windowing Toolkit), 317–318

bidirectional algorithm source code, 146

demo applet, 269–270

FileReader class, transcoding using, 105

locale support, 259–262

sample output, 268

sample string, generating code, 263–268

string normalization, lack of support for, 185

Unicode Standard support, 259–262

JavaScript. *See also* ECMAScript

Netscape ECMA implementation, 251

relationship to ECMAScript, 251

JIS X-0208-1997 encodings, XML support for, 210

JNI (Java Native Interface), 271

jongseong (Jamo trailing consonants/T), 169

JScript, 251. *See also* ECMAScript

example code, 254–257

example code in VBScript, 305–307

relationship to ECMAScript, 251

similarities to VBScript, 302

viewing in Netscape Communicator 4.7, 258–259

Judezmo, Hebrew character block, 34–35

jungseong (Jamo vowels/V), 169

K

Kacchi, Gujarati character block, 34, 36

Kanbun character block, 40, 41

Kangxi Radicals character block, 40, 41

KangXi Zidian dictionary,
164–165
kanji characters, 158
Kannada
 character block, 34, 36
 digits, 127
Karen, Myanmar character
 block, 34, 37
Katakana character block, 40, 41
KC normalization form, 135, 138
KD normalization form, 135,
 138
Khmer
 character block, 34, 38
 digits, 127
Khondi, Oriya character block,
 34, 36
Korean. *See also* CJK Unified
 Ideographs; Hangul
 displaying Korean-style glyphs
  (language tagging),
  143–145
 Hangul Jamo character block,
  34, 37
 Hangul syllable blocks, 168
 Hangul Syllables character set
  for, 43, 44
 hanja characters, 157–168
 in Macintosh systems, 236
 similar/dissimilar ideographs,
  163
 in Solaris 7 systems, 234
 text display conventions, 312,
  313
 unifying characters, rules for,
  25
KSC 5601
 compatibility with, 41
 Hangul syllable orders,
  Unicode matching of, 169

Kuy, Thai character block, 34, 37

L
Ladakhi, Tibetan character
 block, 34, 37
Lahuli, Tibetan character block,
 34, 37
Lambadi, Telugu character
 block, 34, 36
lang attribute
 IE5 (Internet Explorer 5) support, 197–199
 Netscape Communicator 4.7
  support, 201–203
 in HTML documents,
  193–194, 197–198
 in XML documents, 212–213
LANG environment variable
 (Solaris 7), components,
 232
language codes (ISO 639), 214
language identification, 139
language-specific glyphs, 314
LANGUAGE TAG character,
 140
language identification/tagging.
 See lang attribute
 examples, 143
 in higher-level protocols, 140
 history of, 140
 in HTML documents,
  193–194
 limitations of using, 140
 Plane 14 characters for, 24,
  140–145
 in XML documents, 24,
  212–213
languages. *See also* character
 blocks; character sets
Continued

languages *(continued)*
uncommon, including in
Unicode Standard, 77
unification of characters
across, 25–26
Lao character block, 34, 37
LastResort font (Apple), 319
Latin-1 Supplement character
block, 34–35
LATIN CAPITAL LETTER
A, converting from UTF-
16 to ASCII, 89–90
Latin characters
encoding in UTF-8, 93
presentation forms, 45
sorting order, 153
Latin Extended-A character
block, 34–35
Latin Extended Additional
Character block, 34, 38
Latin Extended-B character
block, 34–35
LATIN SMALL LETTER A
character, 23
LATIN SMALL LETTER B,
converting to ASCII,
89–90
LATIN SMALL LETTER LJ,
capitalization, 118
Lavna, Thai character block, 34,
37
Left of Pair property, 131
LEFT SQUARE BRACKET
character, Mirrored prop-
erty with, 125–126
left-to-right text, 145–146. *See
also* bidirectional algorithm
Letter property, 114, 125
Letterlike Symbols character
block, 38, 39

letters, Numeric property values,
127
libutf-8 function library (Whiz
Kid Technomagic), 245
licensing of "Unicode" logo, 14
limited subsets (ISO/IEC
10646), 69
line-breaking algorithm, 57
line breaking property, 114,
125
UTR #14 definitions, 57, 125,
171
LINE character, UTF-7 encoding format, 86
LINE FEED character, Base64
encoding format, 88
LineBreak.txt, 52, 57
Line Breaking property, 114,
125
properties in, 114
Linux systems
Linux Internationalisation
Initiative, 235
Unicode support, limitations
of, 235
little-endian computers, 68, 97
BOM (Byte Order Mark)
character, 98–99
byte order, 173
DataInputStream.writeUTF()
(Java) output, 262
encoding formats, 66
Ll (Lowercase character), 117
Locale-Sensitive Support (regular expression engines),
152
locales
for CJK ideographs, 163
in ECMAScript applications,
253

effects on characters/glyphs, 152
in Java applications, 105
locale-independent versus local-sensitive character support, 152
providing information about, 55
in Solaris 7 systems, 232–233
SpecialCasing.txt fields for, 118
specifying for glyph-matching, 24
support for, in Perl applications, 277–278
Unicode-enabled, 233
logical order, right-to-left text, 24
Lolo, Yi Syllables character set for, 43
Low-half zone (ISO/IEC 10646), 83
Unicode Standard equivalent, 74
Low surrogate (Unicode Standard), ISO/IEC 10646 standard equivalent, 74
Low Surrogates character block, 44, 83–84
encoding in UTF-8, 91
Surrogate property, 129
Lowercase mapping field (Unicode Character Database), properties in, 113
Lt (Titlecase character), 118
Lu (Uppercase character), 117
Lucinda San Unicode, 320

M
Mac OS X Server, Unicode support, 237
Macintosh OS 9.0 systems, Unicode support, 236–237
mail lists, Linux UTF-8 support, 235
Mail-Safe Transformation Format for Unicode. *See* UTF-7 encoding format
Malayalam
character block, 34, 37
digits, 127
Mandarin, Bopomofo character block, 40, 41
mapping
canonical mapping, 122–123
case mapping, 53–55, 118, 172
character-to-glyph mapping, 316–317
character encoding forms, 79
compatibility mapping, 122–123
composition mapping, 188
mapping tables (UTC) for transcoding, 104–105
round-trip mapping, 58, 161, 169–170
Mathematic Operators character block, 38, 39
mathematical operators, 125
Mathematical property, 114, 125
mathematical symbols, private use, 111
MBCS (multi-byte character strings)
in C/C++ applications, 242
Continued

MBCS *(continued)*
  _MBCS macro (C/C++ appli-
    cations), 241–242
  string-handling using, 230
membership in Unicode
    Consortium
  benefits of, 13
  levels, 12
  membership lists, 12
  rates, 12
  Unicode Technical
    Committee, 13
merged blocks, relationship of
    ISO/IEC 10646 collections
    to, 70
<META> element (HTML doc-
    uments), 191, 192–193
MIB (SNMP Management
    Information Base), identi-
    fiers for, 217–218
MIBenum field (character set
    registry files), 217
MICR symbols, Optical
    Character Resolution char-
    acter block, 38, 39
Microsoft text files, BOM (Byte
    Order Mark) character
    with, 68
Microsoft Visual Basic Scripting
    Edition. *See* VBScript
Microsoft Visual C++, Unicode
    support, 242–243
MIME e-mail messages,
    Unicode Standard charac-
    ter encoding in, 216
Mirrored field (Unicode
    Character Database), prop-
    erties, 114
Mirrored property, 114, 125–126

Miscellaneous Symbols character
    block, 38, 40
Miscellaneous Technical
    Character block, 38, 39
Modified Base64 encoding for-
    mat, 88
modular fonts, 315
Mon, Myanmar character block,
    34, 37
Mongolian
  character block, 34, 38
  digits, 127
  fonts, 314
Monotype WordType font,
    320
MSFlexGrid control, in Visual
    Basic output, 299
Myanmar
  character block, 34, 37
  digits, 127

N

N (Unicode Scalar Value), 83
Name field (character set registry
    files), 217
NAMECASE section (SGML
    Declaration), 226
NAMECHAR keyword (SGML
    Declaration), 226
names
  for ISO/IEC characters,
    guidelines for, 11
  declaring allowable characters
    for, 225–226
  for Unicode characters,
    129–130
  in Unicode Character
    Database files, 51
  in XML documents, 207–209

NAMESTRT keyword (SGML Declaration), 226
NAMING section (SGML Declaration), 225–226
National Language Support (NLC), in Windows CE applications, 231
Nd value (Numerical property), 126–127
Netscape Communicator 4.7
 JavaScript, 251
 Unicode Standard support, 199–203
 viewing VBScript output in, 308
network byte order, 193
Neutral Bidirectional category values, 149
Nl value (Numeric property), 127
NLS (National Language Support), in Windows CE applications, 231
No value (Numeric property), 127
non-ASCII characters, in Visual Basic output, 299
Non-Cognate Rule (CJK Unification), 162
non-spacing marks, canonical ordering for, 119
nonambiguity, in Unicode design, 20
normalization
 in ECMAScript applications, 253
 in Java applications, 261–262
 in Web applications, 184–188
 in XML documents, lack of, 208

normalization forms
 early normalization, 184–188
 Normalization Form C, 59, 184, 188, 253
 Normalization Form K, 59
 normalization types, 134–135
 precomposed character sequences, 136–137
 precomposed values for, 59–60
normative fields, 53
normative properties, 112
 Case, 113, 117–118
 Combining Class, 113, 121
 Combining Jamo, 113, 122
 Decomposition, 114, 122–123
 Directionality, 114, 124
 Jamo Short Name, 114, 125
 Line Breaking, 125
 listing of, 113–117
 Mirrored, 114, 125–126
 Numeric, 114, 126–128
 Private Use, 114, 128
 Surrogate, 114, 129
normative requirements, UTRs listing, 172
Norse, Runic character block, 34, 37
NTFS file system (Windows NT), Unicode names for, 230
Number Forms character block, 38, 39
numeric character references
 in ASCII documents, 228
 directionality properties, 146
 in DSSSL applications, 246–247
 in HTML documents, 22, 191
 Continued

numeric character references
(continued)
Ideographic property, 124
in SGML Declaration,
227–228
in XML documents, 22, 206
Numeric property, 23, 114
numeric values, relationship to
digit values (table), 128

O
O-zone (ISO/IEC
10646-1:1993), 73
Unicode Standard equivalent,
74
OBJECT REPLACEMENT
CHARACTER, 132
OCR-A characters, Optical
Character Resolution char-
acter block, 38, 39
octets
versus bytes, 10, 61
receiving in sequence, 66–68
in UCS-4 character set, 81
Ogham character block, 34, 37
OHM SIGN character, 117
Ojibwe, Unified Canadian
Aboriginal Syllabics char-
acter block, 34, 37
OLE interfaces, Unicode sup-
port, 230
OpenType font format, 315
OpenType (Microsoft) font for-
mat, specification, 322
operators, mathematical, 125
Optical Character Resolution
character block, 38, 39
Oriya language
character block, 34, 36
digits, 126

P
P-octet, in UCS-4
Pali, Thai character block, 34, 37
pan-Unicode fonts, 318–320
Paragraph Separator property, 60
parenthesized numbers
(Numeric property values),
127
parsed entities (XML), 204,
211–212
parsing
HTML <META> element,
193
identifiers, 154
language identification, 24,
145, 212
in Macintosh systems, 237
plain text, 20
SGML parser, 224
space/semicolon characters,
51
unparsed entities (XML), 204
in XML documents, 156
pattern matching, 153
Perl programming language
character properties screen
output, 295
character properties support,
283–284
demo program screen output,
282
extended character sequence
support, code listing,
285–286
extended character sequence
support, screen display,
286
new Unicode-supporting regular expression extensions,
277–278

script demonstrating UTF-8 support, 280–282
UTF-8 encoding format for, 90
versions 5.005/5.6, 276
Persian, Arabic character block, 34, 36
plain text, 23–24
Plane 0, 83. *See also* BMP (Basic Multilingual Plane)
Plane 1 character addresses, including new scripts among, 50
Plane 14 Characters for Language Tags (UTR #7), 24, 172, 213, 214
Plane 14 character addresses, language tags, 24, 140–145
Planes 1-16 character addresses pointers to, 82–83
Private Use areas (Planes 15/16), 84
planes, in UCS architecture, 62–63, 81
Policy on Character Sets and Languages (RTF 2277), HTTP referencing of, 215
Polish
  Latin Extended-A character block, 34–35
  Polish diacritics, 312, 314
POSIX interface, with Solaris 7 applications, 235
Postscript (Adobe)
  glyph list, 321–322
  names for Unicode characters, 321
  transition to Unicode support, 321–322

precomposed character sequences
  decomposition versus canonical ordering, 121
  equivalent sequences for, 26–27
  new, with early normalization, 188
  normalization forms, 136–137
  in singleton decompositions, 135–136
predefined windows (SCSU), 100–102
PRIME (U+2032) character, 25
Private Use areas, 33, 65–66, 67
  Adobe assignments in, 322
  assigning characters to, 110–111
  block layout, 45
  code value ranges/character block names, 45
  Corporate/Ender User subareas, 111
  ISO/IEC 10646 standard equivalent, 74
  Planes 15/16 as, 84
Private Use character block, 45
Private Use property, 114, 128
programming languages. *See also* C/C++; DSSSL; Java; Perl; Visual Basic
  parsing identifiers, 154
  test characters/protocol, 239–242
  Unicode support, ranges of, 309–310
properties
  Alphabetic, 113, 177

Continued

properties *(continued)*
  Case, 113, 117–118
  Case mapping, 113, 118
  of characters, listing of, 60–61
  Combining Class, 113, 121
  Combining Jamo, 113, 122
  Dashes, 113, 122
  Decomposition, 114, 122–123
  Directionality, 114, 124
  East Asian Width, 114, 124
  East Asian Width values,
    58–59
  Ideographic, 114, 124
  Jamo Short Name, 114, 125
  Letter, 114, 125
  Line Breaking, 114, 125
  line-breaking, 57
  listing of, 113–117
  Mathematical, 114, 125
  Mirrored, 114, 125–126
  mutually exclusive, 113
  normative versus informative,
    112
  Numeric, 114, 126–128
  Paragraph Separator, 60
  Private Use, 114, 128
  Space, 114, 129
  Surrogate, 114, 129
  Unassigned Code Value, 60
  Unicode 1.0 Name, 114, 129
  in Unicode Character
    Database files, 51
  Unicode Character Name,
    114, 129–130
  for Unicode characters, 23
  Unicode Scalar Value (N),
    108–109
  Zero-width, 60
PropList.txt, 52, 60–61
  Alphabetic property, 113, 117

  directionality listings, 124
  Mathematical property, 114,
    125
  properties in, 130
  surrogate property listings,
    129
punctuation, directionality prop-
    erties, 146
Punjabi, Gurmukhi character
    block, 34, 36
Python scripting language,
    Unicode support, 286–287

R
R-octet, in UCS-2, 82
R-zone (ISO/IEC
    10646-1:1993), 73
  Unicode Standard equivalent,
    74
Raw Native Interface (RNI),
    271
RC-element (ISO/IEC 10646),
    62–63
  Unicode Standard equivalent,
    74
RDF (Resource Description
    Framework) Model appli-
    cations, WD applicability
    to, 183
recomposition, in Normalization
    Form C, 188
registry files, IANA character
    set, 217
regular expressions
  guidelines, 151–152
  in Perl, new extensions for,
    277–278
  in Tcl 8.1 applications, 291
rendering engines, implement-
    ing, 150–151

REPLACEMENT CHARAC-
TER, 133–134
Requirements for String Identity
(W3C/TR draft), 185
reserved planes (ISO/IEC
10646), Unicode Standard
support limitations, 71
RFC 1521, Base64 encoding def-
inition, 85–86
RFC 1641, Unicode Standard,
Version 1.1, 219
RFC 1766 (IETF)
language identifiers, 142
language tagging, 193
RFC 1815, ISO 10646, Japanese
version, 219
RFC 2070 (UCS text-handling
guidelines), 182
RFC 2152, UTF-7 encoding format definition, 84–85
RFC 2277 (IETF), Policy on
Character Sets and
Languages, 213
RFC 2278 (IETF)
character set registration procedure, 216
Policy on Character Sets and
Languages, 189
RFC 2626 (IETF), HTTP/1.1
definition, 215
right-joining, in Arabic/Syriac
characters, 55–56
right-to-left text, 145. *See also*
bidirectional algorithm;
directionality
with left-to-right text,
145–146
logical order, 24
RING ABOVE, compatibility
mapping, 123

RNI (Raw Native Interface),
271
Roman numerals
Number Forms character
block, 38, 39
Numeric property, 127
Rosette C++ Library for Unicode
(Basis Technology), 244
round-trip mapping
in CJK (Han) Unification,
161
of Hangul syllables, 169–170
Unicode Standard support for,
58
Row-octets. *See* R-octet
rows
R-octet representation (UCS-
2), 82
in UCS architecture, 62–63,
81
Runic character block, 34, 37

S
S-zone (ISO/IEC 10646), 73
pointers to Planes 1 to 16,
82–83
Unicode standard equivalent,
74
Sanskrit, Devangari character
block, 34, 36
Santali, Oriya character block,
34, 36
SCOPE DOCUMENT state-
ment (SGML
Declaration), 224
scripting languages, Unicode
support
ECMAScript/JavaScript/JScri
pt, 250–259
Continued

scripting languages *(continued)*
Python scripting language,
286–287
Tcl scripting languages,
287–292
VBScript, 301–307
Scripting Run-Time Library
with VBScript, 302
in Visual Basic applications,
292
scripts
approval process, 50–51
proposed for inclusion in
Unicode standard, 47–50
SCSU (Standard Compression
Scheme for Unicode), 80,
172–173
definition (UTR #6), 100
presumptions, 100–101
searching text (sorting), 152–154
selected subsets (ISO/IEC
10646), 69
semantics
defined, 112
for Unicode characters, 23
semicolons, in Unicode
Character Database files,
51
SGML Declaration
concrete syntax declaration,
224–225
document character set,
221–224
FUNCTION section, 225
NAMECASE section, 226
NAMING section, 225–226
numeric character references,
227–228
SCOPE DOCUMENT
statement, 224

specifying character sets in,
221–224
syntax reference character set,
221–224
for XML, code listing/discus-
sion, 222–226
versus XML Declaration,
221
SGML (Standard Generalized
Markup Language). *See
also* SGML Declaration
document components, 220
flexibility of markup characters, 220
language tagging in, 140
Unicode Scalar Value (N) and,
108–109
Unicode Scalar Value with,
228
Shan, Myanmar character block,
34, 37
Shavian, including in Unicode
Standard, 77
signatures, 66–68, 98, 131, 132.
See also BOM (Byte Order
Mark); endianness
for distinguishing encoding
formats, 209
single-byte applications, 230,
241–242
singleton decompositions, 60,
135–136
Sinhala character block, 34, 37
Small Form Variants character
block, 45, 46
SNMP (Simple Network
Management Protocol),
Management Information
Base (MIB), 217

software, transcoding, Java
    FileReader class, 105
Solaris 7 systems
    character-to-glyph mapping,
        316–317
    e-mail application, 234
    interface conversion utility,
        232–233
    localized versions, 232
    programming using POSIX
        interface, 235
    Unicode-enabled locales,
        232–233
sorting
    culturally-expected, 153
    text/8-bit character strings,
        152–154
Source Separation Rule (CJK
    Unification), 161
SPACE character
    converting from UTF-16 to
        ASCII, 89–90
    SP line-breaking property,
        57
    UTF-7 encoding format,
        86
Space property, 114, 129
Space (SP) line-breaking prop-
    erty, 57
Spacing Modifier Letters charac-
    ter block, 34–35
spacing properties, 23, 57, 114,
    129
Special Casing. txt, 52, 54–55
special characters
    interlinear annotations, 133
    listing of, 131–132
    OBJECT REPLACEMENT
        CHARACTER, 132

special numeric characters,
    Numeric property values,
    127
SpecialCasing.txt
    Case mapping property, 113,
        118
    properties in, 113
Specials character block, 45,
    46
Standard Compression Scheme
    for Unicode (UTR #6),
    172
Standard Generalized Markup
    Language. See SGML
standards. See also ISO/IEC
    10646 standard; Unicode
    Standard
    pre-existing, convertibility of
        Unicode to, 27–28
    Unicode conformance require-
        ments, 171–174
    Unicode Transformation
        Formats, support for,
        172–173
static windows, predefined,
    102–103
    with SCSU compression,
        100–101
storing characters, logical order
    for, 24, 145
StrConv() function (Visual
    Basic), 292
string-handling approaches. See
    also character strings
    ANSI systems, 230
    in C/C++ programs, 241–242
    fixed bytes per character
        (Wide), 230
    MBCS, 230

String objects (ECMAScript),
    referencing characters
    using, 252
stroke count, as CJK unifying
    principle, 158
Strong Bidirectional category
    values, 148
Strong Surrogate Pair support,
    109–110
style language component
    (DSSSL), 246
    example listing for, 248
subscripts, Numeric property
    values, 127
Subset (ISO/IEC 10646)
    Unicode standard equivalent,
        74
    Unicode Standard support
        limitations, 69
Superscripts and Subscripts
    character block, 38, 39
superscripts, Numeric property
    values, 127
Surrogate code point (Unicode
    Standard), ISO/IEC 10646
    standard equivalent, 74
Surrogate Pairs, 172
    accessing script characters
        using, 50
    with C/C++ programming
        language, 242
    character references using,
        109–110
    encoding in UTF-8, 91, 93
    formula for calculating, 83
    levels of support for, 109–110
    number possible, 84
    representing in UCS-4, 81–82
    Unicode Scalar Value (N),
        83

    in XML documents, restric-
        tions on, 212
Surrogate property, 114, 129
Surrogates area, 33, 74
    block layout, 44
    for characters outside BMP,
        79–80
    code value ranges/character
        block names, 44
    pointers to Planes 1 to 16,
        82–83
Swahili, Latin-1 Supplement
    character block, 47
Sybase Unilib, 245
Symbols area, 33
    block layout, 38
    character block names/ranges,
        39–40
symbols, unification across lan-
    guages, 25–26
syntax reference character set
    (SGML), 221–224
Syriac
    character block, 34, 36
    joining/shaping guides,
        55–56
    right-to-left script, 145

T
TAB character, UTF-7 encoding
    format, 86
tag names
    Plane 14 characters for lan-
        guage tagging, 24
    XML restrictions on, 207–209
Tags for the Identification of
    Language (RFC 1766),
    213, 214–215
Tamil
    character block, 34, 36

digits, 126
fonts for, 314
_TCHAR macro (C/C++ applications), 241–242
Tcl scripting languages
example script, screen output, 291
Unicode support, 287–292
Version 8.1, regular expression implementation, 291
TEC (Text Encoding Converter) (Macintosh systems), 236
Telugu
character block, 34, 36
digits, 127
text declaration format (XML), 211
text, displaying. *See also* fonts; glyphs
AAT (Apple Advanced Typography), 316
AWT (Java Abstract Windowing Toolkit) for, 317–318
font requirements, 312–314
font subsetting, 315
modular fonts, 315
monolithic pan-Unicode fonts, 315
OpenType font format, 315
Solaris character-to-glyph mapping, 316–317
typographic conventions, 312–314
wide-coverage Unicode fonts, 318–320
Text Encoding Converter (TEC) (Macintosh systems), Unicode conversions, 236

text, handling. *See also* character strings
bidirectional algorithm, 145–150
converting, in Visual J++, 270–271
language identification, 139
language tagging, 139
normalizing in Web applications, criteria, 186
rendering editors, difficulties, 150–151
sorting/searching, 152–154
Visual J++ Unicode conversion class, 270–271
text utilities (Macintosh systems), 237
Thaana
character block, 34, 36
right-to-left script, 145
Thai
character block, 34, 37
digits, 127
THAI DIGIT NINE, 88–90
Tibetan
fonts for, 314
character block, 34, 37
half-digits, Numeric property values, 127
Titlecase mapping field (Unicode Character Database), properties in, 113
titlecase value, uses for, 118
trademark attribution, "Unicode" logo, 14–15
transcoding
character names and, 11
from other standards to Unicode, 104
Continued

transcoding *(continued)*
software for, 105–106
from Unicode to other standards, 103–105, 164
transmission, of data, ISO/IEC 10646 standards and, 10
TrueType Unicode fonts, 319–320
approved glyph names, 322
code mapping, 230
TSM (Text Services Manager), generating Unicode code values using, 236
Tulu, Kannada character block, 34, 36
Turkish, special case mapping for, 55
Two-level Classification (CJK Unification), 162–164
two-octet BMP. *See* UCS-2
typographic conventions, 312–314

U
UCData (Leisher), 245
UCS-2 character set (16-bit), 21, 62, 65, 82, 218
comparison with UTF-16, 82
ECMAScript support, 252–253
ISO/IEC 10646 standard definition, 10
Unicode-compatibility, 79
XML support for, 210
UCS-4 character set (32-bit), 81–82, 218
architecture, overview, 61–63, 61–63
available characters, 61–62

with big-/little-endian computers, 66
comparison with UTF-32 encoding format, 96–97
as ISO/IEC 10646 default form, 79
ISO/IEC 10646 standard definition, 10
representing Surrogate Pairs, 81–82
specifying in SGML declarations, 223
Unicode Standard support limitations, 69
XML support for, 210
UCS Transformation Format, 7-bit form. *See* UTF-7 encoding format
UCS Transformation Format, 8-bit form. *See* UTF-8 encoding format
UCS Transformation Format for Planes of Group 00. *See* UTF-16 encoding format
UCS (Universal Character Set)
architecture/canonical form, 81
HTML Recommendation support, 190
ISO/IEC 10646-defined, 81
numeric references to in HTML documents, 191
string identity matching problems, 184–185
in Web applications, 183
Ugaritic, including in Unicode Standard, 77
Unassigned Code Value property, 60
undefined characters, 110

UniAPI (Bjondi International), 245

Unicode 1.0 name field (Unicode Character Database), properties in, 114, 129

Unicode bibliography (Beebe), 6

Unicode Canonical Composition (Normalization Form C), applying to Web applications, 184–188

Unicode Character Database, 17
ArabicShaping.txt, 52, 55–56
Blocks.txt, 52, 56–57
CompositionExclusions.txt, 52, 59–60
EastAsianWidth.txt, 52, 57–59
file format, 51
file naming conventions, 51–52
FTP access, 51
General Category field, 261
Jamo.txt, 52
Java programming language support, 259–260
LineBreaking.txt, 52, 57
in Normalization Form C, 188
in Perl applications, 278–279
property sources, listing of, 113–114
PropList.txt, 52, 60–61
Special Casing. txt, 52, 54–55
UnicodeData.txt, 52, 53–54
Unihan.txt, 31–32, 52

Unicode Character Name property, 114, 129–130

Unicode Collation Algorithm (UTR #10), 153, 172

Unicode Consortium, 3. See also Unicode Character Database
administration, 11–12
Default Unicode Collation Element Table, 153–154
incorporation, 6
information about pending scripts, 50
International Unicode Conferences, 15–16
liaisons/overlapping memberships, 16
mailing lists, 13
membership, 12–13
Unicode Character Database, 17
"Unicode" logo, 14

Unicode-enabled locales (Solaris 7 systems), 232–234

Unicode-handling class libraries (Visual J++), 270

"Unicode" logo
correct trademark attribution, 14–15
licensing, 14
non-commercial use, 14
using, restrictions on, 14, 15

_UNICODE macro (C/C++ applications), 241–242

Unicode Newline Guidelines, Version 4 (UTR #13), 171

Unicode Normalization Forms, Version 16 (UTR #15), 171

Unicode processing, Specials character block, 45, 46

Unicode Regular Expression Guidelines (UTR #18), 172

Unicode Scalar Value (N). *See also* BOM (Byte Order Mark)
  ranges, 108
  in SGML documents, 228
  uses for, 108
  UTF-32 encoding, 97
  UTF-8 encoding, 91
Unicode Standard-ISO/IEC 10646 standard comparisons, 5, 10–11, 32, 46, 76
  ISO/IEC 10646 standard, Unicode supported features, 63–68
  ISO/IEC 10646 standard, features unsupported by Unicode, 69–74
Unicode Standard, 4
  adding characters, 8
  approved UTRs, 171
  blocks, 31, 68
  character set aliases, 218–219
  collation/sorting rules, 11
  database support, 308–309
  defined, 6
  diacritics, handling of, 312
  directionality override characters, 194
  endianness, support for, 98
  evaluating conformance with, 96
  font techniques/font suppliers, 315–318
  fonts for, transition to, 321–322
  history of, 3–6
  Jamo/modern Hangul characters in, 169–170
  major allocations (figure), 7

normative requirements, UTRs reflecting, 172
proposed scripts for, 47–50
relationship to XML Recommendation, 174
semantics, 112
submitting new characters, 175–176
transcoding, 103–105
transition to, 321–322
typographical conventions, 312–314
universality of, 76–77
using with Microsoft extensions, 270–271
in Web applications, limited application of, 183–184
wide-coverage fonts, 318–320
Windows 95/98 support, limitations of, 230
Windows CE compliance, 231
Windows NT support, 230
XML support for, 208–212
Unicode Standard Version 1.0/1.1, 6, 219
Unicode Standard Version 2.0
  Unicode-encoded text, 79
  UTF-7 encoding format support, 85
  Version 2.0, 6
  Windows 2000 compliance with, 230–231
  XML Recommendation reference to, 205
Unicode Standard Version 3.0
  added CJK ideographs, 42
  CJK Unified Ideographs, source standards, 159–161

compatibility with BMP (Basic Multilingual Plane) characters, 62

compatibility with ISO/IEC 10646-1:2000, 8

conformance requirements, 171–174

differences from Version 2.0, 32

downplaying of UTF-7 encoding format, 84, 85

Han character set, 318

Hangul syllable blocks, 318

Plane 1 characters in, 50

Unicode Character Database files for, 51–61

UTF-16 encoding, 80

Version 3.0, 7

Unicode support

C/C++ programming language, 242–246

DSSSL (Document Style and Semantic Specification Language), 246–250

ECMAScript, 252–259

HTML 4.0/HTML 4.01 references, comparisons, 189–190

in HTTP applications, 215

Internet Explorer 5, 195

Java programming language, 259–262

Java programming language, example code listing, 263–268

Linux systems, limitations, 235

Macintosh OS 9.0.5 systems, 236–237

Netscape Communicator 4.7, 199–203

Perl applications, 276–286

Python scripting language, 286–287

SGML applications, 220–228

Solaris 7 systems, 231–235

variability among programming languages, 309–310

VBScript, 302

Visual Basic applications, 292

Visual J++ 6.0 programming language, 270–276

in XML documents, 204–215

Unicode Technical Committee (UTC). *See* **UTC (Unicode Technical Committee)**

Unicode Technical Reports (UTR). *See* **UTR (Unicode Technical Reports)**

Unicode Transformation Format, 7-bit form. *See* **UTF-7 encoding format**

Unicode Transformation Format, 8-bit form. *See* **UTF-8 encoding format**

Unicode Transformation Formats, required support for, 172–173

UnicodeData.txt, 52, 53–54

Bidirectional category values, 147–150

Case mapping property, 113, 118

Case property, 113, 117–118

Combining Class property, 113, 121

Dashes property, 113, 122

Continued

UnicodeData.txt *(continued)*
Decomposition property, 114, 122–123
Directionality property, 114, 124
Letter property, 114, 125
Mirrored property, 114, 125–126
Numeric property, 114, 126–128
Private Use property, 114, 128
properties in, 113–116
Space property, 114, 129
Surrogate property, 114, 129
Unicode 1.0 Name property, 114, 129
Unicode Character Name property, 114, 129–130
unification principles, CJK Unified Ideographs, 158
Unified Canadian Aboriginal Syllabics character block, 34, 37
Unified Ideographs characters, Ideographic property, 124
uniformity, in Unicode design, 20
Unihan database
Unihan.txt file, 31–32, 52, 165–168
Web site, 167
Unihan.txt (Unicode Character Database), 31–32, 52, 165–168
Unilib (Sybase UDK component), 245
Universal Character Set. *See* UCS
universality, in Unicode design, 20

Unix systems
Unicode support, 231–236
UTF-8 encoding format for, 90
unknown characters, REPLACEMENT CHARACTER for, 133–134
unparsed entities (XML), 204
unrecognized characters, handling, 111–112
Uppercase mapping field (Unicode Character Database), properties in, 113
Urdu, Arabic character block, 34, 36
US-ASCII equivalents
UTF-16 encoding, 85
UTF-7 direct encoding, 86
user agents (Web browsers), variability in character support, 190–191
user-defined characters, 110–111
user interface, Windows 2000, Unicode-compliant character sets in, 231
UTC (Unicode Technical Committee), 16. *See also* UTR (Unicode Technical Reports)
liaison with ISO/IEC WG2, 8–9
mapping tables, 104–105
membership, 13
merger/relationship with WG2, 4–5
SCSU (Standard Compression Scheme for Unicode), 80
Unicode Standard, 16

UTF-32 encoding, draft
    report on, 80
UTR (Unicode Technical
    Reports), 16
**UTF-1 encoding format, 193,
    218**
UTF-2 encoding format. *See*
    UTF-8 encoding format
UTF-7 encoding format, 218
    applications for, 80, 85
    Base64-encoded data with, 88
    = character in, 85, 88
    control code encoding, 86
    definition (RFC 2152), 85
    direct encoding, 86
    modified Base64 encoding, 85
    Modified Base64 encoding
        format, 88
    modified Unicode encoding
        (Base64), 86
    uses for, 84–85
**UTF-8 encoding format, 65,
    89–90**
    advantages of using, 220
    applications for, 80, 90
    with C/C++ programming
        language, 242
    caveats using, 95
    conversion into Unicode, 95
    development of, 90
    generating HTML in Java,
        sample code, 263–268
    how it works, 91
    IE5 (Internet Explorer 5) sup-
        port, 195–196
    IETF support for, 189
    ISO/IEC 10646 standard def-
        inition, 10
    Java programming language
        support, 259, 262

with Linux systems, 235
lossless transformations using,
    21
Mac OS X Server support for,
    237
with non-Latin characters,
    limitations, 94
in Perl applications, 276–277
Plane 14 language tags,
    141–142
relationship of bytes to code
    values, 92
required bytes, 93
specifying in HTTP message
    headers, 215–216
in Solaris 7 systems, 233, 234
Tcl support for, 288
viewing in IE5 (Internet
    Explorer 5), 257–258
XML support for, 209,
    209–211
**UTF-16 encoding format, 65,
    82–84**
    BOM (Byte Order Mark)
        character with, 68
    with C/C++ programming
        language, 242
    comparison with UCS-2, 82
    definition, 83
    ECMAScript support, 252
    endianness variants, 99
    enlarging Universal Character
        Set using, 21
    High Private Use Surrogates
        character block with, 44
    with HTML documents, 156,
        193
    Java programming language
        support, 259, 262
            Continued

UTF-16 encoding format
(continued)
Mac OS X Server support for,
237
numeric character references,
227–228
Plane 14 language tags,
141–142
Planes 1-16 character
addresses in, 79, 84
Surrogate Pairs representations, 81–82
transcoding into UTF-7,
89–90
VBScipt support, 304–305
viewing in IE5 (Internet
Explorer 5), 257–258
with XML files, 98, 209–211
UTF-16BE encoding format, 66
in Java applications, 268
viewing in IE5 (Internet
Explorer 5), 257–258
UTF-16LE encoding format, 66
in Java applications, 268
Tcl support for, 288
VBScript support, 304–305
viewing in IE5 (Internet
Explorer 5), 257–258
**UTF-32 encoding format, 21,
96**
with C/C++ programming
language, 242
comparison with UCS-4 character set, 96–97
endianness variants, 99
Plane 14 language tags,
141–142
UTC draft report on, 80
variants among, 97

**UTF-EBCDIC encoding for-
mat, 96**
applications for, 80
**UTF (UCS/Unicode
Transformation Format),
65**
utf8 pragma (Perl)
character string handling,
277
enabling UTF-8 encoding for-
mat, 276–277
new regular expression exten-
sions, 277–278
**UTR #6, SCSU (Standard
Compression Scheme for
Unicode) definition, 100,
172**
**UTR #7, Plane 14 Characters for
Language Tags, 24, 140,
142, 143, 172, 213, 214**
**UTR #9, Bidirectional
Algorithm, 124, 145, 146,
171**
**UTR #10, Unicode Collation
Algorithm, 153, 172**
**UTR #11, East Asian Width
property, 124**
**UTR #13, Unicode Newline
Guidelines, Version 4, 171**
**UTR #14, Line Breaking
Properties, 57, 125, 171**
**UTR #15, Normalization Forms,
59, 96, 123, 134, 171, 188**
**UTR #16, EBCDIC formats, 80,
172**
**UTR #17, Character Encoding
Model, 172**
**UTR #18, Regular Expresssion
Guidelines, 151–152, 172,
187**

UTR #19, UTF-32 encoding
    format definition, 21, 96
UTR #21, Case Mappings, 118,
    172
UTRs (Unicode Technical
    Reports), 16
    Web site for, 172

V
valid documents (XML), 205
values, General Category field,
    listing of, 115–116
variable width encoding. *See*
    UTF-16 encoding format;
    UTF-8 encoding format
VBScript scripting language,
    301
    JScript code, 305–307
    sample string, screen output,
        302–303
    sample Unicode string,
        HTML code, 302–303
    Unicode support, 302–305
Vietnamese, CJK Unified
    Ideographs, 158
Visual Basic programming lan-
    guage, 291
    sample form with source code,
        listing, 293–299
    sample form, screen output,
        300, 301
Visual J++ 6.0 programming lan-
    guage
    demo program screen output,
        276
    form with Unicode text, code
        listing, 271–276
    Unicode support, 270–276

W
W3C World Wide Web
    Character Model proposal,
    181–182. *See also* WD
    (W3C Character Model
    Working Draft)
W3C (World Wide Web
    Consortium)
    character model, working draft
        (WD), 181–188
    liaison with Unicode
        Consortium, 12
    User Interface domain, 189
    W3C Draft Requirements for
        String Identity, 185
    W3C MathML
        Recommendation, 111
    XML Recommendation,
        203–204
WD (W3C Character Model
    Working Draft), 181–182
    applicability of, 183–184
    comparison with RFC 2070,
        182
    early normalization, 184–188
    guidelines for early normaliza-
        tions, 186–187
Weak Bidirectional category val-
    ues, 148–149
Weak Surrogate Pair support,
    109–110
Web applications. *See also*
    HTML (Hypertext
    Markup Language) docu-
    ments
    UCS (Universal Character
        Set) with, 182–188
Web browsers
    Unicode Standard support,
        195–203

variability in character support,
190–191
viewing VBScript output in
Netscape, 308
Web sites
Adobe glyph list, 321
Adobe PostScript Unicode
name conventions, 321
Adobe Private Use character
assignments, 322
Apple LastResort font, 319
Batam Unicode conversion
API, 244
BDF Unicode fonts (X
Window systems), 320
bidirectional algorithm imple-
mentation, 146
ECMAScript, 251
font.org, 312
form for submitting proposed
new characters, 176–177
FreeBSD systems, 236
IANA character set registry,
216
IBM Classes for Unicode, 244
IETF HTTP/1.1 definition,
215
IETF (Internet Engineering
Task Force), 182
International Unicode
Conferences, 15
Internet Society, 16
ISO 3166 alpha-2 country
codes, 214
ISO 639 language codes, 214
libutf-8 function library, 245
Linux Internationalisation
Initiative, 235
Microsoft OpenType specifi-
cation, 322

Microsoft Unicode support,
231
Microsoft Windows CE, 231
Perl programming language,
276
proposed character model for
world Wide Web, 181
Python scripting language,
286–287
regular expression guidelines,
152
Rosette C++ Library for
Unicode, 244
SGML declaration for XML,
222
SGML declaration for XML,
allowable name characters,
225–226
Tcl scripting language, 287
TrueType Pan-Unicode fonts,
320
TrueType Unicode fonts, 320
UCData (Leisher), 245
Unicode bibliography (Beebe),
6
Unicode Consortium mem-
bership list, 12
Unicode Consortium, pending
scripts, 50
Unicode FAQ, 68
Unicode for Linux (M. Kuhn),
235
Unicode proposals, status
information, 48
Unihan database, 167–168
Unilib, 245
UniLib, 245
UTP (Unicode Technical
Report) #7 (language tags),
140

UTR (Unicode Technical Reports), sources for, 172
VBScript, 301
Visual J++, 270
Visual Studio/Visual Basic, 292
W3C Draft Requirements for String Identity, 185
W3C MathML Recommendation, 111
W3C User Interface Domain, 189
XML development activities, 204
Webwide Early Uniform Normalization, 184–188
well-formed documents (XML), 205
Welsh, Latin Extended-A character block, 34–35
WG2 (ISO/IEC working group)
CJK-JRG (CJK Joint Research Group), 159
mandate/goals, 9
merger/relationship with UTC, 4–5
Unicode Consortium liaison with, 16
UTC liaison, 8–9
WGL4 (Windows Glyph List 4), 322
wide-coverage Unicode fonts, 318–320
wide-string handling, 230
in C/C++ programs, 242–243
Windows 2000, Unicode support, 230
Windows 95/98 support
imitations of, 230
string-handling functions, 230

Windows CE, Unicode compliance, 231
Windows NT, Unicode support, 230
Windows systems, interfaces, Unicode characters with, 270–271
WordScript I/II language kits (Apple), 236
World Wide Web Character Model, 181–182
World Wide Web Consortium. *See* W3C (World Wide Web Consortium)
wuli kulca. *See* Hangul

X
X/Open consortium, UTF-8 encoding format, 90
XML character references, Unicode Scalar Value (N) and, 108, 109
XML Declaration
character encoding format, 210
versus SGML Declaration, 221
specifying encoding in, 94, 105
text declaration format), 210
XML (Extensible Markup Language)
applications/documents, 204–205
advantages of using, 204–205
avoiding Plane 14 language tags with, 24
BOM (Byte Order Mark) character, 68
case-sensitivity, 209

Continued

XML (Extensible Markup Language) *(continued)*
character encoding, 206
combining standards in, 22
comparison with HTML, 204
directionality controls, 149–150
DSSSL formatting for, 246
identifiers, rules governing, 155
language identification (lang attribute), 144, 212–213
non-standard encoding, declaring, 94
overriding bidirectional algorithm, 146
parsed entities, 156, 211–212
SGML declaration for, 222–226
string normalization, lack of support for, 185
tag naming restrictions, 207–209
W3C activity related to, 203–204
WD applicability to, 183
XML Recommendation
IANA-registered names, 211
inclusion of UCS (Universal Character Set), 183
lang attribute, using, 213
naming guidelines, 226
numeric character references, 22
relationship to ISO/IEC 10646 standard, 174
relationship to Unicode Standard, 174
and revisions to Unicode Standard, 205

standard references, 5
supported encodings, 209–212
UTF-8 support in, 94
well-formedness constraints, 205
XML processors/controllers, 204
XML/UTF-16 encoded files, ZERO WIDTH NO-BREAK SPACE character, 98
xml:lang attribute (XML documents), 24, 144, 164, 212–213
XSL (Extensible Style Language) applications, WD applicability to, 183

Y
Yi radicals character set, 43
Yi Syllables allocation area, 33
block layout, 43
character block names/ranges, 43
Yi Syllables character set, 43
Yiddish
Hebrew character block, 34–35
right-to-left script, 145

Z
zenkaku (full-width) characters, 58
zero. *See also* **digit values; numeric character references**
in Ethiopic, 127
ideographic, Numeric property values, 127
in Tamil, 127

ZERO WIDTH NO-BREAK
     SPACE character, 173
   with BOM (Byte Order
     Mark), 132
   converting from UTF-16 to
     ASCII, 89–90
   as encoding signature, 98–100
   signatures for, 66–68
Zero-width property, 60, 61
Zhuang, Latin Extended-B
   character block, 34–35

Zone (ISO/IEC 10646),
     Unicode standard equiva-
     lent, 74
zones
   BMP, comparison with
     Unicode "areas," 71–72
   in ISO/IEC 10646:1:2000,
     74, 75
Zs value (Space property), 129
Zulu, Latin Extended-B character block, 34–35

my2cents.idgbooks.com